THE
POLITICS OF HATE

Hugo N. Gerstl

THE
POLITICS OF HATE

A PIERCING INSIGHT INTO AMERICAN POLITICS

*How obstructionists, media, and
vested interests are making America
a third world country and*

HOW WE CAN TURN IT AROUND

Hugo N. Gerstl

SAMUEL WACHTMAN'S SONS

DEKEL PUBLISHING HOUSE

Dekel Publishing House
www.dekelpublishing.com

North American rights by
Samuel Wachtman's Sons, Inc.

ISBN 978-1-888820-32-4

Cover design and typesetting by:

For information contact:

Dekel Publishing House	**Samuel Wachtman's Sons, Inc.**
P.O. Box 45094	2460 Garden Road, Suite C
Tel Aviv 61450, Israel	Monterey, CA 93940, U.S.A.
Tel: +972 3506-3235	Tel: +1 831 649-0669
Fax: +972 3506-7332	Fax: +1 831 649-8007
Email: info@dekelpublishing.com	Email: samuelwachtman@gmail.com

There were once two cats of Kilkenny
Each thought there was one cat too many
So they fought and they fit
And they scratched and they bit
'til excepting their nails
and the tips of their tails
Instead of two cats there weren't any.

- Edward Lear

*

The hatred stirred up by politics does what hatred always does:
It breeds hatred in return.
Truth seldom flourishes in an atmosphere of politics or emotion.

CONTENTS

FOREWORD

WAKE UP, AMERICA!

This past weekend my grandson Jake, 17, came to visit us. During dinner conversation, my wife Lorraine asked him, "Are there more Republicans or Democrats in the area where you live?"

His response positively floored us. "I don't know. I'm not really into politics."

* * *

On Thursday, June 28, 2012, in a landmark ruling that is certain to impact the November election and the lives of every American, the United States Supreme Court upheld the controversial health care law championed by President Barack Obama.

Chief Justice John Roberts, ordinarily a conservative Republican stalwart and a George W. Bush appointee – joined the high court's liberal wing -- Justices Stephen Breyer, Ruth Bader Ginsburg, Sonia Sotomayor and Elena Kagan -- in upholding the law. Three dependably conservative justices, Antonin Scalia, Samuel Alito, and Clarence Thomas, as well as conservative-moderate swing vote Justice Anthony Kennedy, largely viewed as the most powerful voice on the Court because he usually tips the scale in 5-4 decisions -- dissented.

The narrow 5-4 ruling was a victory for Obama but will serve as a rallying issue for Republicans calling for repeal of the Affordable Care Act passed by Democrats in 2010.

Republican presidential nominee Mitt Romney immediately said that defeating President Obama in November is the only way to get rid of the law despised by conservatives as a costly expansion of government. Of course, former Massachusetts Governor Romney would be hard-pressed to *honestly* rail against this Act when *he* engineered the passage of a law virtually identical to the Affordable Healthcare Act in Massachusetts in 2006 – something he now, belatedly, claims was "a mistake."

Such is the wondrous game of politics.

Thursday's decision impacts how Americans get medicine and health care, and also provides new court guidelines on federal power.

The most anticipated Supreme Court ruling since the Supreme Court determined the winner of the 2000 presidential election allows the government to continue implementing the health care law, which doesn't take full effect until 2014. That means popular provisions that prohibit insurers from denying coverage for pre-existing medical conditions and allow parents to keep their children on family policies to the age of 26 will continue.

In the ruling, the high court decided the most controversial provision -- the individual mandate requiring people to have health insurance -- is valid as a tax. While the federal government does not have the power to order people to buy health insurance, the federal government does have the power to impose a tax on those without health insurance.

The polarizing law, dubbed "Obamacare" by its detractors, is the most important legislation of Obama's time in office. It helped spur the creation of the conservative tea party movement and will be a centerpiece of the presidential election campaign.

Romney called Obamacare "bad policy and a bad law," adding that defeating Obama in November is the only way to get rid of it.

"What the court did not do in its last session, I will do on the first day if elected president of the United States, and that's to repeal Obamacare," he said Thursday after the court's decision was announced.

Obama used the focus on the issue to spell out the benefits of the law that remains unpopular with many Americans. The principle upheld by the high court's ruling is that no American should go bankrupt because of illness, the president said. "I know the debate over this law has been divisive," Obama said. "It should be pretty clear that I didn't do this because it was good politics. I did it because I believe it is good for the country." He said the country can't afford to "to refight the political battle of two years ago or go back to the way things were." Other Democrats celebrated the policy victory.

In his opinion, Justice Roberts noted the political divisions of the health care law, writing that, "We do not consider whether the act embodies sound policies. ... That judgment is entrusted to the nation's elected leaders. ... We ask only whether Congress has the power under the Constitution to enact the challenged provisions."

On the individual mandate, the opinion said that, "The Affordable Care Act's requirement that certain individuals pay a financial penalty for not obtaining health insurance may reasonably be characterized as a tax. ... Because the Constitution permits such a tax, it is not our role to forbid it, or to pass upon its wisdom or fairness.

Republican Representative Michele Bachmann of Minnesota, a leading tea party voice against the health care law, complained that the ruling "means now for the first time in the history of the country, Congress can force Americans to purchase any product, any service.

This is truly a turning point in American history. We'll never be the same way again," Bachmann said, adding that "this is a more far-reaching decision than anyone had expected or imagined."

In another part of Thursday's decision, the high court ruled that a part of the law involving Medicaid must change. The law calls for an expansion of eligibility for Medicaid, which involves spending by the federal government and the states, and threatens to remove existing Medicaid funding from states that don't participate in the expansion. Thursday's ruling said the government must remove that threat. In his remarks, Obama acknowledged a need to improve those parts of the health care law that need it.

According to a poll released Tuesday, 35% of Americans said they would be pleased if the health care law were deemed unconstitutional by the Supreme Court.

28% said they would be pleased if the Affordable Care Act were ruled constitutional.

But nearly four in 10 Americans surveyed said they would have "mixed feelings" if the justices struck down the whole law. Previous surveys have indicated that some who oppose the law do so because they think it doesn't go far enough.

The Supreme Court heard three days of politically charged hearings in March on the law formally known as the Patient Protection and Affordable Care Act. The landmark but controversial measure was passed by congressional Democrats despite Republican opposition. The challenge focused primarily on the law's requirement that most Americans have health insurance or pay a fine.

Supporters of the plan argued the "individual mandate" is necessary for the system to work, while critics argued it is an unconstitutional intrusion on individual freedom. Four federal appeals courts heard challenges to parts of the law before the Supreme Court ruling, and came up with three different results.

The act passed Congress along strictly partisan lines in March 2010, after a lengthy and heated debate marked by intense opposition from the health insurance industry and conservative groups. When Obama signed the legislation later that month, he called it historic and said it marked a "new season in America." While it was not the comprehensive national health care system liberals initially sought, supporters said the law would reduce health care costs, expand coverage and protect consumers.

In place of creating a national health system, the law bans insurance companies from denying coverage to people with pre-existing medical conditions, bars insurers from setting a dollar limit on health coverage payouts, and requires them to cover preventative care at no additional cost to consumers. It also requires individuals to have health insurance, either through their employers or a state-sponsored exchange, or face a fine beginning in 2014.

There are, however, a number of exemptions. The penalty will be waived for people with very low incomes who are members of certain religious groups, or who face insurance premiums that would exceed 8% of family income even after including employer contributions and federal subsidies.

Supporters argued the individual mandate is critical to the success of the legislation, because it expands the pool of people paying for insurance and ensures that healthy people do not opt out of having insurance until they need it.

Critics say the provision gives the government too much power over what they say should be a personal economic decision.

Twenty-six states went to court to say individuals cannot be forced to have insurance, a "product" they may neither want nor need. They argued that if that provision is unconstitutional, the entire law must go. The Justice Department countered that since every American will need medical care at some point in their lives, individuals do not "choose" whether to participate in the health care market.

The partisan debate around such a sweeping piece of legislation has encompassed almost every traditional hot-button topic: abortion and contraception funding, state and individual rights, federal deficits, end-of-life care, and the overall economy.

During arguments on March 27, Justice Anthony Kennedy said the law appeared to "change the relationship between the government and the individual in a profound way." Roberts argued then that "all bets are off" when it comes to federal government authority if Congress was found to have the authority to regulate health care in the name of commerce.

Liberal justices, however, argued people who don't pay into the health system by purchasing insurance make care more expensive for everyone. "It is not your free choice" to stay out of the market for life, Justice Ruth Bader Ginsburg said during arguments.

The legislation signed by Obama stretched to 2,700 pages, nine major sections and some 450 provisions. The first lawsuits challenging the health care overhaul began just hours after the president signed the measure.

Was this dispute _really_ "for real" or does it have the trappings of *Alice In Wonderland*? The United States of America is the only advanced country in the world that does not have some form of universal health care – 40 million United States citizens do not have medical insurance. The narrow question on which the High Court focused was whether or not the Federal Government has the Constitutional right to compel Americans to buy some form of affordable health care insurance or face a fine if they do not do so.

Shockingly, people across the nation picketed, marched, and demanded that the government leave them alone – and protect their God-given right to be without health care – or to pay the exorbitant rates charged by health insurance companies which gleefully rack up 800 *billion* dollars worth of business a year!

* * *

We elected the first Black president in our history and we have systematically tried to destroy him, not because he doesn't have good ideas, but because in the rarified halls of vested power, without using the "N" word, they will make sure (nod, nod, wink, wink) that this Uppity N*gg*r goes back to where he belongs. Racially-motivated attacks, whether they hide behind the "birthers" curtain of "prove he was born in America" (Thank you, Donald Trump!) or other unspoken "Gentlemen's Agreements" out of the 1940s, hit a new low in the spring of 2012 when bumper stickers on cars started spouting the statement, "Don't Renig America!" – at a time when the word "Nigger" hasn't been used outside the Southeastern United States for more than 75 years!

Playing on the word *renege*, which means to go back on a promise, undertaking, or contract, according to Merriam-Webster, the ever-hateful anti-Obama masses seem to have come up with yet another way to disparage not only the President, but also African Americans. Circulating on Facebook, a picture of a bumper sticker, reading, "Don't Re-Nig In 2012" made feverish rounds. While Obama's iconic red, white and blue logo was crossed out, the bumper sticker made it very clear that Obama opposers descended far beneath the idea of just being against Obama politically.

* * *

The separation of Church and State – which was originally meant not to keep the *Church* safe from the *State*, but to keep the *State* safe from the *Church* – is more tenuous than ever. Protestant Christian Fundamentalists believe in absolute terms that America is first and foremost a *Christian* nation – more than that, a *Fundamentalist Christian* nation. And what the hell are we doing with a (Nigger) President whose name is Barack *Hussein* Obama? Religion belongs in the schools and in rock concerts and in politics – provided it's White Anglo-Saxon Protestant Christianity.

And while we're on the subject, can you believe that they want to keep teaching in public schools that human beings were descended from a goddam *monkey*? Evolution is nothing more than a Communist plot that "they" are trying to foist on us, just like that sh*t about "global warming" that everyone knows is phony as a three dollar bill ...

* * *

America is being systematically destroyed - not by terrorists from without, but by vested interests from within. Politicians, talk show hosts, media moguls, and populist rabble rousers ("Can you believe it, they're saying everyone ought to have the opportunity to go to college? What a bunch of goddam elitists!") who seek to preserve their "territory" at any cost - by obstructing the passage of beneficial laws, by scandalous lies and accusations, by negative campaigning, and by gratuitous insults. These "saviors" studiously ignore the fact that they pose *absolutely no constructive ideas of their own to resolve the morass in which our country now finds itself.*

The politicians think no farther than getting themselves elected or re-elected. The communications *mavens* want nothing more than to secure million dollar media deals. And the moguls who run their media empires thrive on sheer power and unlimited money from advertising revenues built on the backs of those who spend their hard-earned money on Budweiser, Chevrolets, and Exxon-Mobil.

The lure of $100,000 in lecture fees is a powerful aphrodisiac. The lure of power, the adulation, the cheers are an even greater aphrodisiac. These politicians, fearmongers, "talking heads," and captains of industry revel in their fame, their glory, and their self-styled wisdom, when the country is in greater debt than any nation in history, and we are slipping faster and faster into becoming a third world nation each year.

If the public starts putting two and two together and the answer comes out "four," you won't be able to dazzle them with your brilliance or baffle them with your bulls**t anymore. But so far, the "average" American can still be led to believe that 2+2 equals whatever number the spin masters want to make it. Attach "cold war" epithet names to sound fiscal and social policies. Speak louder than the other guy, even if you're using more of the same old scare tactics - tactics which have already propelled our country into being the largest debtor nation in the history of the world.

What is even worse, as the 2010 elections showed – and as the 2012 elections seem to be echoing – more than 40% of Americans are buying into the politics of fear, dissension, and abuse without stopping for even a moment to consider exactly what these political hatemongers are offering in exchange for turning one faction out and securing the benefits of power for themselves. Memories are short. Fear is bewitching.

The lure of a drop-out from several colleges, who finally managed to get a bachelor's degree, whose heavy-handed humor runs to, "Do you know the difference between a soccer mom and a pit bull? Lipstick," who uses an autistic child as a "prop," and who's reasonably attractive and has a largely unused brain, seemed to be hypnotic.

In the 2010 elections, the incredibly well-funded Republican machine (translation: nameless 527(c) (3) tax exempt organizations operating in anonymous offices along the "beltway") managed to convince an electorate impatient that what had taken eight years to ruin under a Republican administration could not be fixed in the first two years, and that "the *American people* had decided that we were going in the wrong direction!" The Democrats lost 52 seats and control of the House of Representatives.

But it would be simplistic and stupidly naïve to blame "the Republicans" for winning the elections. What happened was what has so often happened in our political history. The Democrats swept in on a wave of "Change You Can Believe In!" in 2008. *They had the votes necessary to swiftly and decisively pass a series of programs which could greatly have benefited our nation.* After all, they had effectively campaigned on a platform that Republicans had stonewalled, blockaded, and ruined our economy.

Instead of delivering a *fait accompli* and then promoting it to the public by showing *specifically how their program would benefit us all*, the Democrats became embroiled in what Democrats are historically so successful at doing: splintering, backbiting, cannibalizing their own, and *finally, after the populace was disgusted and confused, and after the Republicans had had all the time they needed to publicize how the Democrats were back to their old "tax and spend" ways,* the Democratically-controlled Congress passed a watered-down healthcare bill (which Republicans immediately derided as "ObamaCare") which no one understood. The Republican minority somehow convinced the American people that the Democrats were "out of touch with mainstream America," and that we should "turn out this do-nothing Congress."

And that's exactly what happened. The Democrats once again shot themselves in their collective feet. They got thrown out *and they deserved to get thrown out*!

But in a harbinger of things to come – maybe – the largest of our United States, California, which has the 6th largest economy *in the world* – bucked the trend. A billionaire businesswoman, Meg Whitman, spent $143 *million* of her own money in an unsuccessful gubernatorial campaign that proved that maybe you couldn't buy a governorship. A former head of Hewlett Packard, Carly Fiorina, who was endorsed by Sarah Palin and much better financed than her opponent, failed to unseat United States Senator Barbara Boxer, a Jew, whom Fiorina had painted as "far to the left of mainstream

America." California voted overwhelmingly Democratic in virtually every contested race.

And in Delaware, the public answered Tea Party darling Christine O'Donnell's much-parroted campaign slogan, "I'm one of you!" with a decisive *"No, you're not!"* and rebuffed her effort to gain the U.S. Senate (for the third time in five years).

While the Democrats have suffered a rude, hard, perhaps well-deserved slap in the face, the dancing-in-the-streets celebration of the Republicans may well be premature. No one has ever won a campaign by overestimating the intelligence of the American voting public. The way the President and Congress are now aligned, no dramatic changes occurred during the 2010-2012 Congressional session. It's gridlock once again. The Republicans did not pass *their* program – whatever that undisclosed program was – and as the Presidential election nears, three things have become increasingly obvious:

1. The economy *is* getting better – not necessarily because one party or the other is in power, but simply because the economy has always been cyclical.

2. The Republicans have – for the first time in memory – failed to "hang together" – they seem to be splintering among their own, and while each major would-be candidate *re*-made himself in a far more conservative image – they seem to forget the lesson taught so well by former President Bill Clinton: the United States of America is basically and essentially a *centrist* society. Veer too far to the right or too far to the left, and you will easily capture the vocal *minority.* But vocal or not, it will still be a *minority* and in order to get elected in a two-person race, you have to win *more than* 50% of the electorate.

3. Whether people love him or hate him, the current occupant of the White house has brought the troops home from an unpopular war in Iraq, a far-off corner of the world where we had no business being in the first place; and it looks like he has a program in place to bring our soldiers home from an even uglier war in an even more remote corner of the world which can't even boast that it has anything of economic value that we need; and under his administration Osama bin Laden, the most vilified villain in the last fifty years, was killed.

Regardless of political infighting or outfighting, what we are doing is akin to two fleas fighting over which one owns the dog. We seem not to realize that we have run out of time and money; that we no longer have the luxury of political gamesmanship and needless, stupid bickering.

Many years ago, I saw the movie *On The Beach*, based on the Neville Shute novel. In that movie, man's desire to dominate other men resulted in a nuclear holocaust that ultimately destroyed the entire world. Just before the end of the movie, the camera panned onto a group of do-gooders carrying signs that read, "There's still time, Brother!" At the very end of the movie, there were no more beings alive. The wind blew and the camera paused on a single sign with the words, "There's still time, Brother!"

INTRODUCTION

It has always seemed strange to me that when men or women run for public office, they always use the term *Fight*. "I will *fight* to lower your taxes!" "I will *fight* the other fellow's corrupt ways!" "I will make sure you have a *fighter* for you in [Congress / City Hall / the office of city dog catcher] whatever."

Forty-six years ago, I became a trial lawyer – and again the term *fight* surfaced more often than not. I somehow amassed a reputation as being a "pit bull," a "junkyard dog," and other, more colorful if less flattering names. It was a reputation I felt really wasn't *me*, but if that kind of reputation brought in business, I could live with it.

As the years passed, I started to wonder and I started to ask questions. Why was it necessary for a politician to say he or she would *fight*? Fight for *what*? Exactly what would a *fight* accomplish that working together – reasoning, compromising, and coming to agreement – would not accomplish easier, better, more efficiently, and cheaper? That was the premise of my book *How To Cut Your Legal Bills In Half*, which promoted mediation instead of ever-costlier court fights.

Think, for a moment: *Exactly what does a _fight_ accomplish?*
I'll tell you what it accomplishes: People get their emotions up.
They feel they cannot compromise or they'll lose face – that they'll
somehow be _less than_ the other fellow. If one's opponent says, "Yes,"
then you say "No" as a knee-jerk reaction, not because you will get
anything done, but because you'll make sure the other guy doesn't
get anything done *either* – so you will have the dubious satisfaction
of knowing you've blocked something your opponent wanted even
if, in your calm, rational mind, you knew that the proposal would
move things forward; not admitting that if you compromised on this
point, the other fellow might compromise on something *you* wanted
and something could get done.

If you think I'm wrong, look at what's happened in the United
States in the past two decades: gridlock, stagnation, inaction, and,
finally, an economic recession the likes of which we haven't seen
since the Great Depression. And rather than try to *do* something
about this recession, the Democrats were so busy blaming the
Republicans for *causing* it, and the Republicans were so busy
blaming the Democrats for *spend and tax* to get us *out* of the
recession, that *nothing at all happened and we were – all of us –
trapped like a deer in the headlights.* Not doing a thing but sitting
there, waiting to get clobbered again.

New voices on the right and on the left exhorted us to "throw
the bums out" and start anew – and that's exactly what happened in
the 2010 elections. The Democrats, who came into the Obama years
with a filibuster-proof majority, immediately started squabbling and
fighting so they couldn't even pass legislation that should have been
a "no brainer." Republicans raised their traditional "politics of fear"
bogeyman to the ever shriller chastisements of the Sarah Palins and
Rush Limbaughs, so that otherwise sensible people got caught up
in the firestorm of frustration and threatened to vote the incumbents
out of office, to get a "fresh start."

Unfortunately, while it was easy to bash the Democratic proposals with such outmoded epithets as "liberal" and "socialist," and say, "Wait 'til we get into office – have we got a program for you!" the Republicans haven't come up with *one single positive idea about what they're going to do or how they're going to do it. NOT ONE!* You think I'm kidding? Tell me one single constructive idea the Republicans have put forth. Can't do it, can you? Of course not. For this is ***The Politics of HATE.***

It doesn't have to be that way. If we all stopped fighting and stonewalling and blaming and dumping garbage on the other fellow, and learned to work *together* for the good of us *all*, just think what we could accomplish. *Trillions of dollars* spent on foreign wars, when all it takes is *one single terrorist* to escape the safety nets and come into the United States, could have been saved and spent on *roads, schools, healthcare, social programs, growing food, and paying off our debt – things that we need, not things that would make us temporarily feel more macho*.

"It'll never work!" naysayers will say. "How dare you be so naïve?" Or, as former president George W. Bush said about the Iraqis before we got so embroiled in the Iraqi War that we won't recover what it cost us for the next hundred years, "I *know* those people. I *understand* those people." Right. That's the same fellow who crowed, "Mission accomplished!" and swore that Saddam Hussein had an arsenal of "weapons of mass destruction."

You think cooperation won't work? Try telling that to the Chinese, who've *made* it work. Or to the Indians, whose economy continues to get better each year. Or to the French or Danish, who, according to the World Health Organization, have the world's best and most affordable system of delivering healthcare. All of these societies, who have learned to *cooperate and work together* rather than *fight*, are moving *up* on the indexes by which we measure quality of life, while we in the United States – the greatest, strongest, richest, most moral country on the face of the planet ("Yes, indeed, Our God is better than their god!") – are, for some absolutely unexplainable reason – moving *down*. *Why? What are we doing wrong?*

* * *

Don't get me wrong. There's a time and a place for everything, including all-out competition. The Olympic games are such a venue. High school football games are an appropriate place for such an outpouring of emotion. Even overpriced professional sports draw more spectators year after year as our overfed, under-exercised, increasingly obese men, women, and children live vicariously through sports heroes that are paid millions of dollars a year, while teachers, whose influence on tomorrow is surely more positive and tangible, struggle and work 100-hour weeks to bring home a modest income.

In the sports arena, there are rules which make the competition fair, controlled, and honorable. In football, "unsportsmanlike conduct" warrants a 15-yard penalty. Pass interference is punished by an automatic first down. In soccer, which is a very secondary sport in the United States, even though it is the most popular sport in the rest of the world, a deliberate act will get you a "red card" – not only are you ejected from the game, but your team has to play the remainder of the game with one less player than the other side.

It is only in the political arena where even the most dishonorable actions are acceptable, where lies are as plentiful and cheap as tap water, and where reputation-killing defamation is sloughed off as "politics as usual."

When was the last time you heard someone running for office say, "Vote *for* me because *I did* ..." rather than "Vote *against* the other fellow" or "Don't vote for so-and-so because *he* (or *she*) is ...

[take your choice of negative images]." Does that really seem right to you? Shouldn't we be voting *for* an idea, a person, a proposal that makes sense rather than *against* someone because of completely unproved allegations thrown against someone's reputation?

Under Bill Clinton's presidency, our budget was balanced (indeed, we had a surplus), we were at peace, people were employed, and life was pretty damned good. Can you say that about our lives today? Simple question: Was the United States better off in 1998 than it is today? Was life better for *you*, easier for *you* 14 years ago than it is today?

"But," you say, "Bill Clinton was an immoral philanderer. How *dare* he do what he did with Monica Lewinsky and *lie* about it to the American people? He *deserved to be impeached and removed from office!*"

Oh, really? From 9 to 5, Bill Clinton did as good a job as anyone has ever done in the White House. While I don't justify his after-hours frolics, he was a damned good president. So was FDR, so was Eisenhower, and so was John F. Kennedy. Would anyone care to go into *their* after-hours bedroom antics? Perhaps all the hypocritical moralists on both sides of the aisle might like to do a little research. Even better, perhaps the American bury-their-head-in-the-sand sheep, who follow honey-worded hypocrites might even (Gasp!) want to open their eyes, their ears, and their *minds* by doing a little research themselves, instead of meekly accepting what the officeholder wannabe *du jour* wants them to hear.

Am I angry that my fellow Americans have become a nation being led to slaughter by their own politicians? Damn right I am! In ads for the United Negro College Fund, the traditional motto is, "A mind is a terrible thing to waste!" *Yet that's just what 95% of us are doing. We are being led around by those who have not even a small percentage of the brains God gave us, who have the morals of a goat, and who are capable of talking "prettier" and spouting venomous attacks in such an attractive manner that we follow them blindly over the cliff.*

And while it's so easy to trample on a dream or a good idea by saying, "That's so stupid it will never work, exactly *what have we got to lose by trying it out?* If it fails, we're in exactly in the same place we are now. And if it succeeds? What then?

WAKE UP, AMERICA!

THE CLASS OF 2012

A PRESIDENTIAL YEAR

ELECTION PRIMER

Handicapping The Race

Human beings have gambled since the dawn of humankind. The oldest known dice were excavated as part of a 5000-year-old backgammon found at an archeological site in southeastern Iran. There are several biblical references to "casting lots," indicating that dice were commonplace during King David's reign. Gambling with two dice was very popular in Greece, and the Romans were passionate gamblers, especially at the peak of the Roman Empire.

Perhaps the earliest form of oddsmaking began with dice, particularly when a pair of dice were used. In a single die, there are six numbers on the cube. Each of these numbers has an equal chance of coming up. On the other hand, when two dice are rolled, any number from 2 to 12 can come up. It didn't take an intelligent oddsmaker long to realize that the chance of rolling a 2 or a 12 is much smaller that rolling a 7. The logic of this is inescapable: there is only one combination – a 1 + a 1 – that will yield a 2, and likewise there is only one combination – a 6 + a 6 – that will yield a 12. On the other hand, you have a much greater chance of rolling a 7 because either a 6 + 1, a 5+2, or a 4+3 will get you 7.

Giving odds became particularly attractive as games and contests of chance became more sophisticated, whether in games such as roulette, cards, and the like, or in horse races. The more likely a horse or a number, or, in politics, the candidate is likely to win, the lower the odds. For example, a "most likely will win" bet would be 1-2, which means that for ever two dollars you bet, if you win, you will get three dollars back. On the other hand, if you bet a "long shot" at, say 20-1, if you bet the same two dollars and you win, your payoff will be $40. Great monetary reward, but, like the risk-reward ration everywhere, you're not likely to win a lot of the time.

With that type of mindset, I thought I'd play a little game of oddsmaking. I "gave odds" on 2012 Presidential candidates as they existed at the beginning of October 2011, and as they existed half a year later in April 2012. Since most handicappers put a little one-line comment about the horse or candidate to let you know *why* the handicapper projected what he or she did, I've added a brief comment for each candidate.

Here is how I viewed the upcoming election at the beginning of October 2011:

Candidat	Part	Odd	Comment
Barack Obama	Dem.	2-1	Incumbent. Slower recovery than normal and continuing wars signal trouble ahead.
Mitt Romney	Rep.	2-1	Centerline candidate has best chance to beat Obama

Sarah Palin	Rep. 5-1	Say what you will, love or her hate her, she's a name to contend with and the Tea Party's darling.
Rick Perry	Rep. 6-1	Texas governor – populist rabble rouser with dangerous, inconsistent ideas and a hypnotic manner reminiscent of some 20th century dictators.
Herman Cain	Rep. 6-1	African-American conservative antithesis to Obama – a spellbinder who's gaining traction.
Michele Bachmann	Rep. 10-1	Sarah Palin-clone who started making points by being pretty, outspoken, and passionate.
Newt Gingrich	Rep. 10-1	Name recognition, former Speaker of the House.
John Huntsman	Rep. 20-1	Good ideas, but too much of a pedant and Mormon.
Rich Santorum	Rep. 30-1	Looks too much like a college student.
Ron Paul	Rep. 30-1	Good ideas, but too old and not handsome enough.

Fast forward to April 2012:

Candidat	Part	Odd	Comment
Barack Obama	Dem.	1-2	Hard to beat the incumbent when the economy is starting to pick up for real, the soldiers are home from Iraq, Afghanistan is winding down, people are starting to feel good about America again, and, most important, the never-ending Republican debates have shown that those who are still running are out of step with America.
Mitt Romney	Rep.	3-1	Probably the best of the Republican bunch, but can't seem to attract passionate supporters – has switched positions too many times to be fully trusted. Too patrician to connect with common folk.
Newt Gingrich	Rep.	40-1	How the heck did he stay in the race as long he has? – and with so-o-o much "baggage?"
Ron Paul	Rep.	100-1	Great, sound, consistent ideas, last of the pre-hate gentleman politicians, but absolutely no traction with the majority of voters.

Sarah Palin	Rep.	WITHDREW. Much more money to be made becoming a writer, king-maker, and "talking head" in the media.
Rick Perry	Rep.	WITHDREW. after a series of gaffes emphasized his hot temper and his inflexibility and scariness.
Herman Cain	Rep.	WITHDREW. Like the downfall of so many politicians he couldn't seem to keep his zipper up, and too many women brought him down.
Michele Bachmann	Rep.	WITHDREW. She was so insistent on saying what *she* wanted to say that she never answered a hard question directly. Why spend money you don't have when the vote count is so low?
John Huntsman	Rep.	WITHDREW. You can't get elected by winning 1%.
Rich Santorum	Rep.	WITHDREW. Underfunded, underesti-mated, who would have thought he'd make it to April 2012? But far too much to the right to attract the numbers which would put him into the White House – and some genuinely scary ideas.

Who are The Candidates?

Obama and Romney

Barack Obama

The current President of the United States would seem to need little introduction, yet a background précis is necessary to identify the *man* rather than what most challengers view as the "target."

Barack Hussein Obama II was born August 4, 1961. He is the 44th and current President of the United States, the first African American to hold the office. Born in Honolulu, Hawaii, Obama is a graduate of Columbia University and Harvard Law School, where he was the president of the *Harvard Law Review*. He was a community organizer in Chicago before earning his law degree. He worked as a civil rights attorney in Chicago and taught constitutional law at the University of Chicago Law School from 1992 to 2004.

Obama ran for the seat of junior United States Senator from Illinois in 2004. He won the election. His presidential campaign began in February 2007. After a close campaign in the 2008 Democratic Party presidential primaries against Hillary Rodham Clinton, he won his party's nomination. In the 2008 presidential election, he defeated Republican nominee John McCain, and was inaugurated as president on January 20, 2009. Nine months later, Obama was named the 2009 Nobel Peace Prize laureate.

As president, Obama signed economic stimulus legislation in the form of the American Recovery and Reinvestment Act of 2009 and the Tax Relief, Unemployment Insurance Reauthorization, and Job Creation Act of 2010. Other domestic policy initiatives include the Patient Protection and Affordable Care Act (derisively called "ObamaCare" by its opponents), the Dodd–Frank Wall Street Reform and Consumer Protection Act, the Don't Ask, Don't Tell Repeal Act of 2010 and the Budget Control Act of 2011. In foreign policy, he ended the war in Iraq, increased troop levels in Afghanistan (which is now starting to wind down), signed the New START arms control treaty with Russia, ordered US involvement in the 2011 Libya military intervention, and ordered the military operation that resulted in the death of Osama bin Laden. In April 2011, Obama declared his intention to seek re-election in the 2012 presidential election.

During the first two years of his Presidency, Obama appointed two women to serve on the Supreme Court. Sonia Sotomayor was the first Hispanic to be a Supreme Court Justice. Elena Kagan, a woman and a Jew, brought the number of women sitting simultaneously on the Court to three (as well as the number of Jewish justices on the Court to three) for the first time in American history.

Obama called the November 2, 2010 election, where the Democratic Party lost 63 seats in, and control of, the House of Representatives, "humbling" and a "shellacking." He said that the results came because not enough Americans had felt the effects of the economic recovery.

According to the Gallup Organization, Obama began his presidency with a 68 percent approval rating before gradually declining for the rest of the year, and eventually bottoming out at 41 percent in August 2010, a trend similar to Ronald Reagan's and Bill Clinton's first years in office. Polls show strong support for Obama in other countries. In a recent poll conducted by Harris Interactive for France 24 and the *International Herald Tribune*, Obama was rated as the most respected world leader, as well as the most powerful. In a similar poll conducted by Harris, Obama was rated as the most popular world leader, as well as the one figure most people would pin their hopes on for pulling the world out of the economic downturn.

On October 9, 2009, the Norwegian Nobel Committee announced that Obama had won the 2009 Nobel Peace Prize "for his extraordinary efforts to strengthen international diplomacy and cooperation between peoples." Obama accepted this award in Oslo, Norway on December 10, 2009, with "deep gratitude and great humility." Obama is the fourth U.S. president to be awarded the Nobel Peace Prize and the third to become a Nobel laureate while in office.

Obama was known as "Barry" in his youth, but asked to be addressed with his given name during his college years. Besides his native English, Obama speaks Indonesian at the conversational level, which he learned during his four childhood years in Jakarta. He plays basketball, a sport he participated in as a member of his high school's varsity team.

In June 1989, Obama met Michelle Robinson when he was employed as a summer associate at a Chicago law firm. Assigned for three months as Obama's adviser at the firm, Robinson joined him at group social functions, but declined his initial requests to date. They began dating later that summer, became engaged in 1991, and were married on October 3, 1992. The couple's first daughter, Malia Ann, was born on July 4, 1998, followed by a second daughter, Natasha ("Sasha"), on June 10, 2001. The Obamas have a Portuguese Water Dog named Bo, a gift from the late Senator Ted Kennedy.

MITT ROMNEY

Willard Mitt Romney, born March 12, 1947, is an American businessman and politician. He was the 70th Governor of Massachusetts from 2003 to 2007 and is the presumptive a candidate for the 2012 Republican Party presidential nomination.

The son of George W. Romney, the former Governor of Michigan, Romney was raised in Bloomfield Hills, Michigan, and later served as a Mormon missionary in France. He married Ann Davies in 1969. They have five children. He received his undergraduate degree from Brigham Young University, and then earned a joint JD and MBA from Harvard University. Romney entered the management consulting business, which led to a position at Bain & Company. Eventually serving as CEO, Romney brought the company out of crisis. His wealth helped fund most of his future political campaigns. Active in his Mormon church, he served as ward bishop and later stake president in his area. He ran as the Republican candidate in the 1994 U.S. Senate election in Massachusetts, losing to long-time incumbent Ted Kennedy. Romney organized and steered the 2002 Winter Olympics as head of the Salt Lake Organizing Committee, and helped turn the troubled games into a financial success.

Romney was elected Governor of Massachusetts in 2002 but did not seek re-election in 2006. He presided over a series of spending cuts and increases in fees that eliminated a $1.5 billion deficit. He also signed into law the Massachusetts health care reform legislation, which provided near-universal health insurance access via subsidies and state-level mandates and was the first of its kind in the nation. During the course of his political career, his positions seem to have shifted more towards conservatism in several areas, giving his opponents ammunition to describe him as an inconsistent "shape shifter."

Romney ran for the Republican nomination in the 2008 U.S. presidential election, winning several primaries and caucuses, but eventually lost the nomination to John McCain. On June 2, 2011, Romney announced that he would seek the 2012 Republican presidential nomination. The results of the caucuses and primaries so far place him as the leader in the race.

In March of his senior year, he began dating Ann Davies, whom he had once known in elementary school. The two informally agreed to marriage around the time of his June 1965 graduation, and married four years later. Romney attended Stanford University for a year, where he worked as a night security guard to fund secret trips home to see Ann. Although the campus was becoming radicalized with the beginnings of 1960s social and political movements, Romney kept a well-groomed appearance and enjoyed traditional campus events

In July 1966, Romney lived for 30 months in France as a Mormon missionary, a traditional duty that his father and other relatives had done. Like most individual Mormon missionaries, he did not gain many converts, with the nominally Catholic but secular, wine-loving French people proving especially resistant to a religion that prohibits alcohol. He became demoralized, and later recalled it as the only time when "most of what I was trying to do was rejected.

Romney developed a lifelong affection for France and its people, and speaks French. The experience in the country also changed him. It instilled in him a belief that life is fragile and that he needed seriousness of purpose. After having been only a half-hearted Mormon growing up: "On a mission, your faith in Jesus Christ either evaporates or it becomes much deeper. For me it became much deeper."

As a result of his business career, by 2007 Romney and his wife had a net worth of between $190 and $250 million, most of it held in blind trusts. An additional blind trust existed in the name of the Romneys' children and grandchildren that was valued at between $70 and $100 million as of 2007. The couple's net worth remains in the same range today. Romney and his wife receive about $21 million a year from investment income, of which about $3 million goes to federal income taxes and about $3.5 million goes to charity, including to the LDS Church.

After unsuccessfully running against Ted Kennedy for the U.S. Senate, Romney threw his hat into the political arena again in 2002. He ran as a political outsider again, saying he was "not a partisan Republican" but rather a "moderate" with "progressive" views. Romney supporters hailed his business record, especially with the Olympics, as the record of someone who would be able to bring a new era of efficiency into Massachusetts politics. Nevertheless, Romney had difficulty connecting with voters and fell behind his Democratic opponent, Massachusetts State Treasurer Shannon O'Brien, in polls for a while before rebounding. He contributed over $6 million to his own campaign during the election, a state record at the time. Romney was elected governor with 50 percent of the vote to O'Brien's 45 percent.

Upon entering office in the middle of a fiscal year, Romney faced an immediate $650 million shortfall and a projected $3 billion deficit for the next year. Unexpected revenue of $1.0–1.3 billion from a previously enacted capital gains tax increase and $500 million in unanticipated federal grants decreased the deficit to $1.2–1.5 billion. Through a combination of spending cuts, increased fees, and removal of corporate tax loopholes, the state ran surpluses of around $600–700 million for the last two full fiscal years Romney was in office, although it began running deficits again after that.

Although in his present incarnation as a Republican Presidential candidate he now harshly criticizes "ObamaCare," Romney was at the forefront of a movement to bring near-universal health insurance coverage to Massachusetts after a close adviser told him at the start of his term that doing so would be the best way he could help people and after the federal government, due to the rules of Medicaid funding, threatened to cut $385 million in those payments to Massachusetts if the state did not reduce the number of uninsured recipients of health care services. Despite not having campaigned on the idea of universal health insurance, Romney decided that because people without insurance still received expensive health care, the money spent by the state for such care could be better used to subsidize insurance for the poor.

Romney formed a team of consultants from different political backgrounds that came up with innovative proposals more ambitious than the one recommended by the Massachusetts Senate and more acceptable to him than one from the Massachusetts House of Representatives that incorporated a new payroll tax. Past rival Ted Kennedy, who had made universal heath coverage his life's work and who, over time, had developed a warm relationship with Romney, gave Romney's plan a positive reception, which encouraged Democratic legislators to cooperate. The effort eventually gained the support of all major stakeholders within the state, and Romney helped break a logjam between rival Democratic leaders in the legislature. On April 12, 2006, Romney signed the resulting Massachusetts health reform law, which requires nearly all Massachusetts residents to buy health insurance coverage or face escalating tax penalties such as the loss of their personal income tax exemption. Surprisingly, this is the very problem that faced the United States Supreme Court, albeit on a national level.

In 2005, Romney revealed a change of view regarding abortion, moving from an "unequivocal" pro-choice position expressed during his 2002 campaign to a pro-life one. He vetoed a bill on pro-life grounds that would expand access to emergency contraception in hospitals and pharmacies. His veto was overridden by the legislature.

Romney formally announced his candidacy for the 2008 Republican nomination for president on February 13, 2007. His assets included a highly-profitable career in the business world and his successful management of the Olympics. A number of commentators noted that with his square jaw and ample hair graying at the temples, Romney physically matched one of the common images of what some believed a president should look like. His liabilities included having run for senator and served as governor in one of the nation's most liberal states, having taken some positions there that were opposed by the party's conservative base, and subsequently shifting those positions. His religion was also viewed with suspicion and skepticism by some in the Evangelical portion of the party.

Romney assembled a veteran group of Republican staffers, consultants, and pollsters, but he was little-known nationally, and stayed around the 10 percent range in Republican preference polls for the first half of 2007. He proved the most effective fundraiser of any of the Republican candidates; he also partly financed his campaign with his own personal fortune. These resources, combined with the mid-year near-collapse of nominal front-runner John McCain's campaign, made Romney a threat to win the nomination and the focus of the other candidates' attacks. Romney's staff suffered from internal strife and the candidate himself was indecisive at times, constantly asking for more data before making a decision.

Romney announced the end of his campaign on February 7, 2008. Altogether, he had won 11 primaries and caucuses, received about 4.7 million total votes, and garnered 280 delegates. Romney spent $110 million during the campaign, including $45 million of his own money. A week later, Romney endorsed McCain for president.

On June 2, 2011, Romney formally announced the start of his 2012 campaign for President. He focused on the economy and criticized President Obama's handling of it.

Romney raised $56 million during 2011, far more than any of his Republican opponents, and refrained from spending any of his own money on his campaign. He initially ran a low-key, low-profile campaign. Michele Bachmann staged a brief surge, then by September 2011, Romney's chief rival in polls was a recent entrant, Texas Governor Rick Perry, and the two exchanged sharp criticisms of each other during a series of debates among the Republican candidates. The October 2011 decisions of Chris Christie and Sarah Palin not to run finally settled the field. Perry faded due to poor performances in those debates, while Herman Cain staged a long-shot surge until allegations of sexual misconduct derailed him.

After the charges of flip flopping that marked his 2008 campaign began to accumulate again, Romney declared in November 2011 that "I've been as consistent as a human being can be." In the final month before voting began, Newt Gingrich enjoyed a major surge, taking a solid lead in national polls and in most of the early caucus and primary states before settling back into parity or worse with Romney following a barrage of negative ads from Restore Our Future, a pro-Romney Super PAC.

Throughout his business, Olympics, and political career, Romney's instinct has been to apply the "Bain way" towards problems. Romney has said, "There were two key things I learned at Bain. One was a series of concepts for approaching tough problems and a problem-solving methodology; the other was an enormous respect for data, analysis, and debate." He has written, "There are answers in numbers – gold in numbers. Pile the budgets on my desk and let me wallow." Romney believes the Bain approach is not only effective in the business realm but also in running for office and, once there, in solving political conundrums such as proper Pentagon spending levels and the future of Social Security. Former Bain and Olympics colleague Fraser Bullock has said of Romney, "He's not an ideologue. He makes decisions based on researching data more deeply than anyone I know." Romney's technocratic instincts have thus always been with him; in his public appearances during the 2002 gubernatorial campaign he sometimes gave PowerPoint presentations rather than conventional speeches. Upon taking office he became, in the words of *The Boston Globe*, "the state's first self-styled CEO governor." During his 2008 presidential campaign, he was constantly asking for data, analysis, and opposing arguments, and has been viewed as a potential "CEO president."

FORMER CANDIDATES WHO DIDN'T MAKE IT!

NEWT GINGRICH AND RON PAUL

NEWT GINGRICH

This section devotes much less space to Gingrich than to the other candidates because he is described in far greater detail in another section – The Contract With America. This writer believes that Gingrich is largely responsible for the current trend of supplanting the politics of cooperation which emerged after World War II with the Politics of Hate. Nevertheless, since he considered himself "in the hunt" for the 2012 Republican nomination, and since, given his background, he did a remarkable job of reinventing himself, a brief biography is in order.

Newton Leroy "Newt" Gingrich is an American politician, author, and political consultant who represented Georgia's 6th congressional district as a Republican from 1979 until his resignation in 1999, and served as the 58th Speaker of the U.S. House of Representatives from 1995 to 1999. In the 1970s, Gingrich taught history and geography at the University of West Georgia. During this period he ran twice (1974 and 1976) for the United States House of Representatives before winning in November 1978. He served as House Minority Whip from 1989 to 1995.

A co-author and architect of the "Contract with America," Gingrich was a major leader in the Republican victory in the 1994 congressional election. In 1995, *Time* named him "Man of the Year" for "his role in ending the four-decades-long Democratic majority in the House." While he was House speaker, the House enacted welfare reform, passed a capital gains tax cut in 1997, and in 1998 passed the first balanced budget since 1969. The poor showing by Republicans in the 1998 Congressional election and pressure from Republican colleagues caused Gingrich's resignation from the speakership on November 5, 1998, and then the House on January 3, 1999. He is a member of the Council on Foreign Relations. He has written or co-authored 27 books. In May 2011, he announced his campaign for the Republican presidential nomination.

Gingrich converted to Roman Catholicism in 2009 after being raised Lutheran and spending most of his adult life as a Southern Baptist. He has been married three times, with the first two marriages ending in divorce. He has two children from his first marriage and has been married to Callista (Bisek) Gingrich since 2000.

RON PAUL

What a tragedy for American politics that "also ran" Ron Paul gained so little traction when his libertarian ideas make such eminent common sense. Although I disagree with most of his positions, he is the *only* candidate who was consistently *consistent*, who discussed *issues*, not personalities, and who was, in the best possible way, perhaps the last of the old-time pre-Politics-of-Hate politicians. I might often disagree with him, but I have the feeling he can disagree *without being disagreeable*. I have the feeling I can trust him, and I'd love to have him in what the British call "the shadow cabinet."

Ronald Ernest "Ron" Paul, born August 20, 1935, 76, has been the U.S. Representative for Texas's 14th congressional district since 1997. He has run for President three times: as a Libertarian in 1988, and as a Republican in 2008 and 2012. He is an outspoken critic of American foreign and monetary policies, including the Military–industrial complex and the Federal Reserve, and is known for advocating libertarian positions and opposing his own party on certain issues.

A native of Pittsburgh, Pennsylvania, Paul is a graduate of Gettysburg College and Duke University School of Medicine, where he earned his medical degree. He served as a medical officer in the United States Air Force from 1963 until 1968 and worked as an obstetrician-gynecologist from the 1960s to the 1980s, delivering more than 4,000 babies. He became the first Representative in history to serve concurrently with a child in the Senate when his son Rand Paul was elected to the United States Senate from Kentucky in 2010.

Ron Paul has been an active writer and publisher since the late 1970s, when he created the first of several newsletters bearing his name. He has published many books and has been called the "intellectual godfather" of the Tea Party movement. On July 12, 2011, Paul announced that he would forego seeking another term in Congress in order to focus on his presidential bid.

Paul has served in Congress three different periods: first from 1976 to 1977, after he won a special election, then from 1979 to 1985, and finally since 1997. He resigned from the Republican Party in 1987 and launched a bid for the presidency running on the Libertarian Party ticket. In the 1988 presidential election, Paul was on the ballot in 46 States, scoring third in the popular vote with 432,179 votes (0.5%). According to Paul, his presidential campaign was about more than obtaining office; he sought to promote his libertarian ideas, often to school and university groups regardless of vote eligibility. He said, "We're just as interested in the future generation as this election. These kids will vote eventually, and maybe, just maybe, they'll go home and talk to their parents."

Paul considered campaigning for President during 1992, but instead chose to endorse Pat Buchanan that year, and served as an adviser to Buchanan's Republican presidential primary campaign against incumbent President George H. W. Bush.

During 1996, Paul was re-elected to Congress after a difficult campaign. Paul narrowly defeated Democratic attorney Charles "Lefty" Morris in the fall election, despite Morris' criticism over controversial statements in several newsletters that Ron Paul published. In 1998 and 2000, Paul defeated Loy Sneary, a Democratic Bay City, Texas, rice farmer and former Matagorda County judge. In the 2008 Republican primary, he defeated Friendswood city councilman Chris Peden, with over 70 percent of the vote and ran unopposed in the general election. In the 2010 Republican primary, Paul defeated three opponents with 80 percent of the vote.

On May 13, 2011, Paul formally announced his candidacy. In December 2011, with Ron Paul's increased support, the controversy over allegedly racist and homophobic statements in several Ron Paul newsletters in the 1980s and early 1990s once again gained media attention. During this time Paul supporters asserted that he was continually ignored by the media despite his significant support, citing examples of where television news shows would fail to mention Paul in discussions of the republican presidential hopefuls even when he was polling second.

Paul came in third in the Iowa Republican Caucus held on January 3, 2012. Out of a turnout of 121,503 votes, Paul took 21% of the certified votes. Rick Santorum and Mitt Romney finished in a virtual tie for first place with 25% each. In the New Hampshire Primary held on January 10, 2012, Paul received 23% of the votes and came in second after Romney's 39%. Ron Paul's results then declined, despite the withdrawal of candidates Michele Bachmann, Jon Huntsman and Rick Perry. He had fourth place finishes in the next two primaries, on January 21st in South Carolina (with 13% of the vote and on January 31st in Florida, where he received 7% of the vote. On February 4, Paul finished third in Nevada with 18.8% of the vote. Three non-binding primaries were held on February 7th; Paul took 3rd place in Colorado and Missouri with 13% and 12% of the vote respectively. He fared better in Minnesota with 27%, finishing second to Rick Santorum.

Paul had been a lifelong supporter of the Republican Party by the time he entered politics in the mid 1970s. He was one of the first elected officials in the nation to support Ronald Reagan's presidential campaign, and he actively campaigned for Reagan in 1976 and 1980. After Reagan's election in 1980, Paul quickly became disillusioned with the Reagan administration's policies. He later recalled being the only Republican to vote against Reagan budget proposals in 1981, aghast that "in 1977, Jimmy Carter proposed a budget with a $38 billion deficit, and every Republican in the House voted against it. In 1981, Reagan proposed a budget with a $45 billion deficit – which turned out to be $113 billion – and Republicans were cheering his great victory. They were living in a storybook land." He expressed his disgust with the political culture of both major parties in a speech delivered in 1984 on resigning from the House of Representatives to prepare for a failed run for the Senate, and he eventually apologized to his Libertarian friends for having supported Reagan.

By 1987, Paul was ready to sever all ties to the Republican Party, as he explained in a blistering resignation letter: "Since 1981 Ronald Reagan and the Republican Party have given us skyrocketing deficits, and astoundingly a doubled national debt. How is it that the party of balanced budgets, with control of the White House and Senate, accumulated red ink greater than all previous administrations put together? ... There is no credibility left for the Republican Party as a force to reduce the size of government. That is the message of the

Reagan years." A month later he announced he would seek the 1988 Libertarian Party nomination for president.

During the 1988 campaign, Paul called Reagan "a dramatic failure" and complained that "Reagan's record is disgraceful. He starts wars, breaks the law, supplies terrorists with guns made at taxpayers' expense and lies about it to the American people." Paul predicted that "the Republicans are on their way out as a major party," and he said that, although registered as a Republican, he had always been a Libertarian at heart.

In 2012 presidential campaign, during which he acknowledged it was unlikely that he would win the Republican Party nomination, Paul again asserted that he was participating in the Republican Party on his own terms, trying to persuade the rest of the party to move toward his positions rather than joining in with theirs. He expressed doubt that he would support any of his rivals should they win the nomination, warning that, "If the policies of the Republican Party are the same as the Democrat Party and they don't want to change anything on foreign policy, they don't want to cut anything, they don't want to audit the Fed and find out about monetary policy, they don't want to have actual change in government, that is a problem for me." On that same theme he said in another interview, "I would be reluctant to jump on board and tell all of the supporters that have given me trust and money that all of a sudden, I'd say, all we've done is for naught. So, let's support anybody at all ... even if they disagree with everything that we do."

Paul has been described as conservative and libertarian. Paul had the most conservative voting record of any member of Congress from 1937 to 2002, and was the most conservative of the candidates seeking the 2012 Republican nomination for president, on a scale primarily measuring positions on the role of government in managing the economy – not positions on social issues or foreign policy matters. Other analyses, in which key votes on domestic social issues and foreign policy factor more heavily, have judged Paul much more moderate. The National Journal, for instance, rated Paul only the 145th most conservative member of the House of Representatives based on votes cast in 2010.

The foundation of Paul's political philosophy is the conviction that "the proper role for government in America is to provide national defense, a court system for civil disputes, a criminal justice system for acts of force and fraud, and little else." He has been nicknamed "Dr. No," reflecting both his medical degree and his insistence that he will "never vote for legislation unless the proposed measure is expressly authorized by the Constitution."

He has pledged never to raise taxes and states he has never voted to approve a budget deficit. Paul believes that the country could abolish the individual income tax by scaling back federal spending to its fiscal year 2000 levels; financing government operations would be primarily by excise taxes and non-protectionist tariffs. He endorses eliminating most federal government agencies, terming them unnecessary bureaucracies.

On April 15, 2011, Paul was one of four Republican members of Congress to vote against Rep. Paul Ryan's budget proposal, known as "The Path to Prosperity."

Paul has a consistent record as an inflation hawk, having warned of the threat of hyperinflation as far back as 1981. While Paul believes the long-term decrease of the U.S. dollar's purchasing power by inflation is attributable to its lack of any commodity backing, he does not endorse a "return" to a gold standard – as the U.S. government has established during the past – but instead prefers to eliminate legal tender laws and to remove the sales tax on gold and silver, so that the market may freely decide what type of monetary standards there shall be. Since 1999, he has introduced bills into each Congress seeking to eliminate the Federal Reserve System in a single year.

Paul's foreign policy of nonintervention made him the only 2008 Republican presidential candidate to have voted against the Iraq War Resolution in 2002. He advocates withdrawal from the United Nations, and from the North Atlantic Treaty Organization, for reasons of maintaining strong national sovereignty. He endorses free trade, rejecting membership in the North American Free Trade Agreement (NAFTA) and the World Trade Organization as "managed trade." He favors increased border security and opposes welfare for illegal aliens, birthright citizenship and amnesty; he voted for the Secure Fence Act of 2006. He voted for the Authorization for Use of Military Force Against Terrorists in response to the September 11 attacks, but suggested war alternatives such as authorizing the president to grant Letters of Marque and Reprisal targeting specific terrorists. An opponent of the Iraq War and potential war with Iran, he has also criticized neo-conservatism and U.S. foreign policy in the Middle East, arguing that both inadvertently cause terrorist reprisals against Americans. Paul has stated that "Israel is our close friend" and that it is not the place of the United States to "dictate how Israel runs her affairs."

Paul endorses constitutional rights, such as the right to keep and bear arms, and *habeas corpus* for political detainees. He opposes the Patriot Act, federal use of torture, presidential autonomy, a national identification card, warrantless domestic surveillance, and the draft. Paul also believes that the notion of the separation of church and state is currently misused by the court system: "In case after case, the Supreme Court has used the infamous 'separation of church and state' metaphor to uphold court decisions that allow the federal government to intrude upon and deprive citizens of their religious liberty."

Citing the Ninth and Tenth Amendments, Paul advocates states' rights to decide how to regulate social matters not cited directly by the Constitution. He opposes federal regulation of the death penalty (although he opposes capital punishment), of education, and of marriage, and endorsed revising the military's "don't ask, don't tell" policy to concern mainly disruptive sexual behavior whether heterosexual or homosexual.

Paul says his years as an obstetrician led him to believe life begins at conception.

He terms himself "strongly pro-life," "an unshakable foe of abortion," and believes regulation or ban on medical decisions about maternal or fetal health is "best handled at the state level." His abortion-related legislation, like the Sanctity of Life Act, is intended to negate *Roe v. Wade* and to get "the federal government completely out of the business of regulating state matters."

Paul has stated that "The government shouldn't be in the medical business." He pushes to eliminate federal involvement with and management of health care, which he argues would allow prices to decrease due to the fundamental dynamics of a free market. Paul also opposes the federal War on Drugs, and believes the states should decide whether to regulate or deregulate drugs such as medical marijuana. He also opposes federal government influenza inoculation programs.

As a free-market environmentalist, he asserts private property rights in relation to environmental protection and pollution prevention. He called global warming a hoax in a 2009 Fox Business interview, saying, "You know, the greatest hoax I think that has been around in many, many years if not hundreds of years has been this hoax on the environment and global warming." He acknowledges there is clear evidence of rising temperatures in some parts of the globe, but says that temperatures are cooling in other parts.

Paul was critical of the Civil Rights Act of 1964, arguing that it sanctioned federal interference in the labor market and did not improve race relations. He once remarked: "The Civil Rights Act of 1964 not only violated the Constitution and reduced individual liberty; it also failed to achieve its stated goals of promoting racial harmony and a color-blind society." Paul opposes affirmative action.

He is an outspoken proponent of increased ballot access for 3rd party candidates, but has sought to repeal the National Voter Registration Act of 1993, also known as the Motor Voter law.

Paul has been married to Carol Wells since 1957. They met in 1952 when Wells asked Paul to be her escort to her 16th birthday party. They have five children, who were baptized Episcopalian: Ronald, Lori, Randal, Robert, and Joy. Paul's son Randal is the junior United States senator from the state of Kentucky. Raised a Lutheran, Paul later became a Baptist.

SANTORUM, PERRY, BACHMANN, CAIN, AND HUNTSMAN

Of the five Republican candidates who withdrew earlier – Sarah Palin never intended a serious run, and since she's described in detail later in this book, I'll go on to the others – I found one genuinely scary, two despicable; one who made a lot of sense – always a dangerous thing for a politician; and one who was downright *fun*. Let's start with the dangerous demagogues.

RICK SANTORUM

Until he announced the suspension of his Presidential campaign on April 10, 2012, Rick Santorum was a formidable candidate, running second only to Mitt Romney. He looks so remarkably clean-cut that even though he's over 50, he could be a choir boy or a freshman in college. He's so devout, he's squeaky clean, and I was seriously worried that if his ideas caught on in this country we'd go back to worst the 1950s had to offer.

Richard John "Rick" Santorum, born May 10, 1958, served as a United States Senator representing Pennsylvania from 1995 to 2007. As of April 2012, he was still a candidate for the Republican Presidential election. Born in Virginia, Santorum was raised primarily in Butler, Pennsylvania. He obtained an undergraduate degree from Pennsylvania State University, an M.B.A. from the University of Pittsburgh, and a J.D. from the Dickinson School of Law. Santorum worked as an attorney in a major Pennsylvania law firm, where he met Karen Garver. They married in 1990, and have seven children; an eighth child died shortly after birth. Santorum was elected to the U.S. House of Representatives in 1990, and was elected as a United States Senator for Pennsylvania in 1994. He served there until losing his re-election bid in 2006.

Santorum holds socially conservative positions, including opposition to same-sex marriage and birth control. In the Senate, he voted for tax cuts and a balanced budget amendment, supported the use of earmarks, and played a leading role in enacting welfare reform. He also voted for spending programs for education and transportation such as No Child Left Behind and funding for Amtrak, which he later disavowed.

In the years following his departure from the Senate, Santorum worked as a consultant, private practice lawyer, and news contributor. As a presidential candidate, he has proposed spending and tax cuts and expressed hawkish views regarding Iran. Despite running in the bottom tier of candidates for several months, he won the caucuses in Iowa, Minnesota, Colorado and the Missouri primary, and quickly rose to the top of national polls, winning Tennessee, Oklahoma and North Dakota on Super Tuesday. He subsequently went on to win primaries in Alabama, Mississippi and Louisiana. But by spring of 2012, as his views became more extreme than the centrist tradition of the United States, the more moderate Mitt Romney started to steamroll ahead, picking up more and more pledged nominating votes.

When asked in November 2011 about his views on evolution, Santorum stated that he believes that evolution occurred "on a tiny, micro level." Santorum is a supporter of the War on Terror. He says the war on Terror can be won and is optimistic about the U.S. occupation of Iraq and Afghanistan for the long-term. Santorum was one of only two senators who voted against confirming the nomination of Robert Gates as Secretary of Defense. Santorum stated that his objection was to Gates's support for talking with Iran and Syria, because it would be an error to talk with radical Islamists. A supporter of enhanced interrogation, he said in 2011 that John McCain, who was tortured as a prisoner of war, did not understand how the process works.

On January 15, 2010, Santorum sent an email and letter to supporters of his political action committee, saying, "I'm convinced that conservatives need a candidate who will not only stand up for our views, but who can articulate a conservative vision for our country's future." He continued, "And right now, I just don't see anyone stepping up to the plate. I have no great burning desire to be president, but I have a burning desire to have a different president of the United States." He formally announced his run for the Republican presidential nomination on June 6, 2011, saying he's "in it to win." Santorum has consistently held socially conservative views and has advocated "compassionate conservatism." He has a more mixed record on fiscal issues. As a member of Congress, he voted for the Bush tax cuts, favored a balanced budget amendment and sought to curb entitlements, playing a key role in enacting welfare reform. However, he has been criticized for supporting costly federal programs in education and transportation and for using earmarks to fund Pennsylvania projects. He says he regrets many of his votes for such programs, and opposes earmarks. He has also specifically disavowed his 2003 support for the unfunded Medicare prescription drug benefit and his vote for the No Child Left Behind Act.

Santorum has been described as having a "confrontational, partisan, 'in your face' style of politics and government." "I just don't take the pledge. I take the bullets," Santorum said. "I stand out in front and I lead to make sure the voices of those who do not have a voice are out in front and being included in the national debate."

In an interview with ABC's television program *This Week*, Santorum said, "I don't believe in an America where the separation of church and state is absolute." Santorum continued, "The First Amendment means the free exercise of religion and that means bringing people and their faith into the public square." In an interview with the *National Catholic Reporter*, Santorum said that the distinction between private religious conviction and public responsibility, espoused according to Santorum by President John F. Kennedy, had caused "great harm in America." He said: "All of us have heard people say, 'I privately am against abortion, homosexual marriage, stem cell research, cloning. But who am I to decide that it's not right for somebody else?' It sounds good, but it is the corruption of freedom of conscience."

In his 2005 book, *It Takes a Family*, Santorum advocated for a more "family values"-oriented society centered on monogamous, heterosexual relationships, marriage, and child-raising. While prior to his running for congress Santorum considered himself pro-choice on abortion, he has since changed his position to pro-life. He opposes same-sex marriage, saying the American public and their elected officials should decide on these "incredibly important moral issues," rather than the Supreme Court, which consists of "nine unelected, unaccountable judges."

Santorum has stated that he does not believe a "right to privacy" is part of the Constitution. He has been critical of the Supreme Court decision in *Griswold v. Connecticut* (1965), which held that the Constitution guaranteed that right and overturned a law prohibiting the sale of contraceptives to married couples. He has described contraception as "a license to do things in a sexual realm that is counter to how things are supposed to be," and said in 2003 that he favors having laws against polygamy, adultery, sodomy, and other actions "antithetical to a healthy, stable, traditional family."

In 2003, Santorum became the subject of a controversy when he juxtaposed same-sex marriage with pedophilia and bestiality during an interview. The remarks drew a retaliatory response from sex advice columnist and gay rights activist Dan Savage, who launched a contest to coin a "Santorum" neologism among his blog's readers.

In June 2011, Santorum said he would continue to "fight very strongly against libertarian influence within the Republican party and the conservative movement." In a National Public Radio interview in the summer of 2005, Santorum discussed what he called the "libertarianish right," saying "they have this idea that people should be left alone, be able to do whatever they want to do. Government should keep our taxes down and keep our regulation low and that we shouldn't get involved in the bedroom, we shouldn't get involved in cultural issues, you know, people should do whatever they want. Well, that is not how traditional conservatives view the world, and I think most conservatives understand that individuals can't go it alone."

In January 2012 The Atlantic Wire characterized Santorum as an "extreme hawk" on Iran. The same month, Santorum criticized Obama for not doing enough to block Iran from developing nuclear weapons. Santorum said that, if elected, he would call upon Iran to open its facilities to international inspection and begin to dismantle them, and that if Iranian leaders did not comply, he would bomb the weapons sites. Speaking in Greenville, South Carolina, and referring to the assassination of an Iranian nuclear scientist, Santorum said Iran "cannot have a nuclear weapon, because you, in Greenville, will not be safe."

Santorum rejects the mainstream scientific opinion on climate change, having referred to it as "junk science"; he also embraces common threads of the global warming conspiracy theory, believing that global warming is a "beautifully concocted scheme" by the political left and "an excuse for more government control of your life." He has stated a policy of "drill everywhere" for oil and that there is "enough oil, coal and natural gas to last for centuries." Santorum has often supported gun rights.

In 1996, the Santorums' son Gabriel was born prematurely after twenty weeks of pregnancy and died in the hospital two hours after birth. Karen wrote that she and Rick slept with the dead infant between them in the hospital that night, then brought his body home the following day and introduced it to their children as "your brother Gabriel." The handling of their infant son's death attracted scrutiny in January 2012 following Santorum's success in the Iowa caucuses. Four of the Santorums' children appeared with their parents on *Piers Morgan Tonight* in January 2012, and said they were all glad to have seen Gabriel, and they hold a place in their hearts for their brother.

RICK PERRY

James Richard "Rick" Perry, born March 4, 1950, is the current Governor of Texas. Perry was elected Lieutenant Governor of Texas in 1998 and assumed the governorship in December 2000 when George W. Bush resigned to become President of the United States. Perry was elected to full gubernatorial terms in 2002, 2006 and 2010. He is the longest continuously serving current U.S. governor and the longest serving governor in Texas history.

On August 13, 2011, Perry announced that he was running for the Republican nomination for President of the United States. Five months later, he suspended is campaign for the Republican nomination, and endorsed Newt Gingrich.

A fifth generation Texan, Perry graduated from Texas A&M University in 1972 with a Bachelor of Science degree in animal science. In the early 1970s, Perry interned during several summers as a door-to-door book salesman. Perry said in 2010. "There is nothing that tests your commitment to a goal like getting a few doors closed in your face."

Upon graduation in 1972, Perry was commissioned in the Air Force and completed pilot training in February 1974. His duty stations included two-month overseas rotations at RAF Mildenhall in England and Rhein-Main Air Base in Germany. His missions included a drought relief effort in Mali, Mauritania and Chad, and two years later, earthquake relief in Guatemala. He left the Air Force as a captain in 1977, and returned to Texas where he went into business farming cotton with his father.

In 1984, Perry was elected to the Texas House of Representatives as a Democrat. He served three two-year terms in office. Perry supported Al Gore in the 1988 Democratic presidential primaries and worked for Gore's campaign in Texas. In 1989, he announced that he was switching parties, becoming a Republican.

In 1998, Perry ran for Governor. During this election, he had a notable falling out with his previous top political strategist Karl Rove, which began the much-reported rivalry between the Bush and Perry camps. Perry became the state's first Republican lieutenant governor since Reconstruction, taking office on January 19, 1999.

As Governor, Perry has been an outspoken opponent of federal health-care reform. Since his election to Governor in 2002, Perry has continually rejected health care reform. He has described the Patient Protection and Affordable Care Act as "socialism on American soil."

During Perry's governorship, Texas rose from second to first among states with the highest proportion of uninsured residents at 26%, and had the lowest level of access to prenatal care in the U.S. Today, Texas ranks next-to-last among states in terms of affordability of health insurance. Perry is pro-life and has signed multiple bills creating new rules or restrictions for abortion procedures and funding. In February 2007, he issued an executive order mandating that Texas girls receive the HPV vaccine, which protects against some strains of the human papilloma virus, a contributing factor to some forms of cervical cancer. Following the move, news outlets reported various apparent financial connections between Perry and the vaccine's manufacturer, Merck.

Perry grew up in the Methodist church, until 2010 when he began attending Lake Hills Church in Austin. In 2006, Perry stated that he believes in the inerrancy of the Bible and that those who do not accept Jesus as their savior will go to hell. He later clarified, "I don't know that there's any human being that has the ability to interpret what God and his final decision-making is going to be." In June 2011, Perry proclaimed August 6 as a Day of Prayer and Fasting, inviting other governors to join him in a prayer meeting hosted by the American Family Association in Houston. The event was criticized as going beyond prayer and fasting to include launching Perry's presidential campaign.

Perry has called himself "a firm believer in intelligent design as a matter of faith and intellect," and has expressed support for its teaching alongside evolution in Texas schools, but has also said that "educators and local school officials, not the governor, should determine science curriculum."

Governor Perry supported the 2005 ballot proposition which amended the Texas constitution by defining marriage as "only a union between a man and a woman" and prohibiting the state from creating or recognizing "any legal status identical or similar to marriage." Perry's supports for a federal constitutional amendment banning same-sex marriage. He supports the death penalty. As of August 10, 2011, Texas has carried out 234 executions since Rick Perry became governor.

On August 13, 2011, Perry officially announced that he would be running for president. In October 2011, the *Washington Post* reported that Perry's family leases a hunting camp once called "Niggerhead." According to some local residents interviewed by the *Post*, the Perrys used the camp for years before painting over a large rock with that name on it, which stands at an entrance to the area. During that time Perry hosted friends and supporters at the camp. Perry's campaign disputed the claims, stating that the Perrys painted over the rock almost immediately after acquiring a lease on the property in 1983.

On December 6, Perry released a Presidential campaign video on YouTube called "Strong" discussing his religious beliefs, as well as criticism of Obama's governance. The video states, "There's something wrong in this country when gays can serve openly in the military, but your kids can't openly celebrate Christmas." Perry announced on January 19, 2012, that he would be dropping out of the 2012 Presidential Race, publicly endorsing Newt Gingrich.

In 1982, Perry married Anita Thigpen, his childhood sweetheart whom he had known since elementary school. They have two grown children, Griffin and Sydney. Anita Perry attended West Texas State University and earned a degree in nursing. She has spearheaded a number of health-related initiatives such as the Anita Thigpen Perry Endowment at the University of Texas Health Science Center at San Antonio, which focuses on nutrition, cardiovascular disease, health education, and early childhood development. Anita also helped develop and host the Texas Conference for Women.

MICHELE BACHMANN

There are two identifiable "Michelles" (or, more accurately, one "Michelle" and one "Michele") in the public spotlight. I adore Michelle Obama, who is everything a First Lady should be – and more;

conversely, I have an almost visceral dislike for Congressperson Michele Bachmann, who, before she withdrew from the race citing "unfair treatment by the media," believed herself to be a serious candidate for the Republican nomination.

Michele Marie Bachmann, née Amble, was born April 6, 1956. She has been a member of the United States Congress from Minnesota since 2007. She was a candidate for the Republican nomination in the 2012 U.S. presidential election, winning the Ames Straw Poll in August 2011 but dropping out in January 2012 after finishing sixth in the Iowa caucuses. Bachmann previously served in the Minnesota State Senate and is the first Republican woman to represent the state in Congress. She is a supporter of the Tea Party movement and a founder of the House Tea Party Caucus.

Bachmann graduated from Anoka High School in 1974 and, after graduation, spent time working on Kibbutz Be'eri in Israel. In 1978, she graduated from Winona State University with a B.A. Subsequently, she attented the O. W. Coburn School of Law, then a part of Oral Roberts University. While there, Bachmann studied with John Eidsmoe, whom she described in 2011 as "one of the professors who had a great influence on me." Bachmann worked as a research assistant on Eidsmoe's 1987 book *Christianity and the Constitution*, which argues that the United States was founded as a Christian theocracy, and should become one again.

In 1978, she married Marcus Bachmann, a clinical therapist with a master's degree from Regent University and a Ph.D. from Union Graduate School, whom she had met while they were undergraduates. After she received an LL.M. in taxation from William & Mary School of Law in 1988, the couple moved to Stillwater, Minnesota, near St. Paul, where they run a Christian counseling center. Bachmann and her husband have five children. She suffered a miscarriage after the birth of their second child, an event which she said shaped her pro-life views. Bachmann and her husband have also provided foster care for 23 other children, all teenage girls.

Bachmann was a longtime member of Salem Lutheran Church in Stillwater. She and her husband withdrew their membership on June 21, 2011, just before she officially began her presidential campaign. They had not attended the congregation for over two years. When challenged about that denomination's belief that the Pope is the Antichrist, Bachmann responded by stating, "I love Catholics, I'm a Christian, and my church does not believe that the Pope is the Anti-Christ, that's absolutely false." A spokesman for the Catholic League for Religious and Civil Rights said they see "no evidence of any bigotry" in Mrs. Bachmann. More recently, according to friends, the Bachmanns began attending Eagle Brook Church, an Evangelical church closer to their home. Bachmann and her husband own a Christian counseling practice.

Bachmann grew up in a Democratic family, but she says she became a Republican during her senior year at Winona State. While still a Democrat, she and her then-fiancé Marcus were inspired to join the pro-life movement. They prayed outside of clinics and engaged in sidewalk counseling, a pro-life protest activity in which activists approach people entering abortion clinics in an attempt to dissuade women from obtaining abortions. Since then, Bachmann has made statements supportive of sidewalk counseling. Bachmann supported Jimmy Carter in 1976; she and her husband worked on his campaign. During Carter's presidency, Bachmann became disappointed with his liberal approach to public policy, support for legalized abortion and economic decisions she held responsible for increased gas prices. In the 1980 presidential election, she voted for Ronald Reagan and worked for his campaign.

On November 20, 2003, while a State Representative, Bachmann proposed a constitutional amendment that would bar the state from legally recognizing same-sex marriage. First elected on November

2006, Bachmann is the first Republican woman to be elected to the U.S. House from Minnesota.

Bachmann has charged that global warming is a hoax and has been a vocal skeptic of global warming. She opposed both versions of the Wall Street bailout bill for America's financial sector. On October 17, 2008, Bachmann gave an interview on MSNBC's *Hardball with Chris Matthews* in support of the presidential campaign of Senator John McCain that brought the Minnesota 6th Congressional District race national attention. During the interview she criticized Barack Obama for his association with Jeremiah Wright and Bill Ayers, saying "Usually we associate with people who have similar ideas to us, and it seems that it calls into question what Barack Obama's true beliefs, and values, and thoughts are... I am very concerned that he may have anti-American views." She noted the bombing campaign orchestrated by Bill Ayers before discussing his association with Barack Obama, arguing that "Bill Ayers is not someone the average American wants to see their president have an association with." Matthews followed up by asking "But Obama is a Senator from the State of Illinois; he's one of the members of Congress you suspect of being anti-American. How many people in the Congress of the United States do you think are anti-American? You've already suspected Barack Obama, is he alone or are there others?" Bachmann answered, "What I would say is that the news media should do a penetrating exposé and take a look ... I wish they would ... I wish the American media would take a great look at the views of the people in Congress and find out are they pro-America, or anti-America. I think people would love to see an exposé like that." The five Democratic members of Minnesota's congressional delegation issued a joint statement in which they questioned her ability to "work in a bipartisan way to put the interests of our country first in this time of crisis." Former Secretary of State Colin Powell and former Minnesota Governor

Republican Arne Carlson said that her comments had influenced their decisions to endorse Obama for president.

Bachmann brought up the interview before business leaders and Republicans during a campaign stop in St. Cloud, Minnesota, on October 21, 2008. She stated that she never intended to question Obama's patriotism. "I made a misstatement. I said a comment that I would take back. I did not, nor do I, question Barack Obama's patriotism. I did not say that Barack Obama is anti-American nor do I believe that Barack Obama is anti-American ... But I'm very concerned about Barack Obama's views. I don't believe that socialism is a good thing for America." However, in March 2010, Bachmann said, "I said I had very serious concerns that Barack Obama had anti-American views-- and now I look like Nostradamus." A year later, in March 2011, Bachmann was asked on *Meet the Press* if she still believed that Obama held un-American views. She responded "I believe that the actions of this government have, have been emblematic of ones that have not been based on true American values." Pressed for clarification, she said "I've already answered that question before. I said I had very serious concerns about the president's views."

In 2009, Bachmann became a critic of what she characterized as proposals for mandatory public service. Speaking in reference to the Edward M. Kennedy Serve America Act, an expansion to AmeriCorps (a federal community service organization), she said in April: "It's under the guise of—quote—volunteerism. But it's not volunteers at all. It's *paying* people to do work on behalf of government. ... I believe that there is a very strong chance that we will see that young people will be put into mandatory service. And the real concerns is that there are provisions for what I would call re-education camps for young people, where young people have to go and get trained in a philosophy that the government puts forward and then they have to go to work in some of these politically correct forums."

On August 31, 2009, Bachmann spoke at an event in Colorado, saying of Democratic health care overhaul proposals that: "This cannot pass. What we have to do today is make a covenant, to slit our wrists, be blood brothers on this thing. This will not pass. We will do whatever it takes to make sure this doesn't pass." She outlined ideas for changing the health care system, including: "Erase the boundaries around every single state when it comes to health care," enabling consumers to purchase insurance across state lines; increase the use of health savings accounts and allow everyone to "take full deductibility of all medical expenses," including insurance premiums; and tort reform.

Bachmann denounced the government-run health insurance public option, calling it a "government takeover of health care" that would "squeeze out private health insurance."

According to an article in the Stillwater Gazette, a local newspaper in Minnesota, Bachmann supports the teaching of creationism alongside evolution in public school science classes. During a 2003 interview on the KKMS Christian radio program Talk The Walk, Bachmann said that evolution is a theory that has never been proven one way or the other.

Bachmann has promised to bring the price of gasoline down to $2 per gallon, without specifying a plan for how to accomplish this. She supports increased domestic drilling of oil and natural gas, as well as pursuing renewable sources of energy such as wind and solar. She is a strong proponent of nuclear power. Bachmann has called for phasing out Social Security and Medicare: "What you have to do, is keep faith with the people that are already in the system, that don't have any other options, we have to keep faith with them. But basically what we have to do is wean everybody else off."

Bachmann says in dealing with Iran, diplomacy "is our option," but that other options, including a nuclear strike, shouldn't be taken off the table. She has also said that she is "a long time supporter of Israel."

Bachmann is against a Reagan type of amnesty. She voted against the DREAM Act, which would have allowed illegal immigrants a road to legitimacy. She has also stated that the current law does not need modification but rather proper enforcement. Bachmann said: "... the immigration system in the United States worked very, very well up until the mid-1960s when liberal members of Congress changed the immigration laws." Bachmann supports both a federal and state constitutional amendment banning same-sex marriage and any legal equivalents. She has identified herself as pro-life. At a debate among presidential candidates in New Hampshire, when asked if abortion should be allowed in cases of rape or incest, Bachmann responded she is "100 per cent pro-life."

Bachmann formally announced her candidacy for the 2012 Republican presidential nomination on June 27, 2011, during an appearance in Waterloo, Iowa.

Although she won the Ames Straw Poll hosted by the Iowa GOP on August 13, 2011, becoming the first woman ever to win the poll, when the actual caucuses were held on January 3, 2012, she finished sixth. Bachmann announced on January 4 that she would be cancelling her scheduled campaign trips to South Carolina, as she was suspending her presidential campaign. On January 25, 2012, Bachmann announced that she would run for reelection for her seat in Congress.

HERMAN CAIN

Despite his conservative views, which I believe were "somewhat to the right of Attila the Hun," there is no question that in a largely lackluster race between the Republicans' version of "the seven dwarfs," Herman Cain was a *fun* candidate – fun to listen to, fun to watch, quick to think on his feet. Like so many politicans on both sides of the aisle, it took a good old-fashioned sex scandal to bring him down, and although I may be condemned in many quarters – especially among those "Holier than Thou" moralists who preach strict morality and practice something else entirely – I'm sorry he's not still in the race.

Herman Cain, 66, is an author, business executive, radio host, syndicated columnist, and Tea Party activist from Georgia. He grew up in Georgia and graduated from Morehouse College in 1967 with a Bachelor's in mathematics. Cain then earned a Master of Science in computer science from Purdue in 1971, while also working full-time for the U.S. Department of the Navy.

In 1977, he joined Pillsbury Company where he later became vice president. During the 1980s, his success as a business executive at Burger King prompted Pillsbury to appoint him as chairman and CEO of Godfather's Pizza, where he served for the next decade. Cain was chairman of the Federal Reserve Bank of Kansas City from 1989-1996. In 1995, he was appointed by Newt Gingrich to the Kemp Commission, and was a senior economic advisor to the Bob Dole presidential campaign. Cain was the CEO of the National Restaurant Association from 1996 to 1999. Cain has served as a member of the board of directors of Nabisco, Whirlpool and Reader's Digest.

In May 2011, Cain announced his presidential candidacy. His proposed 9–9–9 tax plan, along with his debate performances, made him the Republican front-runner in fall of 2011, during which he briefly led President Obama in the polls. In November his campaign struggled to deal with allegations of sexual misconduct, which resulted in Cain suspending his campaign on December 3. The Pew Research Center reported that, of the Republican candidates, "Herman Cain was the most covered candidate in 2011." On January

28, 2012, Cain announced his endorsement of Newt Gingrich for the 2012 Republican Party presidential nomination.

Herman Cain was born in Memphis, Tennessee, to Lenora Davis Cain, a cleaning woman and domestic worker, and Luther Cain, Jr., who was raised on a farm and worked as a barber and janitor, as well as a chauffeur. Cain has said that as he was growing up, his family was "poor but happy." His mother taught him that "success was not a function of what you start out with materially, but what you start out with spiritually." His father worked three jobs to own his own home — something he achieved during Cain's childhood — and to see his two sons graduate. Cain grew up on the west side of Atlanta. Eventually his father saved enough money and the family moved to a modest brick home in the Collier Heights neighborhood.

Cain married his wife Gloria soon after her graduation from Morris Brown College in 1968. His wife of 43 years is a homemaker, with experience as a teacher and a librarian. The couple have two children and three grandchildren. In 2006, Cain was diagnosed with Stage IV cancer in his colon and metastases to his liver and given a 30-percent chance of survival. Cain underwent surgery and chemotherapy following the diagnosis, and has since reported that he is in remission. His wealth is estimated to be as between $2.9 to $6.6 million. His income for both 2010 and 2011 was between $1.1 and $2.1 million. Cain serves as an associate minister at Antioch Baptist Church North in Atlanta, which he joined at the age of 10.

Cain writes a syndicated op-ed column, which is distributed by the North Star Writers Group. From 2008, until February 2011, he hosted *The Herman Cain Show* on Atlanta talk radio station WSB. After he withdrew from the Presidential race in January 2012, Cain began working for WSB again by providing daily commentaries.

Cain received the 1996 Horatio Alger Award and has received honorary degrees from Creighton University, Johnson & Wales University, Morehouse College, University of Nebraska, New York

City Technical College, Purdue University, Suffolk University, and Tougaloo College.

Cain publicly opposed the Clinton health care plan of 1993. He challenged Bill Clinton on the costs of the employer mandate contained within the bill and criticized its effect on small businesses. Cain transformed the debate when he challenged Clinton at a town meeting in Kansas City, Missouri. Cain asked the president what he was supposed to say to the workers he would have to lay off because of the cost of the "employer mandate." Clinton responded that there would be plenty of subsidies for small businessmen, but Cain persisted. "Quite honestly, your calculation is inaccurate," he told the president. "In the competitive marketplace it simply doesn't work that way." Conservative politician and former Housing Secretary Jack Kemp was so impressed with Cain's performance that he chartered a plane to Nebraska to meet Cain after the debate. Cain credits Kemp with his becoming interested in politics.

Cain briefly ran for the Republican presidential nomination in 2000; he says it was more about making political statements than winning the nomination. "George W. Bush was the chosen one, he had the campaign DNA that followers look for." However, Cain went on to state, "I believe that I had a better message and I believe that I was the better messenger." After ending his own campaign, he endorsed Steve Forbes. In 2004, Cain ran for the U.S. Senate in Georgia, but did not win in the primaries.

In 2010, Cain addressed more than 40 Tea Party rallies, hit all the early presidential states, and became a YouTube sensation. On September 24, 2010, he announced that he was considering a run for president in 2012 on the Republican Party ticket. On May 21, 2011, Cain officially announced his candidacy.

A popular speaker, Cain's addresses to conservative groups were well-received. In September and early October 2011, Cain won the straw polls of the Florida Republican Party, TeaCon, and the

National Federation of Republican Women's Convention. Among pollsters, one of the most vocal said, "My focus groups have consistently picked Herman Cain as the most likeable candidate in the debates. Don't underestimate the power of likeability, even in a Republican primary. The more likeable the candidate, the greater the electoral potential."

The centerpiece of Herman Cain's campaign was the "9-9-9 Plan." He plan would replace the current tax code with a 9-percent business transactions tax, a 9-percent personal income tax, and a 9-percent federal sales tax. Cain said his plan "expands the base," arguing that "When you expand the base, we can arrive at the lowest possible rate, which is 9-9-9." An analysis released to Bloomberg News by the campaign claimed that the rate for each of the three taxes could in fact be as low as 7.3%, but "poverty grants" — which Cain has described as a lower rate in targeted "empowerment zones" — necessitated a national rate of 9%. Reaction to the Plan was mixed, largely because during the campaign Cain kept referring to "9-9-9 and we'll all be fine," but scarcely anyone understood the details of the Plan. As a result, Cain's 9-9-9 plan attracted skepticism from his fellow candidates at numerous Republican debates.

In late October 2011, accusations of sexual misconduct during his time as CEO of the National Restaurant Association in the late 1990s began to surface. In all, four women alleged that he had been guilty of sexual harassment and sexual misconduct. Cain denies all allegations of sexual misconduct, while acknowledging that the restaurant organization made financial settlements to the complainants. On November 28, 2011, Cain asserted that a woman named Ginger White would be claiming to have had an affair with him, and that the allegation was not true. An interview with White was aired an hour later on Fox 5 in Atlanta. In the interview, White said the affair lasted 13 years and ended right before Cain announced his presidential campaign. On November 30, 2011, Herman Cain denounced allegations of sexual harassment and adultery as "character assassination" during an event in Dayton, Ohio

On December 3, 2011, Cain announced he was "suspending" his campaign for the presidency following allegations of sexual harassment and adultery, which he denied, but which were widely considered responsible for the sharp drop in his poll numbers.

On January 4, 2012, Cain announced the "Cain's Solutions Revolution." Cain's stated goal is to get commitments from members of Congress to support the 9-9-9 Plan before the 2012 elections. Cain stated that he started a new movement because the "biggest comment I got when I ended my candidacy was to keep 9-9-9 alive. That's what this is about, and I'm going to keep it alive with what I'm calling Cain's Solutions Revolution."

JON HUNTSMAN

Jon Huntsman is everything a president should be – intelligent, articulate, issues-oriented, able to work cooperatively with both parties, balanced, and fair-minded. In short, all the things that do *not* work in an era where politics is a hate-oriented game. Add to that the fact that he is Mormon – which doesn't seem to have hurt Mitt Romney – and the fact that the American electorate seems to be more intrigued by how much mud you can sling rather than how much you can cooperate to bring about constructive change – and Huntsman's dismal pre-election numbers seem to have been preordained.

Jon Meade Huntsman, Jr., born March 26, 1960, is a politician, businessman, and diplomat who served as the 16th Governor of Utah. He served in the administrations of four United States presidents. Huntsman worked as a White House staff assistant for Ronald Reagan, and he was appointed by George H.W. Bush as Deputy Assistant Secretary of Commerce and later as United States Ambassador to Singapore from 1992 to 1993. He served as Deputy United States Trade Representative under George W. Bush, guiding the accession of the People's Republic of China and the Republic of China into the World Trade Organization.

Huntsman has also served as CEO of his family's Huntsman Corporation, was elected Governor of Utah in November 2004, and won re-election in 2008 with nearly 78% of the vote. On August 11, 2009, he resigned as governor to accept an appointment by Barack Obama as the United States Ambassador to the People's Republic of China. He submitted his resignation as ambassador on January 31, 2011, in order to explore a presidential campaign; he launched his campaign in June 2011. After campaigning almost exclusively in New Hampshire but finishing a distant third in that state's primary, he dropped out of the presidential race on January 16, 2012 and endorsed Mitt Romney.

Huntsman was born in Redwood City, California. His mother is the daughter of LDS Church apostle David B. Haight. His father is a billionaire businessman and philanthropist. At age 15, Huntsman earned the rank of Eagle Scout, the highest rank of the Boy Scouts of America. He dropped out of high school before graduating to pursue his passion as a keyboard player in the rock band Wizard. Huntsman later obtained a G.E.D. and enrolled at the University of Utah. He served as a Mormon missionary in Taiwan for two years. He then transferred to the University of Pennsylvania, where he received a bachelor's degree in international politics.

From 1987 to 1988, Huntsman and his family lived and worked in Taipei. After college, Huntsman worked as a White House staff assistant in President Ronald Reagan's administration. Under President George H. W. Bush, he was Deputy Assistant Secretary of Commerce for trade development and commerce for East Asian and Pacific Affairs. In June 1992, Bush appointed him to become U.S. Ambassador to Singapore. Confirmed unanimously, he became the youngest U.S. Ambassador to serve in over 100 years.

In January 2001, after George W. Bush took office as President, the Washington Post reported there was a strong possibility Huntsman would be appointed U.S. Ambassador to China. In March, he reportedly turned down the nomination to be the U.S. Ambassador to Indonesia. On March 28, Bush appointed Huntsman to be one of two Deputy United States Trade Representatives in his administration.

In March 2003, Huntsman resigned his post in the Bush administration. In May 2004, a Republican Party convention was held for the purpose of nominating a candidate. In the June 2004 primary, Huntsman secured 66%. of the Republican vote. In November 2004, Huntsman was elected Governor with 58% of the vote, defeating the Democratic nominee.

Huntsman maintained extremely high approval ratings as Governor of Utah hitting 90% approval at times. In 2008, he won re-election with 77.7% of the vote. He left office with his approval ratings over 80%. During his term as governor, he was successful in having Utah replace its progressive income tax with a flat tax of 5%; cut the statewide sales tax rate from 4.75% to 4.65% and sales tax on unprepared food from 4.70% to 1.75%; and raised motor vehicle registration fees. He proposed a 400% increase in cigarette taxes, but the measure was never signed into law. In 2006 he proposed the largest state budget in the state's history.

Huntsman was one of John McCain's earliest supporters in the 2008 presidential campaign, while most Utah and Mormon politicians supported Mitt Romney. At the 2008 Republican National Convention, Huntsman delivered a nominating speech for Alaska Governor Sarah Palin, the party's nominee for vice president. In 2008, he successively proposed tax credits for families purchasing their own health insurance, as well as income tax credits for capital gains and solar projects.

President Barack Obama nominated Jon Huntsman to serve as the United States Ambassador to China on May 16, 2009, noting his experience in the region and proficiency in Mandarin Chinese. On August 7, 2009, the Senate unanimously confirmed Huntsman and he formally resigned as Governor of Utah and was sworn in as Ambassador to China on August 11, 2009.

In February 2011, Huntsman made a controversial appearance at the site of a planned pro-democracy protest in Beijing. In the wake of the 2010–2011 Middle East and North Africa protests, Chinese democracy activists called for similar protests to be held in major Chinese cities, hoping to engender a large-scale movement they called the "Jasmine Revolution." On February 20, Huntsman was captured on video at the Wangfujing shopping area, where an anonymous online appeal had called for a major demonstration on that date. When approached by an onlooker asking why he was there, Huntsman replied, "I'm just here to look around." When further asked if he wanted to see "chaos" in China, Huntsman replied "No," and left the area. Huntsman resigned from his position as Ambassador, effective April 30, 2011, in order to return to the United States to explore a 2012 Republican presidential bid.

Huntsman's name appeared on lists of potential Republican nominees for the 2012 presidential election as early as 2008 and 2009. John McCain specifically mentioned Huntsman as a potential candidate for the 2012 election in March 2009. Huntsman formally entered the race for the Republican presidential nomination on June 21, 2011

After focusing his energy and resources on the New Hampshire primary in which he finished third, Huntsman announced the end of his campaign on January 16, 2012, endorsing Mitt Romney. Huntsman was appointed to the board of directors of the Ford Motor Co. on February 9, 2012.

Huntsman has been described by the Huffington Post as "a conservative technocrat-optimist with moderate positions who was willing to work substantively with President Barack Obama" and identifies himself as a center-right conservative.

As governor, Huntsman listed economic development, health-care reform, education, and energy security as his top priorities. He oversaw tax cuts and advocated reorganizing the way that services were distributed so that the government would not become overwhelmed by the state's fast growing population. He also proposed a plan to reform health-care, mainly through the private sector, by using tax breaks and negotiation to keep prices down. In 2007, when asked about a healthcare mandate, Huntsman said, "I'm comfortable with a requirement – you can call it whatever you want, but at some point we're going to have to get serious about how we deal with this issue."

In a 2008 evaluation of state governors' fiscal policies, the libertarian Cato Institute praised Huntsman's conservative tax policies, ranking him in a tie for fifth place on overall fiscal policy. He was particularly lauded for his efforts to cut taxes. The report specifically highlighted his reductions of the sales tax and simplification of the tax code. However, the report concluded that: "Unfortunately, Huntsman has completely dropped the ball on spending, with per capita spending increasing at about 10 percent annually during his tenure." He defines his taxation policy as "business friendly."

As part of his presidential campaign, Huntsman claimed that "our tax code has devolved into a maze of special-interest carve-outs, loopholes and temporary provisions that cost taxpayers more than $400 billion a year to comply with." The candidate called for "getting rid of all tax expenditures, all loopholes, all deductions, all subsidies. Use that to lower rates across the board. And do it on a revenue-neutral basis."

In addition, Huntsman has proposed reducing the corporate tax rate from 35% to 25%, eliminating corporate taxes on income earned overseas, and implementing a tax holiday for repatriation of corporate profits. He favors eliminating taxes on capital gains and dividends.

As the governor of Utah, Huntsman signed numerous bills restricting abortion. Huntsman has supported civil unions for years but not same-sex marriage. As Utah's Governor, he supported legislation that would have allowed civil unions for same-sex couples in the state.

In 2007, in response to the issue of global warming, Huntsman signed the Western Climate Initiative, by which Utah joined with other governments in agreeing to pursue targets for reduced production of greenhouse gases. He also appeared in an advertisement sponsored by Environmental Defense, in which he said, "Now it's time for Congress to act by capping greenhouse-gas pollution." In 2011, however, Huntsman said, "Cap-and-trade ideas aren't working; it hasn't worked, and our economy's in a different place than five years ago. Much of this discussion happened before the bottom fell out of the economy, and until it comes back, this isn't the moment." "There's not enough information right now to formulate policies in terms of addressing it over all, primarily because it's a global issue," Huntsman said. "We can enact policies here, but I wouldn't want to unilaterally disarm as a country. I wouldn't want to hinder job creators at a time when our economy is flat."

Huntsman has repeatedly stated, "We need to continue working closely with China to convince North Korea to abandon its nuclear weapons program." He has also named Taiwan, human rights, and Tibet among the "areas where we have differences with China" and vowed "robust engagement" on human rights if confirmed. The governor, who lived in Taiwan as a Mormon missionary, said he felt "personally invested in the peaceful resolution of cross-strait differences, in a way that respects the wishes of the people on both Taiwan and the mainland. He said that current US policy "supports this objective, and I have been encouraged by the recent relaxing of cross-strait tensions." Huntsman is a strong supporter of Israel and has made several visits to Israel.

In June 2007, Huntsman joined other Western governors in urging the Senate to pass comprehensive immigration reform. In 2005, Huntsman signed a bill giving illegal aliens access to "driving-privilege cards," which allowed them to have driving privileges but unlike driver licenses, cannot be used for identification purposes. As Governor, Huntsman threatened to veto a measure repealing in-state college tuition for illegal immigrants.

Huntsman has stated support for a border fence, saying that, "as an American, the thought of a fence to some extent repulses me, but the situation is such that I don't think we have a choice." In the September 9 Republican debate, Huntsman suggested that the country needed more legal immigration, claiming that it will revive America's housing market, citing Vancouver's quickly growing real estate market as evidence. Huntsman also supports granting more H-1B visas to foreigners. Huntsman supported the DREAM Act which proposed a path to citizenship for undocumented young people brought to the United States by their parents.

Huntsman has eight brothers and sisters, and he and his wife, Mary Kaye, have seven children. He is a self-proclaimed fan of the progressive rock genre and played keyboards during high school in the band Wizard. On July 30, 2007, he attended a concert by progressive metal band Dream Theater. Later that day, Huntsman signed a proclamation creating "Dream Theater Day" on that date for the state of Utah. Huntsman also joined REO Speedwagon on the piano for two songs during their concert at the Utah State Fair on September 16, 2005. Huntsman is a fan of riding motocross, and he helped in pushing outdoor sporting activities and outdoor tourism for the State of Utah.

Huntsman has been awarded honorary doctorate degrees from Snow College, Westminster College, the University of Utah, the University of Pennsylvania, and Southern New Hampshire University. He is a founding director of the Pacific Council on International Policy and has served on the boards of the Brookings Institution Asia Policy Board, the Asia Society in New York, and the National Bureau of Asian Research.

Huntsman was brought up as a member of The Church of Jesus Christ of Latter-day Saints (LDS), and stated in a May 2011 interview with George Stephanopoulos of ABC News, "I believe in God. I'm a good Christian. I'm very proud of my Mormon heritage. I am Mormon." However, he told *Newsweek* in December 2010 that the LDS Church doesn't have a monopoly on his spiritual life. In an interview with *Time* magazine, he stated that he is more spiritual than religious and that his membership in the LDS Church is "tough to define." Although still Mormon, Huntsman has said that he and his wife draw from an array of sources for inspiration, stating: "I was raised a Mormon, Mary Kaye was raised Episcopalian, our kids have gone to Catholic school, I went to a Lutheran school growing up in Los Angeles. I have an adopted daughter from India who has a very distinct Hindu tradition, one that we would celebrate during Diwali. So you kind of bind all this together."

Huntsman professes a firm belief in science, rejecting the notion that faith and evolution are mutually exclusive. In response to Rick Perry's creationist world view, Huntsman warned that the Republicans should not become the "anti-science" party, and stated: "To be clear. I believe in evolution and trust scientists on global warming. Call me crazy."

I would rather have called him Mr. President.

PART ONE:

WE'VE BEEN DOWN

THIS ROAD BEFORE

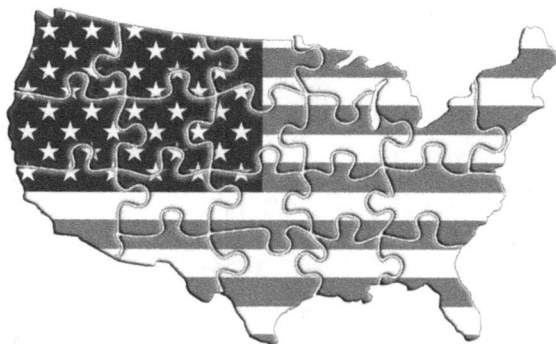

BEFORE THERE WAS A UNITED STATES

If we are to believe the scientists – and nowadays not everyone, especially "Creationists" don't – modern *Homo sapiens* (us) have been around for more than 120,000 years – quite a bit more time than if we take the Bible as literally as Creationist Evolution-deniers want us to believe. The "Great Leap Forward" – the technological and societal advances that made humans beings what they are, took place somewhere between 40,000 and 50,000 years ago, when modern humans started burying their dead, making clothing out of hides, developing sophisticated hunting techniques, and engaging in cave painting. Then came fish hooks, buttons and bone needles.

As humankind progressed, the trappings of "modern" civilization took shape – the use of jewelry, the organization of living space, advanced hunting techniques, farming, the exploration of new geographical areas, and trade with people in other places – and politics. I'm reminded of a cartoon I saw about twenty-five years ago. It showed a group of cavemen sitting around on rocks, staring at a bunch of bones. The caption underneath read: "A motion was made to fight over the meat." "It was pointed out that there *was* no meat." "A motion was made to fight over the bones." It seemed quite amusing to me at the time – until I think how apt the analogy is to politics today. By 4,000 B.C., humankind had advanced from caves to tents, then from tents to more permanent buildings. Settlements of two or three families had grown to towns, then cities, then nations. Much of what we experience today goes back a lot farther than we think. American politicians didn't invent the lust for power, greed, corruption, graft, or name-calling. I'm certain that when the bids went out to put up the pyramids – "lowest responsible responsive bidder gets the job" – Ahmenotep/Halliburton had fixed the winning bid, the Parthenon was built by Georgopoulos/Lockheed, and a likely slogan was "something for everyone and a bit left over for me." Actually, the Athenian city-state tried to clean up its political mess in a novel way: if you had been in political office for ten years, you were banished from Athens for the next ten years. A little more effective than today's "term limits."

Angry rhetoric? Dirty tricks? The 21st Century is an absolute novice compared to ancient Rome. A common bit of political advice in the days before Christ and for four hundred-fifty years thereafter was "*Fortiter calumniare, aliquid adhaerebit*" ("'Sling plenty of mud and some of it will stick.'"). And there was a *lot* of mud slung. "How to screw your neighbor's wife (or, for that matter, his daughter, his son, his ward, or his sheep) for fun, profit, and political power," was more than a scatological exercise. In the upper echelons of the Palatine Hill, it was "business as usual," unless, like Richard Nixon in much later times, you disobeyed the "Eleventh Commandment" – "Thou Shalt Not Get Caught."

But the focus of this book is not on ancient history. For our purposes, we'll start with the 1980 election, when Ronald Reagan, the Great Communicator, ran for President. I could have picked any election prior to 1980, but I believe this is when the *current* climate of organized hate politics began. The era when the media became a serious player in politics, when there were more people and less resources to go around, and the time when we really started to go astray. That's not to say American politics was always "squeaky clean." To the contrary, the Presidential Elections between 1789 and 1976 were often brutal, immoral, and filled with extraordinary vitriol. For those of you interested in such stuff, Appendix "A" to this book furnishes capsule shots of those elections. For now, we'll stick to the elections that took place within the last three decades.

PRESIDENTIAL ELECTIONS: 1980-2008

1980

This election was a contest between incumbent Democrat Jimmy Carter and his Republican opponent, Ronald Reagan, as well as Independent John B. Anderson. Reagan, aided by the Iran hostage crisis and a worsening economy at home, won the election in a landslide. After defeating Ted Kennedy for the Democratic nomination, Carter attacked Reagan as a dangerous right-wing radical. Reagan ridiculed Carter, and won. Republicans won control of the Senate for the first time in 28 years.

Throughout the 1970s, the United States had undergone low economic growth, high inflation and interest rates, and intermittent energy crises. By the beginning of the election season, the prolonged Iran hostage crisis had sharpened public perceptions of a national crisis. Jimmy Carter was blamed for the Iran hostage crisis, in which followers of the Ayatollah Khomeni burned American flags and chanted anti-American slogans, parading the captured American hostages in public, and burning effigies of Carter. Critics saw Carter as an inept bungler who had failed to solve the worsening economic problems at home. His supporters defended the president as a decent, well-intentioned man being attacked for problems that had been building for years.

President Carter entered the party's convention with 60% of the delegates pledged to him on the first ballot. Despite this, Kennedy refused to drop out, and the 1980 Democratic National Convention was one of the nastiest on record. There was a "Draft Muskie" movement in the summer of 1980, since Muskie was polling even with Ronald Reagan at the time, while Carter was seven points down. After a futile last-ditch attempt by Kennedy to alter the rules to free delegates from the first-ballot pledge, Carter was renominated. He warned that Reagan's conservatism posed a threat to world peace and progressive social welfare programs from the New Deal to the Great Society.

Ronald Reagan was the odds-on favorite to win his party's nomination for president after nearly beating then-incumbent President Gerald Ford just four years earlier. He won the nomination on the first ballot, then chose George H. W. Bush, his top rival, as his running mate.

Reagan's supporters praised him for running a campaign of upbeat optimism. Carter emphasized his record as a peacemaker, and said Reagan's election would threaten civil rights and social programs. Immediately after the primaries, a Gallup poll showed Reagan ahead, with 58% of vote. The campaign was largely negative. While Reagan and Carter were religious Christians, Carter had the most support of evangelical Christians, but in the end, Jerry Falwell's Moral Majority lobbying group was credited with giving Reagan two-thirds of the white evangelical vote.

The election of 1980 heralded the new electoral power of the suburbs and the Sun Belt. Reagan's success as a conservative initiated a realignment of the parties. Liberal Republicans and conservative Democrats either left politics or changed party affiliations throughout the 1980s and 1990s, leaving the parties much more ideologically polarized. By 1980, a majority of Americans believed that government held too much power.

Reagan promised to restore the nation's military strength. At that time, 60% of Americans felt defense spending was too low. Reagan also promised an end to 'trust me' government" and to restore economic health by implementing a supply-side economic policy. He promised a balanced budget within three years, which he said would be "the beginning of the end of inflation." He reduced taxes by 30% over those same years. With respect to the economy, Reagan said, "A recession is when your neighbor loses his job. A depression is when you lose yours. And recovery is when Jimmy Carter loses his." Reagan criticized the "windfall profit tax" that Carter and Congress enacted in regards to domestic oil production and promised to attempt to repeal it as president. The tax was not a tax on profits, but on the difference between the price control-mandated price and the market price.

Many feminists were frustrated with Carter, the only candidate who supported the Equal Rights Amendment. After a bitter Convention fight between Republican feminists and antifeminists the Republican Party dropped their endorsement of the ERA. Reagan, however, announced his dedication to women's rights and his intention, if elected, to appoint women to his cabinet and the first female justice to the Supreme Court. He also pledged to work with all 50 state governors to combat discrimination against women and to equalize federal laws as an alternative to the ERA. Carter was criticized by his own aides for not having a "grand plan;" he often criticized Reagan's economic plan, but did not create one of his own in response.

In August, Reagan announced, "Programs like education and others should be turned back to the states and local communities with the tax sources to fund them. I believe in states' rights. I believe in people doing as much as they can at the community level and the private level. I believe we have distorted the balance of our government today by giving powers that were never intended to be given in the Constitution to that federal establishment." He promised to "restore to states and local governments the power that properly belongs to them." Oddly enough, when Democrat Jerry Brown was elected Governor of California in 2010, twenty-five years after his *first* tenure as Governor of the Golden State ended, he called for the same program in his campaign. The more things change, the more they remain the same.

Reagan was widely ridiculed by Democrats for saying that trees caused pollution. He later said that he meant only certain types of pollution and that his remarks had been misquoted. Carter was burdened by a continued weak economy and the Iran hostage crisis. Inflation, high interest rates, and unemployment continued through the course of the campaign. The ongoing hostage crisis in Iran became, to many, a symbol of American impotence during the Carter years.

The most important event of the entire 1980 presidential campaign was the second presidential debate, which was held one week to the day before the election. Over the course of two hours, the entire race changed drastically, and what was considered an extremely tight race with the President slightly ahead became a comfortable Republican victory for Reagan. Nothing of that magnitude has happened since in any televised confrontations. The presidential debate between President Carter and Governor Reagan ranked among the highest ratings of any television show in the previous decade. Debate topics included the Iranian hostage crisis, nuclear arms treaties and proliferation. Carter's campaign sought to portray Governor Reagan as a reckless "hawk." It came as no surprise then, when the candidates repeatedly clashed over the nuclear weapons issue in their debate. But it was President Carter's reference to his consultation with his 12-year-old daughter Amy concerning nuclear weapons policy that became the focus of post-debate analysis and fodder for late-night television jokes. President Carter said he had asked Amy what the most important issue in that election was and she had said, "the control of nuclear arms." A famous political cartoon, published the day after Reagan's landslide victory, showed Amy Carter sitting in Jimmy's lap with her shoulders shrugged asking, "The economy? The hostage crisis?"

Governor Reagan's demeanor, on the other hand, was sunny, tolerant, and almost folksy, somewhat like Andy Griffith's character. When President Carter made a reference to what he saw as the governor's record, voting against Medicare and Social Security benefits, Governor Reagan replied with a nonchalant, "There you go again." In describing the national debt that was approaching 1 trillion dollars, Reagan stated "a billion is a thousand millions, and a trillion is a thousand billions." When Carter attacked the content of Reagan's campaign speeches, Reagan began his counter with "Well, I don't know that I said that, I really don't."

In his closing remarks, Gov. Reagan asked a simple yet devastating question that would resonate with voters in 1980 and beyond: "Are you better off now than you were four years ago? Is it easier for you to go and buy things in the stores than it was four years ago? Is there more or less unemployment in the country than there was four years ago? Is America as respected throughout the world as it was? Do you feel that our security is as safe, that we're as strong as we were four years ago? And if you answer all of those questions yes, why then, I think your choice is very obvious as to whom you will vote for. If you don't agree, if you don't think that this course that we've been on for the last four years is what you would like to see us follow for the next four, then I could suggest another choice that you have." The President's tiny lead turned into a major Reagan landslide over the final weekend.

Ronald Reagan beat Carter by almost 10 percentage points in the popular vote. Republicans also gained control of the Senate for the first time in twenty-five years. The electoral college vote was a landslide, with 489 votes for Reagan and 49 votes for Carter. NBC News projected Reagan as the winner at 8:15 pm EST, even before voting was finished in the West. Carter conceded defeat at 9:50 pm EST. His loss was the worst defeat for an incumbent President since Herbert Hoover lost to Franklin D. Roosevelt in 1932 by a margin of 18%.

1984

Incumbent President Ronald Reagan, helped by a strong economic recovery from the deep recession of 1981–1982, easily defeated Democratic challenger Walter Mondale. Reagan carried 49 of the 50 states, becoming only the second presidential candidate to do so. Reagan came within 3800 votes of winning all fifty states. His 525 electoral votes out of 538 remains the highest total ever received by a presidential candidate. In the national popular vote, Reagan received 58.8% to Mondale's 40.6%.

When he made his acceptance speech at the Democratic Convention, Mondale said, "Let's tell the truth. Mr. Reagan will raise taxes, and so will I. He won't tell you. I just did." Although Mondale intended to expose Reagan as hypocritical and position himself as the "honest" candidate, the choice of taxes as a discussion point damaged his electoral chances. Mondale chose U.S. Rep. Geraldine A. Ferraro of New York as his running mate, making her the first woman nominated for that position by a major party.

Mondale ran a liberal campaign, supporting a nuclear freeze and the Equal Rights Amendment. He spoke against what he considered to be unfairness in Reagan's economic policies and the need to reduce federal budget deficits. At a campaign stop in New Jersey,

Reagan said, "America's future rests in a thousand dreams inside your hearts. It rests in the message of hope in songs of a man so many young Americans admire, New Jersey's Bruce Springsteen." The Reagan campaign briefly used "Born in the U.S.A.," a song criticizing the treatment of Vietnam War veterans, which they mistakenly thought was devoid of anti-war content, as a campaign song, without permission, until Springsteen, a lifelong Democrat, insisted that they stop. Remarkably, in that election, the Republicans preached the politics of hope, while Democrats touted the politics of fear. How times have changed since then.

By 1984, Reagan was the oldest president to have ever served, and there were many questions about his capacity to endure the grueling demands of the presidency, particularly after Reagan had a poor showing in his first debate with Mondale on October 7. However, in the next debate on October 21, Reagan effectively neutralized the issue by quipping, "I will not make age an issue of this campaign. I am not going to exploit, for political purposes, my opponent's youth and inexperience."

Reagan was re-elected in an electoral and popular vote landslide, winning 49 states. He won a record 525 electoral votes total (of 538 possible), and received 58.8 percent of the popular vote. Mondale's defeat was the worst for any Democratic Party candidate in U.S. history in the Electoral College.

1988

Reagan was vacating the position after serving the maximum two terms. His Vice President, George H. W. Bush, won the Republican nomination, while the Democrats nominated Michael Dukakis, Governor of Massachusetts. Bush capitalized on a good economy, a stable international stage (the U.S. was not involved in any wars or conflicts), and on Reagan's popularity. Dukakis's campaign suffered from several miscues. Bush became the first incumbent Vice President of the United States to win a presidential election in 152 years.

After Reagan's image was tarnished in the Iran-Contra scandal, and after the Democrats won back control of the Senate in the 1986 congressional elections, the party's leaders felt more optimistic about winning the Presidency in 1988. The party looked for a new, fresh candidate who could move beyond the traditional New Deal-Great Society ideas of the past and offer a new image of the Democrats to the public. Party leaders tried to recruit the New York Governor, Mario Cuomo, who had impressed many Democrats with his stirring keynote speech at the 1984 Democratic Convention, to run for President. However, Cuomo declined. Gary Hart had made a strong showing in the 1984 presidential election, but questions and rumors about possible extramarital affairs dogged his campaign. On May 8, 1987, a week after the report of his involvement with Donna Rice broke, Hart dropped out of the race. In December 1987, Hart resumed his presidential campaign. However, the allegations of adultery had delivered a fatal blow to his candidacy, and he did poorly in the primaries before dropping out again.

Senator Ted Kennedy ruled himself out of the 1988 campaign. Two other politicians mentioned as possible candidates, both from Arkansas, didn't join the race: Senator Dale Bumpers and Governor (and future President) Bill Clinton. Joe Biden's campaign ended in controversy after the Delaware Senator was accused of plagiarizing a speech by Neil Kinnock, then-leader of the British Labor Party. Dukakis later revealed that his campaign was responsible for leaking the tape, and two members of his staff resigned. Al Gore, a Senator from Tennessee, also chose to run for the nomination. Turning 40 in 1988, he would have been the youngest president ever if elected, surpassing both John F. Kennedy and Theodore Roosevelt.

The Democratic Party Convention was held in Atlanta, Georgia. In his first major national speech, Arkansas Governor Bill Clinton placed Dukakis's name in nomination. The speech lasted for so long that some delegates began booing to get him to finish. The most memorable speech given at the Democratic Convention was by Texas State Treasurer Ann Richards, who two years later was elected the state governor. Richards uttered the famous line: "Poor George [H.W. Bush], he can't help it, he was born with a silver foot in his mouth." Six years later, Bush's son and future President George W. Bush would defeat Richards in her re-election campaign for Texas Governor.

Vice President George H.W. Bush pledged to continue Reagan's policies, but he also pledged a "kinder and gentler nation" in an attempt to win over some more moderate voters. Bush unexpectedly came in third in the Iowa caucus, which he had won in 1980, behind Dole and Robertson. Dole was also leading in the polls of the New Hampshire primary, and the Bush camp responded by running television commercials portraying Dole as a tax raiser, while Governor John H. Sununu campaigned for Bush. Dole did nothing to counter these ads and Bush won, thereby gaining crucial momentum, or what he called "Big Mo." Dole was bitter about his defeat in New Hampshire, going on TV to tell Bush to "stop lying about my record." At the Republican party convention, Bush was nominated unanimously. He selected U.S. Senator Dan Quayle of Indiana as his running mate. In his acceptance speech, Bush made the pledge, "Read my lips: No new taxes," a comment that would come to haunt him in the 1992 elections.

Bush sought to portray Governor Dukakis as a "Massachusetts liberal" who was unreasonably left-wing, attacking him for opposing mandatory recitation of the Pledge of Allegiance in schools, and being a "card carrying member of the ACLU." Dukakis responded that he was a "proud liberal" and that the phrase should not be a bad word in America. Bush derided Dukakis for having "foreign-policy views born in Harvard Yard's boutique." The Dukakis camp tried to tie Bush to Iran-Contra, and argued that Republicans were too hawkish on foreign policy.

Governor Dukakis attempted to quell criticism that he was ignorant on military matters by staging a photo op in which he rode in an M1 Abrams tank outside a General Dynamics plant in Sterling Heights, Michigan. The move ended up being a massive public relations blunder, with many mocking Dukakis's appearance as he stuck his smiling, helmeted head out one of the tank's hatches to wave to the crowd. Footage of Dukakis was used by the Bush campaign as evidence he would not make a good commander-in-chief, and "Dukakis in the tank" remains shorthand for backfired public relations outings.

Dukakis's campaign suffered a setback when staff member Donna Brazile resigned after she spread rumors that Bush was having an extramarital affair with Jennifer Fitzgerald, his secretary throughout the 1970s. Dukakis was badly hurt by the Republican "Willie Horton," "Revolving Door," and "Boston Harbor" campaign ads, the latter of which attacked the governor's failure to clean up environmental pollution in the harbor. Dukakis supported a state prison furlough program, which had begun before he was governor. The program had resulted in the release of convicted murderer Willie Horton, who then committed a rape and assault in Maryland. As Governor, Dukakis had vetoed a 1976 plan to bar inmates convicted of first-degree murder from the furlough program. The program was abolished by the state legislature in April 1988 after public outcry over the Willie Horton case.

A number of false rumors were reported in the media about Dukakis, including the claim by Idaho Republican Senator Steve Symms that Dukakis's wife Kitty had burned an American flag to protest the Vietnam War, as well as the claim that Dukakis himself had been treated for a mental illness. Lee Atwater, who will be mentioned at length later in this book, was accused of having floated these rumors.

Although Dukakis did well in the first presidential debate, Bush seemed to do better in the second debate. Before the second debate, Dukakis had been suffering from the flu and spent quite a bit of the day in bed. His performance was poor and played to his reputation as being intellectually cold. The most memorable moment came when reporter Bernard Shaw asked Dukakis whether he would support the death penalty if his wife were raped and murdered. Dukakis's answer lacked the normal emotions one would expect of a person asked about a loved one's rape and death. Tom Brokaw of NBC reported on his October 14 newscast: "The consensus tonight is that Vice President George Bush won last night's debate and made it all the harder for Governor Dukakis to catch and pass him in the 25 days remaining. In all of the Friday morning quarterbacking, there was common agreement that Dukakis failed to seize the debate and make it his night."

The election resulted in a majority of the popular vote for Bush and a lopsided majority (40 states) in the Electoral College. Although his victory was not a landslide in the popular vote, though it was substantial, Bush in 1988 was the last Republican to carry certain states which have since gained a reputation as "blue states" that favor the Democratic Party in presidential elections. He was the last candidate to secure an absolute majority until his son George W. Bush's 2004 election.

1992

There were three major candidates in this election: Incumbent Republican President George H. W. Bush; Democrat Arkansas Governor Bill Clinton, and independent Texas businessman Ross

Perot. Bush had alienated much of his conservative base by breaking his 1988 campaign pledge against raising taxes, the economy was in a recession, and Bush's perceived greatest strength, foreign policy, was regarded as much less important following the collapse of the Soviet Union and the relatively peaceful climate in the Middle East after the defeat of Iraq in the Gulf War. Clinton won a plurality in the popular vote, and a wide Electoral College margin.

Conservative journalist Pat Buchanan was Bush's primary opponent. However, his best showing was in the New Hampshire primary, where Bush won by a 53-38% margin. Bush and Vice President Dan Quayle easily won renomination by the Republican Party.

After the successful performance by U.S. and coalition forces in the Persian Gulf War, President Bush's approval ratings were 89%. His re-election was considered very likely. As a result, several high profile candidates such as Mario Cuomo refused to seek the Democratic nomination. However, several candidates such as Tom Harkin, Paul Tsongas, Jerry Brown, Bob Kerrey, and Bill Clinton chose to run. Clinton positioned himself as a centrist, or New Democrat. He was still a relative unknown. That quickly changed however, when a woman named Gennifer Flowers appeared in the press to reveal allegations of an affair. Clinton rebutted the story by appearing on *60 Minutes* with his wife, Hillary Rodham Clinton. Ultimately, when the Democratic Convention met in New York City, Governor Clinton was picked to be the standard bearer.

The public's concern about the federal budget deficit and fears of professional politicians allowed the independent candidacy of billionaire Texan Ross Perot to catch fire. At one point Perot was leading the major party candidates in the polls. Perot crusaded against the North American Free Trade Agreement (NAFTA), internal and external national debt, tapping into voters' potential fear of the deficit. His volunteers collected enough signatures to get his name on the ballot in all 50 states. In June, Perot led the national public opinion polls with support from 39% of the voters (versus 31% for Bush and 25% for Clinton). Perot severely damaged his credibility by dropping out of the presidential contest in July and remaining out of the race for several weeks before re-entering.

The 1992 campaign also saw Ralph Nader enter presidential politics. Nader did not formally run, but urged members of both parties to write in his name. Nader received more votes from Republicans than Democrats.

As the economy continued to deteriorate, the President's approval rating continued to slide and the Democrats rallied around their nominee. Clinton promised to bring a "new covenant" to America, and to work to heal the gap that had developed between the rich and the poor during the Reagan/Bush years. The Clinton campaign received the biggest convention bounce in history, which brought him from 25 percent in the spring, behind Bush and Perot, to 55 percent versus Bush's 31 percent.

After the convention, Clinton and Gore began a bus tour around the United States. The Bush/Quayle campaign panicked and began to hammer at Clinton's character, highlighting accusations of infidelity and draft dodging. The Bush campaign emphasized its foreign policy successes such as Desert Storm, and the end of the Cold War. Bush criticized Clinton's lack of foreign policy expertise. However, as the economy was the main issue, Bush's campaign floundered, even in strongly Republican areas, and Clinton maintained leads with over 50 percent of the vote nationwide consistently, while Bush typically saw numbers in the upper 30s. Bush then turned to the socially conservative Republican base. The campaign continued with a lopsided lead for Clinton through September, until Ross Perot decided to re-enter the race. Perot's numbers stayed low, until he was given the opportunity to participate in a trio of unprecedented three-man debates. The race narrowed. Perot's number's significantly improved as Clinton's number's declined, while Bush's numbers remained more or less the same from earlier in the race. Perot and Bush began to hammer at Clinton on character issues once again.

Many character issues were raised during the campaign, including allegations that Clinton had dodged the draft during the Vietnam War, that he had used marijuana, which he claimed he had pretended to smoke, but "didn't inhale." Bush accused Clinton of meeting with communists on a trip to Russia he took as a student. Clinton was often accused of being a philanderer, and that he had engaged in a long-term extramarital affair with Gennifer Flowers, which he denied.

On November 3, Bill Clinton won the election by a wide margin in the Electoral College. He captured 43 percent of the popular vote against Bush's 37 percent and Perot's 19%. It was the second largest electoral vote shift in American history after Jimmy Carter's victory in 1976. It was the first time since 1968 that a candidate won the White House with under 50 percent of the popular vote. President Bush's 37.4% was the lowest percentage total for a sitting president seeking re-election since William Howard Taft in 1912.

Several factors made the results possible. First, the campaign came on the heels of an economic slowdown. 75% of voters thought the economy was in Fairly Bad or Very Bad shape, while 63% thought their personal finances were better or the same as four years ago. The decision by Bush to accept a tax increase adversely affected his re-election bid. Clinton was able to condemn the tax increase effectively on both its own merits and as a reflection of Bush's honesty. Effective Democratic TV ads were aired showing a clip of Bush's infamous 1988 campaign speech in which he promised "Read my lips ... No new taxes." The end of the Cold War allowed old rivalries among conservatives to re-emerge and meant that other voters focused more on domestic policy, to the detriment of Bush, a social and fiscal moderate.

Unlike Bush, Clinton was able to unite his fractious and ideologically diverse party behind his candidacy. Clinton pointed to his centrist record as Governor of Arkansas. He was able to take back a number of southern states that the GOP had been winning for almost two decades, and crucially, the New England states as well. Liberal Democrats were impressed by Clinton's record on abortion and affirmative action. His strong connections to African Americans played a key role. He became a symbol of the rise of the Baby Boomer generation to political power. Supporters remained energized and confident, even in times of scandal or missteps.

In the months after the election, Republicans asserted that Perot had acted as a spoiler, enough to the detriment of Bush to lose him the election. However, the Election Night exit polls not only showed that Perot siphoned votes nearly equally among Bush and Clinton. Of the voters who cited Bush's broken "No New Taxes" pledge as "very important," two thirds voted for Bill Clinton. Perot's best results were in states that strongly favored either Clinton or Bush, or carried few electoral votes, limiting his real electoral impact for either candidate.

Clinton's election ended an era in which the Republican Party had controlled the White House for 20 of the previous 24 years. That election also brought the Democrats full control of the legislative and executive branches of the federal government, including both houses of and the presidency, for the first time since Jimmy Carter. This would not last for very long, however, as the Republicans won control of both the House and Senate in 1994. Reelected in 1996, Clinton would become the first Democratic President since Franklin Delano Roosevelt to serve two full terms in the White House.

1996

Clinton and Vice President Al Gore of Tennessee handily defeated former Senator Bob Dole of Kansas and Jack Kemp of New York. Ross Perot ran as candidate for the Reform Party with economist Pat Choate as his running mate, but he received less media attention and was excluded from the presidential debates. Clinton benefited from an economy which recovered from the early 1990s recession: the economy was in its best shape since the Eisenhower administration of the 1950s.

In 1995, the Republican Party was riding high on the gains it had made in the 1994 congressional elections. Republicans, led by Newt Gingrich, captured the majority of seats in both the House and the Senate.

Bill Clinton was renominated with only token opposition. The fragmented field of Republican candidates debated issues such as a flat tax and other tax cut proposals, and a return to Reagan's supply-side economic policies. Former U.S. Army General Colin L. Powell was widely courted as a potential Republican nominee. However, Powell declined. Dick Cheney was sought out by many as a possible candidate, but he declared his intention not to run. Donald Rumsfeld formed a presidential campaign exploratory committee, but declined to formally enter the race.

Going into the 1996 primary contest, Senate majority leader and former vice-presidential nominee Bob Dole was seen as the most likely winner. Pat Buchanan received early victories in Alaska, Louisiana, a strong second place in the Iowa Caucus, while Steve Forbes finished first in Delaware and Arizona. This put Dole's leadership in doubt. However, Dole won every primary thereafter which locked up the nomination for him. Ross Perot entered the field and Ralph Nader was drafted by the Green Party.

Clinton was able to focus on the general election early, while Dole was forced to move to the right and spend his campaign reserves fighting off challengers. Clinton ran a campaign through the summer defining his opponent as an aged conservative far from the mainstream, before Dole was in a position to respond. Compared to the 50-year old Clinton, the 73-year old Dole appeared especially old and frail, as illustrated by an embarrassing fall off a stage during a campaign event. Dole further enhanced this contrast on September 18 when he made a reference to a no-hitter thrown the day before by Hideo Nomo of the "Brooklyn Dodgers," a team that had left Brooklyn for Los Angeles four decades earlier.

Clinton painted Dole as a clone of unpopular House Speaker Newt Gingrich, warning that Bob Dole would work with the Republican Congress to slash popular social programs like Medicare and Social Security. Dole's tax-cut plan found itself under attack from the White House, who said it would "blow a hole in the deficit," which had been cut nearly in half during Clinton's first term. Clinton maintained comfortable leads in the polls over Dole and Perot. The televised debates featured only Dole and Clinton.

In late September 1995, questions arose regarding the Democratic National Committee's fund-raising practices. In February the following year, the People's Republic of China's alleged role in the campaign finance controversy first gained public attention after the *Washington Post* published a story stating that there was evidence that agents of China sought to direct contributions from foreign sources to the DNC before the 1996 presidential campaign. Seventeen people were eventually convicted for fraud or for funneling funds into the U.S. elections.

In the end, President Clinton won a decisive victory over Dole, becoming the first Democrat to win presidential reelection since Franklin Roosevelt. He outpolled Dole by over 8.2 million votes. The Democrats won 379 electoral votes to the Republican ticket's 159. Reform Party nominee Ross Perot won approximately 8% of the popular vote, less than half of his performance in 1992.

2000

Republican candidate George W. Bush, then-governor of Texas and son of former president George H. W. Bush, and Democratic candidate Al Gore, then-Vice President, squared off in one of the most controversial elections in U.S. Presidential history. Bush narrowly won the election, with 271 electoral votes to Gore's 266. The election was noteworthy for a controversy over the awarding of Florida's 25 electoral votes, the subsequent recount process in that state, and the unusual event of the winning candidate having received fewer popular votes than the runner-up. It was the closest election since 1876.

Vice President Gore's only serious challenge came from former Senator Bill Bradley of New Jersey. Gore easily defeated Bradley in the primaries, largely because of support from the Democratic Party establishment. He easily won the Democratic nomination.

Several Republican candidates challenged Gore's candidacy. Bush became the early front-runner, acquiring unprecedented funding and a broad base of leadership support, name recognition, and connections of the Bush family. Several aspirants withdrew early, leaving Bush, John McCain, Alan Keyes, Steve Forbes, Gary Bauer, and Orrin Hatch as the only candidates still in the race.

Bush was portrayed in the media as the establishment candidate. McCain portrayed himself as a crusading insurgent who focused on campaign reform. McCain supporters blamed his losses on the Bush campaign's mudslinging and dirty tricks, such as push polling that implied that McCain's had adopted Bangladeshi-born daughter, an African-American child he fathered out of wedlock. McCain criticized Bush for accepting the endorsement of Bob Jones University despite its policy banning interracial dating. Bush won the Republican nomination on March 14 and accepted the Nomination of the Republican party.

Although the campaign focused mainly on domestic issues, such as the projected budget surplus, proposed reforms of Social Security and Medicare, health care, and competing plans for tax relief, foreign policy was often an issue. Bush criticized Clinton administration policies in Somalia and in the Balkans. During the second presidential debate, Bush said, "I don't think our troops ought to be used for what's called nation-building," Bush pledged to bridge partisan gaps in the nation's capital, claiming the atmosphere in Washington stood in the way of progress on necessary reforms. Gore questioned Bush's fitness for the job, pointing to gaffes made by Bush in interviews and speeches and suggesting the Texas governor lacked the experience to be president.

Bill Clinton's impeachment and the sex scandal that led up to it cast a shadow on the campaign, particularly on his vice president's run to replace him. Republicans strongly denounced the Clinton scandals. Bush made his repeated promise to restore "honor and dignity" to the White House. Gore studiously avoided the Clinton scandals, as did his vice presidential candidate, Joe Lieberman, even though Lieberman had been the first Democratic senator to denounce Clinton's misbehavior. Some media observers theorized that Gore actually chose Lieberman in an attempt to separate himself from Clinton's past misdeeds, and help blunt the GOP's attempts to link him to his boss.

Ralph Nader was the most successful of third-party candidates, drawing 2.74% of the popular vote. In the aftermath of the campaign, many Gore supporters claimed that many of Nader's voters would have supported Gore, thus siphoning off enough would-be Gore votes to throw the election to Bush. Both vice presidential candidates, Dick Cheney and Joe Lieberman, campaigned aggressively in the 2000 presidential election.

With the exceptions of Florida and Tennessee, Bush carried the Southern states by comfortable margins and secured wins in Ohio, Indiana, most of the rural Midwestern farming states, most of the Rocky Mountain states, and Alaska. Gore swept the Northeast, most of the Upper Midwest, and all of the Pacific Coast states and Hawaii. As the night wore on, the returns in a handful of small-to-medium sized states, including Wisconsin and Iowa, were extremely close. However, Florida would make clear the winner of the election. As the final national results were tallied the following morning, Bush had clearly won a total of 246 electoral votes, while Gore had won 255 votes. 270 votes were needed to win. Two smaller states, New Mexico and Oregon, were still too close to call. The news media focused on Florida. Mathematically, Florida's 25 electoral votes became the key to an election win for either candidate. The outcome of the election was not known for more than a month after the balloting ended because of the extended process of counting and recounting Florida's presidential ballots.

Ten minutes before the polls closed in the largely Republican Florida panhandle, some television news networks declared that Gore had carried Florida's 25 electoral votes. However, Bush began to take a wide lead early in Florida. By 10 p.m. EST those networks had retracted that prediction and placed Florida back into the "undecided" column. At approximately 2:30 a.m., with some 85% of the votes counted in Florida and Bush leading Gore by more than 100,000 votes, the networks declared that Bush had carried Florida and therefore had been elected. However, most of the remaining votes to be counted in Florida were located in three heavily Democratic counties - Broward, Miami-Dade, and Palm Beach. As their votes were reported, Gore began to gain on Bush. By 4:30 a.m., after all votes were counted, Gore had narrowed Bush's margin to just over 2,000 votes. The networks retracted their predictions that Bush had won Florida and the presidency. Gore, who had privately conceded the election to Bush, withdrew his concession. The final result in Florida was slim enough to require a mandatory recount under state law. Bush's lead had dwindled to about 300 votes by the time it was completed later that week. A count of overseas military ballots later boosted his margin to about 900 votes.

Most of the post-electoral controversy revolved around Gore's request for hand recounts in four counties (Broward, Miami Dade, Palm Beach, and Volusia), as provided under Florida state law. Florida Secretary of State Katherine Harris announced she would reject any revised totals from those counties if they were not turned in by November 14, the statutory deadline for amended returns. The Florida Supreme Court extended the deadline to November 26, a decision later vacated by the U.S. Supreme Court. Miami-Dade eventually halted its recount and resubmitted its original total to the state elections board, while Palm Beach County failed to meet the extended deadline. On November 26, the state board certified Bush the winner of Florida's electors by 537 votes. Gore formally contested the certified results. A state court decision overruling Gore was reversed by the Florida Supreme Court, which ordered a recount of over 70,000 ballots previously rejected by machine counters. The U.S. Supreme Court quickly halted the order.

On December 12, the Supreme Court ruled in a 7–2 vote that the Florida Supreme Court's ruling requiring a statewide recount of ballots was unconstitutional, and in a 5–4 vote that the Florida recounts could not be completed before a December 12 deadline. The Supreme Court's decision was an unsigned or "Per Curiam" ruling; the ruling was "limited to the present circumstances" and could not be cited as precedent.

Though Gore came in second in the electoral vote, he received 543,895 more popular votes than Bush. After Florida was decided and Gore conceded, George W. Bush became the President-elect and began forming his transition committee. Bush stated he was reaching across party lines to bridge a divided America, saying, "The President of the United States is the President of every single American, of every race, and every background."

2004

Republican Party candidate and incumbent President George W. Bush defeated Democratic Party candidate John Kerry, the junior U.S. Senator from Massachusetts. Foreign policy was the dominant theme throughout the election campaign, particularly Bush's conduct of the War on Terrorism and the invasion of Iraq.

As in the 2000 presidential election, voting controversies and concerns of irregularities emerged during and after the vote. The winner was not determined until the following day, when Kerry decided not to dispute Bush's win in the state of Ohio. The state held enough electoral votes to determine the winner of the presidency. Both Kerry and Democratic National Committee Chairman Howard Dean stated that voting in Ohio had not proceeded fairly and that, had it done so, the Democratic ticket might have won that state and therefore the election. However, there was far less controversy about this election than in 2000. In the Electoral College, Bush received 286 votes, and Kerry 251.

Eight months into Bush's presidency, the terrorist attacks of September 11, 2001 suddenly transformed Bush into a wartime president. His approval ratings surged to near 90%. Within a month, the forces of a coalition led by the United States invaded Afghanistan, which had been sheltering Osama bin Laden, suspected mastermind of the September 11 attacks. By December, the Taliban had been removed as rulers of Kabul, although a long and ongoing war would follow, severely hampered by on-going turmoil and violence within the country.

The Bush administration then turned its attention to Iraq, and argued the need to remove Saddam Hussein from power in Iraq were urgent. Among the stated reasons were that Saddam's regime had tried to acquire nuclear material and had not properly accounted for biological and chemical material it possessed. Both the possession of these weapons of mass destruction (WMD), and the failure to account for them, violated the U.N. sanctions. Most countries believed the intelligence the U.S. presented, including France, Germany, and Russia. Despite repeated offers for new weapons investigators, Iraq refused entry by U.N. inspectors. The situation escalated to the point that a coalition of forty allied nations invaded Iraq on March 20, 2003. Within three weeks, the invasion caused the collapse of both the Iraqi government and its armed forces. However, the U.S. and allied forces had failed to find any major Weapons of Mass Destruction in Iraq. Nevertheless, on May 1, George W. Bush landed on the aircraft carrier USS *Abraham Lincoln*, in a Lockheed S-3 Viking, where he gave a speech announcing the end of "major combat operations" in the Iraq war. Bush's approval rating in May was at 66%. However, those high approval ratings did not last. First, while the war itself was popular in the U.S., the reconstruction and attempted "democratization" of Iraq lost support as months passed and casualty figures increased. Investigators failed to find the predicted WMD stockpiles, which led to debate over why the U.S. went to war.

Still, Bush's popularity as a wartime president helped ward off any serious challenge to the nomination. Bush focused on two themes: defending America against terrorism and building an ownership society. The ownership society included allowing people to invest some of their Social Security in the stock market, increasing home and stock ownership, and encouraging more people to buy their own health insurance.

By summer of 2003, Howard Dean had become the front runner for the Democrats. He emerged as a left-wing populist, denouncing the policies of the Bush administration (especially the 2003 invasion of Iraq) as well as fellow Democrats, who, in his view, failed to strongly oppose them. Senator Lieberman, a liberal on domestic issues but a hawk on the War on Terror, failed to gain traction with liberal Democratic primary voters. In September 2003, retired four-star general Wesley Clark announced his intention to run in the presidential primary election for the Democratic Party nomination, but his late start left him with few detailed policy proposals.

In March's Super Tuesday, Senator John Kerry won decisive victories in California, Connecticut, Georgia, Maryland, Massachusetts,

New York, Ohio, Rhode Island, and Minnesota. Senator John Edwards finished only slightly behind Kerry in Georgia, but failed to win a single state other than South Carolina, and withdrew from the presidential race. When Kerry was nominated, he announced John Edwards as his running mate. The Kerry/Edwards ticket promised to make America "stronger at home and more respected in the world." Kerry made his Vietnam War experience the prominent theme of the convention. In accepting the nomination, he began his speech with, "I'm John Kerry and I'm reporting for duty." He later delivered what may have been the speech's most memorable line when he said, "The future doesn't belong to fear, it belongs to freedom."

Bush focused his campaign on national security, presenting himself as a decisive leader and contrasted Kerry as a "flip-flopper." He sought to portray Kerry as a "Massachusetts liberal" who was out of touch with mainstream Americans. One of Kerry's slogans was "Stronger at home, respected in the world." People who voted for Bush cited the issues of terrorism and moral values as the most important factors in their decision. Kerry supporters cited the war in Iraq, the economy and jobs, and health care.

Kerry supporters attempted to capitalize on Bush's dwindling popularity to rally anti-war sentiment. During August and September 2004, there was an intense focus on events that occurred in the late 1960s and early 1970s. Bush was accused of failing to fulfill his required service in the Texas Air National Guard. However, the focus quickly shifted to the conduct of CBS News after they aired a segment on *60 Minutes Wednesday* introducing what became known as the Killian documents. Serious doubts about the documents' authenticity emerged, leading CBS to appoint a review panel that eventually resulted in the firing of the news producer and other significant staffing changes.

Meanwhile, Kerry was accused by a group which called itself "Swift Vets and POWs for Truth," who claimed that "phony war crimes charges, his exaggerated claims about his own service in Vietnam, and his deliberate misrepresentation of the nature and effectiveness of Swift boat operations compels us to step forward." The group challenged the legitimacy of each of the combat medals awarded to Kerry. In the beginning of September, Bush gained his first comfortable margin since Kerry had won the nomination.

Three presidential debates and one vice presidential debate were held in autumn 2004. The first debate focused on foreign policy. Kerry accused Bush of having failed to gain international support for the 2003 invasion of Iraq, saying the only countries assisting the USA during the invasion were the United Kingdom and Australia. Bush replied to this by saying, "Well, actually, he forgot Poland." Mainstream pollsters stated that Kerry had won the debate decisively, strengthening what had come to be seen as a weak and troubled campaign. In the days after the debate, coverage focused on Bush's apparent annoyance with Kerry and numerous scowls and negative facial expressions. The Vice Presidential debate was held between Dick Cheney and John Edwards. An initial poll by ABC indicated a victory for Cheney, while polls by CNN and MSNBC gave it to Edwards.

The second presidential debate, conducted in a "town meeting" format, was less formal than the first Presidential debate. Bush attempted to deflect criticism of what was described as his scowling demeanor during the first debate, joking at one point about one of Kerry's remarks, "That answer made me want to scowl." Bush and Kerry met for the third and final debate on October 13. 51 million viewers watched the debate. However, at the time of the ASU debate, 15.2 million viewers watched the Major League Baseball playoffs

Compared to 2000, Bush picked up a net gain of 8 electoral votes. Electoral votes split along sharp geographical lines: the West Coast, Northeast, and most of the Great Lakes region voted for Kerry, and the South, Great Plains, and Mountain States went for Bush. The widespread support for Bush in the Southern states continued the defection of the formerly Democratic Solid South to the Republican South.

2008

The 56th presidential election was held on November 4, 2008. Outgoing Republican President George W. Bush's policies and actions and the American public's desire for change were key issues throughout the campaign. The major party candidates ran on a platform of change and reform in Washington. Domestic policy and the economy emerged as the main themes in the last few months of the election campaign after the onset of the 2008 economic crisis. Democrat Barack Obama, the junior United States Senator from Illinois, defeated Republican John McCain. Obama received 365 electoral votes, and McCain 173.

The election was the first in which an African-American was elected President. It was also the first time the Republican Party nominated a woman, Sarah Palin, then-Governor of Alaska, for Vice President, and the first election in which both major parties nominated candidates who were born outside of the contiguous United States. Voter turnout for the 2008 election was the highest in at least 40 years.

Bush's approval ratings had been slowly declining from their high point of almost 90% after 9/11. They were barely 50% at the time of his reelection in 2004. During his second term, Bush's approval rating dropped more quickly, with the Iraq War and the federal response to Hurricane Katrina in 2005 being most detrimental to the public's perception of his job performance. By September 2006, Bush's approval rating was below 40%. In the November 2006 Congressional elections, Democrats gained the majority in both houses. Bush's approval ratings dropped steadily throughout the rest of his term.

Early polls showed Senators Hillary Clinton and Barack Obama as the most popular potential Democratic candidates. Nevertheless, the media speculated on several other candidates, including Al Gore, John Kerry, John Edwards, Delaware Senator Joseph Biden, and New Mexico Governor Bill Richardson.

Clinton announced her intention to run in the Democratic primaries on January 20, 2007. Obama announced his candidacy on February 10. None of the candidates received a significant bounce in their poll numbers after their official announcements. Through most of 2007, John Edwards and Al Gore each hovered between the third and fourth place spots in the polls behind Clinton and Obama. Clinton led in nearly all nationwide opinion polling until January 2008.

At the start of the year, support for Barack Obama began rising in the polls, passing Clinton for first place in Iowa. Obama's win was fueled by first time caucus-goers and Independents and showed voters viewed him as the candidate of change. Iowa jump-started Obama's campaign and set him on track to win the nomination and the presidency. Obama became the new front-runner in New Hampshire when his poll numbers skyrocketed after his victory in Iowa. The Clinton campaign was struggling after a bad loss in Iowa. Campaign strategists had projected the former first lady wrapping up the Democratic presidential nomination by Super Tuesday on Feb. 5. Clinton won the New Hampshire primary by 2% of the vote, contrary to the predictions of pollsters who consistently had her trailing Obama. On January 30, 2008, Edwards announced that he was suspending his campaign for the presidency, but he did not initially endorse any remaining candidate.

Super Tuesday occurred on February 5, 2008, during which the largest-ever number of simultaneous state primary elections was held. It ended leaving the Democrats in a virtual tie, with Obama amounting 847 delegates to Clinton's 834.

On March 4, Hillary Clinton carried Ohio and Rhode Island in the Democratic primaries. She also carried the primary in Texas, but Obama won the Texas caucuses held the same day and netted more delegates from the state than Clinton. Only one state, Pennsylvania, held a primary in April. Although Obama made a strong effort, Hillary Clinton won the primary by nearly 10%. Obama had outspent Clinton three to one in Pennsylvania, but his comment at a San Francisco fundraiser that small-town Americans "cling" to guns and religion drew sharp criticism from the Clinton campaign and may have hurt his chances in Pennsylvania. Obama was still in a stronger position than Clinton to win the nomination, with a higher number of delegates and popular votes, but Clinton had received the endorsement of more superdelegates.

On May 6, in North Carolina and Indiana, Obama outperformed the polls by several points in both states, winning in North Carolina and losing by only 1% in Indiana. Most experts said it had become increasingly improbable, if not impossible, for Clinton to win the nomination. Although she did manage to win the majority of the remaining primaries and delegates, it was not enough to overcome Obama's substantial lead. She finally conceded the nomination to Obama on June 7, pledging her full support to the presumptive nominee, and vowed to do everything she could to help him get elected.

The Republican race was wide open. Former New York City Mayor Rudolph Giuliani led in the polls, followed closely by Arizona Senator John McCain. The media speculated that Giuliani's pro-choice stance on abortion and McCain's age and support of the unpopular Iraq War would be detriments to their candidacies. Giuliani remained the frontrunner in the polls throughout most of 2007, with McCain and former Tennessee Senator Fred Thompson fighting for second place. McCain eventually displaced Rudy Giuliani and Mitt Romney as the front-runner in New Hampshire.

McCain staged a turnaround victory, having been written off by the experts and polling in single digits less than a month before the race.

In February, McCain was endorsed by California Governor Arnold Schwarzenegger before the California primary took place on Super Tuesday. This gave him a significant boost in the polls for the state's primary, which awarded the greatest number of delegates of all the states. On Super Tuesday, McCain picked up 574 delegates. Huckabee, the surprise performer, won 5 states and 218 delegates, and Romney won 7 states and 231 delegates. Two days later, Romney suspended his presidential campaign and endorsed McCain. After Super Tuesday, John McCain had become the clear front-runner. In March, he clinched the Republican nomination.

His running mate, Sarah Palin, was the first woman nominated for Vice President by the Republican Party. On August 28, 2008, Obama became the first African American to be nominated for President by a major political party. His nomination acceptance speech drew one of the largest attendances of any political speech, attracting some 85,000 people. The television audiences for both McCain's and Obama's acceptance speeches broke records, according to Nielsen ratings.

The unpopular war in Iraq was a key issue during the campaign before the economic crisis took hold. John McCain supported the war; Barack Obama opposed it. McCain's statement that the United States could be in Iraq for as much as the next 50 to 100 years proved costly. Obama used it against him as part of his strategy to tie him to the unpopular President Bush. McCain's support for the troop 'surge' employed by General David Petraeus may have boosted McCain's stance on the issue in voters' minds. However, Obama was quick to remind voters that there would have been no need for a "surge" had there been no war at all, which he then used to question McCain's judgment as well.

Entering 2008, polls consistently showed that only twenty to thirty percent of the American public approved of Bush's job performance. In March 2008, Bush endorsed McCain at the White House, but he did not make a single appearance for McCain during the campaign. For his part, McCain made an effort to show that he had disagreed with Bush on many other key issues. During the entire general election campaign, Obama countered by pointing out in ads and at numerous campaign rallies that McCain had claimed in an interview that he voted with Bush 90% of the time, and congressional voting records supported this for the years Bush was in office.

John McCain adopted the campaign theme of "change" versus "experience" against Obama at the start of the general election campaign. Advantages for McCain and Obama on experience and the ability to bring change, respectively, remained steady through the November 4 election. However, final pre-election polling found that voters considered Obama's inexperience less of an impediment than McCain's association with sitting President Bush, an association which was rhetorically framed by the Obama campaign throughout the election season as "more of the same."

McCain undercut his line of attack by picking first-term Alaska governor Sarah Palin to be his running mate. Palin had been governor only since 2006. Before that, she had been a council member and mayor of Wasilla. She excited much of the conservative base of the GOP with her speech at the 2008 Republican Convention. However, media interviews suggested that Palin lacked knowledge on key issues, and they cast doubt among many voters about her qualifications to even be Vice President, let alone President. In addition, because of Palin's conservative views, there was also concern that, while she would bring conservatives to McCain, she would also alienate independents and moderates, two groups that McCain would need to win the election.

As things came down to the wire, unquestionably the economy was the top concern for voters. News sources reported that the economy was suffering its most serious downturn since the Great Depression. McCain's election prospects faltered when he made several politically unfortunate comments about the economy. On August 20, he said he was uncertain how many houses he and his wife, Cindy, owned; "I think — I'll have my staff get to you." The gaffe was used to portray McCain as unable to relate to the concerns of ordinary Americans. On September 15, the day Lehman Brothers filed for bankruptcy, McCain declared that "the fundamentals of our economy are strong," despite what he described as "tremendous turmoil in our financial markets and Wall Street."

On September 24, after the onset of the 2008 financial crisis, McCain announced that he was suspending his campaign to return to Washington to help craft a $700 billion bailout package for the troubled financial industry. He stated he would not debate Obama until Congress passed the bailout bill. Despite this decision, McCain did not play a significant role in the negotiations for the first version of the bill, which fell short of passage in the House. On September 26, he decided to participate in the first presidential debate, despite Congress' lack of immediate action on the bill. Days later, a second version of the original bailout bill was passed by both the House and Senate, with Obama, his vice presidential running mate Joe Biden, and McCain all voting for the measure.

All these events combined to hurt McCain's standing. All occurred after the economic crisis and after McCain's poll numbers had started to fall. Although sound bites of all of these "missteps" were played repeatedly on national television, most analysts agree that the actual financial crisis and economic conditions caused McCain's large drop

During the first presidential debate, the central issues debated were supposed to be foreign policy and national security. However, due to the economic climate, some questions appeared on this topic.

The second presidential debate was a town meeting format. The third and final debated focused on domestic and economic policy.

Allegations of voter list purges using unlawful criteria caused controversy in at least six swing states: Colorado, Indiana, Ohio, Michigan, Nevada and North Carolina. Virginia election authorities were ordered by a federal judge to preserve late-arriving absentee ballots sent by active-duty military personnel following a suit by the McCain campaign. In Ohio, which was identified by both parties as a key state, allegations surfaced from both Republicans and Democrats that individuals from out of state were moving to the state temporarily and attempting to vote despite not meeting the state's requirement of permanent residency for more than 29 days.

A controversy arose regarding Obama's contact with Bill Ayers, a Distinguished Professor at the University of Illinois at Chicago, and a former leader of the Weather Underground, a radical left organization in the 1970s. Investigations concluded that Obama did not have a close relationship with Ayers. Ayers had served on two nonprofit boards with Obama. Both Ayers and his wife had hosted a gathering at their home in 1995, where Alice Palmer introduced Obama as her chosen successor in the Illinois State Senate. The matter was initially raised by Sean Hannity and other conservative talk show hosts. In October 2008, the matter was mentioned in attack ads, robocalls, mass mailings, and campaign speeches by Republican presidential candidate John McCain and vice presidential candidate Sarah Palin as an issue in the general election campaign. Obama condemned Ayers' past, and stated that he did not have a close association with him.

On election day, a McCain victory quickly became improbable. Obama amassed early wins in Illinois, the Northeast, and the critical battleground states of Ohio and Pennsylvania. By 11 p.m. Eastern time, Obama was only 50 electoral votes shy of victory with only six West Coast states (California, Oregon, Washington, Idaho,

Alaska, and Hawaii) still voting. By that time all of the American networks called the election in favor of Obama. McCain conceded half an hour later in his home state of Arizona. President-elect Obama appeared just before midnight Eastern Time on November 5 in Grant Park, Chicago in front of a crowd of 250,000 people to deliver his victory speech. Following Obama's speech, spontaneous street parties broke out in cities across the United States and around the world in London, Bonn, Berlin, Obama, Japan, Toronto, Rio de Janeiro, Sydney, and Nairobi. The final tally of total votes counted was 131.3 million, compared to 122.3 million in 2004 – the highest turnout since 1960.

Born in Honolulu, Hawaii, Obama was the first president to be born outside the continental United States. Obama, having a white mother and Kenyan father, became the first African American and the first bi-racial president. The Obama-Biden ticket was also the first winning ticket in American history on which neither candidate was a WASP; Biden is Roman Catholic and is the first Roman Catholic to be elected Vice President.

PART TWO:

THE BEGINNINGS OF
THE CURRENT
POLITICS OF HATE

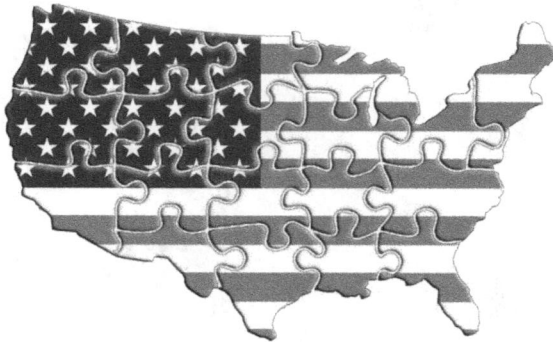

1

DIRTY TRICKS

HAVE ALWAYS BEEN THERE

"Reality is malleable. It can be made to bend to your will. ...
Roger Ailes was a real power player. He played a key role in getting
George H.W. Bush elected over Michael Dukakis in 1988, and his
book, *You Are the Message: Secrets of the Master Communicator*s,
is a 'must read,' along with Sun-T'u'*s The Art of Wa*r, Machiavelli'*s
The Princ*e, and Carl von Clausewitz'*s On Wa*r. He was the guy
who dreamed up the town hall forum for Richard Nixon. He was
Lee Atwater's mentor. All I lacked was influence over other human
beings. No*w the*re was something worth having!" - Allen Raymond,
former GOP Political consultant, author of *How to Rig an Election*
(Simon & Schuster).

Raymond, who went to prison for his role in a scheme to jam the Democratic Party's phone lines during New Hampshire's 2002 Senate elections, says that dirty tricks are commonplace in the political world and reforms are badly needed.

* * *

FROM *ON LANGUAGE: DIRTY TRICKS*

by WILLIAM SAFIRE, February 3, 2008, *New York Times*

Vladimir Putin told a crowd of supporters recently that "'Western specialists' were seeking a 'disorganized and disoriented society' in Russia, so that those sneaky Americans 'can carry out their dirty tricks behind its back." The Russian phrase that the longtime cold warrior used was *delishki*, a colloquialism with a negative connotation variously translated as dirty tricks or shady deals. The American phrase "dirty tricks" is now used most often in politics and is understood around the world.

The first use of the English phrase "dirty tricks" can be traced to Arthur Capel, the Earl of Essex, who wrote in 1670, ''To me he called it a dirty trick." Thirteen years later, the Earl was found with his throat cut in the Tower of London, more dirty deed than dirty trick. The phrase entered the political vocabulary with a vengeance during the Watergate scandal as a phrase that once was equated with ''pranks," ''hardball" and ''borderline slander." In 1973, it gained a more sinister meaning of ''surreptitious disruption of an opponent's campaign." Joe Cummins, author of *Anything for a Vote: Dirty tricks, Cheap Shots and October Surprises in U.S. Presidential Campaigns*, notes that it was George Washington, while commanding general of the American revolutionary forces, who wrote of a British peace proposal, "They are practicing such low and dirty tricks, that men of sentiment and honor must blush at their Villainy." In 1828, *The United States Telegraph*, a newspaper supporting President Andrew Jackson, despite vilification in his re-election campaign for having married Rachel Robards before her divorce was complete, denounced its rival's coverage with *"The Intelligencer* at its dirty tricks again!"

The phrase may have had its modern genesis in the U.S. Navy. In its Nov. 20, 1944 issue, *Time* magazine reported a surprise predawn raid on Japanese land-based air power on the island of Luzon, as "The Dirty Tricksters."

Covert action has been used since time immemorial in both politics and intelligence operations. In the Carter-Reagan campaign of 1980, Carter's briefing book for a television debate mysteriously found its way into the hands of the Reagan camp. James Baker and William Casey were suspected of pulling that dirty trick; both men adamantly denied it. Casey wound up as Reagan's director of Central Intelligence working with Baker as White House chief of staff. Thus ended the Dirty Trick That Never Was.

* * *

The 1988 Bush vs. Dukakis election had an endless barrage of lies and disinformation. The Bush campaign was run by Lee Atwater of Georgia, the ultimate ninja warrior of bad-boy politics. Karl Rove had, in fact, discovered Atwater and introduced him to the Bush family. George W. Bush, who also worked on the campaign, was in awe of Atwater's political savvy and immensely impressed by his take-no-prisoners political sensibility.

After skillful leaks and lies out of the GOP National Committee had defeated Gary Hart, Bob Dole and Pat Robertson, the Bush camp went ballistic on the Democrats' candidate, Michael Dukakis, with skillfully planted stories that Dukakis in the past had consulted a psychiatrist for depression. While the stories were completely untrue, that didn't stop President Reagan from compassionately telling reporters, when asked about this rumor, that he was "not going to pick on a invalid." From there, Atwater was able to destroy Dukakis with an endless carpet-bombing of unprecedented attack ads, like the viciously racist "Willie Horton" commercials about a black man who'd been charged with murder while on work-release in Massachusetts. When the smoke cleared, George Bush the Elder had won the election.

* * *

The source of some of the most outrageous domestic intrigue and international revolutionary conspiracy of its era was 42 Wall Street, the mahogany-lined law offices of Sullivan & Cromwell. Until his death in 1948 at the ripe old age of 94, founding partner William Nelson Cromwell was part court solicitor and part buccaneer-for-hire to the greatest Robber Barons of the day. In 1879, Cromwell incorporated the Edison General Electric Company as a virtual monopoly over the American electric power industry. He did the same thing for Andrew Carnegie's United States Steel Corporation in 1901. Cromwell also orchestrated the enormous land grabs, strike-breaking, and corporate consolidations that led to Edward H. Harriman's takeover of the Union Pacific Railroad in 1898. Cromwell worked hand in glove with the premier Wall Street moneymen of the day, including J.P. Morgan, the Rockefellers, Kuhn Loeb & Co., Otto Kahn and Felix Warburg. So ruthlessly were the tactics of these syndicates in eliminating competitors and rigging prices in American markets, that even a conservative, Big-Business dominated Congress under Republican Senate majority leader Mark "Dollar" Hana was forced to pass the Sherman Anti-trust Act of 1890.

In the realm of international finance and in engineering political revolutions abroad, Cromwell set the world standard. In 1896, Cromwell was retained by the chief engineer of the failed French Panama Canal construction company, to convince the U.S. Government to pay $40 million for a pile of rusting construction equipment and the soon-to-expire development rights from the Colombian government. In one of the most audacious feats of covert corporate political warfare in history, Cromwell paid Hana a record bribe of $60,000, then proceeded to put together a secret syndicate of middleman bankers to surreptitiously buy up a controlling interest in the outstanding shares of "worthless" Compagnie stock at pennies on the dollar.

Beginning in 1902, $3.5 million was quietly paid out by a second syndicate organized by Cromwell that included J.P. Morgan and some of the largest bankers in New York, to repurchase these shares, bought up at the lowest price possible. When the Colombian government learned of the scheme, and balked at the terms in 1903, the deal seemed imperiled as the Colombians threatened to march on Colon in November to throw the Americans out and a crush a Panamanian revolt. At the same time, the scheme met with increasing resistance in Washington and in the press, led by Senator John Tyler Morgan (who had a stake in competing canal plan through Nicaragua) and Joseph Pulitizer, whose New York World newspaper had sought to expose the Panama conspiracy.

Cromwell let loose a team of secret agents, lawyers, and bankers to spark a "nationalist" revolution in Panama. In the meantime, President McKinley, whose support had been lukewarm, was gunned down by an anarchist in Buffalo, New York. After Teddy Roosevelt assumed office, things soon got back on track. As American war ships patrolled the waters off the Panamanian capitol of Colon in November 1903, Cromwell's agents bribed the Colombian Army, sending officers and enlisted men on their way, pockets jangling with silver, all the way back to Bogota. Despite the ensuing scandal, most of the press hailed the revolution of the "Panama Patriots" as a triumph for American-style democracy. The U.S. Congress voted to pay out the $40 million, and authorized another million in public underwriting for the bonds of the Panamanian railroad company owned by Cromwell. The distribution of the U.S. Government payments to stockholders and the Panamanians was, strangely, put in Cromwell's hands, rather than administered by the U.S. Treasury. The conspiracy's principal investors saw as high as a 1,250% return. For his $1.333 million investment, Cromwell personally took at least $18 million, while his law firm billed the United States $832,449 in legal fees

* * *

Black propaganda is false information and material that purports to be from a source on one side of a conflict, but is actually from the opposing side. It is typically used to vilify, embarrass or misrepresent the enemy. Black propaganda contrasts with grey propaganda, the source of which is not identified, and white propaganda, in which the real source is declared and usually more accurate information is given, if also slanted or distorted. Black propaganda purports to emanate from a source other than the true source. This type of propaganda is associated with covert psychological operations. Sometimes the source is concealed or credited to a false authority and spreads lies, fabrications, and deceptions. Black propaganda is the "big lie," including all types of creative deceit.

Ultimately, black propaganda relies on the willingness of the receiver to accept the credibility of the source. If the creators or senders of the black propaganda message do not adequately understand their intended audience, the message may be misunderstood, seem suspicious, or fail altogether. Governments generally conduct black propaganda operations for two different reasons. First, by utilizing black propaganda a government is more likely to succeed in convincing their target audience that the information that they are seeking to influence them with is disguised, and that its motivations are not apparent. Second, there are diplomatic reasons behind the use of black propaganda. Black propaganda is necessary in order to obfuscate a government's involvement in activities that may be detrimental to its foreign policies.

Disinformation is a useful form of black propaganda due to the fact that disinformation campaigns are covert in nature and use various forms of false information. Disinformation can be defined as false information that is deliberately, and often covertly spread in order to influence public opinion and obscure the truth. Prior to, and during the Cold War, the Soviet Union successfully utilized this form of black propaganda on multiple occasions to their benefit. Joseph Stalin's dictatorship firmly believed in black propaganda and disinformation campaigns targeted against Western nations and the United States. One of Stalin's early successes in these operations targeted the United States through the use of the Moscow Bureau Chief at the New York Times, Walter Duranty. Duranty would ultimately win the Pulitzer Prize for his sympathetic writings praising the Soviet dictator, while failing to accurately report on the Ukrainian famine of 1932.

The Soviet Union utilized black propaganda during the Iranian hostage crisis that took place from 1979 until 1981. For strictly political purposes, and to show support for the hostages, Soviet diplomats at the United Nations vocally criticized the taking of the hostages. At this same time however, Soviet "black" radio stations within Iran called the National Voice of Iran openly broadcast strong support for the crisis in an effort to increase anti-American sentiment. This represented a clear utilization of black propaganda by the Soviet Union in order to have anti-American broadcasts appear as if they were actually originating from Iranian sources.

Throughout the Cold War, the Soviet Union effectively utilized the KGB in order to conduct its covert black forms of active measures. The KGB was responsible for clandestine campaigns targeting foreign governments, as well as influencing individuals and specific groups that were hostile towards the Soviet government and its policies.

Following the 9-1-1 attacks against the United States, the Pentagon organized and implemented the Office of Strategic Influence in an effort to improve public support abroad, mainly in Islamic countries. The head of OSI maintained the mission of "circulating classified proposals calling for aggressive campaigns that used not only the foreign media and the Internet, but also covert operations." Defense Secretary Donald Rumsfeld planned for what they called "a broad mission ranging from 'black' campaigns that used disinformation and other covert activities to 'white' public affairs that rely on truthful news releases." Therefore, OSI's operations could include the blackest of activities.

OSI's operations included contacting and emailing media, journalist, and foreign community leaders with information that would counter foreign governments and organizations that are hostile to the United States. In doing so, the emails would be masked by utilizing addresses ending with .com as opposed to using the standard Pentagon address of ".mil," and hide any involvement of the U.S. government and the Pentagon. The Pentagon is forbidden to conduct black propaganda operations within the American media, but is not prohibited for conducting these operations against foreign media outlets. The thought of conducting black propaganda operations and utilizing disinformation resulted in harsh criticism for the program. It closed down in 2002.

In Britain, the Political Warfare Executive operated a number of black propaganda radio stations during World War II. Gustav Siegfried Eins (GS1), which purported to be a clandestine German station, was one of the first such stations. The speaker, "Der Chef," purported to be a Nazi extremist, accusing Hitler and his henchmen of going soft. The station focused on alleged corruption and sexual improprieties of Nazi Party members. Another example was the British radio station *Soldatensender Calais*, which purported to be a radio station for the German military. Under the direction of Sefton Delmer, a British journalist who spoke perfect Berliner German, Soldatensender Calais and its associated shortwave station, *Kurzwellensender Atlantik*, broadcast music, up-to-date sports scores, speeches of Adolf Hitler for "cover" and subtle propaganda.

Radio Deutschland was another radio station employed by the British during the war aimed and designed to undermine German morale and create tensions that would ultimately disrupt the German war effort. The station was broadcast from a signal in close proximity on the radio dial to an actual German station. During the war most Germans actually believed that this station was in fact a German radio station and even gained the recognition of Germany's propaganda chief Joseph Goebbels. There were British black propaganda radio stations in most of the languages of occupied Europe as well as German and Italian.

German black propaganda usually took advantage of European racism and anti-Communism. On the night of April 27, 1944 German aircraft under cover of darkness dropped propaganda leaflets over occupied Denmark. These leaflets used the title of *Frihedsposten*, a genuine Danish underground newspaper, and claimed that the "hour of liberation" was approaching. They instructed Danes to accept "occupation by Russian or specially trained American Negro soldiers" until the first disorders resulting from military operations were over. The German Büro Concordia organization operated several black propaganda radio stations, many of which pretended to broadcast illegally from within the countries they targeted.

The *Protocols of the Elders of Zion* claimed to be the secret protocols of a vast Jewish conspiracy, and was often used as "evidence" by conspiracy theorists and anti-Semitic groups. It was proven to be a forgery produced by the Okhrana, the Tsarist Russian secret police. The Black Panther Coloring Book was distributed in the United States in the late 1960s in an attempt to discredit the Black Panther Party, and the civil rights movement in general. In Dreux, France, in 1982 the National Front distributed anonymous fake letters, supposedly from an Algerian living in France to a brother living in Algeria. These fake letters, which described immigration as a method of conquering France without war, were instrumental in the National Front victory in the 1983 local council elections in Dreux. In the run-up to the 2007 federal election in Australia, flyers were circulated around Sydney under the name of a fake organization called the Islamic Australia Federation. The flyers thanked the Australian Labor Party for supporting terrorism, Islamic fundamentalists, and the Bali bombing suspects. A group of Sydney-based Liberal Party members were implicated in the incident.

* * *

In the "Roorback forgery" of 1844 the *Chronicle* of Ithaca, New York ran a story, supposedly by a German tourist called Baron von Roorback, that James K. Polk, standing for re-election as a Democrat to the United States House of Representatives, branded his slaves before selling them at auction to distinguish them from the others on sale. Polk actually benefited from the ploy, as it reflected badly on his opponents when the lie was found out.

During the 1972 U.S. presidential election, Donald H. Segretti, a political operative for President Richard Nixon's reelection campaign, released a faked letter, on Senator Edmund Muskie's letterhead, falsely alleging that Senator Henry "Scoop" Jackson, against whom Muskie was running for the Democratic Party's nomination, had had an illegitimate child with a seventeen-year-old. Muskie, who had been considered the frontrunner, lost the nomination to George McGovern, and Nixon was reelected. The letter was part of a campaign of so-called "dirty tricks," directed by Segretti, and uncovered as part of the Watergate Scandal. Segretti went to prison in 1974 after pleading guilty to three misdemeanor counts of distributing illegal campaign literature.

The Federal Bureau of Investigation's Counter-intelligence program "COINTELPRO," was intended to "expose, disrupt, misdirect, discredit, or otherwise neutralize the activities of black nationalists, hate-type organizations and groups, their leadership, membership, and supporters." Black propaganda–that is, propaganda that disguises its source–was used famously against Communists and the Black Panther Party. It was also used against domestic opponents of the invasion of Vietnam, labor leaders, and Native Americans. COINTELPRO's use of black propaganda led to their creation of coloring books and cartoons. The FBI's strategy was captured in a 1968 memo: "Consider the use of cartoons, photographs, and anonymous letters which will have the effect of ridiculing the New Left. Ridicule is one of the most potent weapons which we can use against it." The FBI employed a similar tactic in 1968 to disrupt activities of the Ku Klux Klan, as hundreds of 'racist' flyers with misleading information were fabricated and made to appear as if they originated from known Klan leaders.

"The Penkovsky Papers" are an example of a black propaganda effort conducted by the United States' Central Intelligence Agency during the 1960's. The "Penkovsky Papers" were alleged to have been written by a Soviet GRU defector, Colonel Oleg Penkovsky, but was in fact produced by the CIA in an effort to diminish the Soviet Union's credibility at a pivotal time during the Cold War.

2

The Godfathers of

Modern Hate Politics

Lee Atwater, Lynn Nofziger, Karl Rove

Three gurus – all of them somehow Republican (although this is not to say that the Democrats have not had their share of tricksters) – have come to the "forefront," even though they were always in the background, of modern day "dirty trick" svengalis. Although many like to point today's finger at Karl Rove, the "founding father" of the current climate of hate politics was undoubtedly Lee Atwater.

Lee Atwater (1951-1991)

Harvey LeRoy "Lee" Atwater was an American political consultant and strategist to the Republican party. He advised George H. W. Bush, and became Chairman of the Republican National

Committee. Atwater was born in Atlanta and grew up in Aiken, South Carolina. His childhood was marred with tragedy when his three-year-old brother, Joe, was scalded to death when he pulled a deep fryer full of hot oil on himself.

Atwater earned a Master of Arts in communications from the University of South Carolina in 1977. His star started to rise during the 1980 election in the South Carolina Republican party, working on the campaigns of Governor Carroll Campbell and Senator Strom Thurmond. During his years in South Carolina, Atwater became well known for running hard-edged campaigns based on emotional wedge issues. His aggressive tactics were first demonstrated during the 1980 congressional campaigns when he was a campaign consultant to Republican incumbent Floyd Spence in his campaign for Congress against Democratic nominee Tom Turnipseed.

Atwater's tactics in that campaign included push polling in the form of fake surveys by "independent pollsters" to inform white suburbanites that Turnipseed was a member of the NAACP. He also sent out last-minute letters from Senator Strom Thurmond telling voters that Turnipseed would disarm America and turn it over to liberals and Communists. At a press briefing, Atwater planted a "reporter" who rose and said, "We understand Turnipseed has had psychotic treatment." Atwater later told the reporters off the record that Turnipseed "got hooked up to jumper cables," a reference to electroconvulsive therapy that Turnipseed underwent as a teenager.

Turnipseed recalled, "Lee seemed to delight in making fun of a suicidal 16-year-old who was treated for depression with electroshock treatments. In fact, my struggle with depression as a student was no secret. I had talked about it in a widely covered news conference as early as 1977, when I was in the South Carolina State Senate. Since then I have often shared with appropriate groups the full story of my recovery to responsible adulthood as a professional, political and civic leader, husband and father. Teenage depression and suicide are major problems in America, and I believe my life offers hope to young people who are suffering with a constant fear of the future."

After the 1980 election, Atwater went to Washington and became an aide in the Ronald Reagan administration, working under political director Ed Rollins. In 1984, Atwater became the campaign's deputy director and political director. It was Lee Atwater who ran a dirty tricks operation against vice-presidential nominee Geraldine Ferraro including publicizing the fact that Ferraro's parents had been indicted for numbers running in the 1940s. Atwater was described by Rollins as "ruthless," "Ollie North in civilian clothes," and someone who "just had to drive in one more stake." During his years in Washington, Atwater became aligned with Vice President George H.W. Bush, who chose Atwater to run his 1988 presidential campaign.

As a member of the Reagan administration in 1981, Atwater gave an anonymous interview to Political Scientist Alexander P. Lamis, in which he said:

Atwater: "As to the whole Southern strategy that Harry Dent and others put together in 1968, opposition to the Voting Rights Act would have been a central part of keeping the South. Now [the new Southern Strategy of Ronald Reagan] doesn't have to do that. All you have to do to keep the South is for Reagan to run in place on the issues he's campaigned on since 1964 and that's fiscal conservatism, balancing the budget, cut taxes, you know, the whole cluster."

Questioner: "But the fact is, isn't it, that Reagan does get to the Wallace voter and to the racist side of the Wallace voter by doing away with legal services, by cutting down on food stamps?"

Atwater: "You start out in 1954 by saying, 'Nigger, nigger, nigger.' By 1968 you can't say 'nigger' – that hurts you. Backfires. So you say stuff like forced busing, states' rights and all that stuff. You're getting so abstract now that you're talking about cutting taxes, and all these things you're talking about are totally economic things and a byproduct of them is that blacks get hurt worse than whites. And subconsciously maybe that is part of it. I'm not saying that. But I'm saying that if it is getting that abstract, and that coded, that we are doing away with the racial problem one way or the other. You follow me — because obviously sitting around saying, 'We want to cut this,' is much more abstract than even the busing thing, and a hell of a lot more abstract than 'Nigger, nigger.'"

Atwater's most noteworthy campaign was the 1988 presidential election, where he served as campaign manager for George H.W. Bush. A particularly aggressive media program included a television advertisement produced by Floyd Brown comparing Bush and Democratic nominee Michael Dukakis on crime. Bush supported the death penalty for first-degree murderers, while Dukakis opposed the death penalty. Dukakis also supported a felon furlough program originally begun under Republican Governor Francis Sargent in 1972. Prison furlough programs had been long established in California during the governorship of Republican Ronald Reagan, prior to 1980, but never allowed furlough for convicted murderers sentenced to life in prison.

In 1976, Massachusetts passed a law to similarly ban furloughs for first-degree murderers and Dukakis vetoed the bill. Willie Horton was serving a life sentence for first degree murder for stabbing a boy to death during a robbery. Horton, while on weekend furlough, kidnapped a young couple, torturing the young man and repeatedly raping his girlfriend. This issue of furlough for first degree murderers was originally brought up by Democratic candidate Al Gore during a presidential primary debate. Dukakis had tried to portray himself as a moderate politician from the liberal state of Massachusetts. The Horton ad campaign only reinforced the public's general opinion that Dukakis was too liberal, which helped Bush overcome Dukakis's 17-percent lead in early public opinion polls and win both the electoral and popular vote by landslide margins. Although Atwater clearly approved of the use of the Willie Horton issue, the Bush campaign never ran any commercial with Horton's picture, instead running a similar but generic ad. The original commercial was produced by Americans for Bush, an independent group managed by Larry McCarthy, and the Republicans benefited from the coverage it attracted in the national news.

In reference to Dukakis, Atwater declared that he would "strip the bark off the little bastard" and "make Willie Horton his running mate." Atwater's challenge was to counter the "Where was George?" campaign slogan Democrats were using as a rallying cry in an effort to create an impression that Bush was a relatively inexperienced and unaccomplished candidate. Furthermore, Bush had critics in the Republican base who remembered his pro-choice positions in the 1980 primary, and the harder the campaign pursued Dukakis' liberal positions, the bigger his base turnout would be.

During the election, a number of allegations were made in the media about Dukakis' personal life, including the unsubstantiated claim that his wife Kitty had burned an American flag to protest the Vietnam War, and that Dukakis himself had been treated for a mental illness. In the film *Boogie Man: The Lee Atwater Story*, Robert Novak reveals for the first time that Atwater personally tried to get him to spread these mental health rumors. The 1988 Bush campaign overcame a 17-point deficit in midsummer polls to win 40 states. Atwater's skills in the 1988 election led one biographer to term him "the best campaign manager who ever lived."

During that campaign, future president George W. Bush, George H.W. Bush's son, took an office across the hall from Atwater's office, where his job was to serve as "the eyes and ears for my dad," monitoring the activities of Atwater and other campaign staff. In her memoir, Barbara Bush said that the younger Bush and Atwater became friends. After the election, Atwater was named chairman of the Republican National Committee.

Shortly after Atwater took over the RNC, Jim Wright was forced to resign as Speaker of the United States House of Representatives and was succeeded by Tom Foley. On the day Foley officially became speaker, the RNC began circulating a memo to Republican Congressmen and state party chairmen called "Tom Foley: Out of the Liberal Closet." The memo compared Foley's voting record with that of openly gay Congressman Barney Frank, with a subtle implication that Foley was himself gay. It had been crafted by RNC communications director Mark Goodin and House Minority Whip Newt Gingrich. In fact, Gingrich had been trying to get several reporters to print it. The memo was harshly condemned on both sides of the aisle. Republican Senate leader Bob Dole, for instance, said in a speech on the Senate floor, "This is not politics. This is garbage."

Atwater initially defended the memo, calling it "no big deal" and "factually accurate." However, a few days later, he claimed he hadn't approved the memo. Under pressure from Bush, Atwater fired Goodin, replacing him with B. Jay Cooper.

In 1989, Atwater was appointed as a new member of the historically black Howard University Board of Trustees. The university gained national attention when students rose up in protest against Atwater's appointment. Student activists disrupted Howard's 122nd anniversary celebrations, and eventually occupied the university's Administration building. Within days, both Atwater and Howard's President, James E. Cheek, resigned.

Atwater was an accomplished musician. He briefly played backup guitar for Percy Sledge during the 1960s and frequently played with bluesmen such as B.B. King. Atwater recorded an album with King and others on Curb Records in 1990 entitled *Red Hot & Blue,* which featured Carla Thomas, Isaac Hayes, Sam Moore, Chuck Jackson, and B.B. King, who got co-billing with Atwater.

On March 5, 1990, Lee Atwater collapsed during a fundraising breakfast on behalf of Senator Phil Gramm. Doctors searching for an explanation to what was initially thought to be a mere fainting episode discovered an unusually aggressive form of brain cancer in his right parietal lobe. Atwater underwent interstitial implant radiation, a then-new form of treatment, at Montefiore Medical Center in New York City, and received conventional radiation therapy at George Washington University Hospital in Washington, D.C. The treatment for the brain tumor left him paralyzed on his left side, robbed him of his tone discrimination, and swelled his face and body from steroids. He spent the remainder of his life in a wheelchair.

In the months after the severity of his illness became apparent, Atwater said he had converted to Catholicism through the help of Father John Hardon and, in an act of repentance, Atwater issued a number of public and written letters to individuals to whom he had been opposed during his political career. In a letter to Tom Turnipseed dated June 28, 1990, he stated, "It is very important to me that I let you know that out of everything that has happened in my career, one of the low points remains the so-called 'jumper cable' episode," adding, "my illness has taught me something about the nature of humanity, love, brotherhood and relationships that I never understood, and probably never would have. So, from that standpoint, there is some truth and good in everything."

In a February 1991 article for *Life* magazine, Atwater wrote, "My illness helped me to see that what was missing in society is what was missing in me: a little heart, a lot of brotherhood. The '80s were about acquiring – acquiring wealth, power, prestige. I know. I acquired more wealth, power, and prestige than most. But you can acquire all you want and still feel empty. What power wouldn't I trade for a little more time with my family? What price wouldn't I pay for an evening with friends? It took a deadly illness to put me eye to eye with that truth, but it is a truth that the country, caught up in its ruthless ambitions and moral decay, can learn on my dime. I don't know who will lead us through the '90s, but they must be made to speak to this spiritual vacuum at the heart of American society, this tumor of the soul. Atwater died on March 29, 1991 of his brain tumor. Funeral services were held at the Trinity Cathedral Church in Atwater's hometown of Columbia. A memorial service was held at the Washington National Cathedral. Atwater's political career is the subject of the feature-length documentary film *Boogie Man: The Lee Atwater Story.*

In the world of American politics, Lee Atwater was both a product and a symbol of his times. He was one of the Republican Party's best political tacticians, famous and feared for his readiness to attack opponents and his skill in carrying out those attacks. He was best known for his political street-fighting skills, skills that his critics said included a willingness to distort positions, smear opponents and use racial and ethnic messages.

President Reagan was one of Atwater's last visitors in the hospital. After Atwater's death, he said, "Lee Atwater was a person who loved his profession and who brought vigor, energy and enthusiasm to the political process. He was a true patriot and public servant who believed in free elections and the democratic process. He never lost the will to fight,"

To those who complained that the Presidential campaign he ran for Mr. Bush was empty and unpleasant, Atwater replied: "We had only one goal in the campaign: to elect George Bush. That's the purpose of any political campaign. What other function should a campaign have?" Atwater's life was built around a single passion: politics. "My entire adult life, I've had exactly one job, which is managing campaigns. I really had two goals in life: one, to manage a Presidential campaign and to be chairman of my party."

Lee Atwater spent his final months searching for spiritual peace. The man renowned for the politics of attack turned to apologies, including one to Michael Dukakis, the Massachusetts Governor who was the 1988 Democratic Presidential nominee. Dukakis called the death a tragedy. "We obviously were on opposite sides of a tough and negative campaign, but at least he had the courage to apologize," Dukakis said. "That says a lot for the man. My heart goes out to his family."

"Republicans in the South could not win elections by talking about issues," Atwater said. "You had to make the case that the other guy, the other candidate, is a bad guy." From his earliest days, Atwater displayed a skill in the use of racial messages and maneuvers, a crucial part of the effort by Southern Republicans to appeal to white voters.

If Lee Atwater learned one thing during his brief but crowded lifetime, it was how to handle the media. He used the same manipulative skills to orchestrate press coverage as he had applied to developing as a musician over the years. The spin doctor was always in. Even when a reporter had done a little homework, which was surprisingly rare, and tried to get "up close and personal," Atwater knew how to change the topic or cut things short. Magazine writers could be a problem. They usually wanted to hang out for a day or two, and it could be tough to avoid the personal stuff.

Lyn Nofziger (1924-2006)

Franklyn C. "Lyn" Nofziger was a journalist, political advisor, and author. He served as press secretary in Ronald Reagan's administration as Governor of California, as a White House advisor during the Nixon administration, and again during the Reagan presidency.

Nofziger was born and raised in Bakersfield, California. He earned a B.A. in journalism from San Jose State University, then worked for sixteen years as a reporter, editor and Washington correspondent for Copley Newspapers. In 1966, Nofziger was press secretary for Reagan's successful gubernatorial campaign in California. He served two years as Governor Reagan's Director of Communications. After Richard Nixon's election as U.S. President in 1968, Nofziger went to Washington, where he was deputy assistant to the president for congressional relations. He also served as Deputy Chairman of Communications for the Republican National Committee. Nofziger worked for Nixon's presidential re-election campaign in 1972 as executive director of the California Committee to Re-Elect the President.

When Governor Reagan sought the presidential nomination in 1976, Nofziger acted as Reagan's press secretary, convention director, and director of the California campaign. When Gerald Ford won the Republican nomination, Nofziger assisted with the Ford-Dole campaign, which lost the election to Democrat Jimmy Carter. Nofziger then went back to work for Governor Reagan and began laying the groundwork for the 1980 campaign. He was executive vice-chairman of Citizens for the Republic, a political action committee founded by Reagan. With the run at the White House in full gear in 1979, Nofziger served as deputy chairman for finance for the Reagan for President organization. Reagan won the election, defeating Carter's campaign for a second term.

Nofziger never sought to be Press Secretary in the White House. He called it "a young man's job." Jim Brady was named Press Secretary. Nofziger was named assistant to the president for political affairs in the White House, and stayed there for about a year. He then served as senior consultant for the 1984 Reagan-Bush Re-Election Campaign and was a member of the 1985 Inaugural Committee. Afterward, he ran political campaigns for Pat Buchanan and Steve Forbes.

In 1987, Nofziger was investigated for allegedly violating the Ethics in Government Act when he lobbied on behalf of Wedtech Corporation, a defense contractor. Former government officials were prohibited from lobbying their former office for a period of two years after concluding service there. Nofziger knew this. For two years, he did not lobby the Office of Political Affairs at the White House. Federal prosecutors claimed the law made it illegal for Nofziger to contact *any* office at the White House. In spite of the ambiguity, Nofziger was indicted and later convicted of violating the law. Nofziger vigorously fought the indictment and conviction, which was eventually overturned on appeal. The government pressed its case all the way to the United States Supreme Court, which refused to reinstate the conviction. The federal government and the prosecutor, James C. McKay, lost in the end.

Nofziger's political memoir was published in October 1992 by Regnery Publishing. He wrote four Western novels with a hero named Tackett, a drifter who falls into situations that compel him to rescue women in distress. The Tackett series was an homage to Nofziger's friend, Louis L'Amour, famed author of "The Sacketts" and scores of other Westerns. Nofziger died of cancer at the age of 81.

KARL ROVE (1950 -)

The best-known today, and perhaps the most infamous of the "unholy trinity" of political spinmasters, Karl Christian Rove, born on Christmas Day, 1950, was Senior Advisor and Deputy Chief of Staff to former President George W. Bush until his resignation on August 31, 2007. He headed the Office of Political Affairs, the Office of Public Liaison, and the White House Office of Strategic Initiatives. Since leaving the White House, Rove has worked as a political analyst and contributor for Fox News, *Newsweek* and *The*

Wall Street Journal. With the Republicans' mid-term victories in the 2010 elections, his star may be on the ascendant once again.

Prior to his White House appointments, Rove was a Republican political consultant and strategist, who is credited with George W. Bush's successful 1994 and 1998 Texas gubernatorial victories, as well as his successful 2000 and 2004 presidential campaigns. Rove has also been credited for the successful campaigns of John Ashcroft (1994 U.S. Senate), Bill Clements (1986 Texas gubernatorial election), Senator John Cornyn (2002 U.S. Senate), Governor Rick Perry (1990 Texas Agriculture Commission), and Phil Gramm (1982 U.S. House and 1984 U.S. Senate elections). Though no allegations have been proven or sustained, Rove's name has come up in political scandals, including the Valerie Plame affair, the Bush White House e-mail controversy and the related dismissal of U.S. attorneys controversy.

Rove was born in Denver and raised in Sparks, Nevada. His biological father left the family when Rove and his older brother were children. His mother was a gift shop manager. His mother's second husband, who adopted him and whom Rove knew as his father, was a geologist whose ancestry was Norwegian. In 1965, his family moved to Salt Lake City where Rove entered high school, becoming a skilled debater. He says, "I was the complete nerd. I had the briefcase. I had the pocket protector. I wore Hush Puppies when they were not cool. I was the thin, scrawny little guy. I was definitely uncool." Encouraged by a teacher to run for class senate, Rove won the election. As part of his campaign strategy he rode in the back of a convertible inside the school gymnasium sitting between two attractive girls before his election speech.

Rove began his involvement in American politics in 1968. "I was the Olympus High School chairman for (former U.S. Senator) Wallace F. Bennett's re-election campaign, where he was opposed by young, aggressive political science professor J.D. Williams."

Bennett was reelected to a third six-year term. Through Rove's campaign involvement, Bennett's son, Bob Bennett — a future United States Senator from Utah — would become Rove's friend. Williams would later become a mentor to Rove.

In December 1969, the man Rove had known as his father left the family, and divorced Rove's mother. Soon afterward; it became known his stepfather was gay. After the divorce, Rove learned from his aunt and uncle that the man who had raised him was not his biological father; both he and his older brother Eric were the children of another man. Rove has expressed great love and admiration for his adoptive father and for "how selfless" his love had been. In 1981 Rove's mother committed suicide in Reno, Nevada.

In fall 1969, Rove entered the University of Utah on a $1,000 scholarship, as a political science major. He got an internship with the Utah Republican Party, which helped him land a job in 1970 on Ralph Tyler Smith's unsuccessful re-election campaign for Senate from Illinois. Democrat Adlai E. Stevenson III won that election. In fall 1970, Rove used a false identity to enter the campaign office of Democrat Alan J. Dixon, who was running for Treasurer of Illinois. He stole 1000 sheets of paper with campaign letterhead, printed fake campaign rally fliers promising "free beer, free food, girls and a good time for nothing," and distributed them at rock concerts and homeless shelters, In this way, he disrupted Dixon's rally. Rove's role would not become publicly known until August 1973. In his memoir, Rove wrote that when he was later nominated to the Board for International Broadcasting by President George H.W. Bush, Senator Dixon did not kill his nomination. In Rove's account, "Dixon displayed more grace than I had shown and kindly excused this youthful prank."

In June 1971, Rove dropped out of college to take a paid position as Executive Director of the College Republican National Committee. Joe Abate, National Chairman of the College Republicans, became

Rove's mentor. The young, opportunistic Rove traveled extensively, participating as an instructor at weekend seminars for campus conservatives across the country. He was an active participant in Richard Nixon's 1972 Presidential campaign. Rove held the position of executive director of the College Republicans until early 1973.

He left the job to spend five months without pay campaigning full time for the position of national chairman of the organization, for the 1973-1975 term in the same years he attended George Mason University. Lee Atwater, the group's Southern regional coordinator, who was two months younger than Rove, managed Rove's campaign. The two spent the spring of 1973 crisscrossing the country in a Ford Pinto, lining up the support of Republican state chairs.

The College Republicans' summer 1973 convention at the Lake of the Ozarks resort in Missouri was contentious. A number of states had sent two competing delegates, because Rove and his supporters had made credentials challenges at state and regional conventions. In the end, there were two votes, conducted by two convention chairs, and two winners — Rove and Edgeworth, each of whom delivered an acceptance speech. After the convention, both Edgeworth and Rove appealed to Republican National Committee Chairman George H. W. Bush, each contending that he was the new College Republican chairman.

While resolution was pending, Dolan went anonymously to the *Washington Post* with recordings of several training seminars for young Republicans where a co-presenter of Rove's, Bernie Robinson, cautioned against doing the same thing he had done: rooting through opponents' garbage cans. The tape with this story on it, as well as Rove's admonition not to copy similar tricks as Rove's against Dixon, was secretly recorded and edited by Rich Evans, who had hoped to receive an appointment from Rove's competitor in the CRNC chairmanship race. On August 10, 1973, the *Post* broke the story in article titled "GOP Party Probes Official as Teacher of Tricks."

George H.W. Bush had an FBI agent question Rove. As part of the investigation, Atwater signed an affidavit, dated August 13, 1973, stating that he had heard a "20 minute anecdote similar to the one described in the *Washington Post*" in July 1972, but that "it was a funny story during a coffee break." Former Nixon White House Counsel John Dean, who was implicated in the Watergate break-in and became the star witness for the prosecution, said, "Based on my review of the files, it appears the Watergate prosecutors were interested in Rove's activities in 1972, but because they had bigger fish to fry they did not aggressively investigate him."

On September 6, 1973, three weeks after announcing his intent to investigate the allegations against Rove, George H.W. Bush chose Rove to be chairman of the College Republicans. He wrote a letter stating that he had concluded that Rove had fairly won the vote at the convention. Edgeworth wrote back, asking the basis of that conclusion. Not long after that, Edgeworth stated, "Bush sent me back the angriest letter I have ever received in my life. I had leaked to the *Washington Post*, and now I was out of the Party forever."

As National Chairman, Rove introduced Bush to Lee Atwater, who had taken Rove's job as the College Republican's executive director, and who would become Bush's main campaign strategist in future years. Bush hired Rove as a special assistant to the Republican National Committee, a job Rove left in 1974 to become executive assistant to the co-chair of the RNC. Rove also performed small personal tasks for Bush. In November 1973, Bush asked Rove to take a set of car keys to his son George W. Bush, who was visiting home during a break school. It was the first time the two met. "Huge amounts of charisma, swagger, cowboy boots, flight jacket, wonderful smile, just charisma - you know, wow!" Rove recalled years later.

Rove's initial job in Texas was as a legislative aide for a Texas state representative. Later in 1977, Rove got a job as executive director of a political action committee (PAC) in Houston headed by James A. Baker, a Houston lawyer, who was later to become President George H.W. Bush's Secretary of State. The PAC eventually became the genesis of the Bush-for-President campaign of 1979–1980. Rove's work for Bill Clements during the Texas gubernatorial election of 1978 helped Clements become the first Republican Governor of Texas in over 100 years.

In 1981, Rove founded a direct mail consulting firm, Karl Rove & Co., in Austin. The firm's first clients included Texas Governor Bill Clements and Democratic congressman Phil Gramm, who later became a Republican congressman and United States Senator. Rove operated his consulting business until 1999, when he sold the firm to take a full-time position in George W. Bush's presidential campaign. Between 1981 and 1999, Rove worked on hundreds of races. Most were in a supporting role, doing direct mail fundraising. A November 2004 *Atlantic Monthly* article estimated that he was the primary strategist for 41 statewide, congressional, and national races, and Rove's candidates won 34 races.

Rove also did work for non-political clients. From 1991 to 1996, he advised Philip Morris Tobacco Company, and ultimately earned $3,000 a month through a consulting contract. He severed that tie in 1996 because he felt awkward about balancing that responsibility with his role as George W. Bush's top political advisor while Bush was governor of Texas and Texas was suing the tobacco industry.

Rove advised the younger Bush during his unsuccessful Texas congressional campaign in 1978. In 1977, Rove was the first person hired by George H. W. Bush for his unsuccessful 1980 presidential campaign, which ended with Bush as the vice-presidential nominee. Rove handled direct-mail for the 1984 Reagan-Bush campaign.

In 1986, Rove helped Clements become governor a second time. In a strategy memo Rove wrote for his client prior to the race, "The whole art of war consists in a well-reasoned and extremely circumspect defensive, followed by rapid and audacious attack." Just before a crucial debate in campaign, Rove claimed his office had been bugged by Democrats. The police and FBI investigated and discovered that the bug's battery was so small that it needed to be changed every few hours, and the investigation was dropped. Critics, including other Republican operatives, suspected Rove had bugged his own office to garner sympathy votes in the close governor's race.

In 1988, Rove helped Thomas R. Phillips become the first Republican elected as Chief Justice of the Texas Supreme Court. Phillips' election in 1988 was part of an aggressive grassroots campaign called "Clean Slate '88," a conservative effort that was successful in getting five of its six candidates elected. By 1998, Republicans held all nine seats on the Court.

In 1989, Rove encouraged George W. Bush to run for Texas governor, brought in experts to tutor him on policy, and introduced him to local reporters. Eventually, Bush decided not to run, and Rove backed another Republican for governor who lost in the primary. In 1991, U.S. Attorney General Dick Thornburgh resigned to run for a Senate seat in Pennsylvania. Rove's company worked for the campaign, but it ended with an upset loss to Democrat Harris Wofford. Rove subsequently sued Thornburgh alleging non-payment for services rendered. The Republican National Committee, worried that the suit would make it hard to recruit good candidates, urged Rove to back off. When Rove refused, the RNC hired Kenneth Starr to write an amicus brief on Thornburgh's behalf. After a trial in Austin, Rove prevailed.

Rove was fired from the 1992 Bush presidential campaign after he planted a negative story with columnist Robert Novak about dissatisfaction with campaign fundraising chief Robert Mosbacher Jr. In 1993, Rove helped Kay Hutchison Bailey win a special Senate election in June 1993. Hutchison defeated Democrat Bob Krueger to fill the last two years of Lloyd Bentsen's term. Bentsen resigned to become Secretary of the Treasury in the Clinton administration.

In 1993, Karl Rove & Company was paid $300,000 in consulting fees by Ashcroft's successful 1994 Senate campaign. Ashcroft paid Rove's company more than $700,000 over the course of three campaigns. That same year, Rove began advising George W. Bush in his successful campaign to become governor of Texas. Bush announced his candidacy in November 1993. By January 1994, Bush had spent more than $600,000 on the race against incumbent Democrat Ann Richards. $340,000 of that was paid to Rove's firm.

Rove has been accused of using the push poll technique to call voters to ask such things as whether people would be "more or less likely to vote for Governor Richards if they knew her staff is dominated by lesbians." Rove denied being involved in circulating these rumors about Richards during the campaign, although many critics identify this technique as a hallmark of his career.

In 1996, during Harold See's campaign for Associate Justice of the Alabama Supreme Court, a former campaign worker charged that, at Rove's behest, he distributed flyers that anonymously attacked Harold See, their own client. This put the opponent's campaign in an awkward position; public denials of responsibility for the scurrilous flyers would be implausible. Rove's client was elected.

Rove was an adviser for George W. Bush's 1998 gubernatorial reelection campaign. From July through December 1998, Bush's reelection committee paid Rove & Co. nearly $2.5 million, and also paid the Rove-owned Praxis List Company $267,000 for use of mailing lists. Rove's work for the Bush campaign included direct mail, voter contact, phone banks, computer services, and travel expenses. In all, Bush, primarily through Rove's efforts, raised $17.7 million, with $3.4 million unspent as of March 1999.

In early 1999, Rove sold Karl Rove & Co. along with Praxis List Company to two young political operatives who had worked on campaigns of some other Rove candidates. Rove helped finance the sale of the company, which had 11 employees. George W. Bush had insisted that Rove sell the companies. When George W. Bush was first inaugurated in January 2001, Rove accepted an appointment as Senior Advisor and Deputy Chief of Staff to the President. In April 2006, Rove was reassigned to focus on strategic and tactical planning in anticipation of the 2006 congressional elections. Rove ultimately resigned from his position effective August 31, 2007. Bush hugged his old friend saying, "Karl Rove is moving on down the road. I'll be on the road behind you here in a little bit."

Shortly after leaving the White House, Rove was hired to write about the 2008 Presidential Election for *Newsweek*. He was also later hired as a contributor for the *Wall Street Journal* and as a political analyst for Fox News. Rove was an informal advisor to 2008 Republican Presidential candidate John McCain, and donated $2,300 to his campaign. His memoir, *Courage and Consequence*, was published March, 2010.

On June 24, 2008, Rove said of Democratic presidential nominee Barack Obama, "Even if you never met him, you know this guy. He's the guy at the country club with the beautiful date, holding a martini and a cigarette that stands against the wall and makes snide comments about everyone." Rove agreed to debate one-time presidential candidate and former Senator John Edwards on September 26, 2008 at the University at Buffalo. However Edwards later dropped out and was replaced with General Wesley Clark.

On February 23, 2009 Karl Rove was subpoenaed to testify before the House Judiciary Committee concerning his knowledge of the U.S. Attorney firings and the alleged political prosecution of former Alabama Governor Don Siegelman. He did not appear, but since that time Rove and former White House Counsel Harriet Miers later agreed to testify under oath before Congress about these matters.

On July 7, 2009, and July 30, 2009, Rove testified before the House Judiciary Committee regarding questions about the dismissal of seven U.S. Attorneys under the Bush Administration. Rove was also questioned regarding the federal prosecution of former Alabama Governor Don Siegleman who was convicted of fraud.

Rove was the guest host of The Rush Limbaugh Show on August 9, 2010, marking his first time hosting a radio talk show. On December 15, 2011, *The New Republic* described Rove as one of the shrewdest navigators of the political climate after the Supreme Court's *Citizens United* decision which exempted political broadcasts funded by corporations and unions from campaign finance limits. "Rove had no role in creating this new legal environment... but if Rove and his allies did not invent it, they certainly were adroit at exploiting it."

Rove married Houston socialite Valerie Mather Wainwright, on July 10, 1976. They divorced in 1980. He attended the University of Texas at Austin in 1977; he still lacked a degree. In July 1999 he told *The Washington Post* that he did not have a degree because "I lack at this point one math class, which I can take by exam, and my foreign language requirement." In January 1986, Rove married Darby Tara Hickson, a breast cancer survivor, graphic designer, and former employee of Karl Rove & Co. Their son, Andrew Madison Rove is an undergraduate at Trinity University in San Antonio, Texas. On December 29, 2009, Rove and Hickson divorced after 24 years of marriage. Rove left Texas after Bush was elected President. He currently resides in Washington, D.C.

First there was the Tea Party. Then came Grover Norquist. The so-called "Conservative element" has nearly succeeded in wresting control of the Grand Old Party (GOP = Republican Party) from its centrist-right roots. If they prevail, they may well "win the battle but lose the war."

3

GROVER NORQUIST, THE TEA PARTY, AND OTHER NAYSAYERS

THE TEA PARTY

The Tea Party movement is a populist political movement generally recognized as conservative and libertarian. It has sponsored protests and supported political candidates since 2009. It endorses reduced government spending, opposition to excess taxation, reduction of the national debt and federal budget deficit, and adherence to an originalist interpretation of the United States Constitution.

The name "Tea Party" is a reference to the Boston Tea Party, a protest by colonists who objected to a British tax on tea in 1773 and demonstrated by dumping British tea taken from docked ships into the harbor. The Tea Party movement has no central leadership but is composed of a loose affiliation of national and local groups that determine their own platforms and agendas. The Tea Party movement is not a national political party; polls show that most Tea Partiers consider themselves to be Republicans and the movement's supporters have tended to endorse Republican candidates.

The Tea Party's most-noted national figures include Republican politicians Ron Paul, his son Rand Paul, Sarah Palin, Dick Armey, Eric Cantor and Michele Bachmann.

The theme of the Boston Tea Party, an iconic event in American history, has long been used by anti-tax protesters. It was part of Tax Day protests held throughout the 1990s and earlier. More recently, the anniversary of the original Boston Tea Party was commemorated on December 16, 2007, by Republican Congressman Ron Paul supporters who held a "Boston tea-party event" in 2007 which was a fundraiser for the Ron Paul 2008 Presidential Campaign which advocated an end to fiat money and the Federal Reserve System, disengaging from foreign entanglements in Iraq and Afghanistan, and upholding States' rights.

On January 24, 2009, Trevor Leach, chairman of the Young Americans for Liberty in New York State organized a "Tea Party" to protest obesity taxes proposed by New York Governor David Paterson and call for fiscal responsibility on the part of the government. Several of the protesters wore Native American headdresses similar to the band of 18th century colonists who dumped tea in Boston Harbor to express outrage about British taxes.

Some of the protests were partially in response to several Federal laws: the Emergency Economic Stabilization Act of 2008, the American Recovery and Reinvestment Act of 2009, and a series of healthcare reform bills.

On February 19, 2009, in a broadcast from the floor of the Chicago Mercantile Exchange, CNBC Business News editor Rick Santelli criticized the government plan to refinance mortgages, which had just been announced the day before. He said that those plans were "promoting bad behavior" by "subsidizing losers' mortgages." He suggested holding a tea party for traders to gather and dump the derivatives in the Chicago River on July 1. A number of the floor traders around him cheered on his proposal, to the amusement of the hosts in the studio.

Beginning in 2009, the Gadsden flag had become a favorite among the Tea Party movement nationwide for Tea Party protesters who feel patriotism for their country and are upset at the government. It was also seen being displayed by members of Congress at Tea Party rallies. Some lawmakers have dubbed it a political symbol due to the Tea Party connection and the political nature of Tea Party supporters.

The Second Revolution flag gained national attention on January 19, 2010. It is a version of the Betsy Ross flag with a Roman numeral "II" in the center of the circle of 13 stars symbolizing a second revolution in America. The Second Revolution flag has been called synonymous with Tea Party causes and events.

Several polls have been conducted on the demographics of the movement. Though the various polls sometimes turn up slightly different results, they tend to show that Tea Party supporters are mainly white and slightly more likely to be male, married, older than 45, more conservative than the general population, and likely to be more wealthy and have more education. A Gallup poll conducted in March 2010 found that—other than gender, income and politics—self-described Tea Party members were demographically similar to the population as a whole.

Polls have shown that they are to a very great extent more likely to be registered Republican, have a favorable opinion of the Republican Party and an unfavorable opinion of the Democratic Party. 40% of Tea Party supporters are 55 or older, 79% are white, 61% are men, and 44% identify as "born-again Christians."

An October 2010 *Washington Post* canvass of local Tea Party organizers found 99% said "concern about the economy" was an "important factor." Polls have also examined Tea Party supporters' views on race and racial politics. 74% of Tea Party supporters agreed with the statement "While equal opportunity for blacks and minorities to succeed is important, it's not really the government's job to guarantee it." 25% think that the administration favors blacks over whites, and Tea Party adherents are more likely to believe Obama was born outside the United States. A seven state study found that Tea Party movement supporters are "more likely to be racially resentful" than the population as a whole, even when controlling for partisanship and ideology. Of white poll respondents who strongly approve of the Tea Party, only 35% believe that blacks are hard-working. Other figures from various polls: 73% of Tea Party supporters disapprove of Obama's policy of engaging with Muslim countries, 88% approve of the controversial immigration law recently enacted in Arizona, 82% do not believe that gay and lesbian couples should have the legal right to marry, and about 52% believe that "lesbians and gays have too much political power."

The 2010 midterm elections demonstrated considerable skepticism within the Tea Party movement with respect to the dangers and the reality of global warming: only a small percentage of Tea Party supporters considered global warming a serious problem, much less than the portion of the general public that does. The Tea Party is strongly opposed to government-imposed limits on carbon dioxide emissions as part of emissions trading legislation to encourage use of fuels that emit less dioxide. Many of the movement's members also favor stricter measures against illegal immigration.

An October 2010 *Washington Post* canvass of 647 local Tea Party organizers asked "which national figure best represents your groups?" and got the following responses: no one 34%, Sarah Palin 14%, Glenn Beck 7%, Jim DeMint 6%, Ron Paul 6%, Michele Bachmann 4%.

According to many journalists, the Tea Party is more a frustrated state of mind than a classic political movement. 78% are Republican or Republican-leaning, 78% are non-Hispanic whites, 69% are conservatives, 56% are men, and 47% are 55 years or older. Tea Party supporters are united more by their policy views than by their demographics or locations. At the core is a conviction that the federal government has gotten too large and powerful. 90% see the federal deficit as a severe threat, and are unhappy with the country's direction. They are less likely to see discrimination as a hurdle to minorities. 75% say that minorities have equal job opportunities. They are less sympathetic to illegal immigrants: 80% say that in the long run they cost the taxpayers too much.

The Contract from America was the idea of Houston-based lawyer Ryan Hecker. He stated that he developed the concept of creating a grassroots call for reform prior to the April 15, 2009, Tax Day Tea Party rallies. To get his idea off the ground, he launched a website, ContractFromAmerica.com, which encouraged people to offer possible planks for the contract.

1. Identify the constitutionality of every new law

2. Reject emissions trading

3. Demand a balanced federal budget

4. Simplify the tax system

5. Audit federal government agencies for waste and constitu-tionality

6. Limit annual growth in federal spending

7. Repeal the healthcare legislation passed on March 23, 2010

8. Pass an 'All-of-the-Above' Energy Policy

9. Reduce Earmarks

10. Reduce Taxes

The Tea Party Patriots have asked both Democrats and Republicans to sign on to the Contract. No Democrats signed on, and the contract met resistance from some Republicans who since created "Commitment to America."

In October 2011, a Tea Party group proposed that business executives take a pledge not to hire anyone until the Democrats' "war against business" ends.

In an August 2010 article for *Foreign Policy* magazine, Ron Paul outlined foreign policy views the Tea Party movement should emphasize: "We cannot stand against big government at home while supporting it abroad. We cannot talk about fiscal responsibility while spending trillions on occupying and bullying the rest of the world ... I see tremendous opportunities for movements like the Tea Party to prosper by capitalizing on the Democrats' broken promises to overturn the George W. Bush administration's civil liberties abuses and end the disastrous wars in Iraq and Afghanistan. A return to the traditional U.S. foreign policy of active private engagement but government noninterventionism is the only alternative that can restore our moral and fiscal health."

Sarah Palin headlined four "Liberty at the Ballot Box" bus tours, to raise money for candidates and the Tea Party Express. One of the tours visited 30 towns and covered 3,000 miles. Following the formation of the Tea Party Caucus, Michele Bachmann raised $10 million for a political action committee and sent funds to the campaigns of Sharron Angle, Christine O'Donnell, Rand Paul, and Marco Rubio.

In 2010 Tea Party-endorsed candidates upset established Republicans in several primaries, such as Alaska, Colorado, Delaware, Florida, Nevada, New York, South Carolina and Utah, giving a new momentum to the conservative cause in the 2010 elections. In the 2010 midterm elections, *The New York Times* identified 138 candidates for Congress with significant Tea Party support, and reported that all of them were running as Republicans—of whom 129 were running for the House and 9 for the Senate. The *Wall Street Journal*–NBC News poll in mid October showed 35% of likely voters were Tea-party supporters, and they favored the Republicans by 84% to 10%. However the effectiveness of the Tea Party to endorse candidates has come into question as only 32% of the candidates that were backed by the Tea Party won the election

In February 2011, the Tea Party Patriots organized and hosted the American Policy Summit in Phoenix, Arizona. The 1,600 attendees were polled regarding their preference for a 2012 presidential candidate. Herman Cain, the first of the 2012 candidates to form a presidential exploratory committee, won the poll with 22%. Runners up were Tim Pawlenty (16%), Ron Paul (15%) and Sarah Palin (10%). Ron Paul won the Summit's online poll.

In January 2011, approximately 70% of adults, including approximately 9 out of 10 Republicans, felt Republican leaders in Congress should give consideration to Tea Party movement ideas. In August 2011, 42% of registered voters, but only 12% of Republicans, said Tea Party endorsement would be a "negative" and that they would be "less likely" to vote for such a candidate.

After the debt-ceiling crisis, polls became more unfavorable to the Tea Party. According to a Gallup poll, 28% of adults disapproved of the Tea Party compared to 25% approving, and noted that "The national Tea Party movement appears to have lost some ground in popular support after the blistering debate over raising the nation's debt ceiling in which Tea Party Republicans fought any compromise on taxes and spending." Similarly, a Pew poll found that 29% of respondents thought Congressional tea party supporters had a negative effect compared to 22% thinking it was a positive effect. It noted that "The new poll also finds that those who followed the debt ceiling debate very closely have more negative views about the impact of the Tea Party than those who followed the issue less closely." A CNN poll put disapproval at 51% with a 31% approval.

Polls found that just 7% of Tea Party supporters approve of how Obama is doing his job compared to 50% of the general public, and that roughly 77% of supporters had voted for Obama's Republican opponent, John McCain in 2008.

On April 15, 2010, Obama touted his administration's tax cuts, noting the passage of 25 different tax cuts over the past year, including tax cuts for 95% of working Americans. He then remarked, "So I've been a little amused over the last couple of days where people have been having these rallies about taxes. You would think they would be saying thank you. That's what you'd think." On September 20, 2010, at a townhall discussion sponsored by CNBC, Obama said healthy skepticism about government and spending was good, but it was not enough to just say "Get control of spending," and he challenged the Tea Party movement to get specific about how they would cut government debt and spending: "And so the challenge, I think, for the Tea Party movement is to identify specifically what would you do. It's not enough just to say, get control of spending. I think it's important for you to say, I'm willing to cut veterans' benefits, or I'm willing to cut Medicare or Social Security benefits, or I'm willing to see these taxes go up. What you can't do—which is what I've been hearing a lot from the other side—is say we're going to control government spending, we're going to propose $4 trillion of additional tax cuts, and that magically somehow things are going to work."

A Gallup Poll of April 2010 found 47% of Americans had an "unfavorable" image of the Tea Party movement, as opposed to 33% who had a favorable opinion. In November 2011, the New York Times cited opinion polls showing that support for the Tea Party had fallen sharply even in places considered Tea Party strongholds. The Tea Party position in congress was perceived as "too extreme and not willing to compromise."

An October 2010, survey conducted by *The Washington Post* found that the majority of local Tea Party organizers consider the media coverage of their groups to be fair.

Black conservatives have expressed mixed feelings about the Tea Party's inclusiveness and concerns about racism. On March 20, 2010, during a rally at the United States Capitol in Washington, D.C., before the Patient Protection and Affordable Care Bill was voted on, several black lawmakers said that demonstrators shouted racial epithets at them. Congressman Emanuel Cleaver was spat upon, although it is unclear if this was deliberate, and said he heard the slurs. Congressman Barney Frank, who is gay, was called a "faggot" Representative André Carson said that while walking with John Lewis and his chief of staff from the Cannon building, amid chants of "kill the bill," he heard the "n-word at least 15 times." Carson said he heard it coming from different places in the crowd, and one man "just rattled it off several times." Carson quoted Lewis as saying, "You know, this reminds me of a different time."

GROVER NORQUIST

Grover Glenn Norquist, born October 19, 1956, is an American lobbyist, conservative activist, and founder and president of Americans for Tax Reform. He is a member of the Council on Foreign Relations. He is best known as the promoter of the "Taxpayer Protection Pledge," which was signed by 95% of all Republican Congressmen and all but one of the 2012 Republican presidential candidates, to oppose increases in marginal income tax rates for individuals and businesses, as well as net reductions or eliminations of deductions and credits without a matching reduced tax rate.

Norquist grew up in Weston, Massachusetts. He became involved with politics at an early age and in his early teenage years he volunteered for the 1968 Nixon campaign, assisting with get out the vote efforts. He graduated from Weston High School and enrolled at Harvard University in 1974, where he obtained both a B.A. and an M.B.A.. While in college, Norquist was an editor at the *Harvard Crimson* and helped to publish the libertarian-leaning *Harvard Chronicle*. He is quoted as having said, "When I became 21, I decided that nobody learned anything about politics after the age of 21." He attended the Leadership Institute in Arlington, Virginia, an organization that teaches conservative Americans how to influence public policy through activism and leadership.

Early in his career, Norquist was executive director of both the National Taxpayers Union and the national College Republicans, holding both positions until 1983. Afterward, he served as Economist and Chief Speechwriter at the U.S. Chamber of Commerce from 1983 to 1984. Norquist traveled to several war zones to help support anti-Soviet guerrilla armies in the second half of the 1980s. He worked with a support network for Oliver North's efforts with the Nicaraguan Contras and other insurgencies, in addition to promoting U.S. support for groups including Mozambique's RENAMO and Jonas Savimbi's UNITA in Angola and helping to organize anti-Soviet forces in Laos.

Norquist is best known for founding Americans for Tax Reform in 1985, which he says was done at the request of then-President Ronald Reagan. Referring to Norquist's activities as head of ATR, Steve Kroft, in a *60 Minutes* episode that aired on November 20, 2011, claimed that "Norquist has been responsible, more than anyone else, for rewriting the dogma of the Republican Party." The primary policy goal of Americans for Tax Reform is to reduce government revenues as a percentage of the Gross Domestic Product. ATR states that it "opposes all tax increases as a matter of principle." Americans for Tax Reform has supported Taxpayer Bill of Rights legislation and transparency initiatives, while opposing cap-and-trade legislation and Democratic efforts to overhaul health care.

In 1993, Norquist launched his Wednesday Meetings series at ATR headquarters, initially to help fight President Clinton's healthcare plan and eventually becoming one of the most significant institutions in American conservative political organizing. The meetings have been called "a must-attend event for Republican operatives fortunate enough to get an invitation," and "the Grand Central Station of the conservative movement."

In 2009, Norquist received $200,000 in annual compensation for his part-time job (24 hours per week) with Americans for Tax Reform, plus an additional $22,419 in other compensation from ATR and related organizations. As a nonprofit organization, Americans for Tax Reform is not required to disclose the identity of its contributors. Critics have asked Norquist to disclose his contributors; he has declined but has said that ATR is financed by direct mail and other grassroots fundraising efforts. According to CBS News, "a significant portion appears to come from wealthy individuals, foundations and corporate interests."

As of late 2011, 238 of 242 House Republicans and 41 out of 47 Senate Republicans had signed ATR's "Taxpayer Protection Pledge," in which the pledger promises to "oppose any and all efforts to increase the marginal income tax rate for individuals and business; and to oppose any net reduction or elimination of deductions and credits, unless matched dollar for dollar by further reducing tax rates."

In November 2011, Senate Majority leader Harry Reid blamed Norquist's influence for the Joint Select Committee on Deficit Reduction's lack of progress, claiming that Congressional Republicans "are being led like puppets by Grover Norquist. They're giving speeches that we should compromise on our deficit, but never do they compromise on Grover Norquist. He is their leader." Since Norquist's pledge binds signatories to opposing deficit reduction agreements that include any element of increased tax revenue, some Republican deficit hawks now retired from office have stated that Norquist has become an obstacle to deficit reduction. Former Republican Senator Alan Simpson, co-chairman of the National Commission on Fiscal Responsibility and Reform, has been particularly critical, describing Norquist's position as "No taxes, under any situation, even if your country goes to hell."

Working with former Speaker Newt Gingrich, Norquist was one of the co-authors of the 1994 Contract with America, and helped to rally grassroots efforts, which Norquist later chronicled in his book *Rock the House*. Norquist also served as a campaign staff member on the 1988, 1992 and 1996 Republican Platform Committees.

Norquist was instrumental in securing early support for the presidential campaign of then-Governor George W. Bush, acting as his unofficial liaison to the conservative movement. He campaigned for Bush in both 2000 and 2004. After Bush's first election, Norquist was a key figure involved in crafting Bush's tax cuts.

He has long been active in building bridges between various ethnic and religious minorities and the free-market community through his co-founding of the Islamic Free Market Institute, and his involvement with Acton Institute, Christian Coalition and Toward Tradition. In 2010, Norquist, whose wife was born into a Muslim family, emerged as an outspoken Republican foe of politicizing the mosque-in-Manhattan issue, calling it a "distraction." He has also announced his plan to assemble a center-right coalition to discuss pulling out of Afghanistan to save hundreds of billions of dollars.

Norquist is active in Tea Party politics. Talking at a Florida rally he said "tea party groups should serve as the 'exoskeleton' that protects newly elected Republicans" from pressures to increase government spending.

According to a 2011 memoir by former lobbyist Jack Abramoff, Norquist was one of Abramoff's first major Republican party contacts. Norquist and Americans for Tax Reform were also mentioned in Senate testimony relating to the Jack Abramoff Indian lobbying scandal which resulted in a 2006 guilty plea by Abramoff to three criminal felony counts of defrauding of American Indian tribes and corrupting public officials. Records released by the Senate Indian Affairs Committee allege that ATR served as a "conduit" for funds that flowed from Abramoff's clients to surreptitiously finance grass-roots lobbying campaigns. Norquist has denied that he did anything wrong, and has not been charged with any crime.

Norquist's national strategy has included recruiting state and local politicians to support ATR's stance on taxes. Norquist has helped to set up regular meetings for conservatives in many states. These meetings are modeled after his Wednesday meetings in Washington, with the goal of creating a nationwide network of conservative activists that he can call upon to support conservative causes, such as tax cuts and deregulation. There are now meetings in 48 states.

Norquist serves on the boards of directors of numerous organizations including the National Rifle Association, the American Conservative Union, the Hispanic Leadership Fund, the Indian-American Republican Caucus, and ParentalRights.org, an organization that wishes to add a Parental Rights Amendment to the United States Constitution. In 2010, Norquist joined the advisory board of GOProud, a political organization representing conservative gays, lesbians, transgendered people, and their allies, for which he was criticized by the Family Research Council. Norquist also sits on a six-person advisory panel that nominates *Time* magazine's Person of the Year.

Norquist favors dramatically reducing the size of the government. He has been noted for his widely quoted quip: "I'm not in favor of abolishing the government. I just want to shrink it down to the size where we can drown it in the bathtub." Journalist William Greider quotes him saying his goal is to bring America back to what it was `up until Teddy Roosevelt, when the socialists took over. The income tax, the death tax, regulation, all that.` When asked by journalist Steven Kroft about the goal of chopping government "in half and then shrink it again to where we were at the turn of the century" before social security and Medicare, Norquist replied, "We functioned in this country with government at eight percent of GDP for a long time and quite well."

Some smaller government advocates argue that Norquist's "obsession with tax revenue" is actually counterproductive with respect to minimizing the size of government, however. Although the Americans for Tax Reform mission statement is "The government's power to control one's life derives from its power to tax. We believe that power should be minimized," critics at the Cato Institute have argued that "holding the line on taxes constrains only one of the four tools (taxes, tax deductions, spending without taxation, and regulation) used by government to alter economic outcomes."

Norquist has described himself as a "boring white bread Methodist." In 2004, at age 48, he married a Palestinian Muslim named Samah Alrayyes, a Kuwaiti PR specialist who was formerly a director of the Islamic Free Market Institute and specialist at the Bureau of Legislative and Public Affairs at United States Agency for International Development (USAID). The couple has two children adopted from abroad. Norquist is said to live a modest lifestyle. According to friend and former roommate John Fund, Norquist's devotion to his political causes is "monk-like" and comparable to that of Ralph Nader.

4

NEWT GINGRICH VS. BILL CLINTON

THE CONTRACT *WITH* AMERICA OR
THE CONTRACT *ON* AMERICA?

Starting in 1994, the politics of hate took a nasty turn. What had been the dirty tricks of election politics for single candidates of both parties moved into the arena of blocs – the crystallization of party line votes and the inevitable gridlock. In 1992, Bill Clinton won the Presidency of the United States. At the same time, the Democrats won control of both houses of Congress.

Although now portraying himself as "cheerful" in his doomed-to-defeat run for the Republican Presidential standard-bearer in the 2011-2012 run for the nation's highest office, Newton Leroy "Newt" Gingrich has conclusively demonstrated the incredibly short memory of the electorate, reinventing himself yet again. How short-minded we are! In 1994 Newton Leroy "Newt" Gingrich, then a 9-time re-elected Congressman from Georgia, altered the game by changing the stakes. "If you have the Executive branch, I'm going to make sure my side has the Legislative Branch," and vice versa. This was by no means the first time that one party controlled one branch and the other party controlled the other branch. This had often happened in American history during mid-term elections, largely because Americans are impatient and very much "want it *now*." It happened in the November 2010 mid-term election as well. That's the same mentality that's fueled the growth of credit card debt since the 1950's. Why wait 'til you have the cash to buy the "toys" you want? Purchase them *now* and pay on what our English friends across the Pond refer to as "the never never" plan. Somehow the mentality was – and continues to be to this day – if a President can't change things in *one term*, vote him (or her) out of office, and if Congress can't change things in *one two-year session*, vote the representatives and senators out of office as well.

Case in point: In 2008, Barack Obama won the U.S. Presidency on the promise of "Change We Can Believe In." The economy had started its recession shortly after the 2004 election. By mid-2008, the economy had "tanked." Real estate prices had taken a 25% downturn (on its way to a paralyzing 50% loss of value in the single most important asset most Americans cherish), banks had run out of money and begged the Government to bail them out (this during a Republican administration which had always prided itself on a *laissez faire* – hands off – policy). Make no mistake, things were pretty grim in the good ol' U.S.of A.

The Democrats found easy pickings by blaming George W. Bush's policies for the economic collapse of the country – as if one man could possibly be responsible for the downturn of 300,000,000 of his fellow citizens. When Barack Obama was elected President, the American people danced in the streets with glee. The deep recession – which might well have been a Depression, whatever you want to call it – would be over! "Happy Days Are Here Again!" After all, Obama had promised "Change We Can Believe In."

Lost amid the tumult and the shouting of the exuberant victors was a warning that President Obama had given several times during the campaign: "It took us *years* to get into this mess, and it will take us *years* to get out of this mess. It may not happen during my first administration (4 years) – it may take longer." That was not what the people wanted to hear and they didn't bother to listen to that part of the speech.

By 2010 there were some changes. The American Relief & Recovery Act was supposed to get America working once again. But the American public somehow thought that meant that *everyone* would have a job again – *right now*. When it didn't happen, the American public got *mad*. And they blamed the President. And they blamed Congress because there was a 10+% unemployment rate, the banks weren't lending any money, and the value of real estate kept going down and down. The 2010 mid-term elections showed precisely how angry the impatient American populace was.

It would be very easy to blame the Republicans for blocking every measure that President Obama wanted to see passed and for being "obstructionist." Very easy, but not very true. Make no mistake, at one point during President Obama's first term, the Democrats boasted 60 out of 100 Senators. They had the power to steamroll over any attempt at filibuster. In the House, the Democratic majority was even larger. Thus, if every Senator and Congressperson voted along strict party lines, there would have been no way – *none at all* – in which the Republicans could have stopped the social bills demanded by the electorate. While the Republicans railed against a "socialist state," and made other noises which minority parties have always made, the real failure to pass any meaningful laws or programs came from the Democratic disease – shoot yourself in the foot.

Until the current 2012 election, that malaise could be laid at the doorstep of the philosophical differences between the parties: The Republicans, who traditionally represent about 39% of the voters, and who are by nature *laissez faire* Conservatives, tended to hang together, whereas the Democrats, with their free-wheeling spirit, represented almost as many different opinions as there were Congresspersons.

Of course, blaming the Democrats for the gridlock would also be too simplistic. Republicans traditionally have money – and, make no mistake, in the United States "Money talks, B******t walks." Slowly, the Republicans ate away at the Democratic supermajority – one election, one Representative, one Senator at a time. Shortly after President Obama's first year in power, the Democrats no longer had a filibuster-proof majority. Once again, nothing got done, it was a do-nothing Congress (only this time with a truly scary economic Panic), and the American people were *pissed off*.

The current spirit of confrontation rather than cooperation on a large scale did not begin with either Bush I or II. It began in 1993 when the Clinton administration, which had come flying into the White House with a strong Democratic majority, failed to pass its much-heralded plan for Universal Healthcare. It began with two strong politicians, each of whom preached morality while practicing something else entirely. Let's take a moment to examine each of these protagonists, restricting their histories to the "Contract With America," which President Clinton derisively called the "Contract *On* America."

William Jefferson "Bill" Clinton, born August 19, 1946, President of the United States from 1993 to 2001, became the Chief at 46, at the end of the Cold War. He was the first baby boomer president. Both he and his wife Hillary Rodham Clinton earned their Juris Doctor (J.D.) degrees from Yale Law School. During his administration, Clinton presided over the continuation of an economic expansion that would later become the longest period of peacetime economic expansion in American history. There was a budget surplus in 2000, the last full year of Clinton's presidency.

After a failed attempt at health care reform, Republicans won control of the House of Representatives in 1994 for the first time in forty years. They promised, but never-quite-delivered, what they called the "Contract With America," authored in part by Newt Gingrich. Two years later, in 1996, Clinton was re-elected. Later, he was impeached for perjury and obstruction of justice in connection with a scandal involving a White House intern. He was subsequently acquitted by the U.S. Senate. Clinton left office with the highest end-of-office approval rating of any U.S. president since World War II. Pundits quipped that if he had had another sex scandal during his term, his adoring public would have voted to overturn the two-term Presidential limit and he would have been elected again by a landslide.

Clinton and Gingrich came from remarkably similar back-grounds. Bill Clinton was born in Hope, Arkansas. His father, a traveling salesman, died in an automobile accident three months before Bill was born. Following Bill's birth, his mother traveled to New Orleans, leaving Bill in Hope with grandparents, who owned and operated a small grocery store. At a time, when the Southern United States were racially segregated, Clinton's grandparents sold goods on credit to people of all races. When Bill's mother returned from nursing school and shortly thereafter married Roger Clinton, who co-owned an automobile dealership in Hot Springs, Arkansas, the family moved to Hot Springs in 1950. Clinton remembers his stepfather as a gambler and an alcoholic, who regularly abused his mother and half-brother Roger Clinton, Jr., to the point where he intervened multiple times with the threat of violence in order to pro-tect them.

Clinton attended Hot Springs High School, where he was an active student leader, avid reader, and musician. In 1963, Clinton visited the White House as a Boys Nation senator, where he met President John F. Kennedy. That same year, he heard Martin Luther

King's 1963 *I Have a Dream* speech, which so moved him that he committed the entire speech to memory. With the aid of scholarships, Clinton attended Georgetown University, where he received a B.S. in Foreign Service. He spent the summer before his senior year, working as an intern for Arkansas Senator J. William Fulbright. Upon graduation, he won a Rhodes Scholarship to University College, Oxford where he studied Philosophy, Politics and Economics. While at Oxford he participated in Vietnam War protests. In later life, he admitted to smoking marijuana at the university, but famously said that he "never inhaled."

After Oxford, Clinton received his J.D. degree from Yale Law School in 1973. During his time at Yale, Clinton took a job with the McGovern campaign and was assigned to lead McGovern's effort in Texas. After Yale, Clinton became a professor at the University of Arkansas. A year later, he unsuccessfully ran for the House of Representatives, but he was elected Arkansas Attorney General in 1976 and Governor of Arkansas in 1978, becoming the youngest governor in the country at thirty-two. Clinton's defeat in the general election of 1980, made him the youngest ex-governor in the nation's history. He spent the next two years working on his re-election campaign. He was again elected governor and this time he kept his job for ten years.

The Clintons' personal and business affairs during the 1980s included transactions which became the basis of the Whitewater investigation which dogged his later presidential administration, but no indictments were made against the Clintons related to the years in Arkansas.

In 1987, Clinton gave the opening night address at the 1988 Democratic National Convention. This set the stage for his dramatic run for the Presidency. In the first contest, the Iowa caucus, he finished a very distant third. During the campaign for the New Hampshire Primary, rumors circulated about an extramarital affair with Gennifer Flowers. Clinton and his wife Hillary went on *60 Minutes* to refute the charges. Their television appearance was a calculated risk, but Clinton regained several delegates. He finished second in the New Hampshire primary, but after trailing badly in the polls and coming within single digits of winning, the media viewed it as a victory. On election night, Clinton labeled himself "The Comeback Kid," earning a strong second-place finish.

Ultimately, Clinton won the 1992 presidential election against Republican incumbent George H. W. Bush and billionaire populist Ross Perot, who ran as an independent. A significant part of Clinton's success was Bush's steep decline in public approval. By election time, the economy was souring and Bush saw his approval rating plummet. Clinton was inaugurated as the 42nd President of the United States on January 20, 1993. In his inaugural address he declared, "Our democracy must be not only the envy of the world but the engine of our own renewal. There is nothing *wrong* with America that cannot be cured by what is *right* with America."

On February 17, 1993, in a nationally televised address to a joint session of Congress, Clinton unveiled his economic plan: deficit reduction rather than a middle-class tax cut, which had been high on his campaign agenda. Shortly after taking office, Clinton signed the Family and Medical Leave Act of 1993, which required large employers to allow employees to take unpaid leave for pregnancy or a serious medical condition. While this action was popular, Clinton's attempt to fulfill another campaign promise of allowing openly homosexual men and women to serve in the armed forces ended up with a strange compromise, "Don't ask, don't tell," which allowed for homosexuals to serve in the military as long as they kept their sexuality secret

Also in 1993, Clinton supported ratification of the controversial North American Free Trade Agreement. Opposition came chiefly from anti-trade Republicans, protectionist Democrats and Ross

Perot supporters. The Agreement was signed into law by President Clinton on January 1, 1994.

One of the most prominent items on Clinton's legislative agenda was a health care reform plan aimed at achieving universal coverage through a national health care plan. Though initially well-received in political circles, it was ultimately doomed by well-organized opposition from conservatives, the American Medical Association, and the health insurance industry. Despite Clinton's party's holding a majority in Congress, the effort to create a national health care system ultimately died. Does this sound familiar? It was the first major legislative defeat of Clinton's administration. Two months later, after two years of Democratic Party control, the Democrats lost control of Congress in the mid-term elections in 1994, for the first time in forty years, largely due to the Gingrich co-authored promise of a "Contract With America."

* * *

Newt Gingrich was born Newton Leroy McPherson, on June 17, 1943, in Harrisburg, Pennsylvania, to a nineteen-year-old father and a sixteen-year-old mother. His mother raised him by herself until she married Robert Gingrich, who then adopted Newt. Gingrich, the child of a career military family, moved several times during his early years. He ultimately graduated from Baker High School in Columbus, Georgia, received a Bachelor's Degree in history from Emory University in Atlanta in 1965, then received his Masters, and subsequently his Ph.D. in modern European history from Tulane University. While at Tulane, Gingrich began attending the St. Charles Avenue Baptist Church. He was soon baptized.

Gingrich taught history at the University of West Georgia in Carrollton, Georgia, from 1970 to 1978. In 1974 and 1976, he made two unsuccessful runs for Congress in Georgia's sixth congressional district. Gingrich ran for the seat a third time in 1978 and won election by almost 9 percentage points. He was reelected six times from this district.

In 1983, Gingrich demanded the expulsion of fellow representatives Dan Crane and Gerry Studds for their roles in the Congressional Page sex scandal. In May 1988, Gingrich, along with 77 other House members and Common Cause, brought ethics charges against Democratic Speaker Jim Wright, who was alleged to have used a book deal to circumvent campaign-finance laws and House ethics rules. During the investigation, it became public that Gingrich had his own unusual book deal, for *Window of Opportunity*, part of whose publicity expenses were covered by a limited partnership which raised $105,000 from Republican political supporters around the country to promote sales of the book. Wright eventually resigned as a result of the inquiry. Gingrich's success in forcing the resignation was in part responsible for his rising influence in the Republican caucus.

In 1989, after House Minority Whip Dick Cheney was appointed Secretary of Defense, Gingrich was elected to succeed him. Gingrich and others in the house railed against what they saw as ethical lapses in the House, an institution that had been under Democratic control for almost 40 years. The House banking scandal and the Congressional Post Office scandal were emblems of the exposed corruption. Gingrich himself was among those members of the House who had engaged in check-kiting; he had overdrafts on twenty-two checks, including a $9,463 check to the Internal Revenue Service in 1990.

As a result of the 1990 census, Georgia picked up an additional seat for the 1992 elections. However, the Democratic-controlled Georgia General Assembly eliminated Gingrich's old district and created a new 6th District in Fulton and Cobb counties in the wealthy northern suburbs of Atlanta. Gingrich sold his home, moved to Marietta, and won a very close Republican primary. The primary victory was tantamount to election in the new, heavily Republican district.

In the 1994 campaign season, in an effort to offer a concrete alternative to shifting Democratic policies and to unite distant wings of the Republican Party, Newt Gingrich, with the help of other Republicans, came up with a "Contract with America," which had ten items in it. The contract was signed by Gingrich and other Republican candidates for the House of Representatives. It ranged from issues with broad popular support, including welfare reform, term limits, tougher crime laws, and a balanced budget law, to more specialized legislation, such as restrictions on American military participation in U.N. missions. Gingrich's assault on the House was very successful. In the November 1994 elections, Republicans gained 54 seats (they gained 52 seats in the 2010 midterm elections) and took control of the House for the first time since 1954.

Congress fulfilled Gingrich's "Contract" promise to bring all ten of the Contract's issues to a vote within the first 100 days of the session, even though most legislation was held up in the Senate, vetoed by President Bill Clinton, or substantially altered in negotiations with Clinton. The Contract was criticized as a "Trojan horse tactic" that, while trumpeting the notion of reform, would allow corporate polluters to profit at the expense of the environment. It was referred to by opponents, including President Clinton, as the "Contract *on* America." However, future legislation and implementation of the contract put many aspects of it into law in some fashion.

* * *

The Contract with America was introduced six weeks before the 1994 Congressional election, the first mid-term election of President Clinton's Administration, and was signed by all but two of the Republican members of the House and all of the Party's nonincumbent Republican Congressional candidates. It marked the first time since 1918 that a Congressional election had been run broadly on a national level, *i.e.* the politics of an unrelenting bloc. Its provisions represented the view of many conservative Republicans on the issues of shrinking the size of government, promoting lower taxes and greater entrepreneurial activity, tort reform, and welfare reform. When the Republicans gained a majority of seats in the 104th Congress, the Contract was seen as a triumph for Party leaders such as Gingrich.

The Contract's actual text included a list of eight reforms the Republicans promised to enact, and ten bills they promised to bring to floor debate and votes, if they were made the majority following the election. More than half of its text came from Ronald Reagan's 1985 State of the Union Address. On the first day of their majority in the House, the Republicans promised to pass eight major reforms:

- require all laws that apply to the rest of the country to also apply to Congress;
- select a major, independent auditing firm to conduct a comprehensive audit of Congress for waste, fraud or abuse;
- cut the number of House committees and cut committee staff by one-third;
- limit the terms of all committee chairs;
- ban the casting of proxy votes in committee;
- require committee meetings to be open to the public;
- require a three-fifths majority vote to pass a tax increase;
- guarantee an honest accounting of the Federal Budget by implementing zero base-line budgeting.

The Republicans pledged "to bring to the floor ten bills, each to be given a full and open debate, each to be given a clear and fair vote, and each to be immediately available for public inspection." These bills represented significant changes to policy:

- a balanced budget requirement
- tax cuts for small businesses, families and seniors
- term limits for legislators
- social security reform
- tort reform, and
- welfare reform.

A brief description of the proposed laws and their fate follows:

The Fiscal Responsibility Act: An amendment to the Constitution that would require a balanced budget unless sanctioned by a three-fifths vote in both houses of Congress passed by the U.S. House. It was rejected by the U.S. Senate, 65-35. It was enacted with substantial changes on April 9, 1996, but was subsequently ruled by the Supreme Court to be unconstitutional.

The Taking Back Our Streets Act: An anti-crime package including stronger truth-in-sentencing, "good faith" exclusionary rule exemptions, and death penalty provisions. A watered-down version ultimately passed.

The Personal Responsibility Act:
An act to discourage illegitimacy and teen pregnancy by reforming and cutting cash welfare and related programs by prohibiting welfare to mothers under 18 years of age, denying increased AFDC for additional children while on welfare, and enacting a two-years-and-out provision with work requirements to promote individual responsibility. The act included provisions giving food vouchers to unwed mothers under 18 in lieu of cash AFDC benefits, denying cash AFDC benefits for additional children to people on AFDC, requiring recipients to participate in work programs after 2 years on AFDC, complete termination of AFDC payments after five years, and suspending driver and professional licenses of people who fail to pay child support. The

act passed the House and the Senate, but was vetoed by President Clinton. An alternative Personal Responsibility and Work Opportunity Reconciliation Act, which offered many of the same policies was enacted in 1996.

The American Dream Restoration Act: An act to create a $500-per-child tax credit, begin repeal of the marriage tax penalty, and creation of American Dream Savings Accounts to provide middle-class tax relief. The bill passed in the House but stalled in the Senate.

The National Security Restoration Act: An act to prevent U.S. troops from serving under United Nations command unless the President determines it is necessary for the purposes of national security, to cut U.S. payments for U.N. peacekeeping operations, and to help establish guidelines for the voluntary integration of former Warsaw Pact nations into NATO. Passed the House, died in the Senate.

The "Common Sense" Legal Reform Act: An act to institute "Loser pays the winner's lawyers fees," (similar to the English system), limits punitive damages, and weaken product-liability laws to prevent what the bill considered frivolous litigation. The Bill passed both Houses but was vetoed by President Clinton. A softer tort reform bill was enacted in 1995 when Congress overrode a veto by Clinton.

The Job Creation and Wage Enhancement Act
This was a package of measures to spur small-business incentives. Although this was listed as a single bill in the Contract, its provisions ultimately made it to the House Floor as four separate bills:

- H.R.5 required federal funding for state spending mandated by Congressional action and estimated by the Congressional Budget Office to cost more than $50 million per year for the years of 1996-2002, was passed by both the House and the Senate.

- H.R.450 required a moratorium on the implementation of Federal regulations until June 30, 1995. The two bills never emerged from conference.
- H.R.925 required Federal compensation to be paid to property owners when Federal Government actions reduced the value of the property by 20% or more. It was passed by the House but not by the Senate.
- H.R.926 required Federal agencies to provide a cost-benefit analysis on any regulation costing $50 million or more annually, to be signed off on by the Office of Management and Budget, and permitted small businesses to sue that agency if they believed the aforementioned analysis was performed inadequately or incorrectly.

The Citizen Legislature Act
An amendment to the Constitution that would have imposed 12-year term limits on members of the US Congress (i.e. six terms for Representatives, two terms for Senators). The resolution was rejected by the U.S. House and never got to the Senate.

Other sections of the Contract included a proposed Family Reinforcement Act (tax incentives for adoption, strengthening the powers of parents in their children's education, stronger child pornography laws, and elderly dependent care tax credit) and the Senior Citizens Fairness Act (raise the Social Security earnings limit, repeal the 1993 tax hikes on Social Security benefits and provide tax incentives for private long-term care insurance).

The Republicans proudly portrayed the election of 1994 as the "Republican Revolution."

* * *

The momentum of the Republican Revolution stalled in late 1995 during a budget standoff between Congressional Republicans and Democratic President Bill Clinton. Speaker Gingrich and the new Republican majority wanted to slow the rate of government spending. Gingrich allowed previously approved appropriations to expire on schedule, thus allowing parts of the Federal government to shut down for lack of funds. However, Gingrich inflicted a blow to his public image by suggesting that the Republican hard-line stance over the budget was in part due to his feeling "snubbed" by the President during a flight to and from Yitzhak Rabin's funeral in Israel. Gingrich was subsequently lampooned by the media, with one editorial cartoon depicted him as having thrown a temper tantrum. Democratic leaders took the opportunity to attack Gingrich's motives for the budget standoff, which may have contributed to Clinton's re-election in November 1996 and significant losses for the Republican Party in Congress.

* * *

After the firestorm of the Contract With America died down, both Clinton and Gingrich were seen in a "different" light, particularly when it came to morals and ethics.

On January 21, 1997, the House voted 395 to 28 to reprimand Gingrich for ethics violations dating back to September 1994. The House ordered Gingrich to pay a $300,000 penalty, the first time in the House's 208-year history it had disciplined a Speaker for ethical wrongdoing. By 1998, Gingrich had become a highly visible and polarizing figure in the public's eye, making him a target for Democratic congressional candidates across the nation. Republicans lost five seats in the House in the 1998 midterm elections — the worst performance in 64 years for a party that didn't hold the presidency. Polls showed that Gingrich and the Republican Party's attempt to remove President Clinton from office was widely unpopular among Americans.

Facing another rebellion in the Republican caucus, Gingrich announced on November 6, 1998 that he would stand down as Speaker and would leave the House as well. He had been handily reelected to an 11th term, but declined to take his seat. Gingrich said, "I'm willing to lead but I'm not willing to preside over people who are cannibals."

Today, Gingrich, a chameleon like so many politicians everywhere (not just in the United States and not just on one side of the aisle or the other), has recast himself again – this time as a conservative force that will bring back American values "when I am elected President of this great country of ours." But Gingrich's appeal did not take hold. The erstwhile Speaker of the House ran a distant third, or, at times, even a distant fourth.

Gingrich's personal life, like Clinton's, has hardly been a model of fidelity and is somewhat less than beyond reproach. He has been married three times. He first married Jackie Battley, his former high school geometry teacher, when he was 19 and she was 26. Gingrich left his wife in the spring of 1980 after having an affair with Marianne Ginther. According to Battley, Gingrich visited her later that year while she was in the hospital recovering from cancer surgery to discuss the details of their divorce. Six months after it was final, Gingrich wed Ginther. But his second marriage did not result in the cessation of his extracurricular activities. Gingrich began an affair with Callista Bisek, 23 years his junior, in the mid nineties, which, oddly enough, continued during the Congressional investigation of Bill Clinton and the Monica Lewinsky scandal.

In 2000, Gingrich married Bisek shortly after his divorce with second wife Ginther was finalized. A Baptist since graduate school, Gingrich converted to Catholicism, his wife's faith, on March 29, 2009.

Newt Gingrich has been an outspoken critic of Barack Obama, whom he described as "the most radical president in American history." Gingrich has argued that it is necessary to "save America" and stop Obama's "secular socialist machine." He has characterized Obama's universal health care reform as leading America towards authoritarianism, totalitarianism, and the end of democracy.

Although Clinton's morals were certainly questionable, history has, at least thus far, treated him kinder than it has Gingrich. In the 1996 presidential election, Clinton was re-elected by a larger margin than in the first election. The Republicans lost a few seats in the House and gained a few in the Senate, but retained control of both. Clinton received over 70% of the Electoral College votes.

Throughout his career, Clinton has been subject to various allegations of sexual misconduct. In 1998, Kathleen Willey alleged that Clinton sexually assaulted her four years previously. In 1998, Juanita Broaddrick alleged she was raped by Clinton some twenty years previously. These accusations were never brought before a court. Gennifer Flowers, Elizabeth Ward Gracen, Sally Perdue, and Dolly Kyle Browning each said she had had adulterous sexual relations with Clinton during or before his service as governor. Clinton ultimately admitted to only two extramarital sexual relationships, one with Gennifer Flowers, and the second, with Monica Lewinsky, that caused a cataclysm that dogged his second term in office.

In a lame duck session after the 1998 elections, the House voted to impeach Clinton, based on allegations that Clinton had lied about his relationship with Lewinsky in a sworn deposition in the Paula Jones lawsuit. The House began impeachment hearings before the mid-term elections. Although the mid-term elections held in November 1998 were at the 6-year point in an 8-year presidency (a time in the electoral cycle where the party holding the White House usually loses Congressional seats), the Democratic Party actually gained several seats. The Republican leadership called a lame duck session in December 1998 so it could continue the impeachment proceedings.

The two charges passed in the House, largely on the basis of Republican support, were for perjury and obstruction of justice. The perjury charge arose from Clinton's testimony about his relationship with Monica Lewinsky during a sexual harassment lawsuit (later dismissed, appealed and settled for $850,000) brought by former Arkansas state employee Paula Jones. The obstruction charge was based on his actions during the subsequent investigation of that testimony. The Senate later voted to acquit Clinton on both charges. The final vote was generally along party lines, with no Democrats voting guilty. Some Republicans voted not guilty for both charges.

Clinton remained popular with the public throughout his two terms as President, ending his presidential career with a 65% approval rating, the highest end-of-term approval rating of any President since Dwight D. Eisenhower. Clinton also oversaw a boom of the U.S. economy. Under Clinton, the United States had a projected federal budget surplus for the first time since 1969.

The Whitewater controversy began with the real estate dealings of Bill and Hillary Clinton and their associates Jim and Susan McDougal in the Whitewater Development Corporation, a failed business venture in the 1970s and 1980s. In November 1993, David Hale, the source of criminal allegations against Bill Clinton in the Whitewater affair, alleged that Clinton, while governor of Arkansas, pressured him to provide an illegal $300,000 loan to Susan McDougal, the Clintons' partner in the Whitewater land deal. A Securities & Exchange Commission investigation resulted in convictions against the McDougals, but the Clintons themselves were never charged.

Clinton issued 141 pardons and 36 commutations on his last day in office on January 20, 2001. Most of the controversy surrounded Marc Rich and allegations that Hillary Clinton's brother, Hugh Rodham, accepted payments in return for influencing the president's decision-making regarding the pardons. Some of Clinton's pardons remain a point of controversy.

After he left office, Bill Clinton proceeded to give speeches around the world, often for over $100,000 a speech. He has spoken at the last six Democratic National Conventions, dating back to 1988. In the aftermath of the 2005 Asian tsunami, U.N. Secretary-General Kofi Annan appointed Clinton to head a relief effort. After Hurricane Katrina, Clinton and fellow former President George H. W. Bush established the Bush-Clinton Katrina Fund and Bush-Clinton Tsunami Fund.

In March 2010, a Newsmax/Zogby poll asking Americans which of the current living former presidents they think is best equipped to deal with the problems the country faces today, found that a wide margin of respondents would pick Bill Clinton. Clinton received 41% of the vote, while former President George W. Bush received 15%, former President George H. W. Bush received 7%, and former President Jimmy Carter received 5%.

THE RETURN OF THE CONTRACT WITH AMERICA – THE REPUBLICAN "ANSWER" TO THE CHARGE THAT THEY DO NOTHING BUT OBSTRUCT.

On September 23, 2010, a group of Republicans, arguably tired of the charge that they have done nothing but obstruct, went public with their proposal for another "Contract With America." Rather than posit anything *new*, the Republican "initiative" was to unwind what had been done during the first two years of the Obama administration – to wind the clock back to the glory days of George W. Bush. Their new "plan":

- To repeal the Universal Health Care Act
- To repeal the Stimulus Act

- To ensure that substantial tax cuts and tax dodges for the wealthy continue unabated
- To reinstitute the Bush era tax cuts.
- To make government smaller, and
- To ensure that there is complete "accountability in government" – cutting every cent of "wasteful" spending.

Is this supposed to be a new program? It looks surprisingly like a reprise of the same old failed policy. President Obama's justifiable response was: "The voters voted us in to *Change the Guard,* Now we must *Guard the Change.*" However, while the Democrats retained the Senate, they lost the House.

Thus, America is riding the same old do-nothing merry-go-round. I believe that if there is to be any progress, Democrats and Republicans must compromise and work together – something that has not been done in many, many years – to save American from further progressing along the road to becoming a third world country.

5

PROTECTING AGAINST PROGRESS:
NAME CALLING – SOCIALISM
AND OTHER EPITHETS

Americans have always been inventors of labels – an easy shorthand for more detailed explanations. If you think I'm joking, here are some shorthand labels that are quite popular today. Take a mental image "quiz" and see what you think of or picture when you hear the following words:

McDonalds

Coca-cola

Budweiser

Hollywood

New York City

9-1-1

Starbucks

Socialism

Fooled you with the last one, didn't I? Answer truthfully: Did you equate the word "Socialism" with "Communism?" Unquestionably, those whom "Liberals" call "Conservatives" or "Tea Party" would overwhelmingly answer "Yes." Equally unquestionably, "Liberals" would call "Conservatives" such things as "reactionary," "bigoted," and "racist."

Labels have been used both historically and lately as "buzz-words" to negate ideas, some of which just might lead to a better, more equitable society.

Take the current bombast over healthcare. I don't believe there is anyone in the United States who truly believes that the way we deliver healthcare in this country is ideal. Most Americans believe that medical care in the United States is "better than average," even though we rate far below such countries as France and Denmark. It *should* be better than average – *we pay more for our healthcare services and prescription drugs than any other nation on earth.*

I believe every American is entitled to affordable health care. If that makes me a "Communist" or a "Socialist" (more labels) in the eyes of many, so be it. I can live with that. Because the "sin" of "Communism" or "Socialism" is a damned sight easier to swallow than 40 million Americans going without health care.

I can hear the naysayers now: "If you want *socialized medicine* (another label), take a look at Canada and see how bad things are." I am not saying that Canada's system is without its faults - but you can point to exceptions that raise the ire of people in *any* field. For example, despite the tumult and the shouting about how medical fees are so exorbitant because of "huge malpractice verdicts," *less than 1% of medical malpractice cases result in "huge" (or even moderate) verdicts.* In California, medical malpractice non-economic damages have been limited to $250,000 for years.

So-called "Socialized" medicine exists in both France and Denmark and the World Health Organization has proclaimed that these nations furnish their citizens with the best overall health care in the world.

Let's review the naysayers comment again: "If you want *socialized medicine* take a look at Canada and see how bad things are."

Back in 1969, my son Jeff was born while I was in the Air Force. The *total* I paid for prenatal care, obstetrician, hospital, delivery, and postpartum services came to $7.50. My daughter Tracy was born a few years later, after I had gotten out of the military, in a civilian hospital and it cost me *one hundred times as much. Conservatives, who invariably decry "socialized medicine" wave the American flag and salute our military might. Perhaps they conveniently "forget" that we have had "socialized medicine" in the United States for years.* Our military - Army, Navy, Air Force, Marines - have provided full medical coverage for all military personnel and their dependents. After they retire, career military personnel are guaranteed lifelong medical care through Government programs. That is "socialized medicine," and we've had it for more years than I've been alive. I have never suffered because of being subjected to such care.

The same thing applies to Medicare, which, political yammering notwithstanding, is also "socialized medicine." I recently underwent my second cancer scare and went through 7 weeks of radiation therapy. I shudder to think what I would have had to pay but for Medicare and supplemental insurance - and what that would have done to my family's financial picture.

Those opposed to a universal healthcare system can call it "socialized medicine" or anything else they want, but the truth of the matter is that we have too many people who need healthcare and not enough facilities to provide 100% of what 100% of those people *want, immediately when they want it.* So tales of "rationing" are not entirely untrue and there will always be inequality. Those who can afford more and are willing to pay more will get faster, more complete care. Unfair? Yes, but that's the way of the world. England has lived that way since the end of World War II - you can supplement what care the Government provides with private care - which you pay for out of your own pocket.

As I write this book, the Highest Court in the land, the United States Supreme Court, has just concluded, in a dramatic 5-4 decision the government can force its citizens to purchase health insurance – in a form which is much more affordable than what commercial health insurers currently charge – or suffer financial penalties. Are we serious? The alternative is that 40 million Americans go without health insurance because they can't afford it. They crowd into the emergency rooms of hospitals which, by law, *have to* accept them whether they can afford to pay or not – and *all of us* pay that bill by increased insurance premiums and more expensive prices for the delivery of medical care.

Other naysayers condemn the healthcare system on the grounds that it violates freedom of religion because healthcare insurers might offer contraceptive devices – and education about alternatives to unwanted – and unneeded – pregnancies through a system of honest sex education.

I spoke to a radiation oncologist the other day – a wise and humane man named Patrick Feehan. He told me he had just come back from a conference where the point was raised that a 6% value-added tax – essentially a tax on *consumption*, not income – would enable us to provide excellent medical care for every man, woman, and child in America. It would be administered by the Government, which Conservatives warn will "take all our rights away and have death committees." Talk about dirty trick scare tactics! What is so insanely silly is that *we already are paying through the nose for medical care.*

Is there no sense in this Alice-in-Wonderland world called America? Suppose the *exact* amount of income generated by health insurance premiums were, instead, deposited into a government-administered program. Only this time around, the health insurance companies would not be allowed to grab *billions* of dollars each year for their shareholders. Do you seriously believe we would have a lesser grade of healthcare?

Or suppose we went to a single payer system where the ad-ministrator of that system could negotiate with the pharmaceutical companies who make sure that the term "Golden Age" means it's when the big pharmaceutical companies reap the most gold from older America. The United States pays more for medication than any other country in the world. "But," say those who want to keep the system the way it is, "it is only by keeping those prices as they are that we can insure that Americans get *pure* medications that are *up to U.S. standards.*" Balderdash! Most, if not all, of our prescrip-tion drugs are made overseas – in Ireland, Switzerland, Israel, and Germany. And, of course, that means "outsourced jobs" – another dirty word in political parlance.

Here are the results of a recent study by retail giant Costco. I defy anyone to prove these figures wrong.

Did you ever wonder how much it costs a drug company for the active ingredient in prescription medications? Some people think it must cost a lot, since many drugs sell for more than $2.00 per tablet. We did a search of offshore chemical synthesizers that supply the active ingredients found in drugs approved by the FDA. As we have revealed in past issues of Life Extension a significant percentage of drugs sold in the United States contain active ingredients made in other countries. In our independent investigation of how much profit drug companies really make, we obtained the actual price of active ingredients used in some of the most popular drugs sold in America.

- **Celebrex:100 mg**: Consumer price (100 tablets): $130.27; Cost of general active ingredients: $0.60; Percent markup: 21,712%
- **Claritin:10 mg**: Consumer Price (100 tablets): $215.17; Cost of general active ingredients: $0.71; Percent markup: 30,306%
- **Keflex:250 mg**: Consumer Price (100 tablets): $157.39; Cost of general active ingredients: $1.88; Percent markup: 8,372%
- **Lipitor:20 mg**: Consumer Price (100 tablets): $272.37; Cost of general active ingredients: $5.80; Percent markup: 4,696%
- **Norvasc:10 mg**: Consumer price (100 tablets): $188.29; Cost of general active ingredients: $0.14; Percent markup: 134,493%
- **Paxil:20 mg**: Consumer price (100 tablets): $220.27; Cost of general active ingredients: $7.60; Percent markup: 2,898%
- **Prevacid:30 mg**: Consumer price (100 tablets): $44.77; Cost of general active ingredients: $1.01; Percent markup: 34,136%
- **Prilosec: 20 mg**: Consumer price (100 tablets): $360.97; Cost of general active ingredients $0.52; Percent markup: 69,417%
- **Prozac:20 mg**: Consumer price (100 tablets) : $247.47; Cost of general active ingredients: $0.11; Percent markup: 224,973%
- **Tenormin:50 mg**: Consumer price (100 tablets): $104.47; Cost of general active ingredients: $0.13; Percent markup: 80,362%
- **Vasotec:10 mg**: Consumer price (100 tablets): $102.37; Cost of general active ingredients: $0.20; Percent markup: 51,185%

- **Xanax:1 mg**: Consumer price (100 tablets) : $136.79; Cost of general active ingredients: $0.024; Percent markup: 569,958%
- **Zestril:20 mg**: Consumer price (100 tablets) $89.89; Cost of general active ingredients $3.20; Percent markup: 2,809%
- **Zithromax:600 mg**: Consumer price (100 tablets): $1,482.19; Cost of general active ingredients: $18.78; Percent markup: 7,892%
- **Zocor:40 mg**: Consumer price (100 tablets): $350.27; Cost of general active ingredients: $8.63; Percent markup: 4,059%
- **Zoloft:50 mg**: Consumer price: $206.87; Cost of general active ingredients: $1.75; Percent markup: 11,821%

Since the cost of prescription drugs is so outrageous, I thought everyone should know about this. It pays to shop around! This helps to solve the mystery as to why they can afford to put a Walgreen's on every corner.

Steve Wilson, an investigative reporter for Channel 7 News in Detroit, did a story on generic drug prices gouging by pharmacies. He found in his investigation that some of these generic drugs were marked up as much as 3,000% or more. So often we blame the drug companies for the high cost of drugs, and usually rightfully so. But in this case, the fault clearly lies with the pharmacies themselves. For example if you had to buy a prescription drug, and bought the name brand, you might pay $100 for 100 pills.

The pharmacist might tell you that if you get the generic equivalent, they would only cost $80, making you think you are saving $20. What the pharmacist is not telling you is that those 100 generic pills may have only cost him $10!

At the end of the report, one of the anchors asked Mr. Wilson whether or not there were any pharmacies that did not adhere to this practice, and he said that Costco consistently charged little over their cost for the generic drugs.

Recently, I went to the Costco site, where you can look up any drug, and get its online price. It says that the in-store prices are consistent with the online prices. I was appalled. Just to give you one example, I searched for the drug Compazine which helps prevent nausea in chemo patients. 60 generic pills cost $54.99. At Costco, I could have bought 100 pills for $19.89. For 145 of a certain prescription pain pill, CVS charged $72.57. I could have got 150 of the same pills at Costco for $28.08.

* * *

The malaise is not limited to healthcare. Take public education – or *don't* take public education if you have the money not to. When I attended Los Angeles' Alexander Hamilton High School in the late 1950's that school had a full athletic program, a distinguished school newspaper, a symphony orchestra, a marching band, a choir, a drama department, music classes for everyone, special interest after-school clubs for anyone who wanted to join, a fully-stocked school library with the latest books, classes in Latin, French, Spanish, Chemistry, Physics, Biology, etc. We were renowned for the quality of the plays and shows we put on. Even though we usually struggled to a barely winning football season, 75% of the students attended every game and cheered wildly. Most important, they had the Iowa Tests back then, the precursor to the SAT tests. Hamilton's *average* overall score was in the 94th percentile. I was fortunate enough to score in the 99+ percentile and got not so much as a single scholarship offer because so many others had a *higher* 99+ score than I did. Hamilton was not unique. It was made up of middle-class, ordinary students.

Private school? The only ones we ever heard about were the Catholic Schools, and they cost next to nothing. There was more than enough to keep us academically and culturally surfeited at Hamilton.

Contrast that with education in the United States today. My wife teaches in a private school in Monterey, California – a school which offers most of what I enjoyed at Hamilton in the 50s, plus, of course, the requisite computers without which 21st century kids cannot function; and that school teaches *manners*, a forgotten art in today's world. It costs $20,000 per year in grades 1-8, close to $30,000 per year in the upper school. My wife's third grade class has 24 students. She has an assistant for 2/3 of the day, so there is a 12-1 ratio of students to teachers. Lorraine interacts with teachers in both public and private schools and, as always, teachers compare notes.

How do the public schools stack up? The average public elementary school on the Monterey Peninsula in California, a relatively affluent community, has 28-30 students in a class. The teacher has no assistants and, alarmingly, hardly any enrichment classes where he or she can send the children – and get a break to recharge his or her batteries during the day. The average public school has a football program, *no* orchestra, *no* band, *no* choir, *occasionally* a drama department, *no* music classes for anyone, a school library with old books, classes in Spanish, and occasional AP enrichment classes, mostly in math. Because of that spectacular fiasco known as "No Child Left Behind," teachers teach *to the test,* with no time for creativity or anything else. Because of budgetary constraints, our school district loses a couple of teachers each year – and not due to attrition or retirement.

Yet a recent Republican Congress came up with the idea of giving the parents of private school students *vouchers* or tax incentives so they could have a "choice" of whether they wanted to send their children to public or private school. Since the vast majority of children who attend private school go there because their parents can *afford* to place them there, guess who was meant to profit from this scatterbrained idea? This was simply a reverse Robin Hood ploy – take from the *poor* and give to the *rich*. And, of course, since the government would provide vouchers or tax incentives to help out the private schools, that would mean there was that much less money to spend on public schools.

How do we propose to compete in an ever more competitive world when this is the state of our public education and only the wealthy can afford private school? We'd *better* be able to compete, or the middle class will almost totally erode in a generation. And yet, day after day the few remaining newspapers (now that we have the internet), the conservative commentators and politicos, and the Tea Party advocates rail against raising taxes. Exactly how do we propose to save, let alone pay for, public education? By "teaching to the test?" By raising a generation of automatons who can calculate figures but who are soulless because they have never been exposed to fine art or great music? A generation who believes South America is a *country* in Brazil? A generation whose cultural exposure is sated by *America's Got Talent* or *American Idol*.

I could provide at least twenty more examples of how we attach negative labels to mask the cancer of doing *nothing* – and we Americans, like Pavlov's dog – become so attuned to the negative labels we hear each day, that our knee-jerk reaction is to reject the *meaning* of the idea simply because it *sounds* threatening. Our ship of state is becoming much like the *Titanic* – as the huge iceberg looms ever closer, the passengers are fighting over whether or not they should call that brown appetizer in the buffet line "Liver Pâté" or "Chopped liver."

PART THREE:

THE UNTAMING

OF THE MEDIA

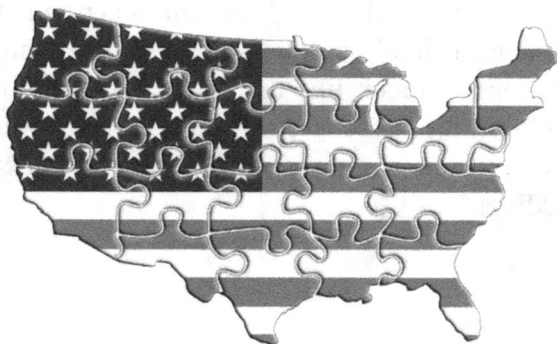

6

THE DECLINE OF THE NETWORKS AND THE EXPANSION OF "FREEDOM OF SPEECH."

"The most stringent protection of free speech would not protect a man in falsely shouting fire in a theatre and causing a panic. ... [T]here is no absolute right of free speech, because there are always circumstances in which unregulated expression can create problematic or dangerous situations. The need for safeguarding the public (or the government) against certain forms of speech creates exceptions that are *not* protected by the First Amendment.

"Words which, ordinarily and in many places, would be within the freedom of speech protected by the First Amendment may become subject to prohibition when [they are] of such a nature and used in such circumstances a to create a clear and present danger that they will bring about the substantive evils which Congress has a right to prevent. The character of every act depends upon the circumstances in which it is done."

> - Justice Oliver Wendell Holmes, Jr., *Schenck v. United States,* 249 US 47 (1919).

* * *

"Joe Klein, president of CNN's U.S. operations, was fired Friday, just weeks after putting the finishing touches on a new nighttime lineup for the cable news network that was aimed at reversing years of declining ratings and bolstering its position against upstart MSNBC and industry leader Fox news. Klein's departure is the latest shakeup in a television news business struggling to adapt to a rapidly changing landscape that increasingly values advocacy and partisanship over news and analysis."

> - Joe Flint, Los Angeles *Times*, September 25, 2010.

* * *

"Jeff Zucker, a lifelong employee of NBC Universal said Friday that he would step down after being told there won't be a place for him once cable giant Comcast Corp. takes over the company at the end of the year. Two weeks ago, Comcast Chief Operating Officer Steve Burke told Zucker that he wanted him to 'move on' as soon as Comcast takes control of the Media conglomerate. Federal regulators are expected to approve the $30 billion Merger between Comcast and General Electric's NBC Universal that includes USA, Bravo, MSNBC, CNBC, E!, the Universal movie studio, and theme parks."

> - Meg James, Los Angeles *Times*, September 25, 2010

* * *

In the 19th Century there were no radios, televisions, or airplanes. The dissemination of information was through the town hall meeting, literary societies, the local newspaper, the local saloon, or the town gossip.

As we entered World War II, and radio had reduced the size of our nation by making news, music, sports, and entertainment programs virtually universal. There were four major networks – CBS, NBC, ABC, and Mutual. There were also "independent" stations, but they were mostly specialized – they played selected types of music depending on their target audience. Their programming was aimed at a certain ethnicity or culture. If we wanted "the news" we relied on the major networks. There were always the crackpots, soap salesmen, preachers, and fringe commentators who found space on some station "far to the right on your AM radio dial" (no FM back then).

In the 1950s. television took off in a big way. By the end of the decade almost every home in America had – or their inhabitants had access to – what was then called the "boob tube." To all intents and purposes, there were the three major networks – CBS, NBC, and ABC – and the "independents." If we wanted to hear the national or international news, we still relied on the major networks. Since the networks were in direct competition with one another, they exerted checks and balances against each other. The news was the *news*. It was usually not colored by opinion of every political stripe. When Walter Cronkite spoke, *you could depend on the integrity – the veritas* – of what he said. News reporters such as Tom Brokaw did not try to "color" the news.

If there were "talking heads," they appeared on game shows such as "What's My Line?" or they spoke on Sunday morning shows reserved for political comment (much as Saturday mornings were reserved for cartoons).

The look and sound of television and radio changed drastically in 1981 when the U.S. Senate Commerce Committee approved a bill that would deregulate the broadcast industry. That bill prevented the Federal Communications Commission from imposing again rules requiring minimum amounts of news and public affairs programming. By 1987, the Fairness Doctrine, which counted broadcast stations as public trustees of the airwaves, was eliminated.

Prior to deregulation, media companies had an obligation to create need-based studies and use them to serve the public interest in the form of relevant public affairs and news programming. One major media outlet could not buy up the other. Broadcasters could not own both a radio and a television station. The rules were set up to prevent media conglomerates from forming. With regulation, the Big Three Networks - Columbia Broadcasting Company, American Broadcasting Company and National Broadcasting Company – would not have been able to grow and diversify. They now even own cable networks and radio stations because of deregulation. Deregulation led to the media conglomerate mergers that we have today. Regulations were based on the idea that there are not enough broadcast channels for all who want them. Because of that "scarcity," the good of the public interest is at stake as it relates to the idea of airwaves as a publicly owned natural resource.

While Deregulation cleared the way for fewer entities to guide and control information for entire broadcast regions, this change opened the way for mass media to form conglomerates, concentrating broadcast air wave ownership among fewer stations. At the same time, we entered the age of Cable Television, broadband, and an almost infinite number of new, largely unregulated, outlets.

The networks now found themselves faced with a dilemma: With well over 100 channels available, although the networks – especially when they combined with other industrial giants, whether or not they were connected to the media industry – could buy up many channels (*e.g.* ABC's ownership of ESPN), they were simply unable to buy <u>all</u> of the channels.

Soon there emerged new forces, new media giants, who didn't care to be saddled with "legacy" network affiliations: CNN and Fox have become major players in that game. As controls started to fall by the wayside, standards started to fall by the wayside. The *nouveau riche* Johnnie-come-latelies realized that *entertainment* trumps truth and accuracy every time. A newscast became more than a newscast – and less *of* a newscast – in their hands. News "anchors" became pedants, commenting on the stories they broadcast. Slowly at first, then faster, what had been "news" morphed into *opinions* – often strong opinions colored by the political persuasion of the powers-at-the-top.

Fox News Network is the best example of the deterioration of objectivity. Do you *really* believe you're getting the true and objective, balanced news from Fox? If you do, I'm sure you believe in fairy tales and Puff the Magic Dragon. Yet, shockingly, *millions* watch Fox News and, like moths drawn to a flame, believe everything they hear on Fox. Sarah Palin is the most brilliant woman that ever lived because Fox *says* she is. And the Tea Party is what we need more than anything else to invigorate America – to bring us back on the right track to true Christianity. That's only natural. The proof that we're the greatest, most God-fearing nation on earth is proved by the fact that the Bible is written in English!

For those of you who think I'm bashing Fox because I'm one of those "Commie Pinko Socialist-Homo-Loving Liberals," I hate to burst your bubble. I'm a flaming centrist, a registered Democrat who has voted for Republicans as often as for Democrats, who has voted "No" on proposals for *unsound* increased taxation, and whose very profession engages a search for truth every day. Yes, I know that MSNBC has been accused of leaning as far to the left as Fox leans to the right. The fact that one station views the world one way and another station takes a contrarian view is guaranteed by the United States Constitution. It's called Freedom of Speech – the freedom to communicate your ideas to whomever you choose, whenever you choose to do so.

But don't call it "news" and don't hide behind mock-seriousness and civility. Call it what it is: "Sensationalism," "Yellow Journalism," even "Entertainment." At least Geraldo Rivera had the integrity to realize he was 10% newscaster and 90% entertainer. In Appendix "B" I have capsule-biographed a random selection of Spin Masters on the Right and Spin Masters on the Left - nine on each side, so I can't be accused of bias one way or the other. However, I have included the biographies of the "Masters of the Spin Masters" in the next chapter, since without these controllers, the Spinners would be largely unheard-of.

My annoyance with the breakdown of objectivity is that people who should know better – and who *do* know better if they really *think* instead of simply using their heads as a lump that sits on top of their shoulders, are mesmerized so that they become *believers, disciples* of the new "religion" – the "news" as brought to you by someone with an axe to grind or money to make. And when that happens, people who *should* know better – and who *do* know better – sacrifice their own objectivity and become adherents of polarization and hate. This has the terrible effect of negating any type of negotiation, working together, or compromise. And it has contributed to the United States being well on its way to becoming a third world country.

7

MASTERS OF THE SPIN MASTERS –

THE HEAVIEST HITTER

AND HIS ADJUTANT

Expansion of the "opinion-based" media has, in my opinion, been the single most effective hydra-headed monster in shaping current public opinion. In the last two chapters, I've described some of the *public* faces of opinion makers on both sides. But these talking heads, no matter how popular or influential, are merely *actors*. They would not be where they are without the money, the clout, and the influence of the "studio heads." In the very old days of Hollywood Stars, we watched, "oohed" and "ahhed" the million megawatt allure of the beautiful and talented actors, forgetting that they were nothing more than the "hired help" – hired and fired at the whim of the movie moguls.

Do you *really* think it's any different today? Well … in Hollywood, the studios are now conglomerates, like as not owned by foreign interests. But in politics? There is still one mogul among moguls – and he happens to be foreign-born as well. Meet the heaviest hitter of all, octogenarian Rupert Murdoch.

Keith Rupert Murdoch, AC, KSG, is an Australian-born media magnate, the founder, chairman, and chief executive officer of News Corporation. His empire includes, among other "subjects," Twentieth Century Fox, the Fox Network in all its permutations, the *Wall Street Journal*, HarperCollins Publishers and William Morrow Publishers. Murdoch began with one newspaper in Adelaide, Australia. He then acquired and started other publications in his native Australia before expanding News Corp. into the United Kingdom, the United States, and Asian media markets. Murdoch's first adventure in TV was in the United Kingdom, where he created Sky Television in 1989. In the 2000s, he became a leading investor in satellite television, the film industry and the Internet.

Murdoch was born in Melbourne. His father was a regional newspaper magnate based in Melbourne. The family was wealthy and Rupert was early groomed as the heir apparent by his father. He went off to study philosophy, politics, and economics at Oxford University, but when he was 22, his father died, and Rupert returned from Oxford to take charge of the family business.

His first acquisition on his own was the *Sunday Times* in Perth, Western Australia. He converted it to a tabloid and it became very successful. Over the next few years, Murdoch expanded his holdings by buying up suburban and provincial newspapers in New

South Wales, Queensland, Victoria and the Northern Territory, including the Sydney afternoon tabloid, *The Daily Mirror.* His first venture outside Australia involved the purchase of a controlling interest in the New Zealand daily *Dominion.*

In 1964, Murdoch launched Australia's first national daily newspaper, *The Australian.* It was intended to give Murdoch new respectability as a 'quality' newspaper publisher, as well as greater political influence. In 1972, he acquired the Sydney morning tabloid *The Daily Telegraph.* In that year's election, Murdoch threw his growing power behind the Australian Labor Party under the leadership of Gough Whitlam and duly saw it elected. As the Whitlam government began to lose public support following its re-election in 1974, Murdoch turned against Whitlam and supported the Governor-General's dismissal of the Prime Minister.

Now it was time for Murdoch to turn his attention to Britain. The Commonwealth Bank financed his biggest venture yet, the takeover of the Sunday *News of the World*, which has the largest circulation in Great Britain. When the Mirror group decided to get rid of its mid-market daily newspaper, *The Sun,* in 1969, Murdoch bought it and turned it into a tabloid. By 2006 it was selling three million copies per day. In 1981, he acquired *The Times* and *The Sunday Times*, from Canadian newspaper interests.

During the 1980s and early 1990s, Murdoch's publications supported Margaret Thatcher. At the end of the Thatcher/John Major era, Murdoch switched his support to Tony Blair. In 1986, Murdoch introduced electronic production processes to his newspapers in Australia, Britain, and the United States, leading to substantial reductions in the number of employees involved in the printing process.

Murdoch's satellite network Sky Television incurred massive losses in its early years of operation, but he merged with British Satellite Broadcasting in 1990. The merged company, BSkyB, has dominated the British pay-TV market ever since. Today, Murdoch's News Corporation has subsidiaries in the Bahamas, the Cayman Islands, the Channel Islands and the Virgin Islands.

Murdoch made his initial foray into the United States in 1973, when he purchased the *San Antonio Express-News*. Soon afterwards, he founded *Star*, a supermarket tabloid. In 1976, he purchased the *New York Post*. He became a naturalized citizen of the U.S. in 1985, in order to satisfy the legal requirement that only U.S. citizens were permitted to own American television stations.

In 1995, Murdoch's Fox Network became the object of scrutiny from the FCC when it was alleged that News Ltd.'s Australian base made Murdoch's ownership of Fox illegal. However, the FCC ruled in Murdoch's favor. In the same year, Murdoch announced a deal with MCI Communications to develop a major news website and magazine, *The Weekly Standard*. That same year, News Corp. launched the Foxtel pay television network in Australia.

In 1996, Murdoch entered the cable news market with the Fox News Channel, a 24-hour cable news station. The heavily-funded Fox News constantly bit into CNN's market share and eventually proclaimed itself as "the most-watched cable news channel." In 2004, Fox News Channel boasted nine of the top ten programs on "Cable News."

Meanwhile, in 1993, Murdoch acquired Star TV, a Hong Kong company and one of the biggest satellite TV networks in Asia, for $1 billion. However, the deal did not work out as Murdoch had planned, because the Chinese government placed restrictions on it that prevented it from reaching most of China. In 2003, Murdoch acquired a 34 percent stake in DirecTV, from General Motors for $6 billion. In 2005, News Corp. bought MySpace.com for $580 million. In 2007, Murdoch acquired Dow Jones, publisher of the *Wall Street Journal*. Recently, Murdoch bought out the Turkish TV channel, TGRT, in a partnership with now-deceased Turkish recording mogul Ahmet Ertegün.

Murdoch's publications generally have conservative leanings in comparison with other national newspapers. Murdoch also served on the board of directors of the libertarian Cato Institute. In May 2006, the *Financial Times* reported that Murdoch would be hosting a fundraiser for Senator Hillary Clinton's Senate re-election campaign. In a 2008 interview, Murdoch was asked whether he had "anything to do with the New York Post's endorsement of Barack Obama in the democratic primaries." Without hesitating, Murdoch replied, "Yeah. He's a rock star. It's fantastic. I love what he is saying about education. I don't think he will win Florida, but he will win in Ohio and the election. I am anxious to meet him. I want to see if he will walk the walk."

In October 2008 Murdoch biographer Michael Wolff wrote a *Vanity Fair* story recounting a meeting between Barack Obama, Murdoch, and Murdoch's lieutenant, Roger Ailes, at the Waldorf-Astoria Hotel in New York early that summer. Obama had initially resisted Murdoch's proposals for a meeting, despite senior News Corp. executives having recruited the Kennedys to act as go-betweens. At the meeting Obama complained of Fox News's portrayal of him "as suspicious, foreign, fearsome – just short of a terrorist," while Ailes said it might not have been this way if Obama had "more willingly come on the air instead of so often giving Fox the back of his hand." Murdoch has met every U.S. President since Harry Truman.

Murdoch has been married three times. In 1956 he married Patricia Booker, a former shop assistant and air hostess from Melbourne with whom he had his first child, Prudence. Rupert and Patricia divorced in 1967. In 1967, he married Anna Torv, an Estonian-born journalist working for his Sydney newspaper *The Daily Telegraph.* During his marriage to Anna Torv, a Roman Catholic, Murdoch was awarded the KSG, a papal honor. Torv and Murdoch had three children: Elisabeth, Lachlan, and James. Anna and Rupert divorced in June 1999. She received a settlement of $1.2 billion in assets. Seventeen days after the divorce, Murdoch, then 68, married Chinese-born Wendi Deng, 30, a recent Yale School of Management graduate. Rupert Murdoch has two children with Deng, Grace Helen and Chloe.

Murdoch's eldest son Lachlan was Murdoch's heir apparent before resigning from his executive posts at the end of July 2005. Lachlan's departure left James as the only Murdoch son still directly involved with the company's operations, though Lachlan has agreed to remain on the News Corporation's board. According to the 2010 list of Forbes billionaires, Murdoch is the 117th-richest person in the world, with a net worth of $6.3 billion.

ROGER AILES – MURDOCH'S ADJUTANT

Roger Eugene Ailes, born May 15, 1940, is president of the Fox News Channel and chairman of the Fox Television Stations Group. He was a media consultant for Richard Nixon, Ronald Reagan, and George H. W. Bush, as well as for Rudy Giuliani's first mayoral campaign in 1989. Ailes was born and grew up in Warren, Ohio. He suffers from hemophilia and was often hospitalized as a youth. Ailes graduated in 1962 from Ohio University, receiving a BA.

Ailes' career in television began in Cleveland and Philadelphia, where he started as property assistant (1962) producer (1965) and executive producer (1967–1968) for KYW-TV, for a then-locally produced talk-variety show, *The Mike Douglas Show*. He later became executive producer for the show, which was syndicated nationally.

Richard Nixon called on Ailes to serve as his executive producer of his TV advertising campaign. Nixon's election victory was Ailes's first venture into the political spotlight. His pioneering work was chronicled in *The Selling of the President 1968* by Joe McGinniss. Ailes founded Ailes Communications, Inc., in New York in 1969, and consulted for various businesses and politicians. Ailes served as a political consultant for many Republican candidates during the 70s and 80s. He returned to presidential campaigning as a consultant to Ronald Reagan in the latter stages of the 1984 campaign. He is widely credited with having helped coach Reagan to victory in the second presidential debate with Walter Mondale. In 1987 and 1988, Ailes and Lee Atwater were credited with guiding George H. W. Bush to victory in the Republican primaries, and the later come-from-behind victory over Michael Dukakis.

Ailes came up with the "orchestra pit theory" regarding sensationalist political coverage in the news media, with the question, "If you have two guys on a stage and one guy says, 'I have a solution to the Middle East problem,' and the other guy falls in the orchestra pit, who do you think is going to be on the evening news?" Ailes's last campaign was the unsuccessful effort of Richard Thornburgh for U.S. Senate in Pennsylvania in November 1991. He announced his withdrawal from political consulting in 1992.

Days after the 9/11 attacks, Ailes gave President George W. Bush political advice indicating that the American public would be patient as long as they were convinced that Bush was using the harshest measures possible. The correspondence was revealed in Bob Woodward's book *Bush At War.* Ailes lashed out against Woodward, saying "Woodward got it all screwed up, as usual," and "The reason he's not as rich as Tom Clancy is that while he and Clancy both make stuff up, Clancy does his research first."

In 1991, Ailes convinced a syndicator to bring Rush Limbaugh from radio to television and became executive producer of the late-night show. In 1993, he became president of the cable channel CNBC and began planning another NBC cable channel, *America's Talking*. The new channel debuted on July 4, 1994. Ailes also hosted his own nightly show, *Straight Forward*, an hour-long talk show.

After the announcement of Microsoft and NBC's partnership to create an online and cable news outlet, MSNBC, Ailes left the network in February 1996 and was hired by Rupert Murdoch to create Fox News Channel for News Corporation. In addition, eighty-nine additional employees of NBC left with Ailes to help with the new channel's creation for launch, on October 7, 1996.

After the departure of Lachlan Murdoch from News Corporation, Ailes was named Chairman of the Fox Television Stations Group on August 15, 2005. His current salary is a reported $5 million per year with bonuses and other compensation extra. His total compensation in 2009 was $23 million. In addition to heading Fox News, Ailes also chairs Fox Television Stations and Twentieth Television as well as MyNetwork TV and Fox Business Network.

Ailes' second marriage was to Norma E. Ailes, who had been a television producer with Mission Media Ministries. The two raised one child, a daughter from Norma's earlier relationship. In 1998, hw married Elizabeth Tilson, formerly a television executive, now a homemaker and titular publisher of The Putnam County News and Recorder. They have one son.

Part Four:

THE POLITICS OF FEAR AND

IRRESPONSIBLE STUPIDITY

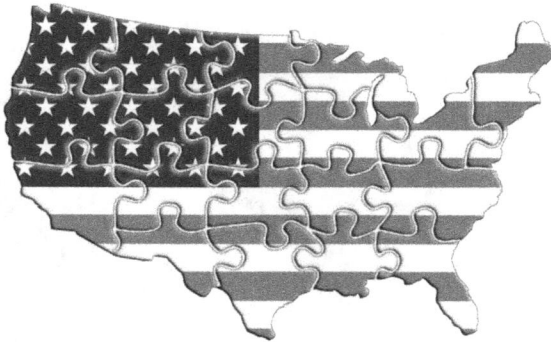

8

PERPETUATING THE POLITICS OF FEAR

Negative campaigning is nothing new. Promising the electorate "something they can count on" is something that started before the ancient Egyptians built the pyramids. The rubric, "Promise them what you have to and pray their memories are short," has been fundamental to politics from time out of mind. "Give them bread and circuses," became entrenched in the political literature of the Roman Empire.

So what's so different about the present state of political affairs in 21st Century America? Simply this: We have unconsciously enshrined in our political consciousness the words attributed to Adolf Hitler (*Mein Kampf*, vol. I, ch. X) and adapted by his propaganda genius, Dr. Josef Goebbels: "*If you repeat a lie often enough, it becomes the truth. If you tell a lie big enough and keep repeating it, people will eventually come to believe it. If you repeat a lie long enough, it becomes truth.*"

Although he may have been one of the most evil geniuses that ever lived, there can be no question that Goebbels was indeed a genius when it came to propaganda. His program almost singlehandedly bound more than fifty million supposedly intelligent, highly cultured people to *Der Fuehrer* for twelve years. Among his more notable quotes:

- "We strive not for truth, but effect. The worst enemy of any propaganda is intellectualism. For the lie to be believable, it should be terrifying. A lie repeated thousands of times becomes a truth."

- "Success is the important thing. Propaganda is not a matter for average minds, but rather a matter for practitioners. It is not supposed to be lovely or theoretically correct. I do not care if I give wonderful, aesthetically elegant speeches, or speak so that women cry. The point of a political speech is to persuade people of what we think right. We do not want to be a movement of a few straw brains, but rather a movement that can conquer the broad masses. Propaganda should be popular, not intellectually pleasing. It is not the task of propaganda to discover intellectual truths."

  - Speech by Joseph Goebbels on 9 January 1928 to an audience of party members at the *Hochschule für Politik*, a series of training talks for Nazi party members in Berlin.

- "One should not as a rule reveal one's secrets, since one does not know if and when one may need them again. The essential English leadership does not depend on intelligence. Rather, it depends on a remarkably stupid thick-headedness. The English follow the principle that when one lies, one should lie big, and stick to it. They keep up their lies, even at the risk of looking ridiculous."

- *"Aus Churchill's Lügenfabrik"* (Churchill's Lie Factory), 12 January 1941, *Die Zeit ohne Beispiel* (Munich: Zentralverlag der NSDAP., 1941), pp. 364-369

* * *

I do not consider Karl Rove, Dick Cheney, or Donald Rumsfeld to be either pillars of honesty or integrity, or, conversely, malignantly evil devils in suits. The Politics of Hate didn't begin with them. However, during the years of the Bush *fils* administration, they appear to have perfected it. They quickly learned that there were no particularly horrendous consequences for lying. Even after it became painfully obvious that "Weapons of Mass Destruction" never existed in Iraq, they kept to the more palatable lie – "No one has ever proved conclusively that there *weren't* Weapons of Mass Destruction – so *there could have been such weapons.* We just haven't be able to find them yet."

I'm sure everyone who reads this book has either heard of – or even been part of – a local scandal, large or small. The pastor ran off with a member of the choir. The manager of the bank embezzled a little bit of money each week so he could support what society expected to be his lifestyle. That well-respected geriatric doctor – the one all the little old ladies loved to death – was found out to be an amoral sexual deviate. The list goes on and on. People's perceived "sins" are really nothing new – they've occurred since the beginning of time in some form or another. Generally everyone loves to hear about a "good scandal," so long as they are not the target. And generally, the scandal will remain "news" for 30 to 60 days – until the *next* juicy scandal rears its titillating head.

9-1-1 was a truly tragic event. We watched with horrified eyes on CNN or one of the networks as that jet plane slammed into the World Trade Center. Thousands of people were killed. It was historically unique in that it was the first time the United States had been "invaded" by a "foreign force." (Never mind that it really *wasn't* the first time – the American Revolution was fought on our soil, the War of 1812 was fought on *our* seas, and the War Between the States (called the Civil War in most history books), pitted brother against brother within the borders of our country).

Yet 9-1-1 has taken on a "Remember the Alamo" (Does *anyone really* remember the Alamo today?) cadence which has propelled the politics of *fear* for the last decade. Every time someone raised the specter of the economy or universal healthcare or the deplorable state of civil rights during the period 2000-2008 (remember the so-called "Patriot Act?"), the Republicans trotted out the need for *Security* because we were sure as hell going to be "*invaded*" by foreigners – "ragheads" – if we didn't tow the party line. And they never let you forget 9-1-1! Never. The "reasoning" behind the Republican propaganda seems to be curiously similar to the Nazi propaganda of the 1930's: *Sometimes the security of the nation is more important than individual "civil rights"* (which is something preached by the Commie-dominated A.C.L.U., and you *know* those people go to court at the drop of a hat to protect the *whackos* who are lucky enough to live in the Land of the Free and the Home of the Brave). *And if you want proof that our security measures are succeeding, you have it right before your very eyes: we have not been invaded or attacked since we put these security measures in place!*

Well … yes … I suppose that's right. But does proof that it hasn't yet happened mean it never *will* happen? Has anyone stopped to consider, for example, that government inspectors, even under the most stringent George W. Bush days, inspected only *6%* of all shipments coming into the U.S. from abroad? It doesn't take a rocket scientist to figure out that *94 out of every 100* shipments did *not* get inspected at all?

Let's take our thinking one step further. Those responsible for the events of September 11, 2001 did not constitute a large, organized army backed by a numerically superior armed force. At the very most, there were a dozen or so active participants. Has the need for *security* that we boasted about during the Bush years stopped every illegal immigrant from pouring across our porous borders? I think not.

The "Swift Boat" approach to politics is a perfect example of perpetuating the politics of fear. "Swift Vets and POWs for Truth," formerly known as the "Swift Boat Veterans for Truth (SBVT)" was a political group of alleged American veterans and former prisoners of war of the Vietnam War, formed during the 2004 presidential election campaign for the sole purpose of opposing John Kerry's candidacy for the presidency. The group disbanded and ceased operations on May 31, 2008. SBVT asserted that Kerry was "unfit to serve" as President based upon his alleged "willful distortion of the conduct" of American servicemen during that war, and his alleged "withholding and/or distortion of material facts" as to his own conduct during that war. This claim caused tremendous controversy during the election, particularly because the "veterans" were partisans who had not been in a place to assess Kerry, while several other Vietnam veterans who served alongside Kerry or under his command disputed the criticisms and supported Kerry in his presidential aspirations. Of the 3,500 Swift boat sailors who served in Vietnam, the names of some 250 appeared on the group's statement against Kerry. Most did not serve at the same time or in the same place as Kerry.

No members of SBVT were aboard Kerry's boat during any of the incidents for which he was decorated. The only member of SBVT who was present at the Silver Star incident, Rood's crew member Larry Clayton Lee, praised Kerry's tactics and stated that he earned his Silver Star. However, he stated that "based on discussions with other SBVT members," he came to question whether Kerry deserved other medals for incidents at which he was not present.

Since the 2004 election, the term "Swift Boating" has become a common expression for a campaign attacking opponents by questioning their credibility and patriotism. The term is most often used with the pejorative meaning of a smear campaign.

9

What's Good for Keeping _Me_ in Power – or Getting _Me_ Back in Power – is Good for The U.S.A.

RIGHT OR WRONG, I LOVE MY COUNTRY – AS LONG AS I GET TO SAY WHAT'S RIGHT.

The past few years may seem a bit vicious, but obstructionism is nothing new. Throughout our history, there have been economic cycles of boom and bust, and, as much as politicians want you to think otherwise, they are not entirely – nor even substantially – based on who's in office at that moment. Those boom and bust waves will take as long they take, and arguing about who's responsible doesn't solve the problem.

The current economic downtown is widespread, well beyond our borders in fact. So who do we blame? George Bush? Nicholas Sarkozy, the former President of France? The Prime Minister of Hungary? The banks, who are easy targets? Or, perhaps, our own greed. It is very easy to use the banks, the mortgage bankers, the mortgage brokers, and something called "stated income," as whipping boys for the morass that now beleaguers us. But stop for a moment and consider: Banks are in the business of making money. If they make it too easy for us to borrow, is this a disease that permeates the entire society?

The current recession / depression is fueled by the same factor that fueled the Great Depression of the late 1920s and early 1930s – unbridled greed.

In the late 1920s the stock market rose to dizzying heights. Quick! Get into the market, even if you have to go on "margin" (borrowing against your expectations) to do it, because you'll miss the fast-rising elevator, or maybe if you get in too late you won't make as much as your neighbor made.

In the early 2000s, the motivation was the same: buy a house for $250,000 *now* because if you don't, it will go up to $650,000 before you know it. The mathematics are so simple any fool can understand them: the house will surely go up to $1,000,000 in the next five years or so. If you buy the house now, today, you'll be able to make a profit before taxes of $750,000. On the other hand, if you wait a couple of years when the market is at $650,000, you'll only make $350,000, less than half the profit. Oh, and by the way, the tax laws are written so that you have 18 months to reinvest in a like house, so taxes are on the "never never," as our British cousins say.

What? You can't afford the $250,000 house? Never mind. Your friendly banker will finance 100% of the purchase price. Why not? His "investment" is absolutely secure. If, for some reason, you can't afford to make the payments on the $250,000 and you lose the home to the bank in 2 years, the bank has $650,000 security on a $250,000 loan, and who do you think will profit? So the bank has a no-risk bet, as long as real estate prices keep rising, and since real estate is finite – there's only so much of it in the United States – how can the prices *not* keep rising.

Then, just about the time the $250,000 house was worth $650,000, the person who tried to buy the house for $650,000 could not afford the payment. No problem at all! The banks would loan money at a "variable interest rate," or, even better, at "negative amortization." That meant that your payments would be much lower than they'd be on a straight fixed-rate loan. The 30-year fixed rate mortgage suddenly became a 40-year fixed rate mortgage, then a 50-year fixed-rate mortgage, and *voila*! You could afford to make the payments on the $650,000 loan even if you couldn't *really* afford to. You see, the "go easy on the borrower" loan would last for anywhere from 3-5 years, and by that time your house would be worth $1,000,000. You'd "refinance" the home then, and actually come out with a profit.

But all of these greed-based hopes depended on the up-spiral never ending. Sort of like a completely legal "Ponzi scheme." And when the bubble finally burst – as bubbles always do – the person who bought the house at $250,000 might still be "all right," but the one who bought the house for $650,000 or more was "under water."

Americans are, by nature, impetuous and, even more so, impatient. We live in a generation on which credit cards were the "mother's milk" of our existence. Why wait for something you could have *right now*? Rather than be weaned off credit by the old, responsible system of "lay away," *i.e.*, pay for what you want over time and when it was paid off you got the product, we became addicted to the *now* mentality – if we didn't have everything wanted *right now*, we would somehow be less socially acceptable, viewed as "poor folk" by our neighbors.

The vast majority of us simply ignored a basic economic truth: *You can't borrow yourself out of debt.*

By the end of 2005, most economists could easily foresee that we were headed for a financial "train wreck." By the end of 2007, most of *us* knew that train wreck was about fifty feet away and there wasn't damned thing we could do about it. And we knew that no matter how hard we slammed on the brakes, the train wasn't going to stop in fifty feet, or, for that matter, two hundred feet.

It took us the better part of ten years to get to the scene of the economic disaster. But Americans being what they are, refused to realize the depth of the "recession" (why not call a spade a "shit shovel" and call it a Depression?) and refused to realize that if it took us this long to get *into* this mess, we sure as hell weren't going to get *out* of this mess in a year or two.

Yet, that's exactly what we demanded, and when candidate Obama warned us, "This recession may not go away in my first term in office, it may take years," we cavalierly said, "Oh, sure, right!" not believing it for one minute. He would be the "man on the white horse." After all, didn't he campaign on the slogan of "Change we can believe in?" And, of course, that meant that if he was elected President in November 2008, all of the stink and shadow of the economic downturn would be erased in his first 100 days in office. He promised an economic stimulus package which we fooled ourselves into believing would cut the unemployment rate to almost nothing in six months. He promised a health care system that would cover everyone. And, he promised, "95% of you won't be paying a dime more in taxes than you're paying now."

Of course, the "not-so-loyal-opposition," which had celebrated *laissez faire* capitalism when it was profitable, immediately took the Holier-than-Thou attitude that, "You can't borrow your way out of debt," and where the hell was all that stimulus money going to come from?

The Republicans shouted, "You caused it!" You promised you'd fix it! You'd better do it right now!" ("Of course, don't expect *us* to vote for anything you propose.") And somehow, the obstructionist politics of the Conservatives caught fire as the Republicans, relying on Americans' short memory, set out to prove that the Democratic-controlled Congress was doing nothing.

Does anyone remember the big fight over the healthcare bill? Yes. Does anyone recall the Opposition publicly putting forth a single specific alternative to what the Majority party proposed? I don't. Rather, the Opposition maintained that the Democrats were headed in the wrong direction, that they would spend our government into bankruptcy, that the government would run your life and take away your freedom of choice. In short, the Republicans successfully used obstructionist tactics to prove that the Democrats were doing nothing – that they were doing no better than the preceding Congress, which they had condemned for doing nothing.

How could such idiocy possibly have succeeded? The Democrats had sixty seats in the Senate – enough to defeat *any* filibuster. They had such a commanding majority in the House that there was no conceivable way they could fail to pass the President's proposals for social programs. How could the Democrats *not* have succeeded by *quickly* moving this country into a new, more socially equitable condition?

And yet, that's exactly what they did!

The Democrats could have – and *should have* – gone on every network or cable channel they could, held town meetings all over the country, and delivered a frank, clear message: *This is all bullshit! You voted us in! You gave us a mandate to change the direction of our society. We are going to give it to you quickly, decisively, and definitively, and in five years you will see how right you were to vote us into office!*

But that's exactly what the Democrats did not do.

Rather, they did what American politicians have done since time out of mind: they squandered their mandate and they lost their direction, one little chip at a time, not by fighting the Republicans, but by fighting one another.

Numerically, the Republicans have generally had a smaller voting base than the Democrats throughout the Twentieth and the early Twenty-first centuries. So why have the Republicans commanded the Presidency and Congress in the majority of elections during the past forty years? The answer is almost too easy to be true: the Democrats have split into factions and fractures and fissures, while the Republicans have cobbled together a united front. There's something comfortable about thinking, "If these guys are all reading from the same sheet of music and the other guys are killing each other, there must be a reason the Republicans are all hanging together. They must know something we don't know."

Let's face it, when a song is being sung by a choir where everyone is singing in harmony and singing the same song, it sounds a lot more pleasing, a lot more comforting, than a mishmash where everyone is singing their own tune in their own rhythm. For the vast majority of classical music and art lovers, Beethoven sounds far better than Arnold Schoenberg and Rembrandt is much easier to understand than Andy Warhol.

But lately, the Republicans seem to have made a few missteps of their own.

No matter what the "Left" and the "Right" will try to tell you, the United States of America is essentially a *centrist* society. No politician in recent memory handled that knowledge better than former President Bill Clinton. By co-opting the center and eschewing "fringe" politics, he maintained his popularity, even in the face of the Monica Lewinsky scandal. Today, he is almost universally revered as a respected elder statesman.

Although the Republicans "recaptured" the House and eliminated the filibuster-proof Democratic hold on the Senate in 2010, they are going to have to deal with a large, very ugly monster, which may turn around and "kick them in the arse" in 2012: the politics of irresponsible stupidity in the guise of a movement called the "Tea Party Express." The two most vocal new "superstars" are emblematic of the intellectual understanding and acumen of the movement.

THE NEW "SUPERSTARS" – "THE EMPEROR HAS NO CLOTHES." – SARAH PALIN, THE TEA PARTY EXPRESS, CHRISTINE O'DONNELL, AND THE POLITICS OF STUPIDITY

SARAH PALIN

The "You betcha'!" mama bear of them all, the "soccer mom," the "pit bull with lipstick." This former mayor of a town in Alaska so small that before the 2008 election 98% of Americans had never even heard of it, struggled through those world-renowned centers of sophisticated education, Hawaii Pacific University, North Idaho College, and Matanuska-Susitna College before taking a bachelor's degree in communications / journalism from the University of Idaho. She worked as a sportscaster and sports reporter before going into town politics, eventually a governorship, and later still the glamour of being thrust into the light as a candidate for Vice President of the United States – a heartbeat away form the Presidency!

John McCain's top campaign strategist and Republican super-spinmaster Steve Schmidt, said in an interview on CBS's "60 Minutes" that Sarah Palin was dishonest as the GOP's vice-presidential nominee and that her untruths have done long-term damage to her public image. "There were numerous instances that she said things that were not accurate that ultimately, the campaign had to deal with, and that opened the door to criticism that she was being untruthful. … [T]hat is something that continues to this day."

Schmidt cited an ethics report on the then-Alaska governor from her home state on an investigation into whether she had improperly used her government position. "She went out and said, 'This report completely exonerates me,' and, in fact, it didn't. It's the equivalent of saying down is up and up is down. It was provably, demonstrably untrue."

Mark Helprin and John Heilemann recounted the days leading up to Palin's shocking selection. With Democrat-turned-Independent Senator Joe Lieberman seen as untenable for the conservative Republican base, McCain's aides were desperate for a similarly outside-the-box pick. So, recalling McCain's urgent need to shake up a race he appeared likely to lose, Halperin said the Arizona senator wound up with a last-minute selection of a "virtual stranger." Her debut speech at the GOP's convention won wide acclaim, but immediately afterward it was clear to McCain's aides that she had significant deficiencies. Even after crash-course tutorials by campaign aides following the convention, Palin was still woefully uninformed about basic policy issues. "She still didn't really understand why there was a North Korea and a South Korea," Heilemann told Anderson Cooper. "She was still regularly saying that Saddam Hussein had been behind 9/11." Palin was ignorant about many matters of national security policy, which could have been forgiven, but she hurt herself in the now-infamous interview with CBS's Katie Couric by not adequately preparing, and by letting herself be distracted by an obsession about her political standing in Alaska. Even on the morning of the Couric interview, Palin was focused on a candidate questionnaire from the small newspaper that circulates in her

Wasilla hometown. And this is, perhaps, the best known "Tea party express" beacon of intellectual enlightenment.

CHRISTINE O'DONNELL

Although she was – mercifully – soundly thrashed in the 2010 election, losing by some 17 percentage points, we may not have heard the last of Christine O'Donnell. Trying to be a Sarah Palin clone, O'Donnell, the 3-time (in 5 years) candidate for the United States Senate from Delaware, seems never to have held a long-term job that called for her to use her brain in her life. This Tea party "golden girl" attended Fairleigh Dickinson University in Teaneck, New Jersey, where she initially majored in theater. In 1993, she attended the graduation ceremony but did not receive a degree. O'Donnell's 2006 senate website stated that she was a "graduate of Fairleigh Dickinson University" and articles that reported on her 2006 and 2008 campaigns said she had a degree from that institution. On September 3, 2010, her campaign said her degree "had been held up for years by unpaid student loans and tuition" and showed reporters a letter from Fairleigh Dickinson indicating she had been awarded her degree *two days earlier, on September 1, 2010*. Her Bachelor of Arts degree is in English literature with a concentration in communications.

In a 2005 lawsuit, O'Donnell implied she was working toward a Master's degree at Princeton University. She later acknowledged she had never taken graduate courses there. She has claimed she studied at Oxford University in England; but her "studies" consisted of taking a single course run by an unaffiliated institution that was renting space at Oxford. As of late September 2010, O'Donnell claimed she had studied Constitutional Government at Claremont Graduate University near Los Angeles, California. That University said it had no record for her. O'Donnell said in response, "I never established a LinkedIn profile or authorized anyone to do so on my behalf." Yet, days earlier, O'Donnell's staff, when asked specifically about her profile on three occasions by the Associated Press and *The Washington Post*, made no reference to the profile being unauthorized. A few days later, when O'Donnell's possible academic embellishments became an issue, O'Donnell's staff asked LinkedIn to remove the profile.

Still, this attractive TV-savvy climber appeared on CNN in a nationally-televised debate. She steadfastly refused to answer whether she believed in Evolution (she has said publicly she does not believe in it, and "I'd like to sit around and have you show me a monkey evolve.") She then said she would do away with the "liberal" Supreme Court. When asked to name a recent United States Supreme Court decision with which she disagreed, she was a "deer caught in the headlights," and asked the moderator, "You obviously have a specific case in mind." When the moderator responded, "No, I am asking *you* to name a specific case," Ms. O'Donnell's response was, "It'll be up on my website tomorrow," before she stumbled into naming *Roe v. Wade*, a case that was decided nearly 39 years ago, as a "recent case."

And this "political phenomenon" wants to be a leader of the United States? When's the next boat leaving for Vanuatu?

THE OBAMA RESPONSE

On April 19, 2009, Senior White House Adviser David Axelrod, when asked about the Tea Party protests on CBS News, said, "I think any time that you have severe economic conditions, there is always an element of disaffection that can mutate into something that's unhealthy. The thing that bewilders me is this President just cut taxes for ninety-five percent of the American people. So I think the tea bags should be directed elsewhere, because he certainly understands the burden that people face."

Ten days later, President Obama commented on the Tea Party protests as follows: "When you see, ... those of you who are watching certain news channels on which I'm not very popular — and you see folks waving tea bags around... let me just remind them that I am happy to have a serious conversation about how we are going to cut our health care costs down over the long term, how we're going to stabilize Social Security. But let's not play games and pretend that the reason is because of the Recovery Act, because that's just a fraction of the overall problem we've got. We are going to have to tighten our belts, but we're going to have to do it in an intelligent way. And we've got to make sure that the people who are helped are working American families, and we're not suddenly saying that the way to do this is to eliminate programs that help ordinary people and give more tax cuts to the wealthy. We tried that formula for eight years. It did not work. And I don't intend to go back to it."

On April 15, 2010, Obama noted the passage of 25 different tax cuts over the past year, including tax cuts for 95% of working Americans. He then remarked, "So I've been a little amused over the last couple of days where people have been having these rallies about taxes. You would think they would be saying 'thank you.' That's what you'd think."

On September 20, 2010, at a town hall discussion sponsored by CNBC, Obama challenged the Tea Party movement to *get specific about how they would cut government debt and spending.* "The challenge for the Tea Party movement is to identify specifically what would you do. *It's not enough just to say, 'get control of spending.' I think it's important for you to say, I'm willing to cut veterans'* *benefits, or I'm willing to cut Medicare or Social Security benefits, or I'm willing to see these taxes go up. What you can't do -- which is what I've been hearing a lot from the other side -- is say we're going to control government spending, we're going to propose $4 trillion of additional tax cuts, and that magically somehow things are going to work."*

10

MY GOD'S BETTER THAN YOUR GOD.

I first heard that term during the George W. Bush administration, when some general or other, in a remark he thought was private and off the record, let slip the reason he thought America would win the war in Iraq: the Christian God was better than the Muslim god. The brilliant poet, Tina Louise, wrote *My God's Better than Your God*, which beautifully sums up all that is truly wrong about so much of the politics of hate in our – and other – nations:

My god's better than your god,
My special book tells me so,
It tells me how to think, who to love,
And how my life should go.

My god's better than your god,
He waits only for me,
Your name's not on his list,
You are my enemy.

My god's better than your god,
His book is filled with truth,
Your book's all wrong you see,
I have all the proof.

My god's better than your god,
His ways are just and right,
His laws are like a roadmap,
That guide me to the light.

My god's better than your god,
Yours is weird and wrong,
I have never heard of him,
And he's been around too long.

My god's better than your god,
He's all shiny and real,
Your god belongs in hell,
He's not the real deal.

My god's better than your god,
Cause he's without sin,
You're a heathen non-believer,
Not good enough for him.

My god's better than your god,
Yours has a silly name,
And your book is stupid,
Really dumb and lame.

I will go to heaven
Cause I'm better than you,
I can do anything,
I'm amongst the chosen few....

Cause my god's better than your god,

You have to say its true,
Cause if you don't,
My god will come,
And make you suffer till you do.[1]

What is so unfortunate is that in America, no matter what religion we espouse, many of us really do think our religion is the only *true* religion and *other people* practice pseudo-religions are have cultures than are "a little bit less than ours." Hitler's concept of the "subhuman" seems to have returned – to our shores – in numbers unimagined since the days of the Ku Klux Klan and other remarkably dangerous, un-American absurdities.

THE "N" WORD AND OTHER CHOICE EPITHETS

In a perfect America – the America we pride ourselves on being, the America we're *supposed* to be, the "N" words and other choice names for "other" religions, national origins, and such, would be anathema, unmentionable, and I'd be justifiably stoned – and I mean with real rocks and clods of dirt, not psychedelic drugs. But this is the land of far too many hypocrites. The same God that is "better than your God," translates into "in" jokes and comments among

---

[1] The poet (not the actress) Tina Louise was born in London in 1962, but was whisked off to Australia at aged four, then on to Hong Kong at 12. She returned to the UK in her early 20's. The reason for all the travel was her mother's employment in the horse racing industry. Tina Louise has lived and traveled in Belgium, Luxembourg and Spain; been a waitress, a writer, a broadcaster, nightclub manager and much else in between. Since 1987, she has been a mother and since 2004 a grandmother. She presently resides in the North of England writing website copy. She has a monthly column in an English language newspaper in Spain. Poetry became her passion since re-discovering it in July 2004. Her website is www.Tinalouise.co.uk.

each of "our" small segments of society. And don't mistake what I say: *Every* small segment of society thinks itself "just a little bit better" than others within that society.

When I was ten years old, standing on Pico Boulevard in Los Angeles, in front of my father and mother's delicatessen, three much bigger, tougher-looking boys came by and contemptuously growled, "Dirty little Jew, go save your pennies." I was hurt, because I didn't understand what I had done to upset them or cause them to say such things. I didn't even know them and never saw them again.

But even though we Jews were "enlightened" and "above that kind of thing," that wasn't quite true. We might not have called African-Americans the "N-word," but we referred to them as "*Schvartzes,*" which was just as bad. And we saw non-Jews as "*Goyim.*" A non-Jewish male was a "*Sheygetz*" and a gentile female was a "*Shiksa.*" Even among European / American Jews, there was a distinct "pecking order." The German Jews thought themselves infinitely superior to their come-lately cousins from Eastern Europe. The Orthodox Jews thought the Conservative Jews and the Reform Jews were not really Jews at all. Am I shocking you be demeaning my own religion and culture? No. It's just that Jews suffer from the same disease as everyone else: *We happen to be human.*

Over the years, I've learned about the prejudices of many human groupings, and I must admit there are many more I *don't* know about. But if you think and reflect honestly, all of us – even you and I – have certain prejudices, certain views of people who are, for whatever reason, "less than we are," or "less intelligent or enlightened" than we are. To many who read this book, I may seem to be "Republican bashing," whether or not *I* see it that way.

I will admit to one prejudice that I have had all my life – and still do. I get terminally annoyed when someone has a good brain (as we *all* do) and does not use it to *think critically.* I get frustrated when someone says, "No," just because it's easier than saying "Yes." And I find it hard to take someone who accepts something "because it's always been that way" and "if it ain't broke, don't fix it."

In 1883, Jewish immigrant Emma Lazarus wrote the poem *The New Colossus*, a part of which has become part of our national lore. It is engraved on the Statute of Liberty.

> **"Give me your tired, your poor,**
> **Your huddled masses yearning to breathe free,**
> **The wretched refuse of your teeming shore.**
> **Send these, the homeless, tempest-tost to me,**
> **I lift my lamp beside the golden door!"**

That was then. This is the Twenty-First Century. In the late Nineteenth and Early Twentieth Centuries, there were mass immigrations to our shores: Jews – "Hebes" from Central and Eastern Europe, who stuck to money like glue; "Eyetalians" from Sunny Italy (who everybody knows were affiliated with "The Mafia") Irishmen (who were dumb cops, who drank way too much, and who were nearly always so stoned out of their mind that they had no need for women); "Portagees" and "Pollacks," (and who the hell needed *them?*). There were a bunch of "Chinks," which meant just about everyone who had Asian forebears. Stereotypes were as abundant then as they are now.

But after World War II, there was a new wave of immigrants and they came from the *other* side of the world. The Japs were an OK bunch – in South Africa under the Apartheid regime they were actually classified as *Honorary Whites*! But we lumped the rest of those "Chinks" – Chinese, Koreans, Filipinos, Vietnamese, Thais, Southeast Asians, and such – together, since they had yellow skin and slant eyes and looked pretty much the same, although we had to admit that their food wasn't all that bad – except for raw fish and *kimchi*, which smelled like the underside of a toilet bowl, and stuff like that.

And then, a bunch of "Wetbacks" swam across the Rio Grande from Mexico, and all hell broke loose, because they soaked up welfare and wanted everything for nothing.

So the land of the free and the home of the brave – the "Golden Land," the land which had been built on the backs, the hearts, and the brains of our polyethnic immigrant population – the "melting pot" which was *never* a melting pot but a "salad bowl" – started to change in ugly ways and to become a land that welcomed the *White European* tired and poor – as long as they weren't *too* poor and didn't *really* create a burden for the rest of us. After all, *we* were already here. We had *our* "Piece of the Rock," and everything was just fine, thank you very much.

And then things got even meaner and uglier. "They've got darker skin, slant eyes, and they wear those *kaffiyehs* – ragheads. Keep 'em off our precious land of the free." Perhaps the most internationally embarrassing moment came in 2010, when a *serious* movement tried to keep Muslims – *American Muslims* – from building a community center for peace within two or three blocks of "Ground Zero," where, on September 11, 2001, a group of *less than twenty* "terrorists" from overseas carried out an attack which destroyed New York City's World Trade Center, killing some 5,000 people.

The circuitous reasoning adopted by those who would kill freedom of religion and freedom of association in America was, "Those ragheads caused it. They're Muslims and everyone knows *all* Muslims – most of them anyway – are a bunch of sicko terrorists controlled by the *Al Khaida* and *Osama ben What's-his-name*." And what's so scary is those who wish to keep the Muslims off property they legitimately purchased and developed, have built a following substantial enough that they may just push through their heinous scheme.

I know I seem to have picked unmercifully on Christine O'Donnell as the poster child for political stupidity, but I was watching a newcast in mid-October 2010 when she actually had the *chutzpah* – the unmitigated gall – to ask, "Where in the Constitution does it say there is a separation of Church and State?"

Excuse me.

While Ms. O'Donnell may be linguistically correct in that there is nothing in the specific and precise language of the United States

Constitution that says, in words of one syllable or less, which Ms. O'Donnell might understand, "There is se-pa-ra-tion of Church and State," but it seems to me that the words of the First Amendment, "Congress shall make no law respecting an establishment of religion, or prohibiting the free exercise thereof ..." as interpreted by the United States Supreme Court for generations, should be understood by an intelligent third grader.

Or has Christianity suddenly become our "state religion?" And if so, *which* branch of Christianity should predominate? Roman Catholicism? Fundamentalist Protestantism? I'm reminded of the words written by the German pastor Martin Niemöller in addressing the Nazi menace:

> They came first for the Communists,
> and I didn't speak up because I wasn't a Communist.
> Then they came for the trade unionists,
> and I didn't speak up because I wasn't a trade unionist.
> Then they came for the Jews,
> and I didn't speak up because I wasn't a Jew.
> Then they came for me
> and by that time no one was left to speak up.

Again I say, "Wake Up, America!" Think of the beacon of light we have been to the nations – the light of fairness and morality and openness. And tremble at what we could become is we don't start using our minds and the morality – the morality that the God who is the *same* God for *all* of us – has prescribed in *every* religion (including the "heathen Muslims").

"Wake Up, America while there's still time. Before it's too late!"

PART FIVE:

SOLVING THE "ISSUES"
THAT DIVIDE US - WHICH ARE
TRULY *NON-ISSUES*

11

DRIVING THE PRIUS OF POLITICS

AND ECONOMICS

By the late 1950's, we had become used to big, snazzy-looking *American* behemoths – cars that were models of "planned obsolescence" that we traded in every two or three years, and which had exhausted their useful life by 100,000 miles at the most. Think the Cadillac Eldorado with its long-swept fins, the Buick, the Mercury Montclair, and the ads for Plymouth – "Suddenly it's 1960!" Oh, sure, there were some foreign cars that reached our shore – the Mercedes Benz, which was the ethereal dream – or the Jaguar, or the Rolls Royce. A lot of "hippie types" even bought a funny-looking little car originally designed under Hitler – the "People's Car" – the *Volkswagen*, which many called "the pregnant roller skate." There were small, cheap foreign cars that were of no better quality than what Americans were building back then: such "classics" as the Nash Metropolitan, the Renault Dauphine, the Opel Kadet, and the Fiat 850 sports car, but since they were "European" they had a certain panache.

In the 1960's Japan started exporting cars to the United States – specifically the Datsun (which became better known when it changed its marque to the company name, Nissan), the Toyota, the Honda, and the Mazda. Americans laughed derisively back then and referred to these small, economical upstart cars as "Rice burners – ha, ha, ha!" These were "different" cars indeed. For one thing, they got much higher than normal gas mileage. For another, they lasted much longer than American cars, were built to much higher quality standards, and were decidedly more dependable. *They didn't break down and you stopped at the gas pump much less frequently.*

General Motors and Chrysler laughed and laughed. By the mid-1990's, they didn't know what had hit them. The government had to bail out Chrysler and GM watched the steady erosion of its sales. Of the "big three" only Ford had the foresight to learn from the Germans and the Japanese. By the late 1990's, the American manufacturers were crying "Unfair!" If Americans continued buying these Japanese imports, Americans would lose their jobs.

In 2001 Toyota and Honda introduced the hybrid car to America. What?!?! How *dare* they? The American manufacturers derided the hybrids by saying, "It's not time to buy one of those newfangled cars. You'll see … they haven't gotten the bugs out yet. They're unsafe. They could catch on fire if they were hit from behind." Turns out, Toyota had been marketing its Prius and Honda had been selling its Insight in Japan since 1997. They'd had four years to work out the bugs.

It's now 2012. My wife and I own two Priuses – a 2001, which has never given us a day of trouble, and a 2005, which generally gets between 42 and 46 miles per gallon and can keep up with anything on the road. Same thing – not a day of trouble – and not a day of "special" maintenance requirements.

And how did the American manufacturers deal with this new phenomenon? By introducing ever bigger, "safer," costlier, more muscular cars that used even more fuel than earlier American models. Think the *Hummer* as the penultimate example of overweening insanity and "keep ahead of the Joneses" mentality at a time when gasoline was going up to $4.00 a gallon in the United States – still less than *half* the price of gasoline in Europe. But that's OK – we were at war in Iraq and Afghanistan and we needed to look ever more *macho* by driving something that looked like it was designed to carry troops and got all of 10 miles per gallon.

Guess what eventually happened? For the past several years, the Toyota Prius has been the best-selling car in America, while the Hummer had all the staying power of the dinosaur. The last I heard, GM was trying to unload that loser on some unsuspecting Chinese company. Meanwhile, some "legacy" makes - Oldsmobile, Plymouth, Pontiac, and Mercury were killed off, and some "newer" American marques – Saturn and Hummer died an unlamented death.

How does this translate into solving The Politics of Hate? What does this discussion about cars have to do with re-creating America as a first world country again? Nothing. And everything.

At the time the Prius was designed and created, Japan was facing some very difficult economic problems. The flying-high economy of Japan's 1980's had crashed and burned. Japan has very few natural resources. OPEC was forcing the price of oil up more and more each year. Japan imports 100% of its petroleum. But Japan – like Germany, India, and China – has one very specific natural resource that ensures its continuing vitality: the *human* resource of creativity and quality-orientation – *pride* in what their country manufactures.

In the early 1990's, the Japanese had not yet perfected the fuel cell car or the electric car. The Americans *could have* perfected such a vehicle, but the big three had long ago purchased all of the existing technology, *and then they had carefully put that technology in some back drawer, while announcing to the world that they were "working on" the new technology!* You see, it was simply much cheaper for the American companies to use the *existing* technology which had been around since the very early 1900's and simply adjust the *outside skin* of their "new" cars to popular tastes.

The Japanese manufacturers were not big enough or powerful enough to take on the Big Three at that time. All they had going for them was innovation and guts. So while the Japanese would have to work for a longer time to perfect their own home-grown fuel cell or electric car, they *could* produce a *combination car* – a *hybrid* car which would utilize a 4-cylinder, efficient gasoline engine *and* an electric motor, which, while not "the perfect answer" still allowed for a credible car which would get *three times the gas mileage of standard gasoline-powered cars.*

They took a chance – just like the early motorcars took a chance that the public would embrace the new technology and move away from the centuries-old horse and buggy. And look what happened!

So it is with politics. Maybe we are not yet ready to wholeheartedly embrace 100% of what the "liberals" want or 100% of what the "conservatives" want, but instead of trying to kill off *every part* of new ideas, wouldn't it be much more constructive – and wouldn't it solve many more problems? – if we constructed a "hybrid" system that allowed Americans the greatest flexibility and freedom *while we designed a more perfect society?* Can the answer to that question really be in doubt? Particularly when we realize that the world's natural resources – whether they are Republican, Democratic, Libertarian, Tea Party, or Green Party – are being depleted at a faster rate than ever?

Case in point: I have been writing books for over twenty years. Until now, those books have all used paper – lots of paper – whether they were hard cover or soft cover books. I have been practicing law for 46 years. I can think of no industry that has used more paper on a regular basis than law. Have you ever looked through a stack of medical records? How many trees were regularly consumed by a hospital's daily output of paper records? By the mid-1990's, the price of paper was skyrocketing just as the supply of trees was rapidly dwindling. What has happened in the last ten years? Without politicizing what happened, and without giving credit (or blame) to Republicans or Democrats, there has been a profound revolution.

Today, at least 90% of the paper which had been used in the law industry is no longer even relevant. The federal government (with the exception of the United States Supreme Court) uses mandatory electronic filing in every United States Court. Using heavy, beautiful books to perform legal research is passé. With the coming of legal research tools such as Westlaw and Lexis, books are best used as doorstops. Of course, this has the concomitant advantage that the excess room we needed for large law offices to house hundreds of volumes of law books is no longer necessary. And mailing voluminous legal documents? E-mail does it better, cheaper, and faster. I recently had a case in Federal Court where there were nearly 10,000 pages of documents. The particular district where the case was filed (and subsequently appealed) required *either forty* copies of those documents *or* the documents could be copied into pdf format and filed electronically. Try a very simple calculation: multiply 10,000 sheets of paper by 40 at a cost of 10 cents per copied sheet, plus mail. Don't even count the number of trees felled to make these copies. Just consider the cost savings by electronically copying and filing.

During the past few years, I have been plagued with the illnesses attendant on growing older (no one ever said growing old was easy) – from cancer to high blood pressure to high cholesterol to … you name it. At least 90% of the doctors and hospitals I have gone to are now "paperless." A friend of mine, an outstanding orthopedic surgeon, loves to golf and regularly goes to Hawaii or Ireland or Scotland to do so. He takes his entire office with him – it will fit on a minicomputer in a small corner of his carry-on suitcase.

Finally, more paper has been used in the book industry than in any other enterprise on earth. Earlier this year, Amazon reported that for every 100 paper books sold, that company sold *143* electronic books on its Kindle apparatus. They could – and did – sell those books at less than half the price of conventional books, and, shock of shocks, the Kindle actually had the heft and *feel* of a "real" book. What's more, you could get *hundreds* – perhaps even *thousands* – of "books" on a single Kindle E-book reader. Amazon is certainly not the only entrepreneur to embrace the new technology. Barnes & Noble has the Nook; Sony has its own reading device; and the new I-Pad proclaims its "reader" is the easiest of all to use. It certainly won't be long before we have the Wal-Martization of the reading devices. After all, when the first hand-held electronic calculator came out, it retailed for over $300. Today you can get a faster, more powerful, smaller, lighter unit that does much, much more for anywhere from $3 to $12 a unit.

I propose a novel, previously untried solution in the political arena: *Let's stop wasting time, energy, emotions, and money fighting and arguing about non-issues. Rather, let us work together and come up with acceptable "hybrid" solutions which will work best for the greatest number of people, regardless of their political, religious, or other persuasions, so we can best mover our society forward.*

Think it can't be successfully done?

On October 12, 2010, 33 miners, who had been trapped in a mine in Chile for 69 days (!) were rescued – *every one of them alive.* The world cheered and cried happy tears. For more than a day, the terrors of a useless war in Afghanistan, the acrimony of the political season in America, and the spewing of hatred was simply wiped off the front pages as a truly *meaningful, miraculous* event – with a large number of very *human heroes* – emerged to take the spotlight.

Why not spend time going through the suggestions I have made? *Challenge them – that's what freedom of expression is all about. Better them!* I certainly don't possess a monopoly on brain cells or good ideas. Then, when you have done all the thinking and discussing and brainstorming you want to do – write, phone, e-mail, and *communicate* with your elected representatives. *Let them know that you want them to use their brains and their good common sense to come up with* solutions *rather than simply doing more of the same fighting and going nowhere.*

And in this way, we – all of us – will take back the America we've known – the America whose best days are ahead of us!

12

IF YOU THINK THERE'S NO SUCH THING AS TAXES, HOW ARE WE SUPPOSED TO RUN THE COUNTRY?

The current political football – the "defining difference" between Republicans and Democrats – or "liberals" and "conservatives" if you prefer to call them that – is that the Republicans claim the Democrats want to "raise your taxes and tax the middle class out of existence," whereas the Democrats say, "The Republicans want to cut the taxes and open loopholes for the *rich*, so that the middle class will be starved out of existence." They're *both* wrong, they're *both* right, and at the end of the day they will *gridlock* the middle class out of existence!

Let's face it: unless you want to pay a private company to build and run every road in this country – and you will pay a goodly sum every single time you drive on that road; unless you want to pay private security services to protect you from crime; unless you want to pay a private school to educate your children … the list goes on and on and on … *someone else is going to have to pay for these things*. In most societies, including our own, that "someone else" is the public sector – the government agencies. Roads cost money; schools cost money; police services cost money; prisons cost money; armies cost money; delivering the mail costs money; general hospitals where they admit the poor cost money; and if you want to build an aqueduct to transport water from a very wet area to a desert, that costs money, too.

And if you believe government agencies can deliver the services we demand without reasonable taxes, you are living in a world of make-believe where the tooth fairy waves her wand and those services magically appear out of nowhere.

For more than half a century, most countries in Europe charge what, to us, seems an exorbitant tax rate, as much as 60-70% of income *plus* Value Added Tax – a consumer tax – on every Euro you spend. Gasoline costs upwards of $10 a gallon, largely because of the incredible amount of taxes charged on a gallon of gas.

This was brought home to me one day in 1996 when a friend of mine, an American expatriate who has Swiss citizenship, but who has lived all over the world for many years, were talking. I asked him why gas cost so much more in Europe than in the U.S. He said, "All of the Arab oil producing countries in OPEC stash their money in Switzerland. Do you *really* think they're going to charge us more than they charge the United States? Of course not. It's just that we *tax* gasoline so much more per gallon." But, he went on to say, "The Swiss government collects that tax and utilizes part of it to build the *public* transportation sector. That's why you can take a train anywhere you want to go in Switzerland for about $2.00."

I heard similar stories from Danish friends and French friends. The overriding theme that came across loud and clear was, "Yes, our *basic* tax rate is much higher than yours, *but* ... our universities are free and, in fact, the government pays you a monthly stipend when you go to college. When someone gets old and infirm here, we provide them with senior care homes, food, and *good* care for free. When you go overseas and you suffer an emergency illness or an accident befalls you, our government will make sure that you don't have to worry – we pay the host medical provider to take care of you." The stories go on and on. You can add any permutation you want to any service which a human being might find necessary.

The more I traveled from country to country in Europe, the more I learned that rather than *destroy* the middle class, the higher tax rate *preserves* the middle class, because the same tax rate applies to everyone – the richer pay more, the poorer pay less, and the government services are more or less the same for everyone. This keeps everyone on a more or less equal footing (no one is ever on a *completely* equal footing). The roads are generally better maintained than any I've seen in the United States. The universities operate successfully and, more important, within the economic grasp of anyone who wants a university education. Have you ever wondered why it is necessary for our young people to go into hundreds of thousands of dollars of debt to pay off their student loans? To a greater or lesser extent, the *average* universal healthcare is neither better nor worse than the *average* healthcare we receive in the United States – you just end up paying less for it because it doesn't matter if you are a doctor, a teacher, or a soccer star, wages are not beyond all rational reason.

It's very easy for those who have not traveled outside the borders of the United States to decry what I've just said, and say, "You're lying! It's not like that at all. *My friends in* ... (England, Canada, pick a place, any place you want) ... *have told me that it's much worse* ..." My answer to those naysayers is to say, "Don't take someone else's word for it, including mine. *Go and see for yourself.* Or, if you feel you can't afford to do that, do a little research on your own – Google makes it very cheap to do – and you can find out *first hand for yourself.* If I'm wrong, don't hesitate to "call" me on it. My purpose is *not* to be combative or to say I'm right and you're "less right." Rather, I want to get you to *think* – and *not* just to take someone else's word – particularly a politician's – for it.

Now, let's look at the United States. We have a basic Federal *income* tax rate of anywhere from 15-35% - *much, much less than the tax rates in Europe, right?* Well, as they used to say in the old Hertz commercials, "Not *exactly.*" Let's take a 25% average Federal tax rate. *State* taxes add another, say, 9% to that. County property taxes add to that. Sales taxes on good or services you buy tacks on more taxes – gasoline taxes are a notorious example, as are so-called "sin taxes" – on alcohol and tobacco. Assessments for the sewer district? The cash register goes "ka-*ching*" once again. I think you're beginning to get the picture. Ben Franklin, one of my great heroes, is quoted as saying, "The only thing that is for absolute certain is death and taxes."

So, regardless of how you're going to slice it, dice it, fold, staple, spindle, or mutilate it, we are going to end up paying taxes. And while no one would dispute that many programs – whether they are for social welfare, purchasing $100 toilet-flushing fixtures, or plain old "Pork" (research that on Google!) – are wasteful and should be guarded against like the plague – there are going to be *necessary* expenditures and there simply has to be revenue sufficient to meet those necessary expenditures.

If you're unwilling to pay taxes and I'm not going to pay taxes, then we can't rely on other people to pay them either. And the result may well be the Californication of America. If you don't believe me, drive on any surface street or freeway in the Golden State that you care to drive on. Lots of potholes. Lots of deferred maintenance. In 2009, my wife and I drove on streets throughout the former Iron Curtain countries of Poland, Lithuania, East Germany, Czech Republic, Slovakia, and Hungary. The only roads we saw that were in an imperfect state were those that were in process of being built. The only derelict buildings we saw were the abandoned border crossings where there are now open borders and the once menacing guard buildings are in a sad, dilapidated, almost ruined state.

A very substantial percentage of our populace is now condemning the current stimulus program – which, believe it or not, turned out to be a bipartisan program. It started during the Bush Administration (TARP) and it continued during the Obama Administration (ARRA). While both sides – now the Republicans more than the Democrats – complain that this has "broken" America and that we can't afford it, once we all felt the horrendous power of the worst "recession" since the Great Depression, what would have been the alternative? Do nothing and watch things get worse? Or do something and at least *take a chance* that we might make things better. There's an old, very apt saying: *If we don't hang together, we sure as hell will all hang separately!* So we did what had to be done. Uncle Sam warmed up the printing press, and while the jury is still out, at least there is hope that we'll be doing better than we would have done had we done nothing at all.

Don't get me wrong: I believe there is something very wrong with the current income tax laws. Would it surprise you to learn that we didn't even have Federal income tax until the early twentieth century? I also believe that we cannot obtain the services we want *without* taxes. Although most Americans I have met are honest, there are always the many who "cheat just a little bit," and the few who cheat "quite a bit more." Is there a simple, fair, and more effective way to collect more revenue, more *fairly*, and in such a way as to discourage the "need" to cheat. I believe so. But remember, this is an intellectual challenge for *you* as well, and the only way you can be part of the *solution* and not just part of the problem is for you to come up with some ideas of your own – and to write these ideas down and send them to your elected representatives.

First, I propose that in addition to – or even as a replacement for – the Federal and State income tax, we have a uniform *consumer* tax on most, if not all, the goods and services we consume. This would be absolutely fair. If you earned more and *saved* what you earned, the only effect it would have would be that you'd get to keep more. If you decided to buy a motor vehicle, you could elect to buy the vehicle you wanted, *but* be aware that if you chose to spend your money on a $250,000 Lamborghini, you'll pay taxes – a *lot* of taxes. And if that Lamborghini roars out of the showroom and down the street getting a munificent 10 miles to the gallon, you will pay a lot of taxes during your stewardship of this behemoth.

On the other hand, if you choose – and it's entirely *your* choice – to buy a Prius for $25,000 and get 45 MPG, you will still be able to get from Point A to Point B in about the same amount of time, but you will pay substantially less taxes. And if you choose to ride public transportation, you'll probably take an even smaller tax bite, and you'll be truly conserving fuel and putting your money where your mouth is. Contrary to what the captains of industry want you to believe, you still have 100% free choice. And as to the claim that you are destroying capitalism, that contention is demonstrably false on its face. What occurs here would be true capitalism – a market-driven economy. Toyota has already proved this can be done because GM and Chrysler, which persisted in telling us we *needed* big gas guzzlers was driven to the brink of collapse when *we* stood up and told them by the most direct, capitalistic way possible, that *they were wrong and we were right*.

Same goes for just about every other product or service you can name.

The next argument advanced by the entrenched special interests is obvious – and equally specious: "If people buy less, there will be less manufacturing activity, less jobs, and the economy, particularly the middle class, will cease to exist."

I concur that if all consumer items are taxed, you'll tend to spend less than you've spent in the past. Perhaps you won't need *five* TVs and *five* personal computers in your 3,000 square foot house. Maybe *two* will be enough. Maybe you'll keep that car an extra year, Or today's I-pad may be *tomorrow's* I-pad for awhile. It won't hurt the economy. Indeed, it will most likely spur industrialists to "invent a better mousetrap."

Does anyone remember that thirty years ago today's ubiquitous PC was virtually nonexistent? Or that if we wanted to send a letter to a friend across the country it took five days (six *weeks* if you sent a postcard from Europe) and all we had to rely on was the postal service? Today it takes about six *seconds* to send the same message around the globe via E-mail. Necessity is the mother of invention. If the need is there, someone will fill it; and if there is no need, whoever wants to make money will discover or invent something else that someone *will* need – enough to pay the consumer tax on it. That's the way of the world.

What could be a fairer or simpler tax? If you want to spend on a toy, you'll pay a little bit more for it. If you don't want to buy that toy, you'll spend less in taxes. And you won't need to spend countless hours and emotional energy figuring out how to cut back on the taxes you have to pay. It's simple, and, what's more, it works. If you don't believe me, I'll refer you to a whole bunch of countries who find it works just fine.

The second idea I have for taxes – assuming you don't want to give up the almighty income tax – is not a new idea. The idea of a "flat tax" instead of a progressive tax has been around for years. Perhaps it never passed because it was too simple and might put

a lot of accountants out of business. But what could be simpler –
and, if you really wanted to be a Rockefeller or J.P. Morgan, could
you even think of asking the conservative politicians for a better
"break?" No figuring, no calculation, no write-offs, no hiding
income in case you might be audited. If you made $100, you would
pay $10 in income tax and you would have $90 left. Period. If you
made $1,000,000, you would pay $100,000 in income tax and you
would have $900,000 left. So the name of the game is to make more
money so you can keep more money. Sounds too simple to be true?

Hey, wait a minute! Did I say *10%* of your gross income?
Impossible! We're now supposed to pay up to 35% of our income
under the current tax laws. Yet, every conceivable public and private
study that's been made, conclusively demonstrates that if there is
a flat tax, the tax rate will go *down* and the government will still
collect much more than it does today. Is this some type of "smoke
and mirrors" trickery? Hardly. The 35% we pay in taxes is 35%
after all those deductions we take for every manner of expenditure.

Those are but two ideas I believe would simplify taxes, make
them much more "painless," to the degree taxes can be painless,
and they would raise more money and enable us to plan ahead and
spend within – rather than above – our means. And that goes for our
government, too.

13

WE *HAVE* TO EQUAL THE PLAYING FIELD – WE HAVE NO OTHER CHOICE

Those who don't learn from history's lessons are doomed to make the same mistakes – over and over and over. It's not as if we haven't heard "Don't fight a land war in Asia" for 3,000 years. It's not as if history hasn't taught us that revolutions *always* come from the bottom. Or that hatred stirred up by anything does what hatred always does - it breeds hatred in return.

It's just that we don't learn from the lessons of the past.

No, it seems we'd rather go on cursing the darkness than lighting a single candle. The "eye for an eye" type of thinking, regardless in what society it takes place, will eventually make the whole world blind.

This worked for more than three thousand years. When we had a million people on earth, it worked just fine. When we had a billion people on earth, it may not have worked quite so well, but it seemed to work. Those rules don't apply anymore. We have more than *six billion people* on the face of the planet. *Six billion people* fighting for the same resources that a million people fought for an hour ago, as time on earth is measured.

My wife, who's a third grade teacher, brought that lesson home to me a few years ago. She was teaching her children about the water cycle on earth. She posed the question, "Do we have more water on earth or less water on earth today than when the world was formed?" The answer shocked me and it may shock you. *We have exactly the same amount of water on earth – to the drop – as when the earth was first populated.* How can that possibly be? People drink water everyday. While they get rid of it as waste, they don't get rid of *all* of it, do they? And when people die, what happens to the water inside them at the time? Surely we must have *less* water than when we started?

Nope. Not so. The earth is a great ball of mud spinning through space, complete with its own atmosphere. Everything that was here when we started is trapped in our atmosphere and is still here – water, gold, steel. It's just that it *seems* like less *because the same finite amount is available, but it must be divided up among more people.* Same applies to medical services, by the way.

Every society has always had its share of "haves" and "have nots," even when there were less people and more to go around. The term "haves" and "have nots," doesn't apply only to natural resources. Wars have been fought from time out of mind for myriad "stated" reasons, but the *real* reasons are few:

- To enable men to carry off women so that they may impregnate them, thus increasing their own progeny. Sounds sexist and archaic, doesn't it? But this is the single most basic aim of war – a carryover from the "lower" animals. Any animal behaviorist will tell you that that when a new male lion becomes king of the hill, one of the first things he does is kill or chase off young *male* lions in the pride. Males who might delete *his* seed.

- To gain a greater share of natural resources, or to protect your own resources from foreign elements.

- To spread "our" *ideas* and our *ideals* to other societies. This has worked exactly *once* in history – with the ancient Roman Empire. And the reason it worked was that when Rome absorbed another people as its subjects, it allowed those people to keep *their own* ideas, their own religion, and their own way of life. All Rome demanded was taxes and conscripts into the Roman army – and back then they weren't so hypocritical that they called their army "defense forces." They were the *offense* – and they proudly acknowledged it.

There are a few other reasons. See how many you can find. But be honest when you do so, because you may be limited to one or two more, if any.

Generally speaking, particularly in a capitalistic system, those who "have" get richer and more powerful. There are proportionately (if not numerically) less "haves" as time goes on, and more "have nots." The ones who get "squeezed" first, are usually on the lowest rung of the socioeconomic ladder, but there are only so many truly poor. Eventually, the so-called "Middle class" is pinched, and its members descend into the lower socio-economic stratum. When that happens, things begin to destabilize.

Think, for a minute, of a wide ship plowing through the ocean. There are rich people standing on the right side of the boat and poor people standing on the left side of the boat. By far the largest number of people standing in the boat – the middle class – are standing in the middle of the boat, and it is very stable. Then a few people from the middle drift over ton the right side, and a few more people drift over to the left side of the ship. The ship is somehow not as stable. By the time this exodus from the middle reaches a critical level, the ship is now very *un*stable, and if something is not done to restabilize the boat, it will capsize in the first storm.

Do a little historical research, and you'll find that in all of history a revolution has *never* started with the rich. Why should it? As people aggrandize wealth and position, they want to keep things exactly as they are. In *Candide*, Voltaire's Dr. Pangloss lives in "the best of all possible worlds," and it was – until the day he lost everything. Thus, it is no real surprise, nor should it be, that the Conservatives in our society, whether you call them Republicans or Whigs or something else, are those who, by and large, enjoy things just the way they are and don't want things to change.

However, it is in the best interests of these "haves" – how could it be otherwise? – to do everything possible to convince the less-advantaged in our society that the way things are is in *their* best interests, too. The words "tax cuts" resonate with poor and middle class people, precisely because the "lower" and "middle" class have less disposable income. Thus *any* law that saves them *any* money is *per se* good. And if the very rich save 10% on their taxes, "You see, they're exactly like the rest of us. They don't get one percent difference in their taxes, so aren't we now equal to them?"

Well ... no. 10% of $50,000 is $5,000. The lower or middle class taxpayer saves $5,000 and that may just be enough to pay the rent or the health insurance premium this year. Thank God and the Republicans for their generous tax cut to us. But 10% of $1,000,000 is somewhat more than $5,000. Try *$100,000* in tax savings. The same $100,000 that could go to pay for universal health care or something that could benefit a far greater number of people.

Eventually, the poor and/or the middle class wake up and realize that they are being "screwed without being kissed." It happens everywhere. It's happened everywhere throughout history. Recall if you will, although many who believe the Bible was originally written in English, would try to have your forget, that *Christianity* started as a movement among the "have nots" of the Roman Empire. And although "Communism" is now a politically disfavored and discarded term, it, too, started not among the "haves" but among the "workers of the world," who were urged to "unite." Unfortunately, what might have been a reasonably good idea, got co-opted by traditional political strongmen, who turned what was intended as an economic idea into a political power base. But if you think "Communism" (with a capital "C") has ceased to exist in the world, it really hasn't. It just goes under another name and, to a greater or lesser degree, it exists everywhere, even in our own society. Examples are:

- Our military
- Social security
- Medicare
- Tenure in certain occupations, such as teaching
- Public education

So the *Titanic* we call American society and politics is now drifting dangerously close to the iceberg called destabilization. The old ways simply don't work anymore. There are too many people and not enough to go around. Ordinary people like you and me are getting more and more disgusted with "the system," with "our politicians," and with everything else that doesn't work the way we think it should.

The "Tea Party Express" has its own ideas of what we should do. While I don't agree with them, I had damned well better listen to some of what they say and not just chalk it off to a bunch of "crazies." Yesterday's "crazies" rule Iran and Afghanistan today. What do we have to lose by *listening* to "their" ideas, and to ideas from *all* shades of the political-economic spectrum? Nothing but our ignorance. I have earlier said that the old ways don't work anymore, that we're running out of time, and that sooner or later a revolution is sure to come if we don't wake up and assume control for our own change. I have said that while we're waiting for the "electric car" or the "fuel cell" car of the new society to arrive, perhaps we should drive a "hybrid" for awhile. It may delay the next revolution. Or, better yet, it may just defuse the need for a revolution before it comes.

Meanwhile, we must equal the playing field for the "have nots" or incipient "have nots" if we want this ship to stay stable enough to bring us safely to the opposite shore.

14

"Capitalism"/"Socialism" –

Bridging The Gap

The classic view of capitalism was initially expressed by Adam Smith, but was even more succinctly stated by President Calvin Coolidge many years ago: "The business of business is *business*." Various others have ventured their own views of that economic theory over the centuries: *Laissez faire*, literally "Let it Be" (with no offense to The Beatles intended). "Trickle down economy." (The term didn't originate with President Reagan). Survival of the fittest – that's the way nature intended it to be. In unregulated capitalism, the entrepreneur, the industrialist, the hard working man who keeps his nose to the grindstone, the one who "builds a better mousetrap," is supposed to always come out ahead. In theory, anyway. You do whatever it takes to get ahead. All too frequently, in every society, this has involved blackmail, graft, bribery, threats, violence, and dirty tricks. Sounds familiar, doesn't it?

Opponents of classic capitalism view it as open class warfare, enabling the rich and powerful to make their filthy lucre on the broken backs of weaker human beings. They point – not entirely without merit – to the fact that unbridled capitalism caused – or at least heavily contributed to – the recession/depression of 2007 and its aftermath, when the great beacons of capitalism, the banks and mortgage lenders, came crawling to the *government* for a bailout, so that they could restart the economy, never mind that they had caused the collapse of the economy to begin with. This, they said, would allow them to loan out money to needy borrowers and entrepreneurs so they, in turn, could restart the engine of commerce.

Somehow, it didn't quite work out that way. The banks borrowed money from our government *at no interest*. They then invested in United States government securities, *which paid them interest*. They parsed out a minuscule percentage of what they had borrowed by way of loans to the "little man." Why should they extend more credit and take a risk? If they were borrowing money at *no* interest from the government and earning 2 or 3% in interest from their investment in government securities, with *absolutely no risk*, one would have to be a "four-cornered meatball" or a head with no brain to figure out which option the banks would take.

So much for flat-out unregulated capitalism.

Of course, there are problems whatever economic system a society chooses to embrace. The other side of the coin is variously called "Socialism," "Communism," or other names, depending on whether it's used as a panacea or an epithet. The short course definition of what we'll call socialism is that, to use Hillary Clinton's words, "It takes a village." The family is now extended to the village and the village is extended to the nation. Since there is a very real chance that not everyone will be able to earn enough to make for a satisfactory life, *society* will provide a "safety net" for all of its members. "To each, according to his needs."

There are instances where socialism has worked very well indeed, and where it has not come in for condemnation, even by hard core capitalist conservatives. One instance is the *Kibbutz* experience in Israel. Another, closer to home, is the Mormon experience in the United States. Members of the Church of Jesus Christ of the Latter Day Saints (LDS) have had a tithing system in place since the inception of that religion. Mormons are expected to *tithe* – to give 10% of their income to the Church. In exchange, the Church has its own social safety net. So far as I know, no Mormon has ever gone on a public Welfare program. The Church looks out for its own. This has been done not only in the LDS, but in other Churches and organizations as well. The Elks, for example, have had an Old Elks home for more than a century. The Screen Actors Guild, of which archconservative Ronald Reagan was once president, has its own old-age home as well. This is nothing more nor less than socialism in its purest form.

But socialism, too, is not immune from excesses and faults. The Communist experience is one classic example. "Communism" (capital "C") failed not because it was an inherently defective economic system, but because it went to the other extreme. If everyone was going to end up more or less equal to everyone else, and no one was going to become wealthier and more powerful than his neighbor, why bother to put in more than the minimal amount of labor necessary to justify one's existence? Why work that much harder than your neighbor to produce a higher quality product? It was much easier to build a Trabant than a Volkswagen, and both eventually got you where you wanted to go. And since there was much less money to go around and all you had to do was go to the commissary, what did it matter that you had to wait endless hours in line to get the wilted head of cabbage or the stunted tomato?

Does that point to the conclusion that capitalism is *ipso facto* superior to socialism? Not really. Man is, by nature, both aggressive *and* gregarious. The aggressive part of man's psyche enables him to climb over his fellow, to better himself at his neighbor's expense – and that is exactly the way it is in the cold, hard, "natural" world of the beast. "Do unto others *before* they do it to you."

On the other hand, unlike solitary animals such as the tiger, we tend to band together in communities, whether for mutual defense, affection, or social necessity. Early on, man learned that he was individually weaker, more susceptible than a whole lot of larger, more powerful animals. Like dogs, he learned that there is safety in numbers, and his large brain, which, unlike most other animals, allowed him to reason, led him to believe that there were areas in his life where it was necessary to cooperate.

Perhaps the first known example of capitalism was when a big, powerful caveman forcibly coerced a smaller, weaker caveman to "trade" him a carrot for a fish. The first known example of socialism was undoubtedly when cavemen went out on a communal hunt. To their surprise, and to their immense satisfaction, they learned that they could trap and kill a much larger animal than themselves – and that this larger animal provided food for the entire group. So they shared the spoils and the group expanded to a village and from there to a town.

The lesson to be learned from this little bit of history is that neither capitalism nor socialism is the perfect answer, particularly where, as now, resources are becoming more scarce. The inescapable conclusion would seem to be that if we stop fighting over inconsequential titles – whether we are "capitalists" or "socialists" – a hybrid system is the sensible way to combine the best of both systems and, at the very least, see how it works before we knee-jerk condemn it.

As I've said earlier, we already have forms of socialized medicine in various pockets of our society, and, to a greater or lesser
degree, it has worked successfully, in some cases for many years.
Social security is an accepted safety net for a large segment of our
society, but 75 years ago it was anathema. Riding public transportation is a form of socialism – while it doesn't give you the privacy
or convenience of getting you to the exact location you want to go
sooner than the next person, it simply costs less if 50 people ride in
a bus that gets 10 miles to a gallon of gas than if 2 people ride in a
car that gets 20 miles per gallon. Is that capitalism or socialism, or
is it some sort of hybrid?

The list of goods and services is virtually endless, just as there
are several countries that successfully use some combination of
capitalism and socialism. Here's an exercise for you to think about:
try to figure what goods are services which are now delivered
entirely individually through a system we call "capitalism" could
use some "socialist" elements to become more efficient, better, or
cheaper, or which could deliver a greater amount of good or services
to a greater amount of people for the same price. Conversely, think
of a similar assortment of goods or services which are presently
delivered in what we'd call a "socialist" system. Could they be better
or more expeditiously delivered if we allowed individual freedom
of choice? Consider the options coolly, using your intellect instead
of your "gut feeling" emotions, and see how many *solutions* you can
come up with for these problems. And how much more productive it
would be to come up with cooperative solutions rather than making
this exercise a territorial battleground for exercising more political
power over the next guy.

15

RELIGION AND SOCIAL/SEXUAL PREFERENCES. ABORTION AND SUCH – IF IT'S A PERSONAL THING, WHY BRING POLITICS INTO IT?

"Never discuss religion, politics, or sex." Historically, these have been bogeymen (or bogeypersons if you want to be politically correct). But if we want to move forward, to make our society a better, gentler, more cooperative, and more progressive place to be, it's high time we shed that old bugaboo and talked frankly about the most sensitive social problems that divide us.

Let me state for the record that I really don't care what your religion is, what your sexual preferences are, or what you feel about abortion or other "taboo" subjects. *Those things are your business and, so far as I'm concerned, your private rights,* as long as they don't directly impact me. Your freedom to put your fist anywhere you wish ends at my chin – but *only* at my chin, not before.

I'm Jewish. Does that mean I have the right to push you into becoming Jewish, or that "my" God is somehow better, more moral, more powerful than your God? I happen not to think so. I happen to believe there's *one* God, whatever you want to call that God, and although we have many pathways that lead us in the direction of that God, the closer we get to the Deity, the closer those paths converge. Come to think of it, you may not believe in a Higher Force, or, if you do, you may not call that Force what I call it. That's your right, too. It's your personal preference, and how dare I invade your privacy?

When I mediate between divorcing couples, I start out my making them promise me one thing: "Promise me that you'll look out for *your own best interests.* The concomitant of that statement is that you do not have the right to tell the other person what his or her best interests are – you simply look out for your *own.*" I feel the same applies to your own interests and concerns, whatever they might be. After all, we're guaranteed freedom of speech *and* freedom of association in America.

Yet, we have somehow politicized these very personal rights. Somehow, a good portion of our population has come to believe we are a *Christian* nation, or, even if we don't express this out loud, Muslims are somehow "less than" the rest of us. If you don't believe that, think about the recent brouhaha over a plan to build a mosque close to "Ground Zero" in New York City. Would the same firestorm have erupted if an Episcopalian Church had announced it was going to build an edifice in the same area? Or if 9-1-1 had never happened? Of course not. It's just that some of us seem to feel that *our* Religion is better than *your* religion, so we should have greater rights than you do.

We can enlarge everything we perceive through the prism of religion. Orthodox adherents of my faith are commanded not to eat such things as pork, shellfish, and animals and birds that scavenge. According to their reading of the Bible, we are not to eat meat and drink milk within six hours of each other ("Thou shalt not eat a calf seethed in its mother's milk"). I'm not Orthodox, and I love pork ribs, bacon, mussels, squid, and lobster. Does that make me a worse human being? Some of my Orthodox brethren certainly think so. But I don't try to tell them how to live their lives, and I take scant notice when they tell me how to live mine.

If you look through the microscope at the most explosive social / political issues that seem to pervade our lives in the United States today – abortion, homosexual rights, including marriage, Darwinism vs. Intelligent Creation, and the like, once you cut through what those who condemn these practices are saying, you find they have absolutely nothing to do with "natural," "scientific," or "moral" rules. They are nothing more nor less than a means of imposition one man's *religious* beliefs on another. As Bill Maher said, "Religion works under the guise of morality but its tenets generally have nothing to do with morality. Just because a religion prohibits abortion or decries homosexuality, that does not mean that having an abortion or having homosexual sex are immoral acts. Instead, an immoral person is one who harms others through murder, rape, or greed."

Take homosexual marriage. Does the fact that I support gay rights means I am going to marry another man? No. Does it mean I am going to think less of another human being because he or she chooses to do something in the privacy of her or his own bedroom, or, for that matter, her or his *mind*? I don't think so. I remember the times when many considered it immoral to date, let alone marry, someone of a different race. I even remember when there were restrictions on selling certain real property to "subjects of the

Ottoman Sultan," which, translated (nod, nod, wink, wink) meant *Jews.* The same motivating force, *"My religion is better than yours,"* propelled those anachronisms.

If you think I'm joking, look at some of the absolutely *immoral* political ads that promoted the passage of California's infamous Proposition 8, which proscribed gay marriage. "Do you know that if Proposition 8 is not passed, they'll *have* to teach *your children* in public school that it's *all right to marry someone of the same sex?"* Such bullsh*t defies credibility, yet *more than 50% of the voters reacted to such drivel by voting it into law!*

"It's easy for you to say," I've been told. "What if *your* [son] [daughter] announced to you that he or she was a homosexual?" My first reaction would be, *What in the world does their sexual preference have to do with whether or not they're my children? What does their sexual preference have to do with whether someone can order me to love them less than I would love my "normal" heterosexual children?* Ask a conservative such as Dick Cheney whether he loves his daughter any less because of her sexual preferences. Or if he'd suddenly disown her. I think not.

Which leads me to my next rant. Of all the hypocrisy I've seen pass through the political gates during the past two decades, none can top the "Don't ask, don't tell" law that permits gays to serve in the military and die for their country – but only if they keep it *private* that they're gay. I happened to walk through Arlington National Cemetery one day, not long ago. I saw a number a flag-draped coffins fresh from the war in Afghanistan. I did not find *one single coffin that announced that its inhabitant had been gay.*

But to keep this in a constructive mode, might I respectfully inquire how any of these attempts to make one segment of our citizens "less than" another in any way promotes the equal rights we are guaranteed under the United States Constitution, or proves which is better and more deserving, the Muslim, the gay, the

African-American, the "illegal" Mexican who is trying to scratch out a living by doing the menial work that no "white man" would do, or the Fundamentalist Christian?

Abortion. Big issue, right? It's murder to abort a fetus, right? It's a *sin* and if you engage in such a sin, you will rot in hell for eternity. Rather, you should be like Sarah Palin and trot a child who was the subject of a tragic genetic accident onto the stage like some heroic stage prop – when you're running for Vice President of the United States. Of course, abortion is positively wrong for White Christian Americans, but everyone knows those illegal hot-blooded Mexicans breed like rabbits and all they do is go on our welfare rolls and *we* have to pay for it.

Come on, my fellow citizens, get real – or if you refuse to get real, at least be consistent. I try to honor every person's moral beliefs, whether or not I agree with them. If someone feels abortion is morally repugnant for him or for her, their belief is certainly as valid as mine. No one compels them to *have* an abortion if they don't want one. I cannot think of a law even proposed – let alone passed in – any state in this Union that *compels* someone to have an abortion. The closest I can come to such a "law" was when certain laws in Nazi Germany mandated sterilization. No one ever said the Third Reich was the ultimate model of moral or ethical law.

The list of social inequities and inconsistencies goes on and on and on. Take stem cell research. *Stem cell research.* Did I hear this right? Politicians want to ban or curtail stem cell research, which is *proven* to lead to incredibly beneficial discoveries in medicine *because a stem cell* may *have once been part of a fetus that* may *have been a potential life*? So now we get to *vote* on whose "life" is more important – a potential Nobel laureate whose life can be saved or, at the very least, made less prone to suffering, or a cell from "someone" who never *was* to begin with?

With all of the *real* problems we have facing a nation that is on its way to becoming a third world country very quickly, do we really have the *luxury* of "confronting" private social issues in the political arena?

If these issues need to be confronted at all, shouldn't they be discussed in the context of one's church or one's private social group or one's family rather than have the proponent's views pushed on others who might not agree?

Again, these issues should be non-issues when it comes to politics. We have better, more urgent, needs to accomplish in our society, and the sooner we deal with what's really important to the socio-economic survival and promotion of our nation, the better off we will all be.

16

WAR? – TO WHAT END?

"Christianity does not forbid the making of war, so long as it is a *just* war. Since every war has its end in peace, and since peace is a divine blessing, then every war can be called just."

from *Scribe*[2]

War, it seems, has been around for as long as man has been around. In an earlier chapter, I've covered what I feel are the basic reasons underlying every war:

- To enable men to carry off women and spread their seed to new societies.

[2] © 2006, 2010 by Hugo N. Gerstl. Published by Dekel Publishing House, Tel Aviv, Israel; U.S. publisher Samuel Wachtman's Sons. Inc.

- To gain a greater share of natural resources, or to protect your own resources from foreign elements. (The territorial imperative).
- To spread our *ideas* and our *ideals* to other societies. (The religious imperative).

How successful have we humans been in these endeavors? By any measure of history, hardly at all, for each "victory" has been fleeting at best – occasionally as long as a generation, but rarely more.

Let's take the first reason for war – to carry off women. Physically, men are generally larger than women, so it's not much of a contest at the inception. And like it or not – "politically correct" or not – men are testosterone-driven. For that matter, *wars* tend to be testosterone-driven. I'm reminded of the Woody Allen movie *Annie Hall* where there is a split-screen view of a man and a woman in a psychiatrist's office. The psychiatrist asks the man, "How often do you have sex?" "Hardly ever," he replies. "Twice a week." When the same question is put to the woman, she responds, "All the time – twice a week." Depends on your point of view.

Another thing I've found: a man can never forgive a woman for a *sexual* dalliance with another man, but if she develops a fond, loving, nonsexual relationship with another man, it's no big deal. Conversely, a woman is capable of forgiving a man for sexual indiscretions with another woman, but she is crushed to the core when a man professes great *emotional love* for another woman.

Historians will tell you that generally men win the *war* but women win the *peace*. A man may start out by taking a woman by force, but this soon loses its luster, particularly if the man falls "in love" with the woman and elects to marry her, or, at the very least, cohabit with her for a long period of time. Children inevitably come, usually as many boys as girls, and of course while the man goes off to war, to work, or whatever, it is the woman who is charged with taking care of the children at home. (This may not always be the case in "advanced" societies like our own, but it still obtains for the majority of the world). That means that all manner of "training" is left to the woman, from potty training to pre-school, and, invariably, to religious training. And here is where man loses the war he had earlier won. Because, for the most part, religion, which stems from the Latin *res ligio*, and means, literally, "rebinding," is geared toward the higher aspirations of humankind, the immortal soul. And *that* is where the woman claims a *"gotcha,"* for religion is usually tied directly to the woman's homeland.

The Romans understood this all too well. They moved into Persia, they captured lovely Persian women, they started marrying and living with Persian women, and, lo and behold, the religion and culture of ancient Persia first hypnotized, then enamored, then captured the conquering Romans. So the Romans left the Persians to their own culture, their own religion, and their own way of life, as long as they paid taxes and formally submitted to Roman rule, and things went along just fine for eleven hundred years.

Take today's wars. One of the least informed (translation: downright stupid) sentences I've ever heard was when former President George W. Bush was talking about *why* we were trying to bring Western-style democracy to the heathen ragheads in Iraq: "*I know those people*." Take that sentence, tear it apart word by word, and you see how meaningless it is.

I – meaning the great enlightened leader of the Western world. The leader who is omniscient, the godlike figure.

Know – this assumes that the speaker has lived in Iraq all his life, that he is as familiar as a native with the religion, culture, and mores that have been in place for over a thousand years, and that he is utterly superior to the inhabitants of that land.

Those – this sets up an "I" versus "you" mentality – note the deliberately capitalized "I" and the lower case "you." "Those" means "not our kind," "foreigners" who are too dumb to realize that they need to learn and take on <u>our</u> ways to advance beyond intelligent monkeys.

People – we are not describing individual human beings here. They are collective – "you've seen one Iraqi, you've seen 'em all." They haven't quite advanced to *our* level yet.

In short, leave it to us to take care of "our little brown brothers." Or, if we want to be Hitleresque about it, the "subhuman Jews." Or you can justify "ethnic cleansing" by any other means you think valid.

Only it doesn't work. At least for more than a generation or so.

So the first reason for war is exposed as a short-term "band aid on a cancer" that doesn't work.

Somewhat more sophisticated is the concept that wars are fought to gain a greater share of natural resources, or to protect your own resources from foreign elements. This has usually worked for a longer period of time. Certainly wars in the Twentieth Century and early Twenty-first Century were fought over sources of energy, primarily petroleum and by most accounts the wars of the later Twenty-first Century will be fought over finite resources like water. One thing is clear, the group/nation/alliance that commands the greatest amount of precious natural resources usually controls the chessboard of world hegemony. Usually, but not always. How do you explain that Japan, which has very few natural resources and has only rarely fought a war for control over something bigger than its chain of islands, has done so well economically? Or that Germany, which has large reserves of coal, water, and forests, but no oil or gold or platinum to speak of, has played such a historically prominent role on the world stage? By the way, both of those nations ended up on the *losing* side of the most recent wars they have fought, yet today they're doing just fine.

Or take Switzerland, one of the wealthiest and most prosperous countries on the face of the planet. Does anyone remember when the Swiss last fought a war? *Any* war?

These three nations are isolated examples that prove the total non-necessity of war. If you'd like, there are several countries you can add to that list: New Zealand, Botswana, Denmark, Costa Rica, and Brazil to name only a few.

For years, the conventional wisdom of American politicians has been, "The best way out of an economic recession / depression is a good war." And for most of the Twentieth Century, that seemed to work. But then, at the end of the 1980's, the Soviet Union, which was either the second or even the first most powerful military force in the world, collapsed in financial bankruptcy. And, sadly, if we look at our own economic balance sheet in the second decade of the Twenty-first Century, *we have gotten to the point where we are the largest debtor nation in the world*. No matter how vaunted our strength and power, it would only take a few keystrokes from a few people in China to bankrupt our country.

Scary, isn't it?

"Wait a minute," you might say. "Aren't you forgetting that wars are fought to gain or protect *territory*?"

Not really. Territory, what the Nazis used to call *lebensraum*, simply means that you control a greater geographical probability of more resources or that you have more room in which to stuff more people. But even territory is finite, just as water, petroleum, and any other resource you can mention is finite.

Which leads us to the final reason for war. To spread your ideas or your ideals. In my opinion, that is the most useless reason for war there is. For anyone to try to impose their will on even another person, let alone another nation, is an invitation to failure. If you think I'm joking, just think for a moment. Picture a scenario where Osama bin Laden, or some equally repugnant character, somehow mounts a force that manages to capture or control the northeastern quadrant of the United States. He proposes that everyone will adhere to his form of government, his religion, and his moral beliefs. How likely are you to willingly and wholeheartedly go along with those ideas? How long before you start fomenting a revolution of sorts, no matter how long the odds, no matter how small the "revolution?"

People have tried to change the minds and ideals of other people since time out of mind. *It has never worked and it never will work.* The "Thousand Year Reich" lasted twelve years. Brittania ruled the waves until it no longer ruled the waves – which was a couple hundred years at most. A man named Gandhi, who never instigated a war, brought down the British Empire in India. 6 million whites kept 50 million blacks under their domination in South Africa. But it didn't last. Lessons taught by force seldom do.

So are there *any* "wars" which have a purpose? Yes. Wars on poverty, on disease, on ignorance, on anything that diminishes the basic human spirit. Wars in which human beings concentrate on what will *save* lives rather than destroy them.

Think about what we could do with the money we've spent thus far on only two regional wars – Iraq (since 1991) and Afghanistan (since the 1980's if you count the Soviet expenditures there) – money which, by the way, is gone forever. The original estimate was that the Iraqi adventure wouldn't cost the U.S. that much – we could fight it "on the cheap" with our National Guard and the oil revenues we'd get after we'd pacified Iraq would more than pay for the war in no time. The latest estimate is that it would take 475 *years* of oil revenue from Iraq to cover the costs of our war there. And by that time, who'll even need oil anymore?

Meanwhile, look at our roads, look at our schools, look at our government budgets? The *real* cost of war is more than we can ever hope to afford, and what then?

So now it's *your* turn to help turn our nation around. Google the expenditures on war during the last twenty-five years. Write a civil engineer in your county or state government to find out what it would cost to resurface every road in your vicinity. What would it cost to bring art and music back into the public school system?

The purpose of this book is not to be a meaningless rant, for that would be contributing to the problem, not to the solution. I am asking you to wake up your minds and project the ten things on a scale of importance that hit you most where you live – that impact *your* quality of life. Is war *truly* one of them? Better yet, how has one war we've fought during your lifetime *improved* the quality of your own life?

17

UNIVERSAL HEALTH CARE

Watch how the politics of hate forces each of us to become inhumane! Remember the insane "death committee" ads when the Democrats were trying to push a universal health care system through Congress? Scare tactics that were as dirty as anything I've ever seen in politics. The spinmasters kicked the rest of us right in the groin, threatening dire consequences if we *dared* embrace a universal healthcare system.

Of course the "nice" thing about it was "there are no vested interests here." *Oh, really?* Think for a moment with your brains instead of your base emotions and consider the following:

* Health care facilities are largely owned and operated by the private sector. Health insurance is primarily provided by the private sector, with the exception of Medicare, Medicaid, TRICARE, the Children's Health Insurance Program and the Veterans Health Administration.

* At least 15.3% of the U.S. population is completely uninsured. 35% of the population is underinsured – not able to cover the costs of their medical needs.

* More money per person is spent on health care in the United States than in any other nation in the world.

* A greater percentage of total income in the United States is spent on health care than in any United Nations member state except for East Timor.

* Medical debt contributes to more than 62% of all personal bankruptcies in the United States.

* The U.S. pays twice as much as almost any other nation for healthcare, yet lags behind other wealthy nations in such measures as infant mortality and life expectancy. The United States life expectancy is 42nd in the world, lagging behind Japan, France, Germany and the United Kingdom, and just *after* Chile and Cuba!

* The World Health Organization ranked the U.S. health care system as the highest in cost, 37th in overall performance, and 72nd by overall level of health.

* A 2009 Harvard study published in the American Journal of Public Health found more than 44,800 excess deaths annually in the United States due to Americans lacking health insurance.

* Current U.S. health care spending is more than 17.3% of our entire Gross Domestic Product, second highest among all United Nations member nations. The Health and Human Services Department expects that the health share of GDP will reach 19.5% of our GDP by 2017. In 1960, we spent 5.2% of our GDP on health care.

* In 2009, the United States federal, state and local governments, corporations and individuals, together spent $2.5 trillion, $8,047 per person, on health care.

* On March 1, 2010, Warren Buffett said that the high costs paid by U.S. companies for their employees' health care put them at a competitive disadvantage. He compared the 17.3% of GDP spent by the U.S. on health care with the 9% of GDP spent by much of the rest of the world, noted that the U.S. has fewer doctors and nurses per person, and said, "That kind of a cost, compared with the rest of the world, is like a tapeworm eating at our economic body."

* Since 2001, premiums for family health care coverage have increased 78%, while wages have risen 19% and inflation has risen 17%.

* In most OECD countries, there is a high degree of public ownership and public finance. The resulting economy of scale in providing health care services enables a much tighter grip on costs. The U.S., on the other hand, does not regulate prices of services from private providers, assuming the private sector can do it better.

* Massachusetts has adopted a universal health care system which mandates that all residents who can afford to do so purchase health insurance, provides subsidized insurance plans so that nearly everyone can afford health insurance, and provides a Health Safety Net Fund to pay for necessary treatment for those who cannot find affordable health insurance or are not eligible.

* Administrative costs for private insurance represent approximately 12% of premiums. In California, billing and insurance-related costs among insurers, physicians, and hospitals in California represented 20-22% of privately insured spending in acute care settings.

* Low reimbursement rates for Medicare and Medicaid have increased cost-shifting pressures on hospitals and doctors, who charge higher rates for the same services to private payers, which directly affects health insurance rates.

* The U.S. Census Bureau estimated that 45.7 million Americans (15.3% of the total population) had no health insurance coverage at some point during 2007. Most uninsured Americans are working-class persons whose employers do not provide health insurance, and who earn too much money to qualify for a local or state insurance programs for the poor, but do not earn enough to cover the cost of enrollment in a health insurance plan designed for individuals.

* 5 million of those without health insurance are considered "uninsurable" because of pre-existing conditions. One large industry survey found that 13% of applicants for individual health insurance who went through medical underwriting were denied coverage in 2004. Declination rates rose from 5% for those under 18 to just under one-third for those aged 60 to 64.

Those in favor of a universal health care system argue that the large number of uninsured Americans creates direct and hidden costs shared by all, and that extending coverage to all would lower costs and improve quality. Both sides of the political spectrum have debated whether people have a fundamental right to have health care provided to them by their government. An impediment to implementing any U.S. healthcare reform that does not benefit insurance companies or the private health care industry is the power of insurance company and health care industry lobbyists. Possibly as a consequence of the power of lobbyists, key politicians have taken the option of single payer health care off the table entirely. A June 2009 NBC News/Wall Street Journal survey revealed that 76% said it was either "extremely" or "quite" important to "give people a choice of both a public plan administered by the federal government and a private plan for their health insurance."

I personally favor a single-payer health care system. This system *works* in other countries, where national government-funded systems produce better health outcomes at lower cost. Opponents have played name-calling games, calling this type of system "socialized medicine." Socialized medicine is a system where the government owns or controls the means of providing medicine. Britain and France are examples of a socialized system. Both of these systems have private insurers to choose from, but the government is the dominant purchaser. In the United States, the Veterans' Administration and Medicare are examples of a mostly single-payer system.

Recently, I saw a debate on CNN between then-candidate (now Senator) Chris Coons and Christine O'Donnell, the tea-party's Barbie Doll *du jour*. I was absolutely floored by Ms. O'Donnell's blatant – and proudly arrogant – ignorance on what universal health care was all about. When prodded by the moderators as to whether she was opposed to universal healthcare because it mandated all citizens to buy affordable health care insurance, she answered, "It's not about the *cost* of *insurance* – it's about medical *care*." She seemed a deer-in-the-headlights when the moderator asked, "If someone who could afford to, *voluntarily* decided *not* to purchase health insurance, and then required the services of an emergency room in the hospital, is it fair that the rest of us who *do* buy insurance end up paying his bill?" The candidate responded about something about why so "many illegal Mexicans use the emergency room." She also pointed out that since what she referred to as "ObamaCare" came into law, health insurance costs had risen. Finally, when asked if she would vote to repeal the Affordable Health Care law – even those things such as the provisions that insurance companies can't cancel you for claims, nor can they limit lifetime pays, and similar basic human rights issues, this rather light-on-brain-cells Sarah Palin-of-the-East-Coast said she would favor scrapping the *entire* health care law and starting over at the beginning to make a *meaningful* law. Of course, one could only imagine what her "meaningful" law would be, since she doesn't believe in the Theory of Evolution and said she'd like to sit and "watch a monkey evolve."

Thank goodness, when Ms. O'Donnell tried to tell the Delaware electorate, "I'm one of *you*," Delaware voters soundly said, "No, you're not!" Otherwise, it might have been time to apply for EU passports, sooner rather than later. And watch the Tea party extremists slam me for that "highly un-American statement."

To return to a serious discussion of the problem, there is no question that affordable health care *should* be available to everyone in what we like to call the richest and most favored country on earth. That seems to me to be a basic right. The legitimate counterpoint is that we simply don't have – and can't afford, no matter how rich we claim to be – "on demand" first-class healthcare for every citizen in the United States. Conservatives are quick to trot out the "horror stories" of the Canadian health care system. I cannot say that system is perfect by any means. Indeed, my late mother-in-law waited in a hospital corridor in Toronto for three days with a broken hip before she was seen. Unfortunately, that is a simple mathematical result of supply and demand.

But the United States already has a better, more affordable system in place – and it works! It is a combination of "socialized medicine" (Medicare) and "free market healthcare" (Supplemental insurance). It's worked remarkably well for me through two onsets of cancer (surgery, radiation, scans and checkups), serious shoulder surgery, and, more important, *preventive medicine*, which is an area in which the United States has fallen far behind the rest of the world. Once again, it is a "hybrid" – a Prius system – and it is a combination that has not, so far, failed me or failed this country.

Once again, this is not a condemnation of the Christine O'Donnells of the country. Rather, it is a clarion call to *cooperate* with one another in *finding answers* rather than tearing down a structure that's already halfway constructed.

* * *

Stem Cell Research – The Phony "Bogeyman"

It has often been said that human beings would rather stumble around cursing the dark than light a single candle. The opponents of the Supreme Court decision in *Roe v. Wade* (1973) 410 U.S. 113, decided in January 1973 – 39 years ago! – now have a new "gather 'round the flag" icon – *stem cell research*. Use of *embryonic* stem cells for research involves the destruction of blastocysts formed from laboratory-fertilized human eggs. For those who believe that life begins at conception, the blastocyst is a human life and to destroy it is unacceptable and immoral. This seems to be the only controversial issue standing in the way of stem cell research in North America.

But this reasoning is the dark of the tunnel – sort of a "My mind is made up, don't confuse me with the facts" mentality. In the summer of 2006 President Bush vetoed a bill passed by the Senate that would have expanded federal funding of *embryonic* stem cell research. Currently, American federal funding can only go to research on stem cells from existing, already destroyed embryos. Thus, not one "life" or living fetus would be used for embryonic stem cell research. That should effectively end the argument right there, but it has become a needless political football which is actually *harming* all Americans because it is standing in the way of a cure – or, at the very least, the promise of hope for millions of Americans suffering from the scariest of all diseases.

First, the "controversial" *embryonic* stem cells only constitute one of many kinds of stem cells. For example, stem cells can be swabbed of the surface of the human tooth with absolutely no risk to the donor. The use of stem cell lines from alternative *non-embryonic* sources has already been demonstrated as a successful option to replace blood-cell-forming cells killed during chemotherapy in bone marrow transplant patients. Adult cells, the use of amnionic fluid, or stem cell extraction techniques that do not damage the embryo, provide alternatives for obtaining viable stem cell lines.

More than 90% of all Americans do not even know what a "stem cell" is – which is why there is such a politicized, knee-jerk reaction to stem cell research. Quick – without looking – do *you* know what a stem cell is, or how it works? When I asked ten randomly selected friends, not one of them knew. About half thought it might have something to do with abortion.

The truth is, stem cells and stem cell research have absolutely *nothing* to do with abortion or a fetus's right to life. A stem cell is a cell which possess two properties:

- *Self-renewal*: the ability to go through numerous cycles of cell division while maintaining the undifferentiated state. This means a stem cell divides into one daughter cell that is identical to the original stem cell, and another daughter cell that is differentiated. When one stem cell develops into two differentiated daughter cells, another stem cell produces two stem cells identical to the original; and
- *Potency*: the capacity to differentiate into specialized cell types. *Potency* specifies the potential to differentiate into different cell types of the stem cell.

The practical definition of a stem cell is the *functional* definition - *a cell that has the potential to regenerate tissue over a lifetime.* For example, the standard test for a bone marrow stem cell is the ability to transplant one cell and save an individual who does not have blood cells and immune cells. In this case, a stem cell must be able to produce new blood cells and immune cells over a long term, demonstrating potency. It should also be possible to isolate stem cells from the transplanted individual, which can themselves be transplanted into another individual without blood cells and immune cells, demonstrating that the stem cell is able to self-renew.

Adult stem cell treatments have been successfully used for many years to treat leukemia and related bone and blood cancers through bone marrow transplants. The use of adult stem cells in research and therapy does not require the destruction of an embryo. Additionally, because in some instances adult stem cells can be obtained from the intended recipient, the risk of rejection is essentially non-existent in these situations. An extremely rich source for adult stem cells is the developing tooth bud of the mandibular third molar. These stem cells eventually form enamel, dentin, periodontal ligament, blood vessels, dental pulp, nervous tissues, and more than thirty different unique end organs. Since there is no risk of death or injury, these cells will probably constitute a major source for research and multiple therapies.

Stem cells are also found in amniotic fluid. All over the world, universities and research institutes are studying amniotic fluid to discover all the qualities of amniotic stem cells. From an ethical point of view, stem cells from amniotic fluid can solve a lot of problems, because it's possible to catch amniotic stem cells without destroying embryos. Even the Vatican newspaper "Osservatore Romano" called amniotic stem cell "the future of medicine."

Now that you've had a most basic lesson – "Stem Cell 101" – can any of you tell me any reason – *any reason at all* – why you still object to stem cell research? Perhaps I should strengthen my "argument" a bit more: Medical researchers believe that stem cell therapy has the potential to dramatically change the treatment of human disease. A number of adult stem cell therapies already exist, particularly bone marrow transplants that are used to treat leukemia. In the future, medical researchers anticipate being able to use technologies derived from stem cell research to treat cancer, Parkinson's disease, spinal cord injuries, Amyotrophic lateral sclerosis (Lou Gehrig's Disease), multiple sclerosis, and muscle damage. However, there still exists a great deal of social and scientific uncertainty which could be overcome through further education of the public.

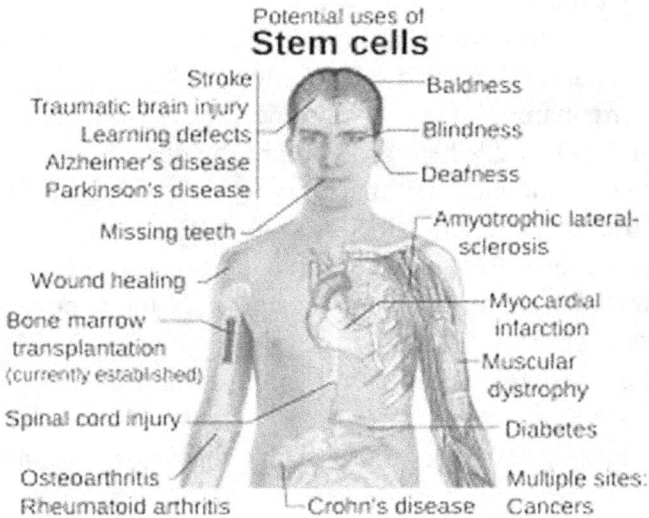

Potential uses of
Stem cells

Stroke
Traumatic brain injury
Learning defects
Alzheimer's disease
Parkinson's disease

Baldness
Blindness
Deafness

Missing teeth

Amyotrophic lateral-sclerosis

Wound healing

Myocardial infarction

Bone marrow transplantation
(currently established)

Muscular dystrophy

Spinal cord injury

Diabetes

Osteoarthritis
Rheumatoid arthritis

Crohn's disease

Multiple sites:
Cancers

* * *

HOW COME THE FRENCH CAN DO IT RIGHT?
HOW COME THE REST OF THE WORLD IS LEAVING US BEHIND?

I have earlier said that we are *not* the beacon of light to the world when it comes to health care. One of the bugaboo words that has become fashionable (or notorious) of late is "outsourcing" – the sending of U.S. jobs overseas. I have experienced this more times than not. When I call United-Continental Airlines to book a reservation or when I call Hewlett Packard to check on why my computer is not running at its optimum speed, chances are I will, without even knowing it, be answered by a reservation agent or technician sitting at a bank of telephones in Mumbai, Jakarta, or San Jose, Costa Rica.

On one such occasion, I had an amusing experience. I could discern that the man answering the phone did not speak with the accent of someone born in Cincinnati, Ohio. I asked his name and he said, "Abraham." I pursued the question. "Would you mind telling me your *last* name?" Without missing a beat, he said, "Lincoln." Bemused, I asked, "Where are you are this moment?" Back came the answer: "Mumbai." By that time, I was getting into the game and my friend "Abraham Lincoln" was just as amused, so I asked him why he used the name "Abraham Lincoln." He answered, "My name isn't really Abraham Lincoln, but the company I work for wants each of us to use an American name so that Americans will feel comfortable talking with us. So I am using a name that is typically American."

Outsourcing has gone much farther than telephone-answerers. College courses – most of them in English or over the internet – are routinely conducted from outside our borders. Much more relevant for this chapter: *Medical care is being rapidly outsourced as Americans realize that they can get equivalent healthcare at one-fourth the cost by going overseas.* Today, it is not the least bit unusual (and becoming less so daily) for someone who needs an operation that would cost $30,000 in the United States to take his or her spouse on a "holiday" to India or Thailand, undergo the entire operation and hospitalization for $5,000, stay in five-star hotels for the duration, dine lavishly, and fly round-trip both ways at a total cost for everything of less than $15,000! Think I'm kidding? Think again – and ask anyone who's done it.

Of course, those hidebound "America-first'ers" decry such barbarity as uncivilized. "How can you trust yourself to *those foreigners*? Everybody knows that their standard of care is *nowhere near what you'll find in the good old U.S. of A.*? Oh, really? I suggest you might want to check out the success-ratio results of overseas operations. People wouldn't keep going if it didn't work. And while we're on the subject, have you checked lately at the number of absolutely outstanding healthcare professionals practicing in the United States who have trained in such "barbaric" places as India, Pakistan, Mexico, and Hungary?

Let's face it: The American healthcare system is pricing itself out of the market. Those who are thoughtful enough to study the statistics are coming to the unassailable conclusion that you can get healthcare better and cheaper overseas than you can here. The rest of the world is leaving us behind – more rapidly every year.

The World Health Organization categorically has stated that the French deliver the best health care system in the world. Let's examine how it works and see if the "shoe would fit" American feet. France, like other countries in Europe, has a system of universal health care largely financed by government through a system of national health insurance. In 2005, France spent 11.2% of GDP on health care, a figure much higher than the average spent by countries in Europe, but far less than in the 17.3% spent in the U.S. Approximately 77% of health expenditures are covered by government.

Most general physicians are in private practice but draw their income from the publicly funded insurance funds. The government has taken responsibility for the financial and operational management of health insurance by setting premium levels related to income and determining the prices of goods and services refunded. It generally refunds patients 70% of most health care costs, and 100% in case of costly or long-term ailments. Supplemental coverage may be bought from private insurers, most of them nonprofit, mutual insurers. The entire population must pay compulsory health insurance. The insurers are non-profit agencies that annually participate in negotiations with the state regarding the overall funding of health care in France. A premium is deducted from all employees' pay automatically. After paying the doctor's or dentist's fee, a proportion is claimed back. This is around 75 to 80%, but can be as much as 85%. The balance is effectively a co-payment paid by the patient, but it can also be recovered if the patient pays a regular premium to a voluntary health insurance scheme. General practitioners are expected to act as "gatekeepers" who refer patients to a specialist or a hospital. The incentive is financial in that expenses are reimbursed at lower rates for patients who go direct to a specialist, except for dentists, ophthalmologists, gynecologists and psychiatrists. 65% of hospital beds in France are provided by public hospitals, 15% by private non-profit organizations, and 20% by for-profit companies.

Patients have freedom of choice where to receive care.

Because the model of finance in the French health care system is based on a social insurance model, contributions to the scheme are based on income. Because the insurance is compulsory, the system can effectively be financed by taxation rather than by traditional insurance, such as auto or home insurance, where risk levels determine premiums.

The founders of the French social security system aimed to create a single system guaranteeing uniform rights for all. However, there was much opposition from certain socio-professional groups who already benefited from the previous insurance coverage that had more favorable terms. *These people were allowed to keep their own systems.* Today, 95% of the population are covered by 3 main schemes. One for commerce and industry workers and their families; a second for agricultural workers; and a third through the national insurance fund for self-employed non-agricultural workers.

All working people are required to pay a portion of their income to a health insurance fund, which mutualizes the risk of illness, and which reimburses medical expenses at varying rates. The government has two responsibilities in this system.

The fixing of the rate at which medical expenses should be negotiated. The Ministry of Health directly negotiates prices of medicine with the manufacturers, based on the average price of sale observed in neighboring countries. A board of doctors and experts decides if the medicine provides a valuable enough medical benefit to be reimbursed. In parallel, the government fixes the reimbursement rate for medical services: this means that a doctor is free to charge the fee that he wishes for a consultation or an examination, but the social security system will only reimburse it at a pre-set rate. These tariffs are set annually through negotiation with doctors' representative organizations.

Oversight of health-insurance funds, to ensure that they are correctly managing the sums they receive, and to ensure oversight of the public hospital network.

All citizens and legal foreign residents of France are covered by one of these mandatory programs, which continue to be funded by worker participation. To counter the rise in health-care costs, the government has installed two plans, which require insured people to declare a referring doctor in order to be fully reimbursed for specialist visits, and which installed a mandatory co-pay for a doctor visit, for each box of medicine prescribed, and a per-day fee of $20–25 for hospital stays and for expensive procedures.

The more ill a person becomes, the less they pay. This means that for people with serious or chronic illnesses, the insurance system reimburses them 100 % of expenses, and waives their co-pay charges. Finally, for fees that the mandatory system does not cover, there is a large range of private complementary insurance plans available. The market for these programs is very competitive, and often subsidized by the employer, which means that premiums are usually modest. 85% of French people benefit from complementary private health insurance.

A government body is responsible for issuing recommendations and practice guidelines. There are recommendations on clinical practice relating to the diagnosis, treatment and supervision of certain conditions, and in some cases, to the evaluation of reimbursement arrangements.

CONCLUSION:

THERE'S STILL TIME, BROTHER!

So now we've explored the fallacies of hate-driven, contrarian politics and disagreements by those who should know better, but who *won't* know better because they don't *want* to know better.

Yesterday, the world held its collective breath and cheered as thirty-three miners who'd been trapped underground for more than two months were lifted to the surface through a Herculean international effort. Today, that same world has let out its breath, concluded that, "Now, those guys are going to make a ton of money," pushed news of the rescue back to page 15 of the second session of the ever-declining print newspaper, and returned to life as usual. My wife and I went to Costco where the most prominently-displayed books were a handful of right-wing and Tea-party written mini-tomes castigating the politicians of the day. I recall the title of one of them, *The Obama Diaries,* which had the face of our President on the cover in a shot that made him look smug, dour, remotely evil. When Lorraine asked if that's the kind of book I was writing, I said, "Not exactly – at least I hope not."

I've just spent an election season listening to the rhetoric of negative political campaigning, which, sad to say, seems to be the *only* kind of campaigning that *works*. Looking at CNN, on my way through the channels to what *really* counts, college football, I come across a rehash of the Christine O'Donnell-Chris Coonts "debate." Mr. Coonts, as well as the moderators, seemed to keep saying, "Can we stick to the debate about the *issues*." Ms. O'Donnell refused. She seemed hell-bent on mouthing ugly platitudes that showed why government is so *evil*. She posited not one new idea of her own. She was a pretty face with a vacuous brain, trying to tear down the infrastructure and replace it with old, failed ideas. And to think she just might have won a legion of voters.

I am reminded of H.G. Wells' short story, "The Country of the Blind," which was first published in 1904. While attempting to climb to the crest of a fictitious mountain in Ecuador, a mountaineer named Nunez slips and falls down the far side of the mountain. At the end of his descent, he finds a valley, cut off from the rest of the world on all sides by steep precipices. Unbeknown to Nunez, he has discovered the fabled Country of the Blind. The valley had been a haven for settlers fleeing the tyranny of Spanish rulers until an earthquake reshaped the surrounding mountains and cut it off from future explorers. The isolated community prospered over the years, despite a disease that struck its inhabitants early on, rendering all new-borns blind. As the blindness slowly spread over the generations, their remaining senses sharpened, and by the time the last sighted villager had died, the community had fully adapted to life without sight.

Nunez finds an unusual village with windowless houses and a network of paths, all bordered by curbs. Upon discovering that everyone is blind, Nunez begins reciting to himself the refrain, "In the Country of the Blind, the One-Eyed Man is King." He realizes that he can teach and rule them. But the villagers have no concept of sight and do not understand his attempts to explain this fifth sense to them. Frustrated, Nunez becomes angry but they calm him and he reluctantly submits to their way of life because returning to the outside world is impossible.

Nunez is assigned to work for a villager named Yacob, and becomes attracted to Yacob's youngest daughter. They soon fall in love. Having won her confidence, Nunez slowly starts trying to explain sight to her. The daughter, Medina, however, simply dismisses it as his imagination. When Nunez asks for her hand in marriage he is turned down by the village elders on account of his "unstable" obsession with "sight." The village doctor suggests that Nunez's eyes be removed, claiming they are diseased and are affecting his brain. Nunez reluctantly consents to the operation because of his love for Medina. But at sunrise on the day of the operation, while all the villagers are asleep, Nunez, the failed King of the Blind, sets off for the mountains without provisions or equipment, hoping to find a passage to the outside world and escape the valley. He is eventually caught. The fact that he even dared to try escape is proof that his brain is addled, and his eyes are removed, so that now he is like all the rest.

We can learn several "lessons" from this story: An isolated community will generally overcome any disability like blindness after a few generations and will establish its own "truth." Having adapted to cope with such disabilities, an isolated community will believe that its modified behavior is normal, while those who don't conform are abnormal. An isolated community will tend to be closed-minded and xenophobic, and will persecute and, if necessary, reject anyone who is different and/or non-conformist.

This story is an allegory of society's treatment of those with ability or intellect beyond the understanding of the many: the fear of the 'barbarian' or at least the fear of the unenlightened masses.

In 2008, Barack Obama, the nation's first would-be President of color, campaigned on the promise of "Change We Can Believe In." Unfortunately, while this was a wonderful slogan, half of our nation did not believe in "change," did not *want* to believe in "change," and would unremittingly and savagely attack *any* "change." President Obama had something his immediate predecessor did not have: a commanding majority in both houses of Congress so great that he could have moved quickly and decisively to have his programs in place by the time the opposition woke up to what had hit them. Another President, Franklin D. Roosevelt, had a similar majority and had the command, the courage, and the *chutzpah* to drive his programs through – and, thank God (or Roosevelt) many of those socially enlightened programs exist and make our lives better today.

But as intelligent and as filled with hope as he was, Obama, who had the power to demand the use of the national media and who could very simply have told the American public, "Wake up and see what the obstructionists are doing!" – over and over and over again, morphed from Obama the campaigner into Obama the President. Somewhere in the midst of the first half of his Presidency he seemed to have lost his drive and lost his focus. Perhaps, like so many other recent Presidents, he found the problems that came with the job so daunting that his resolve collapsed and it became easier to simply "go with the flow." Whatever it was, by the end of his first two years in office, Obama was facing a revolution from the right – the horrifying specter that the more Americans *said* they wanted change, the less they actually wanted anything new, untried, "different." In the Country of the Blind ...

Meanwhile, as the United States slips ever closer to becoming what we once derisively referred to as a "Third World Country," we become more of an outlaw among nations, an embarrassment to our "friends" and a symbol of a warmongering "cowboy" to our increasing number of "enemies" – oops, I'm sorry, I meant "terrorists." For we continue to be the most adept of nations at using meaningless epithets to define those with whom we don't agree.

We have more than enough real problems in this country without manufacturing "non-problems" of our own. Examples:

- Who is going to fix the potholed roads of California, once our wealthiest state, when that state suffers a $20 *billion* deficit?

- Never mind the battle over "illegals." How are we going to take back control of our *neighborhoods* from the gangs that roam the street like uncontrolled packs of stray dogs?

- Instead of fighting one another over "water rights" that each competing "side" has, what steps are we taking to gather water from alternative sources?

- We spend billions of dollars each year fighting a "drug war" that we've been losing for seventy years, while "drug bosses" become ever richer and more powerful. Never mind that the most vigorous adherents of "Keep drugs illegal" are the alcohol interests that want to preserve their own territory. Wouldn't a more simple expedient be to legalize drugs and control it by *taxing* its sale? Or is that too easy and common-sense a solution?

It is time for us to stop being led around by our collective noses – willing victims to those whose money and influence speak the loudest. Perhaps it is time for us to *listen* to what those voices are saying, take the time and make the effort to analyze them, and come up with honest, *real* opinions on what is "wheat" and what is "chaff."

I challenge you to listen to *every single negative campaign*, then *study* what's being said and learn how much of it is true and how much of it is hyperbolic overstatement. *It is time to put a leash on everyone who insists on telling you what the other person has done wrong and demand to know what the naysayer has done right. It is time to demand: Don't tell me that what the other fellow proposes is so bad and won't work. Tell me what you intend to do – and be specific, don't just mouth platitudes.*

When was the last time you heard someone give *specifics* about a plan he or she proposed? And I mean this from *both* sides of the political spectrum. President Obama promised "healthcare reform." He called for a few specific items, but softened his stance significantly when faced with *realpolitik*. Most of the time it is necessary to negotiate in good faith with your other-party counterparts, but in this situation, when the Republicans had made it known from January 20, 2009 forward that they weren't going to pass *any* of President Obama's proposed programs and that they were going to blockade *every* attempt to change the status quo Obama made the drastic mistake of not corralling members of his own party and saying, in no uncertain terms, "We have the power and the numbers to pass our program *without* the opposing party. *Let's stop fiddling around and do it.* You're worried about your chances of reelection if you do? We're facing an impatient group of voters who don't like the healthcare system and a lot of other things that went on during the Bush administration. I can only tell you this – if you *don't* act decisively *now* – and if we don't get out on the stump and explain exactly *what* our program is and, even more important, *why* it's necessary for America, the one thing I can promise you is that you *are* going to lose your seats in 2012!"

He didn't say this, or, if he did, he didn't say it with enough force to move the programs along as they were designed to move along. What about the recalcitrant members of his own party? President Obama appears to have kowtowed to them, came with hat in hand as a supplicant rather than convincing them of the disaster their obstructionism was causing. What would FDR have done? Plain and simple, Roosevelt would have gone directly to the voters in the hesitant representative's district and been the stern taskmaster: "Voters of the 218th district of Ohio, are you aware that we need your Representative, Congressman Jones, to pass this bill? Are you aware that he won't do it? Is that what you elected him not to do? Write him, call his office, besiege him with your personal interest – let him know that the next election is just around the corner, and if he won't get with the program, you'll elect someone who will!"

What we in America seem to have forgotten is that *we are* not *a democracy*. We are a democratic republic in that we elect *representatives*, but we don't, in the true democratic sense, run "town hall meetings" anymore, even if that seems to have become a popular fiction among both parties in 21st century America.

One of the most enlightened views of what our type of government should be like the one that came from Emil Constantinescu, the President of Romania from 1996-2000. Speaking with American journalist and writer Robert D. Kaplan in 1998, he said,

"My job is to be a modern democratic ruler – not a ruler from on high looking down on the population – someone who is here today and back in private life tomorrow, someone who has to beg the people for their vote. The hardest thing I've had to learn is that we are not all equal. In discovering our individuality, we find that some are more intelligent than others, some work harder, some are more innovative, some are luckier and in a better position to acquire wealth. Competition means unsentimental selection of the best. This was done with the utmost toughness in Britain and America. It is only important that there be equality of *opportunity*, not equality of *result*. To say to a people like the Romanians, whose individuality has been crushed by Communism, that they are all equal is an insult. Because this was a hard truth to accept during the early phase of industrialization, Communism seduced intellectuals with the lie of equality, which, in practice, turned out to be rule by the lowest among us.[3]"

Alas, Constantinescu's presidency seems to reflect eerily on what has gone on in the United States during the past few years. His presidency was marred by an economic recession. With dashed expectations of an immediate improvement in daily life, Romanians exhibited strong disillusionment with the major parties and politicians. A disenchanted Constantinescu, who lost popularity and failed to fulfill his reformist agenda, announced on July 17 that he would not run for a second term. He withdrew from political life at the end of his term in November 2000.

I would like to suggest some definitive points for you to consider when evaluating political candidates from every part of the spectrum:

1. Wake up, *LISTEN* to, and ANALYZE what's said.

Does it make sense? Does it propel our nation, our state, our county, or our town forward, or does it simply dwell on past mistakes allegedly made by others? Consider exactly what is said. Use your own common sense – which each of us has – and use it *honestly*. Consider what Mark Twain wrote over a hundred years ago:

"The loud little handful will shout for war. The pulpit will warily and cautiously protest at first…The great mass of the nation will rub its sleepy eyes, and will try to make out why there should be a war, and they will say earnestly and indignantly: 'It is unjust and dishonorable and there is no need for war.' Then the few will shout even louder…Before long you will see a curious thing: anti-war

---

[3] Kaplan, Robert D., Eastward to Tartary: Travels in the Balkans, the Middle East and the Caucusus, 2000, New York, Vintage Books division of Random House, Inc.

speakers will be stoned from the platform, and free speech will be strangled by hordes of furious men who still agree with the speakers but dare not admit it ... Next, statesmen will invent cheap lies, putting blame upon the nation that is attacked, and every man will be glad of those conscience-soothing falsities, and will diligently study them, and refuse to examine any refutations of them; and thus he will by and by convince himself that the war is just, and will thank God for the better sleep he enjoys after this process of grotesque self-deception."

All humankind seems to love a scandal – provided that *another* human being is the target of that scandal. Thus, it is so easy to be misled by honeyed words of negative campaigning. If you and I truly want a decent, positive, representative government, we must work a little harder than we have been. We must make the extra effort, uncomfortable as it may be, to unearth what, to us, is the *truth* as it is – and not "the truth" as some politician or media pundit with an "agenda" wants it to be. It's time for us to dig beneath the surface and, perhaps, *learn* something in the process.

2. **All God's chilluns got brains – *USE 'EM.***

It is easy for us to say, "These politicians, commentators, or experts are insiders. They have more information than we do, and thus they know better." Balderdash! I urge you to read Appendix B of this book to learn about the true background of these so-called, self-styled "experts." Is this a true-to-life profile of someone who is better-educated than you or I? More honest? More worthy of being elected to the United States Senate? *I don't think so*, but again, I am asking you to use *your* brain – not the candidate's.

3. **Question what's *really* behind the words of hate.**

If you answer that question by saying, "The desire and willingness to say *anything* – true or untrue – to get elected," score 100% for using your brain and your common sense.

4. Consider what we can *all* gain by cooperation rather than conflict.

Throughout this book, I have shown numerous instances where, by working *together*, people have been able to arrive at common-sense, positive solutions to problems that confront their society. I have also pointed out equally numerous times when gridlock and paralysis have stymied our better selves from accomplishing what we could accomplish. And this is not only a problem in the United States – it has arisen in every civilization since time out of mind, and, sadly, it will continue to do so.

Cooperation rather than conflagration seems to me to be an idea whose time has come. We simply no longer have the time or the luxury to continue arguing over how many angels are dancing on the head of a pin. We are descending into the Third World we have so often condemned. It is only by working together – as we did during the Great Depression and in many other crises in our history – that we prevailed and came out the stronger for it.

5. It's time for us to "lengthen our memories."

Throughout political history, the politician's unofficial credo has been, "Promise the electorate whatever you have to promise to get elected – and then pray that the electorate's memory is short enough to forget what I promised as soon after the election as possible."

This has worked wonderfully – and contributed to nothing getting done. Human beings are eager for excitement, for titillation of any kind. Politicians know that. Yes, we all *mean* to hold the politicians to their promises, but you know how it is – other, more important things seem to get in the way. Such as my child's grades in elementary school. Or who my teenage daughter is dating. Or what kind of crazy clothing she's wearing? *Or why she doesn't keep her room clean?*

Read the newspapers or listen to the evening news on TV. More than 90% of the "news" stories involve scandals, crimes, *bad* news. The "heroes" segment, if it's broadcast at all, is usually toward the very end of the newscast. Or think about the best selling "news" papers (the "National Enquirer," "Us," etc.) and the top TV "news" programs – scandal, and the juicier the better. "Sorry, I didn't have time to consider what my representative promised, I was too busy watching the latest on Lindsay Lohan's escapades or *Dancing With The Stars*."

What ever happened to the word "accountability?"

I suggest you and I – each of us – make a list of specific promises made by political candidates, whether incumbent or elect-me-wannabes, that we publicize that list, and, just like "report cards" that are issued to our children from Kindergarten through University, we issue report cards on how our elected officials are doing in respect of those promises at least twice a year. Unquestionably, that would require more effort – and less laziness – from all of us, but wouldn't the end result be worth it in the long run?

6. **It's up to all of us – *ALL* OF US – to come up with solutions**.

Probably the most famous *Pogo* quotation is "We have met the enemy and he is us." Perhaps more than any other words written by the late Walt Kelly, it perfectly sums up his attitude towards the foibles of mankind and the nature of the human condition. The finalized version of the quotation appeared in a 1970 anti-pollution poster for Earth Day. If we are "the enemy," *i.e.* the problem, then it is within us *all* to be part of the solution as well. And we *can* be part of the solution. All we need to do is what politicians on both sides have been hypocritically exhorting us to do for decades: *Take back our country*. But in order to do that, we must decide what it is about our country that makes it *our country*. I close this book with a number of pertinent quotes from the late John F. Kennedy, President of the United States of America:

A man does what he must — in spite of personal consequences, in spite of obstacles and dangers, and pressures — and that is the basis of all human morality. (*Profiles in Courage,* 1956)

The New Frontier of which I speak is not a set of promises — it is a set of challenges. It sums up not what I intend to offer the American people, but what I intend to ask of them. (Acceptance Speech as the Democratic presidential nominee, July 15, 1960),

If by a "Liberal" they mean someone who looks ahead and not behind, someone who welcomes new ideas without rigid reactions, someone who cares about the welfare of the people — their health, their housing, their schools, their jobs, their civil rights, and their civil liberties — someone who believes we can break through the stalemate and suspicions that grip us in our policies abroad, if that is what they mean by a "Liberal," then I'm proud to say I'm a "Liberal." (Acceptance of the New York Liberal Party nomination, September 14, 1960).

We must know all the facts and hear all the alternatives and listen to all the criticisms. Let us welcome controversial books and controversial authors. (*Saturday Review*, October 29, 1960).)

The great enemy of the truth is very often not the lie — deliberate, contrived and dishonest — but the myth — persistent, persuasive, and unrealistic. (Commencement address, Yale University, New Haven, CT, June 11, 1962).

The problems of the world cannot possibly be solved by skeptics or cynics whose horizons are limited by the obvious realities. We need men who can dream of things that never were and ask "why not?" (Speech delivered to the Dail, the Parliament of Ireland, June 28, 1963).

And so, my fellow Americans: ask not what your country can do for you — ask what you can do for your country. My fellow citizens of the world: ask not what America will do for you, but what together we can do for the freedom of man. (Inauguration address, January 1960).

The End-

APPENDIX A

PRESIDENTIAL ELECTIONS

1789-1976

1. Presidential Elections – 1789-1860

2. From The Civil War to The Twentieth Century

3. The Going Gets Rougher – 1900-1976

* * *

1. Presidential Elections – 1789-1860

1789 AND 1792

The enormously popular George Washington essentially ran unopposed. The only real issue was who would be chosen as vice president. All 69 electors cast one vote each for Washington. Their other votes were divided among eleven other candidates. John Adams received the most, becoming vice president. Each of the original 13 states appointed electors, in addition to Kentucky and Vermont. Washington ran unopposed for a second term. Washington was elected unanimously with 77 electoral votes. John Adams finished second in voting and was re-elected Vice President.

1796

The first contested American presidential election and the only one to elect a President and Vice President from opposing tickets. George Washington, who could easily have won a third term, refused to run.

However hotly disputed, the election of 2000 was far from the most controversial of presidential contests. The 1796 election witnessed vote-rigging, name-calling and dirty tricks on a monumental scale. Federalist leader Alexander Hamilton decided that his presidential candidate, John Adams, was too stubborn to be easily controlled. Voters cast ballots for whichever of the presidential and vice-presidential candidates they pleased. If a potential vice president polled more votes than his running mate, he would go to the White House in his colleague's place. Hamilton plotted to have Adams's name dropped from the ballot papers in South Carolina, gambling that so many of that state's Federalist voters would vote for vice presidential candidate Thomas Pinckney that Pinckney would be propelled into the White House. When New England Federalists got wind of the plot and retaliated by removing Pinckney's name from their own ballots, the double manipulation cost the party so many votes that Adams scraped to victory by a narrow margin. Pinckney was beaten for vice presidency by the Republicans' Thomas Jefferson. Democratic-Republicans campaigned heavily for Jefferson. Federalists campaigned heavily for Adams. The debate was acrimonious. Federalists tied the Democratic-Republicans to the violence of the French Revolution. The Democratic-Republicans accused the Federalists of favoring monarchism and aristocracy.

1800

The election of 1800 stands as one of the dirtiest and most vicious campaigns in American history. To say that there was no love lost between President John Adams and his Vice President, Thomas Jefferson, is an understatement. Writer James Callendar, secretly hired by Thomas Jefferson, assailed then-President John Adams as a "repulsive pedant" and "a hideous hermaphrodite." The campaign was bitter and characterized by slander and personal attacks on both sides. Federalists spread rumors that the Democratic-Republicans were radicals who would murder their opponents, burn churches, and destroy the country. The Democratic-Republicans accused Federalists of destroying republican values. They accused Federalists of favoring Britain in order to promote aristocratic, anti-republican values. The Federalists claimed that Jefferson had cheated his creditors and defrauded a widow out of her estate, and that he was the child of a "half-breed Indian squaw, sired by a Virginia mulatto father," who fed young Tom bacon, hominy, and fricasseed bullfrog.

Republicans argued that President Adams had planned to marry one of his sons to the daughter of England's King George III, and start an American monarchy; Adams had supposedly abandoned the plan only after George Washington threatened to run him through with a sword. Further, Adams' vice president, General Pinckney had been sent to England to procure pretty girls as mistresses — two for Adams, and two for Pinckney. Remarked Adams, "I declare upon my honor, if this be true, General Pinckney has kept them all for himself and cheated me out of my two."

Hamilton, in his third sabotage attempt towards Adams, schemed to elect Vice Presidential candidate Pinckney to the Presidency. One of Hamilton's letters, providing a scathing criticism of Adams, became public when it came into the hands of a Republican, embarrassing Adams and damaging Hamilton's efforts on behalf of Pinckney, not to mention speeding Hamilton's own political decline.

Hamilton and Jefferson, as leaders of their respective political parties, were bitter political enemies. But the rift between Hamilton and Aaron Burr was a personal one. The two men detested each other with a scorn that went far beyond the political disagreements between Hamilton and Jefferson. When Hamilton saw that Burr had a chance of becoming President, he worked behind the scenes to ensure that Burr would not be the new president. The House of Representatives eventually, on the 36th ballot, chose Jefferson. Burr became vice-president.

When the electoral ballots were opened and counted on February 11, 1801, it turned out that the certificate of election from Georgia was defective. (Shades of the "hanging chad" 200 years later!).

While it was common knowledge that Jefferson was the candidate for President and Burr for Vice President, the lame-duck House was controlled by the Federalists, who were unwilling to vote for Jefferson (with one exception, Alexander Hamilton). Jefferson had been the Federalists' principal opponent since 1789. Seizing an opportunity to elect Burr, as opposed to Jefferson, most Federalists voted for Burr, giving Burr six of the eight states controlled by Federalists.

Over the course of seven days from February 11 to February 17, the House cast a total of 35 ballots, with Jefferson receiving the votes of eight state delegations each time, one short of the necessary majority of nine. During the confusion, Alexander Hamilton said he supported Jefferson because he was "by far not so dangerous a man" as Burr; in short, he would much rather have someone with wrong principles than someone devoid of any. Hamilton embarked on a frenzied letter-writing campaign to get delegates to switch votes, and narrowly succeeded. On Tuesday, February 17, on the 36th ballot, Jefferson was elected.

Still, this was the first peaceful transfer of federal executive power from one political faction to another. Both Adams and his predecessor, George Washington, had been aligned with the Federalist Party; although Washington had voluntarily relinquished power at the end of his term in 1797, Adams was widely viewed as Washington's heir apparent and a continuation of the Federalist agenda. However, when defeated by Jefferson's Democratic-Republicans, the Federalists voluntarily handed over executive authority to their political opposition.

1804

Attacks on Jefferson's policies proved fruitless; Jefferson's victory was overwhelming, even winning most of the New England states in the Federalist heartland.

1808

Democratic-Republican candidate James Madison defeated Federalist candidate Charles Pinckney. Madison had served as United States Secretary of State under Thomas Jefferson. Pinckney had been the unsuccessful Federalist candidate in 1804. The election was marked by opposition to Jefferson's Embargo Act of 1807, a halt to trade with Europe that disproportionately hurt New England merchants and was perceived as favoring France over Britain. Nonetheless, Jefferson was still very popular with Americans and Pinckney was soundly defeated. Pinckney carried only a handful of votes outside New England.

1812

This election took place in the shadow of the War of 1812. It featured competition between incumbent Democratic-Republican President James Madison and dissident Democratic-Republican, DeWitt Clinton, nephew of Madison's late Vice President. The Federalist opposition threw their support behind Clinton, but Madison was re-elected.

1816 AND 1820

The 1816 election came at the end of Madison's two-term presidency. With the Federalist Party in collapse, Madison's

Secretary of State, James Monroe, won the nomination against a divided opposition. Jefferson and Madison both favored Monroe. When the votes were counted, Monroe had won all but three of the nineteen states. The 1820 presidential election was the third and last presidential election in United States history in which a candidate ran effectively unopposed. President James Monroe and Vice President Daniel D. Tompkins were re-elected without a serious campaign. Despite the continuation of single party politics (known as the Era of Good Feelings), serious issues emerged during the election in 1820. The nation had endured a widespread depression following the Panic of 1819. The momentous issue of the extension of slavery into the territories was taking center stage. Nevertheless, Monroe faced no opposition party or candidate in his reelection bid.

1824

John Quincy Adams was elected President after the election was decided by theHouse of Representatives. The Democratic-Republican Party splintered as four separate candidates sought the presidency. Later, the faction led by Andrew Jackson would evolve into the Democratic Party, while the factions led by John Quincy Adams and Henry Clay would become the National Republican Party and later the Whig Party. This election was notable for being the only time since the passage of the Twelfth Amendment in which the presidential election was decided by the House of Representatives, as no candidate received a majority of the electoral vote. This presidential election was also the only one in which the candidate receiving the most electoral votes did not become president (because a majority, not just a plurality, is required to win). It was also the first election in which the president did not win the popular vote.

The election was a contest among: (1) General Andrew Jackson, a charismatic hero of the War of 1812, a former United States Representative, and a then-current United States Senator from Tennessee. (2) John Quincy Adams of Massachusetts, son of former President John Adams, then-current Secretary of State. (3) William H. Crawford, then-Secretary of the Treasury; and (4) Henry Clay of Kentucky, the "Great Compromiser," and the then-Speaker of the House. Not surprisingly, the results of the election were divided and inconclusive. Adams won in New England; Jackson had success in states throughout the nation. With Clay's votes coming from the west and Crawford's from the east, Andrew Jackson received more electoral and popular votes than any other candidate, but not the 131 electoral votes to constitute a majority and win the election. As no candidate received the required majority of electoral votes, the presidential election was decided by the House of Representatives.

Campaigning for this presidential election occurred in many forms. Well-known songs and tunes were lyrically altered and used to promote political agendas and presidential candidates. Another form of campaigning, newsprint, included political cartoons and partisan writings. Most candidates involved in early 19th century elections did not run their own political campaigns. Instead it was left to volunteer citizens and partisans to speak on behalf of and promote the candidates.

1828

The "Era of Good Feeling" was more than over. This was one of the most vicious and vitriolic campaigns in American history. Supporters of conservative candidate John Quincy Adams distributed a pamphlet which claimed that Democratic candidate Andrew Jackson's mother "was a common prostitute brought to this country by British solders. She afterwards married a mulatto man with whom she had several children of which General Jackson is one!!" Jackson's marriage came in for attack: when he had married his wife Rachel, the couple had believed that she was divorced; however, the divorce was not yet finalized, so he had to remarry her once the legal papers were complete. In the Adams campaign's hands, this became a scandal. Charles Hammond in his *Cincinnati Gazette* asked: "Ought a convicted adulteress and her paramour husband to be placed in the highest offices of this free and Christian land?"

The notorious Coffin Handbills attacked Jackson for his court martial and execution of deserters, for his massacres of Indian villages, and for his habit of dueling. Other elements of the Adams campaign suggested that Jackson was a loose cannon who would drag the United States into bloody foreign wars.

The Jackson campaign gave as well as it got. It charged that Adams, while serving as Minister to Russia, had surrendered an American servant girl to the appetites of the Czar. Adams was also accused of using public funds to buy gambling devices for the presidential residence. It turned out these were a chess set and a pool table. Jackson wrote that a lavish government combined with contempt of the constituents could lead to despotism, if not checked by the "voice of the people." John Quincy Adams was nicknamed "The Pimp" by Jackson's campaign.

A goal of the pro-Adams press was to depict Jackson as a "mere military chieftain." Edward Coles recounted that Thomas Jefferson had told him in a conversation in August 1825 that he feared the popular enthusiasm for Jackson: "It has caused me to doubt more than anything that has occurred since our Revolution." Gilmer said Jefferson had told him at Monticello before the election of Adams in 1825: "One might as well make a sailor of a cock, or a soldier of a goose, as a President of Andrew Jackson." Daniel Webster, who was also at Monticello at the time, made the same report. Webster said Jefferson told him that Jackson was a dangerous man unfit for the presidency.

Gilmer, in turn, accused Coles of misrepresentation, and said that Jefferson had become friendly to Jackson's candidacy as early as the summer of 1825. He thought of Jackson as "an honest, sincere, clear-headed and strong-minded man; of the soundest political principles" and "the only hope left" to reverse the increasing powers assumed by the federal government.

The selection of electors began on October 31 with elections in Ohio and Pennsylvania and ended on November 13 with elections in North Carolina. The Electoral College met on December 3. Adams won almost exactly the same states that his father had won in the election of 1800: the New England states, New Jersey, and Delaware. In addition, Adams picked up Maryland. Jackson won everywhere else, resulting in a landslide victory.

Rachel Jackson had been having chest pains throughout the campaign, and she became aggravated by the personal attacks on her marriage. She became ill and died on December 22, 1828. Jackson accused the Adams campaign, and Henry Clay even more so, of causing her death, saying, "I can and do forgive all my enemies. But those vile wretches who have slandered her must look to God for mercy."

When the results of the election were announced, a mob entered the White House, damaging the furniture and lights. Jackson escaped through the back and large punch bowls were set up to lure the crowd outside. Conservatives were horrified at this event, and held it up as a portent of terrible things to come from the first Democratic president. Andrew Jackson was sworn in as President on March 4, 1829.

1832

The first national convention of the Democratic Party, was held in May 1832. On the first contested roll call vote in convention history, the convention voted to deprive D.C. of its voting rights in the convention. Each state was allotted as many votes as it had Presidential Electors. Balloting was taken by states, not by individual delegates. No roll call vote was taken to nominate Jackson for a second term. Instead, the convention passed a resolution stating that "we most cordially concur in the repeated nominations which he has received in various parts of the union." Martin Van Buren was nominated for vice president.

The election campaign revolved around the Second Bank of the United States. Jackson, who disliked banks and paper money in general, vetoed the renewal of the Bank's charter and withdrew federal deposits from the bank. Clay hoped to divide Jackson's supporters and curry favor in Pennsylvania, the bank's headquarters, by attacking Jackson. His supporters attacked Jackson's use of presidential veto power, calling him as "King Andrew." However, the attacks on Jackson generally failed, in spite of heavy funding by the bank, as Jackson convinced the ordinary population that he was defending them against a privileged elite. Jackson campaign events were marked by enormous turnouts. Andrew Jackson easily won reelection against National Republican Henry Clay of Kentucky. This was the first national election for Martin Van Buren of New York. Four years later he would succeed Jackson as President.

1836

This campaign was the last election until 1988 to result in the elevation of an incumbent Vice President to the nation's highest office through means other than the president's death or resignation. It was the only race in which a major political party, the Whigs, intentionally ran four different candidates in different regions of the country, hoping that each would be popular enough to defeat Democratic standard-bearer Martin Van Buren in their respective areas. The House of Representatives could then decide between the competing Whig candidates. This strategy failed: Van Buren won a majority of the electoral vote and became President. And it was the first (and to date the only) time in which a Vice Presidential election was thrown into the Senate.

Incumbent president Andrew Jackson decided to retire after two terms and supported his Vice President, Martin Van Buren. Although Southerners disliked the New Yorker Van Buren as well as his intended running mate, Colonel Richard Mentor Johnson of Kentucky, Van Buren secured the nomination at a meeting in Baltimore, at the 1835 Democratic National Convention. The Whig Party had emerged during the 1834 midterm elections as the chief opposition to the Democratic Party. It absorbed the National Republican Party and the Anti-Masonic Party. Some Southerners, who were angered by Jackson's opposition to states' rights, were temporarily part of the Whig coalition.

Beginning at the end of 1835, some Whig state conventions in the North began to shift from Webster to popular former general William Henry Harrison. By the middle of 1836, Harrison had replaced Webster in all free states except Massachusetts as the Whig nominee. The Whigs attacked Van Buren on all sides, even disrupting the Senate where he presided. No less than Davy Crockett accused Van Buren of wearing women's corsets! Harrison was the most effective of Van Buren's opponents, but the Vice President's superior party organization carried the day, earning him a majority. Van Buren defeated Harrison by a 51-49% vote in the North, and he defeated White by a similar 51-49% margin in the South.

Anticipating a challenge to the results, Congress resolved on February 4, 1837 that during the counting four days later the final tally would be read twice, once with Michigan and once without Michigan. The counting proceeded in accordance with the resolution. The dispute had no bearing on the final result: either way Van Buren was elected and either way no one had a majority for Vice President.

1840

President Martin Van Buren was faced with an economic depression and a Whig Party unified for the first time (sound familiar?) behind war hero William Henry Harrison. This election was the only one in which electors cast votes for four men who had been or would become President of the United States: Van Buren, William Henry Harrison, John Tyler, who would succeed Harrison upon his death; and James K. Polk, who received one electoral vote for Vice President. Because Harrison was considered a Northerner, the Whigs balanced their ticket with a Southerner, former Senator John Tyler of Virginia.

Because of the Panic of 1837, Van Buren was widely unpopular. Harrison, ran as a war hero and man of the people while presenting Van Buren as a wealthy snob living in luxury at the public expense. Although Harrison was comfortably wealthy and well educated, his "log cabin" image caught fire, sweeping all sections of the country. Harrison avoided campaigning on the issues. His Whig Party was a broad coalition with few common ideals. Although his popular vote margin was only 6 points, Harrison's electoral victory was overwhelming. Rallying under the slogan "Tippecanoe and Tyler, too," the Whigs easily defeated Van Buren.

Harrison, the oldest President second to Ronald Reagan, died little more than a month after his inauguration. The choice of Tyler for Vice President proved to be disastrous for the Whigs: he was a former Democrat and a passionate supporter of states' rights who blocked the Whigs' political program in office.

Harrison's campaign slogan, "Tippecanoe and Tyler too," caught fire, and to this day the history books write about it. Van Buren's responsive song, to the tune of "Rockabye Baby," was clever, but didn't save the election for him.

"Rockabye, baby, Daddy's a Whig
When he comes home, hard cider he'll swig
When he has swug
He'll fall in a stu
And down will come Tyler and Tippecanoe.

"Rockabye, baby, when you awake
You will discover Tip is a fake.
Far from the battle, war cry and drum
He sits in his cabin a'drinking bad rum.

"Rockabye, baby, never you cry
You need not fear of Tip and his Ty.
What they would ruin, Van Buren will fix.
Van's a magician, they are but tricks."

1844

Democrat James Knox Polk defeated Whig Henry Clay in a close contest that turned on foreign policy. Polk favored the annexation of Texas. Clay opposed it. Polk embraced American territorial expansionism, an idea soon to be called Manifest Destiny. At their convention, the Democrats called for the annexation of Texas and to the whole of the Oregon Territory. Polk went on to win a narrow victory over Whig candidate Henry Clay, in part because Clay had taken a stand against expansion, although economic issues were also of great importance. This was the last presidential election to be held on different days in different states, as starting with the presidential election of 1848 all states held the election on the same date in November.

The incumbent President in 1844 was John Tyler, Harrison's successor. Although Tyler had been nominated on a Whig ticket, his policies had alienated the Whigs and they actually kicked him out of the party on September 13, 1841, while he was president. Tyler sought an issue that could create a viable third party to support his bid for the presidency in 1844. He found that issue in the annexation of Texas. Going into the presidential campaign season, Texas annexation, which was explicitly tied to southern slavery, suddenly emerged as the top issue.

While Van Buren held a slim majority of delegates, his public stand against immediate annexation had increased the hostility of the opposition. On the eighth ballot, a new name was introduced: James K. Polk, who had intended to seek the vice presidential nomination. While he did not receive the necessary votes to win on this ballot, the momentum was clearly in his direction, and he won the necessary 2/3 on the following ballot, making Polk the first "dark horse" candidate.

Tyler spent much of the summer with his new bride on their honeymoon in New York City. While there, he discovered his support was almost nonexistent. He received appeals from Democrats to withdraw, including a letter from Andrew Jackson. Tyler withdrew from the race at the end of August for fear that his candidacy would divide the votes going to Polk, and potentially lead to Clay's election.

The Whigs initially played on Polk's comparative obscurity, asking "Just Who is James K. Polk?" as part of their campaign to get Clay elected. Polk favored the annexation of Texas. To deflect charges of pro-slavery bias in the Texas annexation issue, Polk combined the Texas annexation issue with a demand for the acquisition of the entire Oregon Territory, which was at the time jointly administered by the United States and Great Britain. This proved to be an immensely popular message, especially compared to the Whigs' economic program. It forced Clay to move on the issue of Texas annexation, saying he would support annexation if it could be accomplished without war and upon "just and fair" terms.

Some historians have speculated that Clay's ambiguous stance on Texas cost him critical anti-slavery votes in New York, and tipped the overall election to the Democrats. On the other hand, Clay won an extremely narrow victory in largely pro-Texas Tennessee. If he had adopted a more forthright anti-Texas position, he may well have lost that state's 13 electoral votes, enough to give the election back to Polk in any case.

Polk's election confirmed the American public's desire for westward expansion. Mexico refused to accept the annexation of Texas and the Mexican-American War broke out in 1846. With Polk's main issue of Texas settled, instead of demanding all of Oregon, he compromised and the United States and Great Britain negotiated the Buchanan-Pakenham Treaty, which divided up the Oregon Territory between the two countries.

1848

President James Polk, having achieved all of his major objectives in one term and suffering from declining health that would take his life less than four months after leaving office, kept his promise not to seek re-election.

In 1846-47, the Whigs had focused all their energy on condemning Polk's war policies. But when Polk surprised everyone in February 1848 with the Treaty of Guadalupe Hidalgo, which ended the Mexican-American War and gave the U.S. vast new territories (including California, Nevada, Utah, and parts of Wyoming,

Colorado, Arizona, and New Mexico), the Whigs quickly reversed course, voting 2-1 to approve the treaty. (You see what cooperation can do!)

In the summer of '48, the Whigs nominated war hero Zachary Taylor. While Taylor promised no more future wars, he did not condemn the Mexican-American war or criticize Polk, and Whigs had to follow his lead. They shifted to the new issue: whether slavery should be banned from the new territories. While Taylor was not clearly committed to Whig principles, he was popular for leading the war effort. The Democrats had a record of victory, peace, prosperity, and the acquisition of both Oregon and the Southwest; they appeared almost certain winners unless the Whigs picked Taylor. Taylor's victory made him one of only two Whigs to be elected President before the party ceased to exist in the 1850s. The other Whig to be elected President was William Henry Harrison, who had also been a general and war hero, but who died a month into office. Zachary Taylor had never voted in an election himself, but he was openly courted by both the Democrats and the Whigs. After Daniel Webster turned down the vice presidential candidacy, the party nominated Millard Fillmore for Vice President.

The Democrats nominated Lewis Cass, former Governor and Senator from Michigan. They chose a platform that remained silent on slavery. With Cass suspected of pro-slavery leanings, many anti-slavery Democrats walked out of the Baltimore convention and started the Free Soil party, which was organized for the 1848 election to oppose further expansion of slavery into the western territories. Former President Martin Van Buren was chosen as its Presidential hopeful.

Whig campaigners like Abraham Lincoln talked up Taylor's "antiparty" opposition to the Jacksonian commitment to the spoils system and yellow-dog partisanship. In the South, they stressed that Taylor was a Louisiana slaveholder, while in the North they highlighted his willingness to defer to Congress on major issues. Democrats repeated their opposition to a national bank, high tariffs, and federal subsidies for local improvements. The Free Soilers branded both major parties lackeys of the Slave Power, arguing that the rich planters controlled the agenda of both parties, leaving the ordinary white man out of the picture. They had to work around Van Buren's well-known reputation for compromising with slavery. Whigs highlighted Taylor's military glories.

With Taylor remaining vague on the issues, the campaign was dominated by personalities and personal attacks: the Democrats called Taylor vulgar, uneducated, cruel and greedy; the Whigs attacking Cass for graft and dishonesty. The division of the Democrats over slavery allowed Taylor to dominate the Northeast.

With the exception of South Carolina, the election of 1848 marked the first time in which every state in the union voted for President and Vice President on the same day: November 7, 1848. Taylor won election over Cass, capturing 163 of the 290 electoral votes cast. However, Taylor won barely more than 47% of the popular vote, mainly because of the 10% the Free Soil Party had won. When Zachary Taylor died of acute gastroenteritis in 1850, he was succeeded in office by his Vice President, Millard Fillmore, who served as President from 1850 until 1853. He was the last member of the Whig Party to hold that office. He became the second Vice President to assume the presidency after the death of a sitting president. Fillmore was never elected president.

1852

Once again, the incumbent President was a Whig who had succeeded to the presidency upon the death of his war hero predecessor. In this case, it was Millard Fillmore, who followed General Zachary Taylor. The Whig party passed over Fillmore in favor of General Winfield Scott. The Democrats nominated a "dark horse" candidate, Franklin Pierce. The Whigs once again campaigned on the obscurity of the Democratic candidate, and once again that strategy failed. Pierce won what was at the time one of the nation's largest electoral victories, trouncing Scott, 254 electoral votes to 42. After the 1852 election the Whig Party collapsed, and its members failed to nominate a candidate for the next presidential race; it was soon replaced as the Democratic Party's primary opposition by the new Republican Party – today's G.O.P..

The 1852 Whig National Convention was bitterly divided. Supporters of President Fillmore pointed to the successful Compromise of 1850 and the failure of a secession movement in the Southern states in 1850–1851. The northern Whigs believed that the Compromise of 1850 favored the slaveholding South over the North. Northern Whigs favored heroic Mexican-American War General Winfield Scott of New Jersey, who had earned the nickname of "Old Fuss and Feathers" due to his insistence on military appearance and discipline. While respected, he was also seen as somewhat foppish. Most New England delegates supported Daniel Webster. Scott was nominated on the 53rd ballot by a margin of 159-112.

As Democrats convened in Baltimore in June 1852, four major candidates vied for the nomination: Lewis Cass, James Buchanan, Stephen A. Douglas of Illinois, and William L. Marcy. Franklin Pierce of New Hampshire, a former Congressman and Senator, did not even get on the board until the 35th ballot, when the Virginia delegation brought him forward as a compromise choice. He consolidated his support in subsequent voting and was nominated nearly unanimously on the 49th ballot.

The Whigs' platform was almost indistinguishable from that of the Democrats, reducing the campaign to a contest between personalities. The lack of clear-cut issues resulted in voter turnout being at its lowest level since 1836. The decline was further exacerbated by Scott's anti-slavery reputation, which decimated the Southern Whig vote at the same time as the pro-slavery Whig platform undermined the Northern Whig vote. Finally, Scott's status as a war hero was somewhat offset by the fact that Pierce was himself a Mexican-American War brigadier general. Shortly before the election Union party candidate Daniel Webster died, causing many Union state parties to remove their slates of electors.

When America went to the polls Pierce won by a landslide. As a result of this devastating defeat, and because of the growing tensions within the party between pro-slavery Southerners and anti-slavery Northerners, the Whig Party fell apart after the 1852 election and ceased to exist.

1856

Filth, mud-slinging, and dirty tricks were a hallmark of this unusually heated election campaign that led to the election of James Buchanan. Republican candidate John C. Frémont crusaded against Slave Power and the expansion of slavery. Democrat Buchanan warned that the Republicans were extremists whose victory would lead to civil war. Former President Millard Fillmore represented a third party, the relatively new American Party or "Know-Nothings," who ignored the slavery issue altogether in favor of anti-immigration policies, and won a little over 20% of the vote.

Incumbent President Franklin Pierce was defeated in his effort to be renominated by the Democrats, thanks in part to the fact that the Kansas-Nebraska Act divided Democrats. The Democratic Party was wounded from its devastating losses in the 1854-1855 midterm elections. The delegates to its National Convention were deeply divided over slavery. For the first time in American history, a man who had been elected President was denied re-nomination. On the 17th ballot, Buchanan was unanimously nominated.

The first Republican National Convention was held in Philadelphia. The convention approved an anti-slavery platform, calling for congressional sovereignty of the territories, an end to polygamy in Mormon settlements, and federal assistance for a transcontinental railroad. John C. Fremont was nominated for President over John McLean, and William L. Dayton was nominated for Vice President over Abraham Lincoln.

During the campaign, none of the three candidates took to the stump. Republicans opposed the extension of slavery into the territories. Their slogan was "Free speech, free press, free soil, free men, Frémont and victory!" The Republicans crusaded against the Slave Power, warning it was destroying Republican values. Democrats counter-crusaded by warning that a Republican victory would bring civil war. The Republicans accused the Pierce administration of allowing a fraudulent territorial government to be imposed upon the citizens of the Kansas Territory, allowing the violence that had raged in Bleeding Kansas, and advocated the immediate admittance of Kansas as a free state. Along with opposing the spread of slavery into the continental territories of the United States, the party also opposed the annexation of Cuba from Spain.

The Democratic platform supported the Kansas-Nebraska Act and the system of popular sovereignty established in the Western territories. The party supported the pro-slavery territorial legislature elected in Kansas, opposing the free state elements within Kansas and castigated the Topeka Constitution as an illegal document written during an illegal convention. The Democrats supported the plan to annex Cuba, which Buchanan helped devise while serving as minister to Britain. The most influential aspect of the Democratic campaign was a warning that a Republican victory would lead to the secession of numerous southern states.

Political dirty tricks were the norm. Democrats marked badges "Black Republican" depicting a runaway slave and made frequent jabs at Frémont's out-of-wedlock birth. Republicans countered with remarks about Buchanan's age and bachelorhood as well as the nickname "Ten-Cent Jimmy" after he unwisely said in public that he considered ten cents a day a fair wage for manual laborers. They also suggested that Buchanan's trademark tendency to tilt his head stemmed not from deficient eyesight but because he had once tried to hang himself.

On the actual campaign issues, Buchanan supported allowing individual states to allow or ban slavery. Fremont was a staunch abolitionist. The Know-Nothing Party actually helped Buchanan - charging Fremont with Catholicism and taking away some of his voter base. Buchanan carried the South and the border states, but with deep divisions in the North, still only took about 1/2 of the popular vote.

The campaign had a different nature in the free states from that in the slave states. Fremont won with 45% of the vote to 41% for Buchanan and 13% for Fillmore. That translated into an electoral vote margin of 114-62 in favor of Fremont. In the South, the campaign was strictly a Buchanan vs. Fillmore race. Buchanan won there by a 56-44% margin, good for a 112-8 electoral vote margin. Nationwide, Buchanan won 174 electoral votes, a majority, and was thus elected. Ultimately, history was unkind to James Buchanan. He made the top of the worst President list.

1860

This election set the stage for the American Civil War, the War Between the States. The nation had been divided throughout most of the 1850s on questions of states' rights and slavery in the territories. In 1860, this issue finally came to a head, fracturing the formerly dominant Democratic Party into Southern and Northern factions and bringing Abraham Lincoln and the Republican Party to power without the support of a single Southern state.

Hardly more than a month following Lincoln's victory, South Carolina declared its secession, which were rejected as illegal by the then-current President, James Buchanan and by the President-elect Abraham Lincoln.

The origins of the American Civil War lay in the complex issues of slavery, competing understandings of federalism, party politics, expansionism, sectionalism, tariffs, and economics. After the Mexican-American War, the issue of slavery in the new territories had led to the Compromise of 1850. While the compromise averted an immediate political crisis, it did not permanently resolve the issue.

Six Democratic candidates were nominated during the first convention in April 1860. When no candidate achieved majority by May 3, the delegates agreed to stop voting and adjourn the convention. The Democrats reconvened in Baltimore on June 18. This time 110 southern delegates walked out when the convention would not adopt a resolution supporting extending slavery into territories whose voters did not want it. After two ballots, the remaining Democrats nominated the ticket of Stephen A. Douglas of Illinois for President.

The Republican had a rich and varied plateful of candidates: Abraham Lincoln, former U.S. representative from Illinois; William H. Seward, U.S. senator from New York; Simon Cameron, U.S. senator from Pennsylvania; Salmon P. Chase, former U.S. senator and governor from Ohio; and Edward Bates, former U.S. representative from Missouri.

William H. Seward was considered the front runner, followed by Abraham Lincoln, Salmon P. Chase, and Edward Bates. However, Seward, Chase, and Bates had each alienated factions of the Republican Party. Since it was essential to carry the West, and because Lincoln had a national reputation from his debates and speeches as the most articulate moderate, he won the party's nomination on the third ballot on May 18, 1860. The party platform stated that slavery would not be allowed to spread any further. It also promised tariffs protecting industry, a Homestead Act granting free farmland in the West to settlers, and the funding of a transcontinental railroad. All of these provisions were highly unpopular in the South.

The contest in the North was between Lincoln and Douglas, but only Douglas took to the stump and gave speeches and interviews. Stephen A. Douglas was the first presidential candidate in American history to undertake a nationwide speaking tour. He traveled to the South where he did not expect to win many electoral votes, but he spoke for the maintenance of the Union.

Throughout the general election, Lincoln did not campaign or give speeches. This was handled by the state and county Republican organizations, who used the latest techniques to sustain party enthusiasm and thus obtain high turnout. There was little effort to convert non-Republicans, and there was virtually no campaigning in the South except for a few border cities such as St. Louis and Wheeling, Virginia. The party did not even run a slate in most of the South. In the North, there were thousands of Republican speakers, tons of campaign posters and leaflets, and thousands of newspaper editorials. These focused first on the party platform, and second on Lincoln's life story, making the most of his boyhood poverty, his pioneer background, his native genius, and his rise from obscurity. His nicknames, "Honest Abe" and "the Rail-Splitter," were exploited. The campaign's goal was to show that a common farm boy could work his way to the top by his own efforts. On the other hand, Lincoln's detractors accused him of having stinky feet.

In 1860, every pundit calculated that the Republicans had an almost unbeatable advantage in the Electoral College, since they dominated almost every northern state. Republicans felt victory at hand, and used paramilitary campaign organizations like the

Wide Awakes to rally their supporters. The election was held on November 6 amidst the exaggerated sectionalism of the vote in a country that was soon to dissolve into civil war. Lincoln captured less than 40% of the popular vote, but almost all of his votes were concentrated in the free states, where he won every state except New Jersey. He won outright majorities in enough of the free states to win the Presidency by an Electoral College vote, even if the 60% of voters who opposed him nationally had united behind a single candidate. The voter turnout rate in 1860 was the second-highest on record (81.2%, second only to 1876, with 81.8%).

A brief footnote to modern times: In 1864, Lincoln wrote,

"I see in the near future a crisis approaching that unnerves me and causes me to tremble for the safety of my country... Corporations have been enthroned and an era of corruption in high places will follow, and the money power of the country will endeavor to prolong its reign by working upon the prejudices of the people until all wealth is aggregated in a few hands and the Republic is destroyed."

* * *

2. From The Civil War to The Twentieth Century

1864

Abraham Lincoln was re-elected as president over his former top general, George B. McClellan. McClellan was the "peace candidate," but he did not personally believe in his party's platform. None of the states loyal to the Confederate States of America participated in this election. Lincoln won by nearly 450,000 popular votes and easily clinched an electoral majority. Lincoln's second term ended just 6 weeks after his inauguration when he was assassinated.

Before the election, the War Democrats joined the Republicans to form the National Union Party. With the outcome of the Civil War still in doubt, Salmon Chase, Benjamin Wade, and Horace Greeley opposed Lincoln's renomination on the ground that he could not win. But the National Union Party nominated Lincoln for a second term. President. Lincoln successfully urged the convention to nominate Military Governor Andrew Johnson of Tennessee, a War Democrat, as his running mate. Johnson had strongly supported the Union, he was a Southerner, and he was a leading member of the War Democrats.

The Democratic Party was bitterly split between the War Democrats and the Peace Democrats. After Gettysburg, when it was clear that the South could not win the war, moderate Peace Democrats proposed a negotiated peace that would secure Union victory. They believed that an armistice could finish the war without finishing the South. Radical Peace Democrats declared the war to be a failure and favored an immediate end to hostilities without securing Union victory.

George B. McClellan and former Connecticut Governor Thomas H. Seymour vied for the presidential nomination. On the day before the Convention, Seymour pulled out of the election. General McClellan emerged as a compromise candidate for president. The convention adopted a peace platform — a platform McClellan personally rejected. McClellan supported the continuation of the war and restoration of the Union, but the party platform was opposed to this position.

For much of 1864, Lincoln himself believed he had little chance of being re-elected. The prospect of a long and bloody war started to make the idea of "peace at all costs" offered by the Democrats look more desirable. McClellan was thought to be a heavy favorite because Frémont's campaign had gotten off to a good start. But as time passed, several political and military events made Lincoln's re-election inevitable. First, the Democrats had to confront the severe internal strains within their party at the Democratic National Convention. Contradicting political compromises made McClellan's campaign inconsistent and difficult. Second, the Democratic National Convention influenced Frémont's campaign. Frémont's was appalled at the Democratic platform, which he described as "union with Slavery," and withdrew from the race in September 1864. In his statement, Frémont stated that winning the Civil War was too important and, although he still felt that Lincoln was not going far enough, the defeat of McClellan was of the greatest necessity. McClellan's chances of victory faded after Frémont withdrew from the presidential race. Finally, with Sherman marching toward Atlanta and General Grant pushing Lee into the outer defenses of Richmond, it became increasingly obvious that a Union military victory was inevitable and close at hand. The Lincoln/Johnson ticket ran with the slogan "Don't change horses in the middle of a stream."

Only 25 states participated, because 11 had seceded from the Union and claimed to have formed their own nation: the Confederate States of America (CSA). Three new states participated for the first time: Nevada, West Virginia, and Kansas. McClellan won just three states: Kentucky, Delaware, and his home state of New Jersey.

1868

When Lincoln was assassinated, Andrew Johnson became President. He is remembered largely because he escaped impeachment and removal from office by a single vote. Johnson was unsuccessful in his attempt to receive the Democratic presidential nomination because he had alienated so many people and had not built up a political base. Instead the Democrats nominated Horatio Seymour to take on the Republican candidate, Civil War hero General Ulysses

S. Grant, one of the most popular men in the North due to his effort in winning the Civil War. Although Seymour gave Grant a good race in the popular vote, he lost the electoral vote.

Reconstruction was a hotly debated issue north and south. Seymour wanted to carry out a Reconstruction policy based on peaceful reconciliation with the South, a policy similar to that advocated by Lincoln and President Andrew Johnson. Grant, on the other hand, was willing to support the Reconstruction plans of the Radical Republicans, wanted to punish the South.

By 1868, the Republicans felt strong enough to drop the Union Party label. They badly needed a popular hero. The Democratic Party still controlled many large Northern states that had a great percentage of the electoral votes. General Grant announced he was a Republican and was unanimously nominated on the first ballot as the party's candidate. The Republican platform supported black suffrage in the South and favored Radical Reconstruction as distinct from the more lenient policy of President Johnson. Initially, the Democrats had twelve potential nominees. The unpopular Johnson, having narrowly survived impeachment, reached his peak on the first ballot, with less than one-third of the total necessary for nomination. For twenty-one ballots, the opposing candidates were at loggerheads. On the twenty-second ballot, Horatio Seymour, over his own objection, was unanimously voted the Democratic candidate.

The 1868 campaign of Horatio Seymour versus Ulysses S. Grant was conducted vigorously. The Republicans were fearful as late as October that they might be beaten. The Democrats were the disinherited party, Seymour had been called a traitor, a troublemaker, the votes of thousands of southern Democrats would not be counted, yet everyone knew that Seymour, a man of charity and peace, would give the warrior Grant a hard race. Grant took no part in the campaign and made no promises. A line in his letter of acceptance of the nomination became the Republican campaign theme—"Let us have peace." After four years of civil war, three years of wrangling over Reconstruction, and the attempted impeachment of a president, the nation craved peace. Voters were told that if they wanted to reopen the Civil War they need only elect Horatio Seymour, spreading lurid tales of murder and massacre in the south to prove that the south needed the heavy foot of the conqueror on her neck. Despite the fervent thanks of Lincoln and Stanton for his quick dispatch of troops to Gettysburg, Seymour was branded in the press as disloyal to the Union.

The Radical Republicans, who had tried to impeach Johnson for his peaceful attitude toward the south, did their best to smear Seymour. They alleged that insanity ran through the Seymour family, citing as evidence the suicide of his father. Henry Ward Beecher branded him a coward and a traitor by declaring him to be "a man who, through all the years of 1860 to 1868, studied how to help southern treason without incurring the risks and pains of overt courageous treasonable acts." Newspaper descriptions Seymour's life and character were staggering. The New York Tribune led the cartoon campaign with the picture of Seymour standing on the steps of the City Hall calling a mob of murderers "my friends." The New York Post called him "childless, scheming, stupid, selfish, stealthy, feeble, insincere, timid, closefisted, inept, and weak." The Hartford Post called him "almost as much of a corpse" as ex-President Buchanan, who had just died. "Seymour is a little creation; his face is an outlined wriggle; its expression is a dodge. He has a smooth tongue, feeble health, a constant fear of aberration. His art is to wheedle the vain, promise the ambitious, and charm the religious."

Seymour refused to answer any of the charges leveled against him, but went his quiet way, making a few key speeches, indulging in no violence, no slander, and no fraud. The bitterness and abuse heaped upon him seeped into history through the medium of the unrestrained newspaper. Yet his conduct of the campaign did his country and the institution of free elections great good and helped to keep the two-party system alive.

Seymour received 2,708,744 votes against 3,013,650 for Grant. The Democrats in the South had worked hard, but Radical regimes controlled the election machinery and carried all of the states except Georgia and Louisiana. The closeness of the race startled the nation. That Grant should lose New York to Seymour by a majority of 10,000 votes was a source of shame and anger to Republicans, who demanded a federal investigation. The Republican Party claimed credit for saving the Union and was bound, bent, and determined to continue to rule it.

1872

Incumbent President Ulysses S. Grant was easily re-elected, despite a split within the Republican Party that resulted in a defection of many Liberal Republicans to his opponent Horace Greeley. After the popular vote, but before the Electoral College cast its votes, Greeley died. As a result, electors previously committed to Greeley voted for four different candidates for President.

Liberal Republican candidates for nomination included Greeley, former U.S. representative from New York, Charles Francis Adams, former U.S. representative from Massachusetts, Benjamin Gratz Brown, governor of Missouri, Salmon P. Chase, Supreme Court Chief Justice from Ohio, and David Davis, Associate Justice from Illinois. Horace Greeley was nominated for President on the sixth ballot. The Liberal platform called for an end to the hatreds of Civil War and Reconstruction. The Republicans renominated President Grant by acclamation. Their platform boasted of the party's achievements:

Victoria Woodhull became the first woman to be nominated for the Presidency, running on the platform of the Equal Rights Party. Her running mate was famed abolitionist and former slave Frederick Douglass. Woodhull was ineligible to be President on Inauguration Day, not because she was a woman—the Constitution and the law were silent on the issue—but because she would not reach the constitutionally prescribed minimum age of 35 until September 23, 1873. Woodhull and Douglass are not listed in "Election results," as the ticket received a negligible percentage of the popular vote and no electoral votes.

Grant's administration had been widely accused of corruption. The Liberal Republicans demanded civil service reform and an end to the Reconstruction process including the withdrawal of federal troops from the South. Both Liberal Republicans and Democrats were disappointed in their candidate Greeley. Wits asked, "Why turn out a knave just to replace him with a fool?" Greeley turned out to be a poor campaigner with little political experience. His career as a newspaper editor gave his opponents a long history of eccentric public positions to attack. Grant, on the other hand, was not only unassailable, but he had a large campaign budget to work with. A large portion of his campaign budget came from entrepreneurs such as Jay Cooke, Cornelius Vanderbilt, and John Astor. As an added plus for the Grant campaign, Greeley's running mate, B. Gratz Brown, committed several gaffes due to his drinking problem. For instance, at one campaign picnic he became so drunk that he tried to butter a watermelon.

This was the first election after the formation of the National Woman's Suffrage Association and the American Woman Suffrage Association in 1869. Protests for women's suffrage became more prevalent. Several suffragettes attempted to vote in the election. Susan B. Anthony was arrested and fined $100 for attempting to vote. Woodhull herself was in jail on Election Day for indecency.

Ultimately, Grant won an easy re-election over Greeley by a margin of 56% to 44%. Greeley died just twenty-four days after the election and before any of the electors could cast their votes.

1876

The bitter 1876 contest between Rutherford B. Hayes and Samuel Tilden was the most sordid and legally questionable presidential election in American history.

Does this sound eerily familiar? Election night comes and goes. The race between two American presidential candidates is too close to call. The popular vote supports the reticent Democrat, but the well-connected Republican is named president after a lengthy and controversial fight over recounts and electoral votes. Of course, we're speaking of the 1876 contest between Rutherford B. Hayes and Samuel Tilden. The Electoral College was unable to declare a winner after Louisiana, South Carolina, and Florida submitted multiple "official" ballots with different victorious candidates. Numerous shady deals were worked out to Hayes's favor while forces loyal to Tilden threatened to march on Washington and install their man by force, if necessary. The most damaging result of the mess was the pervasive mood of distrust and acrimony on the part of Congress, a mood that would contribute to the South's notorious Jim Crow laws.

For those who think the election of George W. Bush over Al Gore in 2000 represented the nadir of American electoral politics, in 1876, New York Democrat Samuel Tilden almost certainly won the popular vote over Ohio Republican Rutherford B. Hayes. But contested returns in Florida, Louisiana and South Carolina, as well as a legal issue in Oregon, eventually led to a 15-member congressional commission awarding Hayes all 20 contested electoral votes, giving him an improbable *one-vote victory* in the Electoral College. Tilden ultimately chose to concede the election rather than drag the nation down a dangerous path. It was an act of supreme patriotism for a man who had won, if not the presidency, at least the election. In sharp contrast to the contested election of 2000, dominated by hanging chads and confusing ballots, the 1876 election reminds us that character can triumph over politics. With partisans still claiming that George W. Bush stole the presidential election of 2000, it is pertinent to look back more than a century to another election that may have been hijacked. The election of Republican Rutherford B. Hayes over Democrat Samuel B. Tilden was a sordid affair in which graft, blatantly undemocratic procedures, and racial politics ruled the day. New York governor Tilden had a reputation as a reformer, but the southern wing of his party included both recalcitrant rebels and hard-line racists. Hayes encouraged Northerners to "vote as you fought," further inflaming sectional passions. Although Tilden won the popular vote decisively, massive fraud in Florida, Louisiana, and South Carolina denied both men a majority in the Electoral College. Eventually, a special Electoral Commission anointed Hayes, guaranteeing the removal of federal troops from the South and ushering in the Jim Crow era.

Riding a wave of popular revulsion at the numerous scandals of the Grant administration and a sluggish economy, Tilden received 260,000 more votes than his opponent. But contested returns ultimately led to Hayes's being declared the winner by a specially created, Republican-dominated Electoral Commission after four tense months of political intrigue and threats of violence. President Grant took the threats seriously: he ordered armed federal troops into the streets of Washington to keep the peace.

Tilden was a wealthy lawyer, a New York sophisticate, whose passion for clean government propelled him to the very brink of the presidency. Hayes was a family man whose Midwestern simplicity masked a cunning political mind. On election night, both candidates went to bed believing Tilden had won. A one-legged former Union army general, "Devil Dan" Sickles, stumped into Republican headquarters and hastily improvised a devious plan to subvert the election in the three disputed southern states. Tilden's physical stamina, never very great to begin with, had been sorely taxed by a brutal political campaign that, for all its public protestations of reform, had quickly descended into a vicious personal attack on the governor's honesty, patriotism, morals, and even his sanity.

Many historians believe that an informal deal was struck to resolve the dispute: the Compromise of 1877. In return for the Democrats' acquiescence in Hayes' election, the Republicans agreed to withdraw federal troops from the South, ending Reconstruction. The Compromise effectively ceded power in the Southern states to the Democratic Redeemers.

When the Republican National Convention convened, it appeared that James G. Blaine would be the nominee. On the first ballot, Blaine was just 100 votes short of a majority. His vote began to slide after the second ballot, as many Republicans feared that Blaine could not win the general election. On the seventh ballot, Hayes was nominated with 384 votes to 351 for Blaine. The Democratic National Convention assembled in St. Louis – the first political convention held west of the Mississippi River. The platform, with its sharp cry for immediate and sweeping reforms, drove delegates into near- hysteria. The historical conjunction of Tilden, the country's greatest reformer, with the crying need for reform brought Tilden more than 400 votes on the first ballot and the nomination by a landslide on the second. The Democratic platform pledged to replace the corruption of the Grant administration with honest, efficient government and to end "the rapacity of carpetbag tyrannies" in the South; called for treaty protection for naturalized U.S. citizens visiting their homeland, restrictions on Oriental immigration, and tariff reform; and opposed land grants to railroads. Tilden's nomination was received by the voting Democrats with more enthusiasm than any leader since Andrew Jackson.

Tilden, who had prosecuted machine politicians in New York and sent legendary William "Boss" Tweed to jail, ran as a reform candidate against the background of the Grant administration. Both sides mounted mud-slinging campaigns, with Democratic attacks on Republican corruption being countered by Republicans raising the Civil War issue, a tactic ridiculed by Democrats who called it "waving the bloody shirt." Republicans chanted, "Not every Democrat was a rebel, but every rebel was a Democrat!" The Democratic strategy was to actively suppress black and white Republican voter turnout by disrupting meetings and rallies and even using violence and intimidation. They saw themselves as the military wing of the Democratic Party. Because it was considered improper for a candidate to actively pursue the presidency, neither Tilden nor Hayes actively stumped as part of the campaign, leaving that job to surrogates.

After the vote, facing an unprecedented constitutional crisis, on January 29, 1877, the U.S. Congress passed a law forming a 15-member Electoral Commission to settle the result. Five members came from each house of Congress, and they were joined by five members of the Supreme Court. The majority party in each house named three members and the minority party two. As the Republicans controlled the Senate and the Democrats the House of Representatives, this yielded five Democratic and five Republican members of the Commission. Of the Supreme Court justices, two Republicans and two Democrats were chosen, with the fifth to be selected by these four.

The justices first selected a political independent, Justice David Davis. No one knew which presidential candidate he preferred. Just as the Electoral Commission Bill was passing Congress, the

Legislature of Illinois elected Davis to the Senate. Democrats in the Illinois Legislature believed they had purchased Davis' support by voting for him. However, they miscalculated: instead of staying on the Supreme Court so that he could serve on the Commission, he promptly resigned as a Justice in order to take his Senate seat. All the remaining available justices were Republicans, so the four justices already selected chose Justice Joseph P. Bradley, who was considered the most impartial remaining member of the court. This selection proved decisive.

The commission first decided not to question any returns that were *prima facie* lawful. Bradley joined the other seven Republican committee members in a series of 8-7 votes that gave all 20 disputed electoral votes to Hayes, giving Hayes a 185-184 electoral vote victory. The commission adjourned on March 2; two days later Hayes was inaugurated without disturbance.

Tilden became the first presidential candidate in American history to lose in the electoral college despite winning a majority of the popular vote. It is not possible to conclude definitively what the result would have been if a fair election had been held without the violence and intimidation throughout the South that disenfranchised many African-Americans explicitly eligible to vote under the 15th amendment. Nevertheless, in the likeliest fair scenario Hayes would have won the election with 189 electoral votes to Tilden's 180 by winning all of the states that he did ultimately carry, plus Mississippi but minus Florida. A strong case can be made that South Carolina, Louisiana, and Mississippi, states with an outright majority African-American population, would have gone for Hayes since nearly all African-Americans during this time voted Republican, while nearly all whites in the South during this time voted Democratic. Florida, with a majority white population, would have likely gone to Tilden in a fair election. Clearly Hayes would have won appreciably more of the popular vote in a fair election, albeit arguably still not a plurality or majority.

1880

There were no pressing issues except tariffs. The Republicans supported higher tariffs and the Democrats supported lower ones. Incumbent President Rutherford Hayes did not seek re-election, keeping a promise made during the 1876 campaign. The Republican Party chose James A. Garfield as their standard-bearer. The Democrats chose Civil War General Winfield S. Hancock as their nominee. In the smallest popular vote victory in American history, despite capturing fewer than 2,000 more popular votes than Hancock, Garfield was easily elected, capturing 214 of the states' 369 electoral votes.

While Hayes didn't seek renomination, former President Ulysses S. Grant openly sought nomination to a third term. Going into the Republican Party convention in Chicago, he was the front-runner, but on the 36th ballot, Garfield outlasted Grant, Blaine, and Sherman to win the nomination. The convention was noteworthy in that it was the first at which delegates cast votes for an African-American, Blanche Kelso Bruce. At the Democratic national convention, Winfield S. Hancock won on the second ballot.

Democrats began the national campaign by attacking the contested 1876 election. Republicans brought up the Civil War again, but the campaign soon shifted to personality. Garfield campaigned as a hard-working, self-made man. Republicans avoided direct attacks on Hancock, who was widely-respected for his service at Gettysburg, but claimed that the general would act as a figurehead for corrupt Democrats like the ones who tried to defame Garfield. The Democrats campaigned on Republican corruption, attacking Garfield and especially his running mate, Chester A. Arthur. The end of the effects of the Panic of 1873 combined with a well-funded and well-run campaign gave the advantage to Garfield.

In 1880, California's electoral votes were split between the two candidates with Garfield getting one and Hancock getting five, giving Garfield nineteen states plus one electoral vote. Notably, Garfield won the presidency without California. No presidential candidate managed to reproduce this feat until Woodrow Wilson's victory in the 1912 election and no Republican presidential candidate managed to reproduce this feat until George W. Bush's victory in the 2000 election.

President Garfield was mortally wounded by Charles J. Guiteau on July 2, 1881. He did not die until September 19 of that year. Vice President Chester Arthur was sworn in as president and served until the inauguration of the next President on March 4, 1885.

1884

The 1884 Presidential Election was marked by excessive mudslinging and personal acrimony. Governor Grover Cleveland narrowly defeated Republican James G. Blaine to become the first Democrat elected President of the United States since 1856.

The Republicans convened in Chicago. Former U.S. Senator and former Speaker of the House James G. Blaine, President Chester A. Arthur, and Senator George F. Edmunds led the contest. Blaine was ahead on the first ballot, with Arthur in second, and Edmunds in third. This order did not change on successive ballots as Blaine increased his lead, and he won a majority on the fourth ballot. The famous Civil War general, William Tecumseh Sherman was considered a possible Republican candidate, but ruled himself out with the famous words, "If drafted, I will not run; if nominated, I will not accept; if elected, I will not serve."

The Democrats held their convention in Chicago. Grover Cleveland was the clear front-runner. Edward S. Bragg of Wisconsin roused the delegates with a memorable seconding speech: "They love him and they respect him, not only for himself, for his character, for his integrity and judgment and iron will, but they love him most of all for the enemies he has made." Cleveland won the Democratic nomination in a landslide on the second ballot.

The campaign was marked by the issue of personal character. In 1876, a Boston bookkeeper named James Mulligan located some letters showing that Blaine had sold his influence in Congress to various businesses. One such letter ended with the phrase "burn this letter," from which a popular chant of the Democrats arose - "Burn, burn, burn this letter!" In just one deal, he had received over $1.5 million in today's dollars from the Little Rock and Fort Smith Railroad for securing a federal land grant. Democrats and anti-Blaine Republicans made unrestrained attacks on his integrity. Governor Cleveland, on the other hand, was known as "Grover the Good" for his personal integrity. In the space of the three previous years he had become the Mayor of Buffalo and then the Governor of the state, cleaning up large amounts of Tammany Hall's graft.

Thus, it was a huge shock when, on July 21, the Buffalo *Evening Telegraph* reported that Cleveland had fathered a child out of wedlock, that the child had gone to an orphanage, and that the mother had been driven to an asylum. Cleveland's campaign decided that candor was the best approach to this scandal: they admitted that Cleveland had formed an "illicit connection" with the mother and that a child had been born and given the Cleveland surname. They also noted that there was no proof that Cleveland was the father, and claimed that, by assuming responsibility and finding a home for the child, he was merely doing his duty. Finally, they showed that the mother had not been forced into an asylum; her whereabouts were unknown. Blaine's supporters condemned Cleveland in the strongest of terms, singing "Ma, Ma, Where's my Pa?" After Cleveland's victory, his supporters responded to the taunt with: "Gone to the White House, Ha, Ha, Ha." Cleveland campaign's approach worked well enough and the race remained close through Election Day. In fact, many Republican reformers, known as "Mugwumps," who were put off by Blaine's scandals, worked for Cleveland's election.

In the final week of the campaign, Blaine's campaign suffered a catastrophe. At a Republican meeting attended by Blaine, a group of New York preachers castigated the Mugwumps. Their spokesman, Rev. Dr. Samuel Burchard, made this fatal statement: "We are Republicans. We don't propose to leave our party and identify ourselves with the party whose antecedents have been rum, Romanism, and rebellion." Blaine did not notice Burchard's anti-Catholic slur, nor did the assembled newspaper reporters, but a Democratic agent did, and Cleveland's campaign managers made sure it was widely publicized. The statement energized the Catholic vote in New York City heavily against Blaine, costing him New York state and the election by the narrowest of margins.

1888

The tariff was the main issue in the election of 1888. Benjamin Harrison, the Republican candidate, opposed tariff reduction. Cleveland's attitude toward the spoils system had antagonized party politicians. He had made enemies among veterans, farmers, and industrialists. Even with these enemies, Cleveland had more popular votes than Harrison, but Harrison won the election in the electoral college.

This was the third election in which the President-elect did not receive a majority or a plurality of the popular vote. The first was in 1824 and the second was in 1876. The fourth would happen 112 years later in the 2000 election.

The Democrats renominated President Cleveland unanimously without a formal ballot. The Democratic platform largely confined itself to defending the Cleveland administration, supporting reduction in the tariff and taxes, and statehood for the western territories. By the time Republicans convened in Chicago, front-runner James G. Blaine had withdrawn from the race because he believed that only a harmonious convention would produce a Republican candidate strong enough to upset incumbent president Grover Cleveland. After he withdrew, Blaine expressed confidence in both Benjamin Harrison and John Sherman. Harrison was nominated on the eighth ballot.

Cleveland set the main issue of the campaign when he proposed a dramatic reduction in tariffs in his annual message to Congress in December 1887. The Republicans responded that the high tariff would protect American industry from foreign competition, guaranteeing high wages, high profits, and high growth. In practice, the tariff was meaningless, since the United States was the low-cost producer in most areas and could not be undersold by the less efficient Europeans. Nevertheless the tariff issue motivated both sides to a remarkable extent.

Harrison, well-funded by party activists, gave many speeches from his front porch in Indianapolis, which were covered by the newspapers. Cleveland believed that presidential candidates did not campaign. He left his vice presidential candidate, Thurman, to spearhead his campaign.

A California Republican, George Osgoodby, wrote a letter to the British ambassador to the U. S., using the pseudonym "Charles F. Murchison." "Murchison" described himself as a former Englishman and asked how he should vote in the upcoming presidential election. The ambassador wrote back and suggested that Cleveland was probably the best man from the British point of view. The Republicans published this letter two weeks before the election. Its effect was comparable to the "Rum, Romanism, and Rebellion" blunder of the previous election: Cleveland lost New York state and the presidency and the British ambassador was fired.

Cleveland led the popular, 48.6% to 47.8%, but Harrison won the Electoral College by 233-168, largely because of his 1% win in Cleveland's home state of New York. Had Cleveland won New York, he would have won the electoral vote 204-197. Cleveland thus became one of only four men (Andrew Jackson in 1824, Samuel Tilden in 1876, and Al Gore in 2000) to win the popular vote but lose the presidency. As Frances Cleveland and the outgoing president left the White House, she assured the staff that they would return in four years, which they did.

1892

Former President Grover Cleveland ran for re-election against incumbent President Benjamin Harrison also running for re-election. Cleveland defeated Harrison. He was the only person in U.S. history to be elected to a second, non-consecutive presidential term. Cleveland had won the popular vote against Harrison in 1888, but lost the electoral vote which cost him re-election. In the rematch election, he won both the popular and electoral vote. The campaign centered mainly on the issue of a sound currency. While the new Populist Party polled more than a million votes, Cleveland still won easily.

Although Thomas C. Platt and other disaffected party leaders mounted a dump-Harrison movement coalescing around veteran candidate James G. Blaine, the president had the nomination locked up by when the convention started and won 535 to 183 for Blaine on the first ballot. The Republican platform supported the high tariff, stiffer immigration laws, free rural mail delivery, and a canal across Central America. The Republicans expressed sympathy for Ireland's struggle for home rule and for the plight of Jews under persecution in czarist Russia.

As for the Democrats, by the end of Harrison's term, many Americans were ready to return to Cleveland's harder policies. Cleveland was the front-runner for the nomination but faced formidable opposition. The New York delegation, packed with Tammany men, demonstrated their hostility to Cleveland on the convention floor. Still, Cleveland squeaked by on the first ballot.

The tariff issue dominated a lackluster campaign. Harrison defended the protectionist McKinley Tariff passed during his term. Cleveland assured voters he opposed absolute free trade, but continued his campaign to reduce the tariff. William McKinley campaigned extensively for Harrison, setting the stage for his own run four years later.

The campaign took a somber turn when, in October, First Lady Caroline Harrison died. On a trip to California with her husband in the spring of 1891, she caught a cold, which quickly deepened into her chest. She was eventually diagnosed with tuberculosis. A summer in the Adirondack Mountains failed to restore her to health. She died in the White House two weeks before the national election. As a result, all of the candidates ceased campaigning.

1896

Republican William McKinley defeated Democrat William Jennings Bryan in a campaign that was one of the most dramatic and complex in American history. The 1896 campaign is often considered to be the realigning election that ended the old Third Party system. McKinley, who forged a coalition in which businessmen, professionals, skilled factory workers and prosperous farmers were heavily represented, was the last veteran of the American Civil War to be nominated for President by either major party. Bryan was the nominee of the Democrats, the Populist Party, and the Silver Republicans.

A superb orator, Bryan was widely regarded as a prominent spokesman for millions of rural Americans who were suffering from the economic depression following the Panic of 1893. At the Democratic Convention, Bryan delivered what many historians regard as one of the greatest political speeches in American history, the "Cross of Gold" Speech. In that speech, Bryan offered a passionate defense of farmers and factory workers struggling to survive the economic depression. He attacked big-city business owners and leaders as the cause of much of the economic suffering. He called for reform of the monetary system, an end to the gold standard, and he promised government relief for farmers and others hurt by the economic depression. Bryan's speech was so dramatic that after he had finished many delegates carried him on their shoulders around the convention hall. The speech earned Bryan the presidential nomination. At just 36 years of age, Bryan was only a year older than the minimum age required by the Constitution to be President. He was the youngest man ever nominated by a major party for President.

Economic issues such as the gold standard, free silver, and the tariff, were crucial. Republican campaign manager Mark Hanna pioneered many modern campaign techniques, and had a hefty $3.5 million budget (over $3 billion in today's dollars) with which to do it. He outspent Bryan by a factor of five to one. The primary issue of the 1896 campaign involved this economic question: would America remain on the gold standard, as McKinley and the Republicans wished, or would the nation's economy switch to following the free silver theories called for by Bryan and the Populists?

Bryan argued that by leaving the gold standard and having paper money backed by silver instead of gold, it would allow more paper currency to enter the national economy. Bryan and his supporters argued that this "easy money" would allow impoverished farmers in the South and West to get out of debt and pay their bills, and that having more paper money circulating in the economy would help lift the nation out of the economic depression which had started in 1893.

McKinley and the Republicans countered that the gold standard was vital to the American economy, that if the nation went off the gold standard paper currency would lose its value by half and inflation would soar. To ridicule what they believed were Bryan's radical and unwise economic policies, the Republicans printed fake dollar bills which had Bryan's face and which read "In God we Trust. For the Other, 53 Cents," thus illustrating their claim that a dollar bill would be worth only 47 cents if it was backed by silver instead of gold.

Since he was being outspent, Bryan decided his best chance to win the election was to conduct a vigorous national speaking tour by train; in that way he could speak to the voters directly. He was the first presidential candidate to travel across the nation and meet voters in person. Prior to 1896, it had been considered undignified for presidential candidates to widely travel before an election. The novelty of such an event, combined with Bryan's spellbinding oratory, led to huge crowds. Bryan supporters welcomed him with parades, speeches, and wild demonstrations of support. Bryan focused his efforts on the Midwest, which he believed would be the decisive battleground in the election. In just 100 days, he gave over 500 speeches, a remarkable feat at the time. Relying on just a few hours of sleep a night, he traveled 18,000 miles in three months to address an estimated five million people.

In contrast, McKinley conducted a traditional "front porch" campaign from his home in Canton, Ohio. Instead of having McKinley travel to see the voters, Mark Hanna brought thousands of voters by train to McKinley's home. McKinley labeled Bryan's proposed social and economic reforms as a serious threat to the national economy. With the depression following the Panic of 1893 coming to an end, support for McKinley's more conservative economic policies increased, while Bryan's more radical policies began to lose support among Midwestern farmers and factory workers.

The Democratic Party's repudiation of their pro-business wing, represented by incumbent President Grover Cleveland, set the stage for 16 years of Republican control of the White House, which ended only when the Republicans split in 1912. Although Bryan lost the election, his coalition of "outsiders" would dominate the Democratic Party well into the twentieth century, and would play a crucial role in the liberal economic programs of Presidents Wilson, FDR, and Lyndon Johnson.

McKinley received a little more than seven million votes, Bryan a little less than six and a half million. The vote was so close that any one of a dozen factors could have changed the result.

1900

A rematch of the 1896 race between Republican President William McKinley and his Democratic challenger, William Jennings Bryan. The return of economic prosperity and recent victory in the Spanish-American War helped McKinley score a decisive victory. President McKinley chose New York Governor Theodore Roosevelt as his running mate.

The Republican delegates renominated William McKinley by acclamation. Although Theodore Roosevelt was reluctant to accept the vice-presidency, which he regarded as a relatively trivial and powerless office, his great popularity among most Republican delegates led McKinley to pick him as his new running mate.

After Admiral George Dewey's return from the Spanish-American War, many Democrats suggested he run for President on the Democratic ticket, but his candidacy was plagued by public relations missteps. He was quoted as saying the job of president would be easy since the chief executive was merely following orders in executing the laws enacted by Congress and that he would "execute the laws of Congress as faithfully as I have always executed the orders of my superiors." Shortly thereafter he admitted to never having voted in a presidential election. He drew yet more criticism when he offhandedly told a newspaper reporter that, "Our next war will be with Germany." Dewey also angered some Protestants by marrying Catholic Mildred McLean Hazen, the daughter of the owner of *The Washington Post*, in 1899, and giving her the house that the nation had given him following the war. Dewey withdrew from the race in mid-May and endorsed William McKinley. William Jennings Bryan was easily nominated after Dewey withdrew from the race.

The economy was booming in 1900, so the Republican slogan of "Four More Years of the Full Dinner Pail," and the victory in the brief Spanish-American War in 1898, had a powerful electoral appeal. Teddy Roosevelt had become a national hero fighting in Cuba during the war, so he was a popular spokesman for the Republican ticket. In his speeches he repeatedly argued that the war had been just and had liberated the Cubans and Filipinos from Spanish tyranny:

Bryan's campaign repeated his major issue from 1896, free silver. His campaign attacked McKinley's imperialism, arguing that instead of liberating Cuba and the Philippines, the McKinley administration had simply replaced a cruel Spanish tyranny with a cruel American one. Both candidates repeated their 1896 campaign techniques. McKinley campaigned from the front porch of his home in Canton, Ohio. Bryan took to the rails, traveling 18,000 miles to hundreds of rallies across the Midwest and East. This time, he was matched by Theodore Roosevelt, McKinley's running mate, who campaigned just as energetically in 24 states, covering 21,000 miles by train.

The triumph of the American army and navy in the war against Spain was a decisive factor in building Republican support. Republicans pledged that the fighting in the Philippines would die down of its own accord within sixty days of McKinley's reelection. However, as one lieutenant wrote to his wife, "It looks good on paper, but there really has been no reduction of the force here. These battalions being sent home are made up of men about to be discharged." (Sounds like Iraq / Afghanistan today). The majority of soldiers in the Philippines did not support Bryan. Soldiers' indicated overwhelming support for McKinley and Roosevelt.

Despite Bryan's efforts, McKinley gained a comfortable victory. His popular and electoral-vote margins were both larger than in 1896. Bryan did best in the traditionally Democratic "Solid South" and among farmers in the West. While he won New York City, President McKinley won the state of New York, winning all the state's electoral votes. Ironically, Roosevelt would be elevated to the Presidency in September 1901 when McKinley was assassinated in Buffalo, New York.

* * *

3. THE GOING GETS ROUGHER – 1900-1976

1904

The Republican Party unanimously nominated incumbent President Theodore Roosevelt at their 1904 national convention. The Democrats nominated Alton B. Parker, Chief Judge of the New York Court of Appeals. Roosevelt won 56.4% of the popular vote, a mandate of more than 2½ million popular votes.

A dump-Roosevelt movement had centered around the candidacy of Senator Mark Hanna of Ohio, but Hanna's death in February 1904 ended any real opposition to Roosevelt within the GOP. Roosevelt was nominated unanimously on the first ballot. The Republican platform insisted on maintenance of the protective tariff, called for increased foreign trade, pledged to uphold the gold standard, favored expansion of the merchant marine, promoted a strong navy, and praised Roosevelt's foreign and domestic policy.

Among the Democrats, both William Jennings Bryan and former President Grover Cleveland declined to run for president. The Democrats knew Roosevelt was colorful and popular with the people and that only a good man could defeat a good man. Alton B. Parker was respected by both Democrats and Republicans in his state. He won the nomination on the first ballot. To make his position clear, Parker informed the convention that he firmly supported the gold standard. In a letter to the Convention, he said, "As the Democratic platform is silent on the subject, if my view on the gold standard is unsatisfactory to the majority, I request you to decline to nominate me at once, so that another may be nominated before adjournment." It was the first time a candidate had made such a move. It was an act of daring that might have lost him the nomination, made him an outcast from the party he had served and believed in all his life.

The Democratic platform called for reduction in government expenditures and a congressional investigation of the executive departments "already known to teem with corruption," condemned monopolies, and pledged an end to government contracts with companies violating antitrust laws. The Democrats opposed imperialism, insisted upon independence for the Philippines, and opposed the protective tariff. It favored strict enforcement of the eight-hour work day, construction of a Panama Canal, the direct election of senators, statehood for the western territories, and the extermination of polygamy.

The Election of 1904 was the first election in which the Socialist Party, a coalition of local parties based in industrial cities, participated. Prominent Socialist Eugene V. Debs was nominated for President.

The campaigning done by both parties was much milder than it had been in 1896 and 1900. The good will of this campaign went a long way toward mending the damage done by the previous class-war elections. So close were Roosevelt and Parker that voters found little to differentiate them. Both were for the gold standard; both believed in fair treatment for the Filipinos and eventual liberation; and both believed that labor unions had the same rights as individuals before the courts. Democratic radicals denounced Parker as a conservative; conservative Republicans denounced Roosevelt as a radical. Joseph Pulitzer's *New York World* carried a full page story about alleged corruption in the Roosevelt's Bureau of Corporations. Roosevelt admitted certain payments had been made, but denied any "blackmail." In appointing George B. Cortelyou as his campaign manager, Roosevelt had purposely used Parker's former secretary of commerce because Cortelyou, knowing the corporations' secrets, could demand large contributions from them. The charge created quite a stir and in later years was proven to be true. In 1907, it was learned that insurance companies had contributed heavily to the Roosevelt campaign and that only a week before the election Roosevelt himself had called E. H. Harriman, the railroad king, to Washington to ask him to raise funds to carry New York state. However, this issue never gained traction. Theodore Roosevelt won in a landslide, taking every Northern and Western state. He also picked up Missouri.

1908

Popular incumbent President Theodore Roosevelt, honoring a promise not to seek a third term, persuaded the Republican Party to nominate William Howard Taft, his close friend and Secretary of War, to become his successor. The Democrats turned to two-time loser William Jennings Bryan. Bryan remained extremely popular among the liberals and populists. Although he ran a hard-fought campaign, Bryan suffered the worst loss in his three presidential campaigns, and Taft won by a comfortable margin.

The only two Republican contenders running nationwide campaigns for the presidential nomination were William Howard Taft and Joseph B. Foraker, both of Ohio. Taft was nominated on the first ballot. The 1908 Democratic Convention was held in Denver. Despite a challenge by Minnesota governor John Albert Johnson, Bryan quickly won the overwhelming support of his party.

Bryan campaigned on a progressive platform attacking "government by privilege." His campaign slogan, "Shall the People Rule?" was featured on numerous posters and campaign memorabilia. However, Taft undercut Bryan's liberal support by co-opting some of his reformist ideas. Roosevelt's progressive policies blurred the distinctions between the parties. Republicans used the slogan "Vote for Taft now, you can vote for Bryan anytime," a sarcastic reference to Bryan's two failed previous presidential campaigns. Bryan ended up with the worst of his three drubbings in the national popular vote, losing the popular vote by eight percentage points. This would be Bryan's last campaign for the presidency; however, he would remain a popular figure within the Democratic Party and in 1912 he would play a key role in securing the presidential nomination for Woodrow Wilson.

1912

This campaign was fought among three major candidates. President Taft was renominated by the Republicans. After former President Theodore Roosevelt failed to receive the Republican nomination, he called his own convention and created the Progressive Party (nicknamed the "Bull Moose Party"). Democrat Woodrow Wilson was nominated on the 46th ballot of a contentious convention, thanks to the support of William Jennings Bryan, who still had a large and loyal following. Wilson defeated both Taft and Roosevelt in the general election, winning 42% of the popular vote and a huge majority in the Electoral College, Wilson became the only elected Democratic President between 1892 and 1932. This was the first election where the 48 states of the continental United States participated.

During Taft's administration, a rift grew between Roosevelt and Taft. Roosevelt's liberal wing of the Republican Party favored restrictions on the employment of women and children, ecological conservation, a more favorable view toward labor unions, free trade, and popular election of federal and state judges. Taft's conservatives favored high tariffs on imported goods to encourage consumers to buy American-made products and business leaders over labor unions. By 1910 the split between the two wings of the Republican Party was so deep that this caused Roosevelt and Taft to turn against one another, despite their personal friendship.

When the Convention gathered, Roosevelt challenged the credentials of nearly half of the delegates. By that time, however, it was too late. Not since the 1872 election had there been such a major schism in the Republican party. With the Democrats holding about 45% of the national vote, any schism would be fatal. Roosevelt's only hope at the convention was to form a "stop-Taft" alliance with Lafollette, but he found this impossible to do. Roosevelt struck back by asking his supporters to leave the Convention. His progressives reconvened in Chicago and endorsed the formation of a national progressive party. The new party chose Roosevelt as its presidential nominee. Roosevelt said he felt as strong as a "bull moose." Thenceforth known as the "Bull Moose Party," the Progressives promised to increase federal regulation and protect the welfare of ordinary people. In his in a famous acceptance speech, Roosevelt compared the coming presidential campaign to the Battle of Armageddon and stated that the Progressives were going to "battle for the Lord." However, many of the nation's newspapers harshly depicted Roosevelt as an egotist who was only running for president to spoil Taft's chances and to feed his large ego.

The Democratic Convention proved to be one of the more memorable presidential conventions of the twentieth century. Champ Clark, Speaker of the House, received a majority of the delegate votes early in the balloting. However, Clark was never able to get the necessary two-thirds majority to win the nomination. His chances were hurt when Tammany Hall, the powerful and corrupt Democratic political machine in New York City, threw its support behind him. William Jennings Bryan, the three-time Democratic presidential candidate and still leader of the party's liberals, turned against Clark and threw his support to New Jersey Governor Woodrow Wilson. Wilson was on the verge of having a concession speech read for him when Bryan's defection led many other delegates to start looking elsewhere. Wilson. received the nomination on the 46th ballot. The Socialists once again ran Eugene V. Debs as their candidate.

The 1912 presidential campaign was bitterly contested. Vice President James S. Sherman died less than a week before the election, leaving Taft without a running mate. Wilson captured the presidency handily. Many thought that had Roosevelt not been in the race, it is doubtful that Wilson would have defeated Taft.

While Roosevelt was campaigning in Milwaukee on October 14, 1912, a saloonkeeper named John F. Shrank shot him, but the bullet lodged in his chest only after penetrating both his steel eyeglass case and passing through a 50 page single-folded copy of the speech he was carrying in his jacket. Roosevelt conducted a vigorous national campaign for the Progressive Party, denouncing the way the Republican nomination had been "stolen." He bundled his reforms under the title "The New Nationalism" and stumped the country for a strong federal role in regulating the economy, and, especially, watching and chastising bad corporations and overruling federal and state judges who made unprogressive decisions. Taft, knowing he had no chance to win, campaigned quietly, and spoke of the need for judges to be more powerful than elected officials. The conservatives were firmly in control of the Republican Party. Many of the Old Guard leaders distrusted Taft as too progressive for their taste, especially on matters of antitrust and tariffs. Much of the Republican effort was designed to discredit Roosevelt as a dangerous radical, but this had little effect.

Roosevelt's strong candidacy resulted in the only instance in the 20th century of a third party candidate receiving more votes than one of the major party candidates. Although he failed to win, Roosevelt succeeded in his vendetta against Taft, who received just 23% of the popular vote compared to Roosevelt's 27%. Wilson easily won election despite getting fewer votes and a lower percentage than William Jennings Bryan had for the Democrats four years previously. Debs' 6% was the all-time high for the Socialist Party in presidential elections and made 1912 the first (and last) election since 1860 in which four candidates each cleared 5%.

This was the first 48-state election, with Arizona and New Mexico having joined the Union earlier in the year. Failing to make itself a believable third party, the Bull Moose Party ended up losing strength. Its candidates did poorly in 1914. It vanished in 1916 with most members following Roosevelt back into the Republican party.

1916

Public sentiment toward World War I was still neutral, although the United States leaned towards the British and French forces, due to the harsh treatment of civilians by the German Army. Still, despite their sympathy toward the allies, most Americans wanted to stay out of the war. President Wilson sought reelection against Republican Supreme Court Justice Charles Evans Hughes. After a hard-fought contest, Wilson defeated Hughes by a narrow margin.

A major goal of the Republican national convention was to heal the bitter split within the Party that cost them the 1912 presidential campaign. The party's bosses, who wanted a moderate acceptable to both factions of the party, turned to Supreme Court Justice Charles Evans Hughes, who had served on the court since 1910. Although he had not actively sought the nomination, Hughes made it known that he would not turn it down. He won the nomination on the third ballot. The Democrats renominated the enormously popular Wilson. The Progressives renominated former President Theodore Roosevelt, but he withdrew from the race and supported Hughes.

The fighting in Europe dominated the campaign. Wilson campaigned on a pledge of continued neutrality: "He Kept Us out of War." Hughes called for greater mobilization and preparedness. Wilson had successfully pressured the Germans to suspend unrestricted submarine warfare. Thus it was difficult for Hughes to attack Wilson's peace platform. Hughes attacked Wilson for his support of various "pro-labor" laws, such as the eight hour workday, on the grounds that they were harmful to business interests. Hughes was helped by the support of popular former President Roosevelt and by the fact that the Republicans were still the nation's majority party at the time. However, just before the election Hughes made a campaign swing through California. He stayed in the same hotel as Hiram Johnson, the powerful Republican Governor. But Hughes never made the short trip to greet Johnson in his hotel suite; Johnson took this as a deliberate affront and never gave Hughes his full support. Given the extremely narrow loss Hughes suffered in California, this unintentional slight may have cost him the Presidency.

On election night, Hughes took an early lead in the Eastern and Midwestern states, and several newspapers declared him the winner.

However, Wilson refused to concede, and as returns came in from the South and West, Wilson eventually took the lead. Wilson won California by only 3,800 votes out of nearly a million cast. The electoral vote was one of the closest in American history. If Hughes had carried California and its 13 electoral votes, he would have won the election. Wilson took 49% of the popular vote to Hughes' 46%. A popular legend from the 1916 campaign states that Hughes went to bed on Election Night thinking he was the newly-elected president. When a reporter tried to telephone him the next morning to get his reaction to Wilson's comeback, someone answered the phone and told the reporter that, "The President is asleep." The reporter retorted, "When he wakes up, tell him he isn't the President."

1920

The wartime boom had collapsed. Politicians were arguing over peace treaties and the question of America's entry into the League of Nations. 1919 had been marked by major strikes and large race riots in Chicago and other cities. Terrorist attacks on Wall Street produced fears of radicals and terrorists. Outgoing President Wilson had become increasingly unpopular. Following a severe stroke in 1919, he could no longer speak on his own behalf. The economy was in a recession, the public was weary of war and reform, the Irish Catholic and German communities were outraged at his policies, and his sponsorship of the League of Nations produced an isolationist reaction.

Former President Roosevelt had been the front runner for the Republican nomination, but his health collapsed in 1918 and he died in January 1919. Both major parties turned to dark horse candidates from the electoral vote-rich state of Ohio. The Democrats nominated Governor James M. Cox. The Republicans turned to Senator Warren

G. Harding. To help his campaign, Cox chose Franklin D. Roosevelt as his running mate. Harding ignored Cox and campaigned against Wilson's policies, calling for a return to "normalcy." With a 4-to-1 spending advantage, he won a landslide victory. Harding's victory was the largest popular-vote percentage margin (60.3% to 34.1%) since 1820.

The Republican race was wide open. Harding was nominated for President on the tenth ballot, after some voting shifted in their allegiance. His nomination, said to have been secured in negotiations among party bosses in a "smoke-filled room," was engineered by Harry M. Daugherty, Harding's political manager who, after Harding's election, became United States Attorney General.

At the Democratic Convention, although William Gibbs McAdoo, Wilson's son-in-law and former Treasury Secretary, was the strongest candidate, Wilson blocked his nomination in hopes a deadlocked convention would demand that he, Wilson, run for a third term. At the time, Wilson was physically immobile and in seclusion. The Democrats nominated Governor James M. Cox, as their presidential candidate, and 38 year-old Assistant Secretary of the Navy Franklin D. Roosevelt, a fifth cousin of the late president Teddy Roosevelt, for vice president.

Harding played upon the weariness of the American public after the social upheaval of the Progressive Era. World War I and the Treaty of Versailles had proved deeply unpopular, causing a reaction against Wilson. Irish Americans were powerful in the Democratic party and had opposed going to war alongside their enemy Britain. Wilson had won them over in 1917 by promising to ask Britain to give Ireland its independence. Wilson had won the election of 1916 largely because of his slogan "He kept us out of war." At the Versailles Peace Conference in 1919, however, he reneged and the Irish American community vehemently denounced him. Wilson in turn blamed the Irish Americans and German Americans for the lack of popular support for his unsuccessful campaign to have the U.S.A. join the League of Nations. Supporters of the Irish Republic in the U.S.A. in 1919-20 raised $5,500,000 in campaign funds, but the Irish American city machines sat on their hands during the election, allowing the Republicans to roll up unprecedented landslides in every major city. Many German American Democrats voted Republican or stayed home, giving the GOP landslides in the rural Midwest.

Wilson had hoped for a "solemn referendum" on the League of Nations, but did not get one. Harding waffled on the League, thereby keeping "irreconcilables" like Senator William Borah in line. Cox also hedged. He went to the White House for Wilson's blessing and apparently endorsed the League, but he said that he wanted the League only with reservations, particularly on Article Ten, which would require the United States to participate in any war declared by the League. False rumors circulated that Harding had "Negro blood," but this did not hurt Harding's election campaign.

Cox's campaign took him to rallies, train station speeches, and formal addresses, reaching audiences of two million. Harding relied on a "Front Porch Campaign," similar to William McKinley in 1896. The GOP spent over $8,00,000, four times the money Cox spent. The Republicans used national advertising in a major way. Their theme was "America First." The GOP used catch phrases like "absolute control of the United States by the United States," "Independence means independence, now as in 1776," "This country will remain American. Its next President will remain in our own country," and "We decided long ago that we objected to foreign government of our people."

Commercial radio broadcast coverage of election returns for the first time during the 1920 elections. Announcers at KDKA-AM in Pittsburgh read telegraph ticker results over the air as they came in. Harding's landslide victory came from all directions except the deep

South. This was the first election in which women from every state were allowed to vote, following the passage of the 19th Amendment to the Constitution in August 1920. Despite the fact that Cox was defeated badly, his running-mate, Franklin Delano Roosevelt, became a well-known political figure because of his active and energetic campaign. In 1928 he was elected Governor of New York, and in 1932 he was elected President and remained in power until his death in 1945, as the longest-serving President ever. Socialist Party candidate Eugene V. Debs received 3.4% of the popular vote, despite the fact that he was in prison at the time for advocating non-compliance with the draft in the war. The Eighteenth Amendment starting Prohibition had passed the previous year.

1924

Incumbent President Calvin Coolidge, the Republican candidate, who had became president in 1923 following Harding's death, won the election. Coolidge was given credit for a booming economy at home and no visible crises abroad. The regular Democratic candidate was John W. Davis, a conservative from West Virginia. Many liberal Democrats bolted the party and backed Wisconsin Senator Robert M. LaFollette, Sr., who ran as the candidate of the Progressive Party. Coolidge's 25.2-point victory margin in the popular vote is one of the largest ever.

The Republican Convention had an easy choice and immediately nominated Coolidge. In the Democratic Convention, the two leading candidates were William G. McAdoo of California and Governor Al Smith of New York. In some cases McAdoo's delegates were also supporters of the Ku Klux Klan (KKK), which was at its peak of nationwide popularity in the 1920s, with chapters in all 48 states and 5 million members. Governor Smith was supported by the anti-Prohibition forces, many Roman Catholics and other ethnic minorities, big-city delegates in the Northeast and urban Midwest, and by liberal delegates opposed to the influence of the Ku Klux Klan.

In a brutal floor fight over a proposal to publicly condemn the Klan, the motion failed to carry by a single vote. Three-time Democratic presidential candidate William Jennings Bryan argued against condemning the Klan for fear that it would permanently split the party. The bitter fight between the McAdoo and Smith delegates over the KKK set the stage for the nominating ballots to come. The deadlock between McAdoo and Smith continued for several days. Ballot after ballot was taken. Neither McAdoo nor Smith received sufficient votes to win the nomination. Eventually the convention would go to over 100 ballots, becoming the longest-running political convention in American history. Will Rogers, a popular comedian of the era, joked that New York had invited the Democratic delegates to visit the city, not to live there.

The convention might have gone on for a great deal longer. However, on the 100th ballot both Smith and McAdoo mutually withdrew as candidates. This allowed the convention's delegates to search for a compromise candidate. Finally, on the 103rd ballot the convention turned to John W. Davis, an obscure former Congressman from West Virginia. This prompted Will Rogers' quip: "I'm not a member of any organized political party, I'm a Democrat!"

Senator Robert M. La Follett, Sr., who had left the Republican Party and formed his own political party, the Progressive Party, in Wisconsin, was so upset over both political parties choosing conservative candidates that he decided to run as a third-party candidate to give liberals an alternative. La Follette was a fiery orator who had dominated Wisconsin's political scene for more than two decades. Backed by radical farmers, the AFL labor unions, and Socialists, LaFollette ran on a platform of nationalizing large industries. He also strongly supported increased taxation on the wealthy and the right of collective bargaining for factory workers.

With the disastrous Democratic Convention having badly divided the Democrats, and with the economy booming, there was little doubt that Coolidge would win the election. His campaign slogan, "Keep Cool with Coolidge," was highly popular. Davis lost the popular vote to Coolidge by 25 percentage points.

1928

Republican Herbert Hoover versus Democrat Al Smith. The Republicans were identified with the booming economy of the 1920s. Smith, a Roman Catholic, suffered politically from anti-Catholic prejudice, his anti-prohibitionist stance, and his association with Tammany Hall. Hoover won a landslide victory.

With President Coolidge choosing not to enter the race, the race for the Republican nomination was wide open. A draft-Coolidge movement failed to gain momentum and failed to persuade Coolidge himself to run. The Convention nominated Hoover on the first ballot. In his acceptance speech a week after the convention ended, Hoover said: "We in America today are nearer to the final triumph over poverty than ever before in the history of this land. We shall soon, with the help of God, be in sight of the day when poverty will be banished from this land."

With the memory of the Teapot Dome scandal rapidly fading, and the current state of prosperity making that year's Presidential nomination not worth all that much, most of the major Democratic leaders were content to sit this one out. Smith became the candidate on the first ballot. He was the first Roman Catholic to gain a major party's nomination for President, and his religion became an issue during the campaign. Many Protestants feared that Smith would take orders from church leaders in Rome in making decisions affecting the country. Republican candidate Herbert Hoover won election by a wide margin on pledges to continue the economic boom of the Coolidge years.

1932

The effects of the 1929 Wall Street Crash and the Great Depression were being felt intensely across the country. President Hoover's popularity was falling. Voters felt he was unable to reverse the economic collapse or deal with prohibition. Franklin D. Roosevelt promised reform in his policy called the New Deal. Roosevelt won by a landslide.

As the year 1932 began, the Republican Party still had hopes that the worst of the Depression was over. Hoover's managers at the Republican National Convention ran a tight ship, not allowing expressions of concern for the direction of the nation. The sitting President was nominated on the first ballot with 98% of the delegate vote. The leading candidate for the Democratic presidential nomination in 1932 was New York Governor Franklin D. Roosevelt. On the first three ballots Roosevelt had well over a majority of the delegate vote, but still lacked the two-thirds majority. Before the fourth ballot his managers struck a deal with House Speaker John Nance Garner, who was also a candidate. Garner agreed to drop out of the race and support FDR. In exchange, FDR agreed to name Garner as his running mate. With this agreement Roosevelt won the two-thirds majority and with it the presidential nomination.

After making an airplane trip to the Democratic convention, Roosevelt accepted the nomination in person. In a history-making speech, he committed himself to battling the Great Depression in the United States when he stated: "I pledge you, I pledge myself, to a New Deal for the American people." Large crowds greeted Roosevelt as he traveled around the nation; his campaign song,

"Happy Days Are Here Again," became one of the most popular in American political history.

In contrast, Hoover was widely blamed for the Great Depression. In a scene scarily similar to today's political climate, for more than two years, Hoover had been issuing statements that the worst was over, only to have the economy make further downturns. His chances of a second term were slim to none. His attempts to campaign in public were a disaster. Rotten fruit and vegetables were thrown at him as he rode through city streets. Hoover attacked Roosevelt as a dangerous radical who would only make the Depression worse by raising taxes and increasing the federal debt to pay for expensive welfare and social-relief programs. Sound familiar?

However, with unemployment at 23.6%, Hoover's criticisms of the New Deal plan did nothing more than further lower his popularity with the public. Hoover even received a letter from an Illinois man that said "Vote for Roosevelt and make it unanimous." Hoover called Roosevelt a "chameleon in plaid" and Roosevelt called Hoover a "fat, timid capon (a castrated rooster)." In the last days of campaigning, Hoover criticized Roosevelt's "nonsense, tirades, glittering generalizations, ignorance, and defamation."

Roosevelt and the Democrats won a landslide victory over Hoover and the Republicans. The Democrats won control over both the House and the Senate. Until 1932, the Republicans had controlled the Presidency for 56 of the previous 72 years, dating to Abraham Lincoln's election in 1860. After 1932, the Democrats would control the Presidency for 28 of the next 36 years. Hoover's 17.76% margin of loss was the largest-ever margin of defeat for an incumbent President. He lost 42 of 48 states.

1936

This was the most lopsided presidential contest in the history of the United States in terms of electoral votes. The election took place as the Great Depression entered its eighth year. Incumbent President Franklin D. Roosevelt was still working to push the provisions of his New Deal economic policy through Congress and the courts. However, the New Deal policies he had already enacted, such as Social Security and unemployment benefits, had proven highly popular with most Americans. Roosevelt's Republican opponent Alf Landon of Kansas, was a political moderate. Although some experts predicted a close race, Roosevelt won the greatest electoral landslide since the beginning of the current two-party system in the 1850s, carrying all but 8 electoral votes. Roosevelt carried every state except Maine and Vermont.

Roosevelt received 98.49% of the electoral vote. He also won the largest number of electoral votes ever recorded at that time, so far only surpassed by Ronald Reagan in the 1984 election when 7 more electoral votes were available. In addition, Roosevelt won 60.8% of the national popular vote, the second highest popular-vote percentage won by a U.S. presidential candidate since 1820.

Although many candidates sought the Republican nomination, only two, Governor Landon and Senator Borah, were considered to be serious candidates. The party machinery almost uniformly backed Landon, a wealthy businessman and centrist, who dominated in the caucuses and at state party conventions. The delegates to the Democratic National Convention unanimously renominated Roosevelt.

Many people expected Huey Long, the colorful Democratic senator from Louisiana, to run as a third-party candidate with his "Share Our Wealth" program as his platform, but his bid was cut short when he was assassinated in September 1935. Father Coughlin and the Reverend Gerald L.K. Smith, a well-known white supremacist and spokesman for the Christian Right, were eventually forced to run Congressman William Lemke as the candidate of the newly-created "Union Party." Lemke barely managed to capture 2% of the vote, and the party was dissolved the following year.

George Gallup, an advertising executive who had begun a scientific poll that year, predicted that Roosevelt would win the election, based on a quota sample of 50,000 people. His correct predictions made public opinion polling a critical element of elections for journalists and for politicians. The Gallup Poll would become a staple of future presidential elections, and remains one of the most prominent election polling organizations to this day.

Roosevelt carried 46 of the 48 states and brought in many additional Democratic members of Congress. Republicans, whom many voters blamed for the Great Depression, would soon become an extinct political party. However, the Republicans would make a strong comeback in the 1938 congressional elections and would remain a potent force in Congress, although they were not able to win the presidency again until 1952.

1940

This campaign was fought in the shadow of World War II as the United States was emerging from the Great Depression. FDR broke with tradition and ran for a third term, which became a major issue. The surprise Republican candidate was Wendell Willkie, a dark horse who crusaded against Roosevelt's failure to end the Depression and his eagerness for war. Roosevelt, aware of strong isolationist sentiment in the U.S., promised there would be no foreign wars if he were reelected. Willkie managed to revive Republican strength in the Midwest and Northeast. However, Roosevelt won a comfortable victory by building strong support from labor unions, big-city political machines, ethnic voters, and the traditionally Democratic Solid South.

This election was the only time in American history in which a candidate was elected to a third term as president. Roosevelt was elected to a fourth term in 1944, but he died only a few months into that term.

In the months leading up to the opening of the 1940 Republican National Convention, the GOP was deeply divided between the party's isolationists, who wanted to stay out of the war at all costs, and the party's interventionists, who felt that Britain and her allies needed to be given all aid short of war to prevent the Germans from conquering all of Europe. The three leading candidates, Senator Robert Taft of Ohio, Senator Arthur Vandenberg of Michigan, and District Attorney Thomas E. Dewey of New York, were all isolationists in varying degrees. This left an opening for a dark horse candidate to emerge. Wall Street-based industrialist Wendell Willkie had never before run for public office. Nevertheless, he emerged as the unlikely compromise nominee. Willkie had supported Roosevelt in the 1932 presidential election and was considered an improbable choice. He had first come to public attention as a critic of Roosevelt's attempt to break up electrical power monopolies. In 1933 President Roosevelt had created the Tennessee Valley Authority, which promised to provide flood control and cheap electricity to the impoverished people of the Tennessee River Valley. However, the government-run TVA competed with Willkie's Commonwealth & Southern company. This led Willkie to oppose the TVA's attempt to compete with private power companies. Willkie argued that the government had unfair advantages over private corporations, and should thus avoid competing directly against them.

Unlike the leading Republican candidates, Willkie was an outspoken advocate of aid to the Allies, especially Britain. His support of giving all aid to the British "short of declaring war" won him the support of many Republicans on the East Coast. Many of the leading media of the era supported Willkie. Even so, he remained a long-shot candidate. The May Gallup Poll showed Dewey at 67% support among Republicans, followed by Vandenberg and Taft, with Willkie at only 3%.

The German Army's rapid blitz into France in May 1940 shook American public opinion, even as Taft was telling a Kansas audience that America needed to concentrate on domestic issues to prevent Roosevelt from using the war crisis to extend socialism at home. Sympathy for the embattled British was mounting daily, and this aided Willkie's candidacy. By mid-June, a little over one week before the Republican Convention opened, the Gallup poll reported that Willkie had moved into second place with 17%, and that Dewey was slipping. Fueled by his favorable media attention, Willkie's pro-British statements won over many of the delegates. As the delegates were arriving in Philadelphia, Gallup reported that Willkie had surged to 29%, Dewey had slipped 5 more points to 47%, and Taft, Vandenberg and former President Herbert Hoover trailed.

At the 1940 Republican National Convention itself, keynote speaker Harold Stassen, Governor of Minnesota, announced his support for Willkie and became his official floor manager. Willkie's amateur status appealed to delegates as well as voters. As the pro-Willkie galleries repeatedly yelled "We Want Willkie," the delegates on the convention floor began their vote. Dewey led on the first ballot but steadily lost strength thereafter. By the fourth ballot, it was obvious that either Willkie or Taft would be the nominee. The key moments came when the delegations of large states switched to Willkie, giving him the victory on the sixth ballot.

Throughout the winter, spring, and summer of 1940 there was much speculation as to whether Roosevelt would break with long-standing tradition and run for an unprecedented third term. The "two-term" tradition, although not yet enshrined in the U.S. Constitution, had been established by President George Washington when he refused to run for a third term in 1796. Roosevelt refused to give a definitive statement as to his willingness to be a candidate again, and he even indicated to some ambitious Democrats, such as James Farley, that he would not run for a third term and that they could seek the Democratic nomination. However, as Nazi Germany swept through Western Europe and menaced Britain in the spring and summer of 1940, Roosevelt decided that only he had the necessary experience and skills to see the nation safely through the Nazi threat. At the 1940 Democratic Convention in Chicago Roosevelt easily swept aside challenges from Farley and John Nance Garner, his Vice-President.

Willkie crusaded against Roosevelt's attempt to break the two-term presidential tradition, arguing that "if one man is indispensable, then none of us is free." Even some Democrats who had supported Roosevelt in the past disapproved of FDR's attempt to win a third term. Willkie criticized what he claimed was incompetence and waste in the New Deal welfare programs. He said he would keep most of FDR's government programs but would make them more efficient.

Similar to today, many Americans still blamed business leaders for the Great Depression. The fact that Willkie symbolized "Big Business" hurt him with many working-class voters. Willkie accused Roosevelt of leaving the nation unprepared for war, but Roosevelt preempted the military issue by expanding military contracts and establishing the lend-lease program to supply the British with badly-needed weapons and warships. Willkie then reversed his approach and charged Roosevelt with secretly planning to take the nation into World War II. This accusation cut into Roosevelt's support. In response FDR promised that he would "not send American boys into any foreign wars." On election day, Roosevelt received 27 million votes to Willkie's 22 million. In the Electoral College, Roosevelt defeated Willkie 449 to 82.

1944

The United States was now fighting World War II. FDR had been in office longer than any other president. There was little doubt that he would run for another term as the Democratic candidate. His

Republican opponent was New York Governor Thomas E. Dewey. There was no question that in the midst of a world war, FDR would win a fourth term.

As 1944 began the frontrunners for the Republican nomination were Willkie, Taft, and Dewey. The Wisconsin primary proved to be the key contest, as Dewey won by a surprisingly wide margin. At the 1944 Republican National Convention, Dewey was nominated on the first ballot. Roosevelt was a popular, war-time incumbent who faced little formal opposition and was renominated easily. Numerous party leaders privately told Roosevelt that they would fight Vice President Wallace's renomination. They proposed Missouri Senator Harry Truman, a moderate who had become well-known as the chairman of a Senate wartime investigating committee, as FDR's new running-mate. Roosevelt reluctantly agreed to accept Truman as his new running mate to preserve party unity. The fight over the vice-presidential nomination would prove to be historic, as FDR's declining health led to his death in April 1945, and Truman thus became the nation's 33rd President instead of Wallace.

The Republicans campaigned against the New Deal, seeking a smaller government and less-regulated economy as the end of the war seemed in sight. Roosevelt's continuing popularity was the main theme of the campaign. To quiet rumors of his poor health, Roosevelt insisted on making a vigorous campaign swing in October, and rode in an open car through city streets. A high point of the campaign occurred when Roosevelt, speaking to a meeting of labor union leaders, gave a speech carried on national radio in which he ridiculed Republican claims that his administration was corrupt and wasteful with tax money. He particularly ridiculed a GOP claim that he had sent a US Navy warship to pick up his Scottish terrier Fala in Alaska, noting that "Fala was furious" at such rumors. The speech was met with loud laughter and applause from the labor leaders. In response, Dewey gave a blistering partisan speech in Oklahoma City a few days later on national radio, in which he accused Roosevelt of being "indispensable" to corrupt big-city Democratic organizations and American Communists. However, American battlefield successes in Europe and the Pacific during the campaign made Roosevelt unbeatable. In the election on November 7, 1944, Roosevelt scored a comfortable victory over Dewey. Roosevelt took 36 states for 432 electoral votes.

1948

Most historians consider the United States presidential election of 1948 as the greatest election upset in American history. Virtually every prediction indicated that incumbent President Harry S. Truman would be defeated by Republican Thomas E. Dewey. Truman won, overcoming a three-way split in his own party. Truman's surprise victory was the fifth consecutive win for the Democratic Party in a presidential election. The Democrats regained control of both houses of Congress.

Both major parties courted General Dwight D. Eisenhower, the most popular general of World War II. Ike flatly refused the nomination of any political party. The contest for the Republican nomination was between Dewey, former Minnesota Governor Harold Stassen, Ohio Senator Robert Taft, California Governor Earl Warren, General Douglas MacArthur and Arthur Vandenberg, the senior Republican in the Senate. Governor Dewey, who had been the Republican nominee in 1944, was regarded as the frontrunner when the primaries began. Dewey's only handicap was that many Republicans disliked him; he often struck observers as cold, stiff and calculating. The "surprise" candidate of 1948 was Stassen, the former "boy wonder" of Minnesota politics, who had been elected governor of Minnesota at 31, Stassen was widely regarded as the most liberal of the Republican candidates, yet during the primaries he was criticized for being vague on many issues. Stassen stunned Dewey and MacArthur in the Wisconsin primary; virtually eliminating General MacArthur. Stassen defeated Dewey again in the Nebraska primary, thus making him the new frontrunner. He then made the strategic mistake of trying to beat Senator Taft in Taft's home state of Ohio. Dewey agreed to debate Stassen in Oregon on national radio - it was the first-ever radio debate between presidential candidates. The sole issue of the debate concerned whether to outlaw the Communist Party of the United States. Stassen, despite his liberal reputation, argued in favor of outlawing the party, while Dewey forcefully argued against it. At one point, he stated, "You can't shoot an idea with a gun." From this point forward, the New York governor had the momentum he needed to win his party's second nomination.

The 1948 Republican National Convention was the first presidential convention to be shown on national television. Dewey was believed to have a large lead in the delegate count. His major opponents planned a "stop-Dewey" movement. However, the three men refused to unite behind a single candidate to oppose Dewey. Instead, all three men simply agreed to try to hold their own delegates in the hopes of preventing Dewey from obtaining a majority. This proved to be futile, as Dewey's efficient campaign team methodically gathered the remaining delegates they needed to win the nomination.

Spirits were low as the Democrats convened in Philadelphia. The Republicans had taken control of both houses of Congress and a majority of state governorships during the 1946 midterm elections. Public opinion polls showed Truman trailing Dewey, sometimes by double digits. Some liberal Democrats had joined Henry A. Wallace's new Progressive Party. Party leaders feared that Wallace would take enough votes from Truman to give the large Northern and Midwestern states to the Republicans. Several Democratic party bosses began working to dump Truman and nominate a more popular candidate. At the Democratic Convention, a group of Northern liberals, led by Minneapolis Mayor Hubert Humphrey, successfully pushed through a platform, over vigorous Southern opposition, promoting civil rights for blacks. Humphrey stated, "The time has come for the Democratic Party to get out of the shadow of states' rights and walk forthrightly into the bright sunshine of *human* rights!" While Truman and his staff were ambivalent about supporting the civil rights plank, many of the big-city party bosses felt that the civil rights platform would encourage the growing black population to vote for the Democrats. The passage of the civil rights platform caused three dozen Southern delegates, led by South Carolina Governor Strom Thurmond, to walk out of the convention. Nonetheless, Truman emerged as the Democratic nominee.

As the Democratic party fragmented, a new Progressive Party nominated former Vice President Henry Wallace. Wallace opposed Truman's Cold War policies, including the Marshall Plan and Truman Doctrine. The Progressives proposed stronger government regulation and control of Big Business and the end of discrimination against blacks and women. They backed a minimum wage and called for the elimination of the House Committee on Un-American Activities, which was investigating the issue of communist spies within the U.S. government and labor unions. The Progressive Party Convention was highly contentious, Several famous newspaper journalists, such as H.L. Mencken and Dorothy Thompson, publicly accused the Progressives of being covertly controlled by Communists.

The Southern Democrats, who had quit the Democratic Convention over Truman's civil rights platform, formed yet another political party, the "States' Rights" Democratic Party, more commonly known as the "Dixiecrats." That party's main goal was continuing the policy of racial segregation in the South. Governor

Strom Thurmond, who had led the walkout, became the party's presidential nominee. Their strategy was to take enough Southern states from Truman to force the election into the United States House of Representatives, where they could then extract concessions. Despite being an incumbent President, Truman was not placed on the ballot in Alabama. In Louisiana, Mississippi, Alabama, and South Carolina, the Dixiecrats were labeled as the main Democratic Party ticket. Outside of these four states, however, it was only listed as a third-party ticket.

Given Truman's sinking popularity and the seemingly fatal three-way split in the Democratic Party, Dewey appeared unbeatable. He carefully avoided risks. He spoke in platitudes, avoided controversial issues, and was vague on what he planned to do as President. Speech after speech was filled with non-political, optimistic assertions of the obvious, including the quote "You know that your future is still ahead of you." (Does this sound like a malapropism of the type later attributed to George W. Bush?)

Truman adopted a slashing, no-holds-barred campaign. He ridiculed Dewey, criticizing Dewey's refusal to address specific issues, and scornfully targeted the Republican-controlled 80th Congress with a wave of relentless, and blistering, partisan assaults. He nicknamed the Republican-controlled Congress as the "do-nothing" Congress. Dewey rarely mentioned Truman's name during the campaign, which fit into his strategy of appearing to be above petty partisan politics.

The Republicans had enacted a platform plank that called for expanding social security, more funding for public housing, civil rights legislation, and promotion of health and education by the federal government. These positions were unacceptable to the conservative Congressional Republican leadership. Truman exploited this rift in the opposing party by calling a special session of Congress in late July and daring the Republican Congressional leadership to pass its own platform. Truman ignored the fact that Dewey's policies were more liberal than most of his fellow Republicans. Instead, he concentrated on what he characterized as the conservative, obstructionist tendencies of the unpopular 80th Congress.

Once again, history seems to be repeating itself in our current economic climate. How could the Democrats, with a clear mandate – and a filibuster-proof majority in both houses after the 2008 election – have resorted to squandering their munificent political capital by once again fighting among themselves so that by 2010 there seemed to be no clear-cut program passed by Congress?

Truman toured much of the nation with his fiery rhetoric, playing to large, enthusiastic crowds. "Give 'em hell, Harry!" was a popular slogan shouted out at stop after stop along the tour. However, the polls all held that Dewey's commanded an insurmountable lead, and that Truman's efforts would be for naught. Indeed, Truman's own staff considered the campaign a last hurrah. The only person who appears to have considered Truman's campaign to be winnable was the President himself, who confidently predicted victory to anyone and everyone who would listen. Even Truman's own wife, Bess, had private doubts that her husband could win.

In the final weeks of the campaign, American movie theatres played two short newsreel-like campaign films in support of the two major-party candidates. Each film had been created by its respective campaign organization. The Dewey film, shot professionally on an impressive budget, featured very high production values, but reinforced Dewey's mage as cautious and distant. The hastily-assembled Truman film, assembled on virtually no budget, relied on newsreel footage of the President taking part in major world events and signing important legislation. The Truman film reinforced an image of the President as engaged and decisive. In the campaign's final days many newspapers, magazines, and political experts were so confident of Dewey's impending victory that they wrote articles to be printed the morning after the election speculating about the new "Dewey Presidency." As Truman made his way to his hometown of Independence, Missouri to await the election returns, not a single reporter traveling on his campaign train thought that he would win.

On election night, Dewey, his family, and his campaign staff, confidently awaited the returns. Truman sneaked away from reporters covering him in Kansas City and made his way to Excelsior Springs, Missouri, where he took a room in the local hotel, had dinner and a Turkish bath, and went to sleep.

As the returns came in Truman took an early lead which he never lost. However, leading radio commentators confidently predicted that once the late returns came in Dewey would overcome Truman's lead and win. Around 4 a.m. Truman awoke, heard on the radio that his lead was nearly two million votes, and decided to ride back to Kansas City. Dewey, meanwhile, realized he was in trouble when early returns from New York and New England showed him running well behind his expected vote total. He was also troubled when the early returns showed that Henry Wallace and Strom Thurmond, the two third-party candidates, were not taking as many votes away from Truman as had been predicted. Dewey stayed up throughout the night examining the votes as they came in. By 10:30 the next morning he was convinced that he had lost. He then sent a gracious telegram of concession to Truman.

The key states in the 1948 election were Ohio, California, and Illinois. Truman narrowly won all three states by a margin of less than 1%. Had Dewey carried all three states by the same narrow margins, he would have won the election in the electoral college while still losing the popular vote. Truman's victory can be attributed to his aggressive, populist campaign style; Dewey's complacent, distant approach to the campaign, and his failure to respond to Truman's attacks; the major shift in public opinion from Dewey to Truman during the late stages of the campaign; broad public approval of Truman's foreign policy, notably the Berlin Airlift of that year; and widespread dissatisfaction with the institution Truman labeled as the "do-nothing, good-for-nothing 80th Republican Congress." As of 2008, Truman was the most unpopular leader to win re-election, though his standing with all Americans increased so much in the ensuing decades that he is now remembered by many historians as one of the greatest presidents of the 20th century.

1952

The Cold War tension between the U.S. and the Soviet Union was escalating rapidly. Republican Senator Joseph McCarthy of Wisconsin had become a national figure after chairing congressional investigations into the issue of Communist spies within the U.S. government. McCarthy's "witch hunt," combined with national weariness after two years of bloody stalemate in the Korean War and the early 1950s recession, set the stage for a hotly-fought presidential contest. Unpopular President Truman decided not to run. The Democrats nominated Governor Adlai Stevenson of Illinois; who had gained a reputation as an intellectual and eloquent orator. The Republican Party nominated war hero General Dwight D. Eisenhower. The Republican landslide victory ended 20 consecutive years of Democratic control of the White House.

The expected candidate for the Democratic nomination was incumbent President Harry S. Truman. Since the newly passed 22nd Amendment (no more than two terms as President) did not apply to whoever was president at the time of its passage, he was eligible to run again. But Truman's popularity was declining rapidly. The indecisive Korean War was dragging into its third year and Senator Joseph McCarthy's anti-Communist crusade was stirring public fears of an encroaching "Red Menace." Polls showed that Truman had a 66% disapproval rating, a record only surpassed decades later by Richard Nixon. With Truman's withdrawal from consideration, Tennessee Senator Estes Kefauver became the front-runner for the nomination. He won most of the primaries. However, most states still chose their delegates to the Democratic Convention via state conventions, which meant that the party bosses – especially the mayors and governors of large Northern and Midwestern states and cities – were able to choose the Democratic nominee. These bosses strongly disliked Kefauver. His investigations of organized crime had revealed connections between Mafia figures and many of the big-city Democratic political organizations. The party bosses thus viewed Kefauver as a maverick who could not be trusted, and they refused to support him for the nomination. Instead, with Truman's backing, they began to search for other, more acceptable, candidates.

One candidate soon emerged who seemingly had few political weaknesses: Governor Adlai Stevenson of Illinois. Truman tried to convince Stevenson to take the presidential nomination, but Stevenson refused, stating he wanted to run for reelection as Governor of Illinois. As the Democrats convened in Chicago, Governor Stevenson, who still proclaimed that he was not a presidential candidate, was asked to give the welcoming address to the delegates. He proceeded to give a witty and stirring address that led his supporters to begin a renewed round of efforts to nominate him, despite his protests. Stevenson gradually gained strength until he was nominated on the third ballot.

The fight for the Republican nomination was between Eisenhower, who became the candidate of the party's moderate eastern establishment; Senator Taft, the longtime leader of the GOP's conservative wing; and Governor Earl Warren of California.

When the 1952 Republican National Convention opened, most political experts rated Taft and Eisenhower as neck-and-neck in the delegate vote totals. The mood at the convention was one of the most bitter and emotional in American history. When Senator Everett Dirksen of Illinois, a Taft supporter, pointed at Dewey on the convention floor and accused him of leading the Republicans "down the road to defeat," mixed boos and cheers rang out from the delegates, and there were even fistfights between some Taft and Eisenhower delegates. In the end, Eisenhower took the nomination on the first ballot. Following Eisenhower's nomination, the convention chose young Senator Richard Nixon of California as Eisenhower's running mate. The Republicans felt that Nixon's credentials as a fierce campaigner and anti-Communist would be valuable.

The Eisenhower campaign was one of the first presidential campaigns to make a major, concerted effort to win the female vote. Many of his radio and television commercials discussed topics such as education, inflation, ending the war in Korea, and other issues that were thought to appeal to women. The Eisenhower campaign made extensive use of female campaign workers. These workers made phone calls to likely Eisenhower voters, distributed "Ike" buttons and leaflets, and gave parties to build support for the GOP ticket in their neighborhoods. Eisenhower won a solid majority of the female vote. Eisenhower attacked "Korea, Communism and Corruption." The Republicans charged that Soviet spies had infiltrated the government. This became a major campaign issue for Eisenhower. Republicans blamed the Democrats for the military's failure to be fully prepared to fight in Korea; they accused the Democrats of harboring Communist spies within the federal government; and they blasted the Truman Administration for the numbers of officials who had been accused of various crimes.

The Democrats criticized Senator Joseph McCarthy and other GOP conservatives as "fearmongers" who were recklessly trampling on the civil liberties of government employees. Many Democrats were particularly incensed when Eisenhower, on a scheduled campaign swing through Wisconsin, decided not to give a speech he had written criticizing McCarthy's methods, and then allowed himself to be photographed shaking hands with McCarthy as if he supported him. Truman never forgot what he saw as a betrayal.

Despite these mishaps, Eisenhower had retained his enormous personal popularity from his leading role in the Second World War. His campaign slogan, "I Like Ike," was one of the most popular in American history. Stevenson concentrated on giving a series of thoughtful speeches around the nation. He too drew large crowds. Although his style appealed to intellectuals and academics, some political experts wondered if he were speaking "over the heads" of most of his listeners, and they dubbed him an "egghead." Eisenhower maintained a comfortable lead in the polls throughout most of the campaign.

A notable event of the 1952 campaign concerned a scandal that emerged when Richard Nixon, Eisenhower's running mate, was accused by several newspapers of receiving $18,000 in undeclared "gifts" from wealthy donors. Nixon, who had been accusing the Democrats of hiding crooks, found himself on the defensive. Eisenhower and his aides considered dropping Nixon from the ticket and picking another running mate. However, Nixon saved his political career with a dramatic half-hour speech on live television. In the speech Nixon denied the charges against him, gave a detailed account of his modest financial assets, and offered a glowing assessment of Eisenhower's candidacy. The highlight of the speech came when Nixon stated that a supporter had given his daughters a gift – a dog named "Checkers" – and that he would not return it, because his daughters loved it.

Both campaigns made use of television ads. A notable ad for "Ike" Eisenhower was an issue-free, feel-good animated cartoon with a soundtrack song by Irving Berlin called *I Like Ike*. For the first time the candidates' personal medical history was released publicly, as were the candidates' financial histories. Near the end of the campaign Eisenhower, in a major speech, announced that if he won the election he would go to Korea to see if he could end the war. His great military prestige, combined with the public's weariness with the conflict, gave Eisenhower the final boost he needed to win. On election day, Eisenhower won a decisive victory, taking over 55% of the popular vote and winning 39 of the 48 states.

1956

Popular Dwight D. Eisenhower successfully ran for re-election in a rematch of the 1952 election, handily defeating Adlai Stevenson once again. While Eisenhower remained immensely popular, his health conditions became a quiet issue. While Stevenson remained attractive to his core of liberal Democrats, he had no real, substantial base. He and Eisenhower largely ignored the civil rights issue. Eisenhower had ended the Korean War and the nation was prosperous, so a landslide for Eisenhower was never in doubt. This was the last presidential election where at least one of the major candidates was born in the 19th century.

As 1956 began there was some speculation that Eisenhower would not run for a second term, primarily due to concerns about his health. In 1955 he had suffered a serious heart attack, and in early 1956 he underwent surgery for ileitis. However, he quickly recovered. After being cleared by his doctors he decided to run for a second term. "Ike" was renominated with no opposition at the Republican Convention. In the spring of 1956 Eisenhower publicly announced that Nixon would again be his running mate. Adlai Stevenson, the Democratic Party's 1952 nominee, fought a tight primary battle with Estes Kefauver for the 1956 nomination. After Kefauver upset

Stevenson in the Minnesota primary, Stevenson, realizing that he was in trouble, agreed to debate Kefauver in Florida. Stevenson and Kefauver held the first televised presidential debate on May 21, 1956 before the Florida primary. By the California primary in June 1956 Kefauver's campaign had run low on money and could not compete for publicity and advertising with the well-funded Stevenson. When Stevenson won the California primary by a 63-37% margin, Kefauver withdrew from the race. At the Democratic National Convention, New York Governor Averill Harriman challenged Stevenson for the nomination. However, Stevenson's delegate lead was much too large for Harriman to overcome, and Stevenson won the nomination on the first ballot.

The highlight of the 1956 Democratic Convention came when Stevenson made the surprise announcement that the convention's delegates would choose his running mate. The two leading contenders were Senator Kefauver and young Senator John F. Kennedy of Massachusetts, who was relatively unknown at that point. Although Stevenson privately preferred Senator Kennedy to be his running mate, he did not attempt to influence the balloting for Kennedy in any way. Kennedy surprised the experts by surging into the lead on the second ballot. At one point, he was only 15 votes shy of winning. However, Kefauver prevailed. The defeat was actually a boost for Kennedy's long-term presidential chances; by coming so close to defeating Kefauver he gained much favorable national publicity, yet by losing to Kefauver he avoided any blame for Stevenson's expected loss to Eisenhower.

Stevenson campaigned hard against Eisenhower, with television ads for the first time being the dominant medium for both sides. Stevenson proposed significant increases in government spending for social programs and treaties with the Soviet Union to lower military spending and end nuclear testing on both sides. He proposed to end the military draft and switch to an "all-volunteer" military. Eisenhower publicly opposed these ideas. Eisenhower maintained a comfortable lead in the polls throughout the campaign. He was helped by two foreign-policy crises that developed in the weekend before the election. In Soviet-occupied People's Republic of Hungary, many citizens revolted against the Soviet Army; their insurrection was crushed within a few days. In Egypt, a combined force of Israeli, British, and French troops seized the Suez Canal; Eisenhower condemned the seizure and pressured the allied forces to return the canal to Egyptian control. The Eisenhower administration had also supported the *Brown vs. Board of Education* ruling in 1954, in which the Supreme Court ended legal segregation in public schools. As a result, Eisenhower won the support of nearly 40% of black voters. On election day Eisenhower took 57% of the popular vote and won 41 of the 48 states.

1960

1960 marked the end of Eisenhower's two terms as President. His Vice President, Richard Nixon was the Republican candidate. The Democrats nominated Massachusetts Senator John F. Kennedy. The electoral vote was the closest in any presidential election since 1916. In the popular vote, Kennedy's margin of victory was among the closest in American history. The 1960 election also remains a source of debate among some historians as to whether vote theft in selected states aided Kennedy's victory.

The major candidates for the 1960 Democratic presidential nomination were Kennedy, Senator Wayne Morse of Oregon, Senator Lyndon Johnson of Texas, Senator Hubert Humphrey of Minnesota, Senator Stuart Symington of Missouri, Governor

Edmund G. Brown of California, and former Illinois Governor Adlai Stevenson. Symington, Stevenson, and Johnson all declined to campaign in the presidential primaries. Each hoped that the other leading contenders would stumble in the primaries, thus causing the convention's delegates to choose him as a "compromise" candidate acceptable to all factions of the party.

Kennedy was initially plagued by suggestions that he was too young and inexperienced to serve as President (shades of Barack Obama!); that he should agree to be the running mate for a "more experienced" Democrat. Kennedy responded, "I'm not running for vice president, I'm running for president." Another problem for Kennedy was his Roman Catholic religion. Many wondered if anti-Catholic prejudice would hurt Kennedy's chances of winning. In the months leading up to the Democratic Convention, Kennedy traveled around the nation persuading delegates from various states to support him. However, as the convention opened, Kennedy was still a few dozen votes short of victory. In the week before the Democratic convention opened in Los Angeles, Kennedy received two new challengers when Senate Majority Leader Lyndon B. Johnson and Adlai Stevenson, the party's nominee in 1952 and 1956, officially announced their candidacies. However, neither Johnson nor Stevenson was a match for the talented and highly efficient Kennedy campaign team led by Robert Kennedy. Johnson challenged Kennedy to a televised debate. Kennedy accepted. Most observers felt Kennedy won the debate, and Johnson was not able to expand his delegate support beyond the South. Many liberal delegates who might have supported Stevenson were already pledged to Kennedy, and Stevenson, despite the support of former First Lady Eleanor Roosevelt, was unable to break their allegiance. Kennedy won the nomination on the first ballot. Then, in a move which surprised many, Kennedy asked Johnson to be his running mate. To this day there is much debate regarding the details of Johnson's nomination.

In 1959, it looked as if Vice President Richard Nixon might face a serious challenge for the GOP nomination from New York Governor Nelson Rockefeller. However, Rockefeller announced he would not be a candidate for president after a national tour revealed that the great majority of Republicans favored Nixon. After Rockefeller's withdrawal, Nixon faced no significant opposition for the Republican nomination. Nixon chose United Nations Ambassador Henry Cabot Lodge, Jr. as his Vice Presidential candidate.

During the campaign Kennedy charged that under Eisenhower and the Republicans the nation had fallen behind the Soviet Union in the Cold War, both militarily and economically, and that as President he would "get America moving again." Nixon responded that, if elected, he would continue the "peace and prosperity" that Eisenhower had brought the nation in the 1950s. Nixon also argued that Kennedy was too young and inexperienced to be trusted with the Presidency. Both Kennedy and Nixon drew large and enthusiastic crowds throughout the campaign. In August 1960, most polls gave Vice-President Nixon a slim lead over Kennedy, and many political commentators regarded Nixon as the favorite to win. However, in August, President Eisenhower, who had long been ambivalent about Nixon, held a televised press conference in which a reporter, Charles Mohr of *Time*, mentioned Nixon's claims that he had been a valuable administration insider and adviser. Mohr asked Eisenhower if he could give an example of a major idea of Nixon's that he had heeded. Eisenhower responded with the flip comment, "If you give me a week, I might think of one." Although both Eisenhower and Nixon later claimed that Ike was merely joking, the remark undercut Nixon's claims of having greater decision-making experience than Kennedy. The remark proved so damaging to Nixon that the Democrats turned Eisenhower's statement into a television commercial criticizing Nixon.

At the Republican Convention, Nixon had pledged to campaign in all 50 states. However, in August Nixon injured his knee on a car door while campaigning in North Carolina. The knee became infected and Nixon had to cease campaigning for two weeks while the infected knee was injected with antibiotics. When he left Walter Reed Hospital, Nixon refused to abandon his pledge to visit every state; he thus wound up wasting valuable time visiting states that he had no chance to win, or which had few electoral votes and would be of little help in the election.

Choosing Johnson as JFK's running mate proved to be a masterstroke for JFK. Johnson was instrumental in helping the Democrats to carry several Southern states, especially Johnson's home state of Texas. Meanwhile, Ambassador Lodge, Nixon's running mate, ran a lackluster campaign and made several mistakes which hurt Nixon. Among them was a pledge - not approved by Nixon - that as President Nixon would name a black person to his cabinet. This remark offended many blacks who saw it as a clumsy attempt to win their votes. Conversely, many Southern whites who still supported racial segregation and may have voted for Nixon were also angered.

The turning point of the campaign were the four Kennedy-Nixon debates. The first presidential debates held on television attracted enormous publicity. Nixon insisted on campaigning until just a few hours before the first debate started. He had not completely recovered from his hospital stay and thus looked pale, sickly, underweight, and tired. He also refused makeup for the first debate. As a result, his beard stubble showed prominently on the era's black-and-white TV screens. Kennedy, by contrast, rested before the first debate and appeared tanned, confident, and relaxed during the debate. An estimated 80 million viewers watched the first debate. Most people who watched the debate on TV believed Kennedy had won, while radio listeners believed Nixon had won. After it had ended, polls showed Kennedy moving from a slight deficit into a slight lead over Nixon. For the remaining three debates Nixon regained his lost weight, wore television makeup, and appeared more forceful than his initial appearance. However, 20 million fewer viewers watched the three remaining debates than the first debate.

A key factor that hurt Kennedy in his campaign was the widespread prejudice against his Roman Catholic religion. Some Protestants believed that if he were elected President, Kennedy would take orders from the Pope in Rome. Kennedy famously told the Greater Houston Ministerial Association on September 12, 1960, "I am not the Catholic candidate for President. I am the Democratic Party's candidate for President who also happens to be a Catholic. I do not speak for my Church on public matters — and the Church does not speak for me." He promised to respect the separation of church and state and not to allow Catholic officials to dictate public policy to him. Kennedy also raised the question of whether one-quarter of Americans were relegated to second-class citizenship just because they were Roman Catholic.

Kennedy's campaign took advantage of an opening when the Rev. Martin Luther King, Jr., the civil-rights leader, was arrested in Georgia while leading a civil rights march. Nixon refused to become involved in the incident, but Kennedy placed calls to local political authorities to get King released from jail. He also called King's father and wife. As a result, King's father endorsed Kennedy, and he received much favorable publicity in the black community. On election day, Kennedy won the black vote in most areas by wide margins. This may have provided his margin of victory in states such as New Jersey, South Carolina, Illinois, and Missouri. Both candidates also argued about the economy and ways in which they could increase the economic growth and prosperity of the 1950s and make it accessible to more people, especially minorities. As the campaign moved into the final two weeks, the polls and most political pundits predicted a Kennedy victory. However, President Eisenhower, who had largely sat out the campaign, made a campaign tour for Nixon over the last 10 days before the election. Eisenhower's support gave Nixon a badly needed boost, and by election day the polls indicated a virtual tie.

The election on November 8 remains one of the most famous election nights in American history. As the early returns poured in from large Northern and Midwestern cities, Kennedy opened a large lead in the popular and electoral vote, and appeared headed for victory. However, as later returns came in from rural and suburban areas in the Midwest, the Rocky Mountain states, and the Pacific Coast states, Nixon began to steadily close the gap with Kennedy. It was not until the afternoon of Wednesday, November 9 that Nixon finally conceded the election, and Kennedy claimed victory. In the national popular vote, Kennedy beat Nixon by just one tenth of one percentage point - the closest popular-vote margin of the 20th century. In the Electoral College, Kennedy's victory was larger, as he took 303 electoral votes to Nixon's 219. Kennedy carried 12 states by three percentage points or less, while Nixon won six states by the same margin.

Many Republicans, including Nixon and Eisenhower, believed that Kennedy had benefited from vote fraud, especially in Lyndon Johnson's state of Texas, and Illinois, home of Mayor Richard Daley's Chicago political machine. If Nixon had carried both of those states, he would have won the election in the electoral college. Republican Senators such as Everett Dirksen and Barry Goldwater also believed that vote fraud played a role in the election. Republicans tried and failed to overturn the results in both these states at the time—as well as in nine other states. Nixon's campaign staff urged him to pursue recounts and challenge the validity of Kennedy's victory in several states, particularly those where large majorities in Catholic precincts had handed Kennedy the election. However, Nixon gave a speech three days after the election stating that he would not contest the election. The actual number of popular votes received by Kennedy in Alabama and Georgia was seriously questioned.

1964

President Lyndon B. Johnson had come to office less than a year earlier following the assassination of his predecessor, John F. Kennedy. Johnson had successfully associated himself with Kennedy's popularity and, in a fierce election called one of the dirtiest in modern times, Johnson successfully painted his opponent, Republican Senator Barry Goldwater of Arizona, as a right-wing extremist who wanted to abolish the social welfare programs created in the 1930s, such as Social Security. LBJ advocated more such programs, and after 1965, he instituted three: Medicare, Medicaid, and the War on Poverty. Johnson easily won the Presidency, carrying 44 of the 50 states and the District of Columbia. The election is also remembered due to Goldwater's status as a pioneer in the modern conservative movement. No post-1964 Democratic candidate has managed to better LBJ's 1964 electoral result.

President Kennedy was assassinated in Dallas on November 22, 1963. Supporters were shocked by the loss of the charismatic Kennedy, while opposition candidates were put in the awkward position of running against the policies of a slain president. During the period of mourning, Republican leaders called for a political moratorium, so as not to appear disrespectful. Little politicking was done by the candidates of either major party until January 1964, when the primary season officially began. At the time, most political experts saw Kennedy's assassination as leaving the nation politically unsettled.

The nomination of Johnson was assured, but he wanted to control the convention and avoid a public fight over civil rights. Nonetheless, Johnson faced challenges from two sides over civil rights issues over the course of the nomination season. At the Democratic National Convention, Johnson faced trouble from Robert F. Kennedy, President Kennedy's younger brother and the U.S. Attorney General. Bobby Kennedy and Johnson had personally disliked one another since the 1960 Democratic National Convention. In early 1964, despite his personal animosity for the president, Kennedy had tried to force Johnson to accept him as his running mate. Johnson announced that none of his cabinet members would be considered for second place on the Democratic ticket. Shortly after the 1964 Democratic Convention, Kennedy decided to leave Johnson's cabinet and run for the U.S. Senate in New York. He won the general election in November. Johnson chose Senator Hubert Humphrey of Minnesota, a liberal and civil rights activist, as his running mate.

The Republican Party was badly divided in 1964 between its conservative and moderate-liberal factions. Nixon, who had been beaten by Kennedy in the 1960 election, decided not to run. In his absence the way was clear for the two factions to engage in an all-out political civil war for the nomination. Barry Goldwater, a Senator from Arizona, was the champion of the conservatives. The conservatives favored a low-tax, small federal government which supported individual rights and business interests and opposed social welfare programs. The conservatives also resented the dominance of the GOP's moderate wing. The conservatives believed the Eastern moderates were little different from liberal Democrats in their philosophy and approach to government. Goldwater's chief opponent for the Republican nomination was Nelson Rockefeller, Governor of New York and the longtime leader of the GOP's liberal-moderate faction.

Initially, Rockefeller was considered the front-runner. However, in 1963, two years after Rockefeller's divorce from his first wife, he married Margarita "Happy" Murphy, a woman 15 years younger who had just divorced her husband and surrendered her four children to his custody. The fact that Murphy had suddenly divorced her husband before marrying Rockefeller led to rumors that Rockefeller had been having an extramarital affair with her. This angered many social conservatives and female voters within the GOP, who claimed Rockefeller was a "wife stealer." Rockefeller's lead among Republicans lost 20 points overnight. Senator Prescott Bush of Connecticut, the father of President George H. W. Bush and grandfather of President George W. Bush, was among Rockefeller's fiercest critics

The final showdown between Goldwater and Rockefeller was in the California primary. In spite of the previous accusations regarding his marriage, Rockefeller led Goldwater in most opinion polls in California, and he appeared headed for victory when his new wife gave birth to a son, Nelson Rockefeller, Jr., three days before the primary. His son's birth brought the issue of adultery front and center, and Rockefeller lost ground in the polls. Goldwater won the primary by a narrow 51% - 49% margin, thus eliminating Rockefeller as a serious contender and all but clinching the nomination. The party's moderates and liberals turned to William Scranton, Governor of Pennsylvania, in the hopes that he could stop Goldwater. However, as the Republican Convention began Goldwater was seen as the heavy favorite to win the nomination.

The 1964 Republican National Convention was one of the most bitter on record. The party's moderates and conservatives openly expressed contempt for each other. Rockefeller was loudly booed when he came to the podium. In his speech he criticized the party's conservatives, which led many conservatives in the galleries to yell and scream at him. A group of moderates tried to rally behind Scranton to stop Goldwater, but Goldwater's forces easily brushed his challenge aside, and Goldwater was nominated on the first ballot. The vice-presidential nomination went to little-known Republican Party Chairman William E. Miller, a Congressman from upstate York. Goldwater stated he chose Miller simply because "he drives President Johnson nuts." In what might be seen as an intriguing comeuppance, today, Miller's daughter, Stephanie Miller, is a popular liberal Democratic "talking head," both on radio and on TV, primarily CNN.

In accepting his nomination, Goldwater uttered his most famous phrase: "I would remind you that extremism in the defense of liberty is no vice. And let me remind you that moderation in the pursuit of justice is no virtue." For many GOP moderates, Goldwater's speech was seen as a deliberate insult, and many of these moderates would defect to the Democrats in the fall election. Although Goldwater had been successful in rallying conservatives, he was unable to broaden his base of support for the general election. Shortly before the Republican Convention, he had alienated most moderate Republicans by his vote against the Civil Rights Act of 1964, which Johnson signed into law. The Johnson camp used this to paint Goldwater as a racist (despite the fact that Goldwater supported the civil rights cause in general, and had voted in favor of the 1957 and 1960 Civil Rights Acts). Goldwater argued that it was a matter for the individual states rather than federal legislation. Goldwater was famous for speaking "off-the-cuff" at times, and many of his former statements were given wide publicity by the Democrats. In the early 1960s, Goldwater had called the Eisenhower administration "a dime store New Deal." The former president never fully forgave him, nor offered him his support in the election. In December 1961, Goldwater had told a news conference that "sometimes I think this country would be better off if we could just saw off the Eastern Seaboard and let it float out to sea," a remark which indicated his dislike of the liberal economic and social policies that were often associated with that part of the nation. That comment came back to haunt him, in the form of a Johnson television commercial, as did remarks about making Social Security voluntary – shades of George W. Bush! In his most famous verbal gaffe, Goldwater once joked that the U.S. military should "lob one (a nuclear bomb) into the men's room of the Kremlin" in the Soviet Union. Goldwater was also hurt by the refusal of many prominent moderate Republicans to support him.

The *New York Herald-Tribune* supported Johnson in the general election. Some moderates even formed a "Republicans for Johnson" organization, although most prominent GOP politicians avoided being associated with it. Eisenhower's strong backing could have been a plus for the Goldwater campaign. Its absence was clearly noticed. When questioned about the presidential capabilities of the former President's younger brother, university administrator Milton S. Eisenhower, in July 1964, Goldwater replied, "One Eisenhower in a generation is enough." However, Eisenhower did make one television commercial for Goldwater's campaign. One prominent Hollywood celebrity who vigorously supported Goldwater was Ronald Reagan, who gave a well-received televised speech supporting Goldwater. Some historians consider this speech to mark the beginning of Reagan's transformation from an actor to a political leader. In 1966, Reagan would be elected Governor of California in a landslide.

Johnson positioned himself as a moderate and succeeded in portraying Goldwater as an extremist. Goldwater's warnings about the overreach of government seemed hyperbolic to 1964 voters, with only 30% of them agreeing at that point that government was too powerful. These numbers would increase in the coming years, up to and including the present. Goldwater's habit of making blunt statements about war, nuclear weapons, and economics were turned against him. Most famously, the Johnson campaign broadcast a television commercial on September 7 dubbed the "Daisy Girl" ad, which featured a little girl picking petals from a daisy in a field, counting the petals, which then segues into a launch countdown and a nuclear explosion. The ads were in response to Goldwater's advocacy of "tactical" nuclear weapons use in Vietnam. Another Johnson ad, "Confessions of a Republican," tied Goldwater to the Ku Klux Klan. Voters increasingly viewed Goldwater as a right wing fringe candidate. His slogan "In your heart, you know he's right," was successfully parodied by the Johnson campaign into "In your guts, you know he's nuts," or "In your heart, you know he might," (as in push the nuclear button), or even "In your heart, he's too far right."

The Johnson campaign's greatest concern may have been voter complacency leading to low turnout in key states. To counter this, all of Johnson's broadcast ads concluded with the line: "Vote for President Johnson on November 3. The stakes are too high for you to stay home." The Democratic campaign used two other slogans, "All the way with LBJ," and "LBJ for the USA." The election campaign was disrupted for a week by the death of former president Herbert Hoover on October 20, 1964, because it was considered disrespectful to be campaigning during a time of mourning.

In the general election, Johnson crushed Goldwater, winning over 61 percent of the popular vote. Goldwater won only his native state of Arizona and five Deep South states that had been increasingly alienated by Democratic civil rights policies. The Johnson landslide defeated many conservative Republican congressmen, giving him a majority that could overcome the conservative coalition.

While losing quite badly in the 1964 election, some historians believe Goldwater laid the foundation for the conservative revolution to follow. Ronald Reagan's speech on Goldwater's behalf, grassroots organization, and the conservative takeover of the Republican party would all help to bring about the "Reagan Revolution" of the 1980s. Indeed, many of today's leading politicians first entered politics to work for Goldwater, including Hillary Clinton.

Johnson went from his victory in the 1964 election to launch the Great Society program at home, signing the Voting Rights Act of 1965 and starting the War on Poverty. But he also escalated the Vietnam War, which eroded his popularity. By 1968, Johnson's popularity had declined and the Democrats became so split over his candidacy that he withdrew as a candidate. Moreover, his support of civil rights for African-Americans helped split union members and Southerners away from Franklin Roosevelt's Democratic New Deal Coalition, which would later lead to the phenomenon of the "Reagan Democrats." The election also furthered the shift of the African-American voting electorate away from the Republican Party. Democratic presidential candidates have almost consistently won at least 80-90% of the African-American vote in each presidential election since that time.

1968

The 1968 election was a wrenching national experience, conducted against a backdrop of the assassination of Martin Luther King, Jr., race riots across the nation, the assassination of Robert F. Kennedy, widespread demonstrations against the Vietnam War, and violent confrontations between police and anti-war protesters at the 1968 Democratic National Convention. Republican nominee Richard Nixon won the election over Democrat Hubert Humphrey.

Nixon ran on a campaign that promised to restore "law and order." The election also featured a strong third party effort by former Alabama Governor George Wallace. Because Wallace's campaign promoted segregation, he proved to be a formidable candidate in the South. No third-party candidate has won an entire state's electoral votes since.

In 1964, Lyndon Johnson had won the largest popular vote landslide in U.S. Presidential election history over Republican Barry Goldwater. During his term, Johnson had seen many political successes: the passage of his sweeping Great Society domestic programs, landmark civil rights legislation, and the continued exploration of space. At the same time, however, the country had experienced large-scale race riots in the streets of its larger cities, along with a generational revolt of young people and violent debates over foreign policy. The emergence of the hippie counterculture, the rise of New Left activism, and the emergence of the Black Power movement fostered social and cultural clashes between classes, generations and races.

A major factor in the decline of President Johnson's popularity was the Vietnam War, which he greatly escalated during his time in office. By late 1967 over 500,000 American soldiers were fighting in Vietnam and suffering thousands of casualties every month. Johnson was especially hurt when, despite his repeated assurances that the war was being "won," the American news media began to show just the opposite. (Mission Accomplished!) The Tet Offensive of February 1968, in which Communist Vietcong forces launched major attacks on several large cities in South Vietnam, led to increased criticism from antiwar activists that the war was unwinnable. In response to the Tet Offensive, the U.S. military claimed that the war could only be won by adding several hundred thousand more soldiers to the American forces already in South

Vietnam. In the months following Tet, Johnson's approval ratings fell below 35%, and the Secret Service refused to let the President make public appearances on the campuses of American colleges and universities, due to his extreme unpopularity among college students. The Secret Service also prevented Johnson from appearing at the 1968 Democratic National Convention in Chicago, because of their fear that his appearance might cause riots.

It was widely assumed when 1968 began that President Johnson would run for another term and that he would have little trouble winning the Democratic nomination. Despite the growing opposition to Johnson's policies in Vietnam, no prominent Democratic candidate was prepared to run against a sitting President of his own party. Only Senator Eugene McCarthy of Minnesota proved willing to challenge Johnson openly. Running as an antiwar candidate, McCarthy was boosted by thousands of young college students who shaved their beards and cut their hair to be "Clean for Gene." These students organized get-out-the-vote drives, rang doorbells and distributed McCarthy buttons and leaflets, and worked hard in New Hampshire for McCarthy. McCarthy won 42% of the primary vote to Johnson's 49%, an amazingly strong showing for such a challenger, and one which gave McCarthy's campaign legitimacy and momentum. The momentum ended, however, when Senator Robert Kennedy announced his candidacy four days later. Thereafter McCarthy and Kennedy would engage in an increasingly bitter series of state primaries. Although Kennedy won most of the primaries, he could never shake McCarthy and his devoted following of antiwar activists, which included many Hollywood celebrities such as Paul Newman, Gene Wilder, Barbra Streisand, and Burt Lancaster.

On March 31, 1968, the President announced to the nation that he was suspending all bombing of North Vietnam in favor of peace talks. Johnson concluded his speech and startled the nation by announcing "With America's sons in the fields far away, with America's future under challenge right here at home, with our hopes and the world's hopes for peace in the balance every day, I do not believe that I should devote an hour or a day of my time to any personal partisan causes or to any duties other than the awesome duties of this office – the Presidency of your country. Accordingly, I shall not seek, and I will not accept, the nomination of my party for another term as your President." Not discussed publicly at the time was Johnson's concern he might not survive another term – Johnson's health was poor, and he had suffered a serious heart attack in 1955 while serving in the U.S. Senate; indeed, he died on January 22, 1973, two days after his term would have ended.

With Johnson's withdrawal, the Democratic Party quickly split into four factions: The first faction comprised labor unions and big-city party bosses, rallied to support Hubert Humphrey, Johnson's Vice President. The second faction, which rallied behind Senator Eugene McCarthy, was composed of college students, intellectuals, and upper-middle-class whites. The third group was primarily composed of Catholics, African-Americans, Hispanics, and other racial and ethnic minorities, who rallied behind Senator Robert F. Kennedy; and the fourth group consisted of white Southern Democrats – Dixiecrats – who supported George C. Wallace and the Alabama governor's third-party campaign in the general election.

Since the Vietnam War had become the major issue that was dividing the Democratic Party, and Johnson had come to symbolize the war for many liberal Democrats, Johnson believed that by withdrawing from the race he could avoid the stigma of defeat, and he could keep control of the party machinery by giving the nomination to Humphrey, who had been a loyal Vice President. As the year progressed, Johnson believed he could secure his place in the history books by ending the war before the election in November, thus giving Humphrey the boost he would need to win.

After Johnson's withdrawal, Vice President Hubert Humphrey announced his candidacy. Kennedy's surprising defeat in Oregon at the hands of McCarthy, the California primary was seen as crucial to both Kennedy and McCarthy. Kennedy and McCarthy engaged in a television debate a few days before the primary. It was generally considered a draw. On June 4 Kennedy narrowly defeated McCarthy in California, 46%–42%. However, McCarthy refused to withdraw from the race and made it clear that he would contest Kennedy in the upcoming New York primary. The New York primary quickly became a moot point, however, for in the early morning of June 5, Kennedy was shot shortly after midnight; he died twenty-six hours later. Kennedy had just given his victory speech in a crowded ballroom of the Ambassador Hotel in Los Angeles; he and his aides then entered a kitchen pantry on their way to a banquet room to meet with reporters. In the narrow pantry Kennedy and five others were shot by Sirhan Sirhan, a Palestinian militant who disliked Kennedy because of his support for Israel.

Robert Kennedy's death altered the dynamics of the race. Although Humphrey appeared the prohibitive favorite for the nomination, thanks to his support from the traditional power blocs of the party, he was an unpopular choice with many of the antiwar elements within the party, who identified him with Johnson's controversial position on the Vietnam War. Some of Kennedy's support went to McCarthy, but many of Kennedy's delegates, remembering their bitter primary battles with McCarthy, refused to vote for him. Instead, they rallied around Senator George McGovern of South Dakota, a Kennedy supporter in the spring primaries. This dividing of the antiwar votes at the Democratic Convention made it easier for Humphrey to gather the delegates he needed to win the nomination.

When the Democratic National Convention opened in Chicago, thousands of young activists from around the nation gathered to protest the Vietnam War. In a clash which was covered on live television, Americans were shocked to see Chicago police brutally beating antiwar protesters in the streets. While the protesters chanted "The whole world's watching," the police used clubs and tear gas to beat back the protesters, leaving many of them bloody and dazed. The police claimed that their actions were justified because numerous police officers were being injured by bottles, rocks, and broken glass that were being thrown at them by the protestors; the protestors had also yelled verbal insults at the police, calling them "pigs" and other epithets. The antiwar riots divided the Democratic Party's base: some sympathized with the police and condemned the protestors, while some liberal Democrats supported the protestors and were outraged by the police actions. Meanwhile, the convention was marred by the strong-arm tactics of Chicago's mayor Richard J. Daley, who publicly cursed Senator Abraham Ribicoff of Connecticut, who had made a speech at the convention denouncing the excesses of the Chicago police in the riots. The nomination itself was anticlimactic. Humphrey easily beat McCarthy and McGovern on the first ballot.

The front-runner for the Republican nomination was former Vice President Richard M. Nixon. Nixon was always the front runner because of his superior organization. By early spring, California Governor Ronald Reagan, the leader of the GOP's conservative wing, had become Nixon's chief rival. Reagan's victory in California gave him a plurality of the nationwide primary vote, but his poor showing in most other state primaries left him far behind Nixon in the actual delegate count. As the 1968 Republican National Convention opened, Nixon's only remaining obstacles were Reagan and Rockefeller, who were planning to unite their forces in a "stop-Nixon" movement. However, the strategy fell apart when neither Reagan nor Rockefeller agreed to support the other for the nomination. Nixon won the nomination on the first ballot.

The American Independent Party was formed by former Alabama Governor George Wallace, whose pro-segregation policies had been rejected by the mainstream of the Democratic Party. Wallace won the electoral votes of several states in the Deep South. He took many votes which might have gone to Humphrey. Although Wallace did not expect to win the election, his strategy was to prevent either major party candidate from winning a preliminary majority in the Electoral College, which would then give him bargaining power to determine the winner.

Nixon's campaign was carefully managed and controlled. He often held "town hall" type meetings in cities he visited, where he answered questions from voters that had been screened in advance by his aides. Since he was well behind Nixon in the polls, Humphrey opted for a slashing, fighting campaign style. He repeatedly, and unsuccessfully, challenged Nixon to a televised debate. Humphrey predicted that he, like Truman, would surprise the experts and win an upset victory. Nixon campaigned on a theme to restore "law and order," which appealed to many voters angry with the hundreds of violent riots that had taken place across the country in the previous few years. Vice-President Humphrey criticized the "law and order" issue, claiming that it was a subtle appeal to white racial prejudice. Nixon also mentioned his opposition to desegregation busing. He believed in combating segregation in other ways, such as promoting better education to blacks. During the campaign, Nixon offered government tax incentives to African Americans for small businesses and home improvements in their existing neighborhoods. Nixon also emphasized his opposition to Chief Justice Earl Warren of the Supreme Court. Many conservatives were critical of Chief Justice

Warren for using the Supreme Court to promote liberal policies in the fields of civil rights, civil liberties, and the separation of church and state. Nixon promised that if he were elected President, he would appoint justices who would take a less-active role in creating social policy. In another campaign promise, he pledged to end the draft.

Humphrey promised to continue and expand the Great Society welfare programs started by President Johnson, and to continue the Johnson Administration's "War on Poverty." He also promised to continue the efforts of Presidents Kennedy and Johnson, and the Supreme Court, in expanding civil rights and civil liberties for minority groups. Early in his campaign Humphrey often found himself the target of antiwar protestors, some of whom heckled and disrupted his campaign rallies. After the Democratic Convention in late August, Humphrey trailed Nixon by double-digits in most polls, and his chances seemed hopeless. As election day approached and Wallace's support in the North and Midwest began to wane, Humphrey finally began to climb in the polls. In the end, the Vietnam War became the one remaining problem Humphrey could not overcome. In October, Humphrey, who still trailed Nixon in the polls, began to publicly distance himself from the Johnson administration on the Vietnam War, calling for a bombing halt. The key turning point for Humphrey's campaign came when President Johnson officially announced a bombing halt, and even a possible peace deal, the weekend before the election. The "Halloween Peace" gave Humphrey's campaign a badly needed boost. In addition, Senator Eugene McCarthy finally endorsed Humphrey in late October after previously refusing to do so, and by election day the polls were reporting a dead heat.

Tipped off in advance by Henry Kissinger of the bombing halt and the possible peace deal, and fearing this 'October surprise' might cost them the election, the Richard Nixon campaign privately assured the South Vietnamese military rulers that an incoming Republican regime would offer them a better deal than would a Democratic one. The tactic "worked," in that South Vietnam withdrew from the talks on the eve of the election, thereby destroying the peace initiative on which the Democrats had based their campaign.

The election on November 5, 1968 proved to be extremely close. It was not until the following morning that the television news networks were able to call Nixon the winner. The key states proved to be California, Ohio, and Illinois, all of which Nixon won by three percentage points or less. Nixon won the popular vote with a plurality of 512,000 votes, or a victory margin of about one percentage point. In the electoral college Nixon's victory was larger, as he carried 32 states with 301 electoral votes, to Humphrey's 13 states and 191 electoral votes.

Nixon's victory is often considered a realignment election. From 1933 to 1968, the Democratic Party was the majority party. During that period, the Democrats won seven out of nine presidential elections. The election of 1968 reversed the situation completely. From 1968 to 2008, the Republican Party was the majority party. During that time period, the Republicans won seven out of ten presidential elections. From 1968 to 2008 only two Democrats were elected President, both native Southerners - Jimmy Carter of Georgia and Bill Clinton of Arkansas. Not until 2008 did a Northern Democrat, Barack Obama, win a presidential election.

1972

The Democratic Party's nomination was eventually won by Senator George McGovern, who ran an anti-war campaign against incumbent Republican President Richard Nixon, but was handicapped by his outsider status, as well as by the scandal and subsequent firing of vice presidential nominee Thomas Eagleton. Nixon won the election in a massive landslide with a 23.2% margin of victory in the popular vote, the fourth largest margin in presidential election history. He received 18 million more popular votes than McGovern, the widest margin of any U.S. presidential election.

Senate Majority Whip Ted Kennedy, the Kennedy's younger brother, had been the odds-on favorite to win the 1972 nomination, but his hopes were dashed by his role in the 1969 Chappaquiddick incident and he was not a candidate. The favorite for the Democratic nomination then became Ed Muskie. However, prior to the New Hampshire primary, the "Canuck letter" was published in the *Manchester Union-Leader*. The letter, whose authenticity was later questioned, claimed that Muskie had made disparaging remarks about French-Canadians. Subsequently, the paper published an attack on the character of Muskie's wife Jane, reporting that she drank and used off-color language. Muskie made an emotional defense of his wife in a speech outside the newspaper's offices during a snowstorm. The press reported that Muskie broke down and cried. Muskie did worse than expected in the primary, while McGovern came in a surprisingly close second. McGovern now had the momentum, which was well orchestrated by his campaign manager, Gary Hart.

New York Representative Shirley Chisholm became the first African American to run for the Democratic or Republican presidential nomination and the first woman to run for the Democratic presidential nomination. South Dakota Senator McGovern entered the race as an anti-war, progressive candidate, picking-up where Eugene McCarthy had left off. McGovern was able to pull together support from the anti-war movement together with the youth block and other grassroots support to win the nomination.

Alabama Governor George Wallace did well in the South, but Wallace was shot while campaigning, and left paralyzed in an assassination attempt. The shooting effectively ended his campaign. In the end, McGovern succeeded in winning the nomination by winning primaries through grassroots support in spite of establishment opposition.

Richard Nixon was a popular incumbent president in 1972. He seemed to have reached détente with the People's Republic of China and the Soviet Union. Polls showed that he held a strong lead in the Republican primaries. He was challenged by two minor candidates, liberal Pete McCloskey of California and conservative John Ashbrook of Ohio. Nixon easily won renomination on the first ballot.

George McGovern ran on a platform of ending the Vietnam War and instituting guaranteed minimum incomes for the nation's poor. His campaign was greatly crippled because of the electro-shock therapy controversy involving his original running mate, and because his views during the primaries had alienated many powerful Democrats. The Republicans successfully portrayed him as a half-crazy radical, and McGovern suffered a landslide defeat of 61%–38%. The election had the lowest voter turnout for a presidential election since 1948. Only 55% of the electorate voted. Nixon won a majority vote in 49 states, with only Massachusetts and the District of Columbia voting for McGovern, resulting in an even more lopsided Electoral College tally.

As part of the continuing investigation in 1974–75, Watergate scandal prosecutors offered companies that had given illegal campaign contributions to Nixon's re-election campaign lenient sentences if they came forward. Many companies complied, including Northrop-Grumman, 3M, American Airlines and Braniff Airlines. By 1976, prosecutors had convicted 18 American corporations of contributing illegally to Nixon's campaign.

1976

The United States presidential election of 1976 followed the resignation of President Richard Nixon in the wake of the Watergate scandal. It pitted then-sitting incumbent President Gerald Ford, the Republican candidate, against the relatively unknown former governor of Georgia, Jimmy Carter. Ford was handicapped by a slow economy and he paid a political price for his pardon of Nixon. Carter ran as a Washington outsider and reformer and won a narrow victory. He was the first president elected from the Deep South since 1848.

When the primaries began, Carter was relatively unknown at the national level. However, in the wake of Watergate, Carter realized that his status as a Washington "outsider," centrist, and moderate reformer could give him an advantage over his better-known "establishment" rivals. Carter took advantage of the record number of state primaries and caucuses in 1976 to eliminate his better-known rivals one-by-one. By June 1976 he had captured more than enough delegates to win the Democratic nomination. Carter easily won the nomination on the first ballot. The contest for the Republican Party's presidential nomination was between two serious candidates, Gerald Ford, the leader of the GOP's moderate wing, and Ronald Reagan, the leader of the GOP's conservative wing. The primary contest was hard-fought and relatively even. Ford defeated Reagan by a narrow margin on the first ballot and chose Senator Robert Dole of Kansas as his running mate. Eugene

McCarthy, a former Democratic Senator from Minnesota, ran as an independent candidate.

As President, Ford presided over events dealing with the United States Bicentennial, resulting in favorable publicity, part of Ford's "Rose Garden" strategy to win the election. Instead of appearing as a typical politician, Ford presented himself as a "tested leader," who was busily fulfilling the role. Not until October did Ford leave the White House to actively campaign. Jimmy Carter ran as a reformer who was "untainted" by Washington political scandals, which many voters found attractive in the wake of Watergate. Ford, although personally unconnected with Watergate, was seen by many as too close to the discredited Nixon administration, especially after Ford granted Nixon a presidential pardon for any crimes he may have committed during his term of office. Ford's pardon of Nixon caused his popularity to tank. His refusal to publicly explain his reasons for pardoning Nixon also hurt his image.

Ford unsuccessfully asked Congress to end the 1950s-era price controls on natural gas, which had caused a dwindling of American natural gas reserves after the 1973 Oil Crisis. Carter stated during his campaign that he opposed the ending of the price controls and thought such a move would be "disastrous."

After the Democratic Convention, Carter held a 33-point lead over Ford in the polls. As the campaign continued, the race greatly tightened. The closeness of the race is normally attributed to three causes. Carter confirmed a promise of a full pardon to Christian and other religious and political refugees and other opponents to the Vietnam War (draft dodgers) in response to a question posed by a reporter during the presidential debates. Americans viewed the pardon as the only true way to end the bitterly hated Vietnam War. *Playboy* magazine published a controversial interview with Carter, in which he admitted to having "lusted in my heart" for women other than his wife, which cut into his support among women and evangelical Christians. Also, on September 23, Ford performed well in the first televised presidential debate since 1960. Polls taken after the debate showed that most viewers felt that Ford was the winner. Carter was also hurt by Ford's charges that he lacked the necessary experience to be an effective national leader, and that Carter was vague on many issues.

However, Ford also committed a costly blunder in the campaign that halted his momentum. During the second presidential debate, Ford stumbled when he asserted that "there is no Soviet domination of Eastern Europe and there never will be under a Ford administration." He added that he did not "believe that the Poles consider themselves dominated by the Soviet Union," and made the same claim with regards to Yugoslavia and Romania. Ford refused to retract his statement for almost a week after the debate. Neo-conservatives, who were becoming increasingly anti-Soviet, were appalled. Combined with Carter's pledge of a pardon for all Vietnam War opponents and refugees, Ford's surge stalled and Carter was able to maintain a slight lead in the polls.

A vice-presidential debate between Robert Dole and Walter Mondale hurt the Republican ticket when Dole asserted that military unpreparedness on the part of Democratic presidents was responsible for all of the wars the U.S. had fought in the twentieth century. By election day the race was judged to be even. It took most of election night and the following morning to determine the winner. At 3:30 a.m., NBC announced that Carter had accumulated more than the 270 electoral votes needed to win. Seconds later, ABC News also declared Carter the winner. CBS News announced Carter's victory at 3:45 a.m. Carter defeated Ford by two percentage points in the national popular vote. The electoral vote was the closest since 1916; Carter took 23 states with 297 electoral votes, while Ford won 27 states and 240 electoral votes. Carter's victory came primarily from his near-sweep of the South and his narrow victories in large

Northern states such as New York, Ohio, and Pennsylvania. Ford did well in the West, carrying every state except Hawaii. The states that ultimately decided the election were Wisconsin and Ohio, both won by Carter. Had Ford won these states, he would have won the presidency. The 27 states Ford won were and remain the most states ever carried by a losing candidate. Carter's 50.1% of the vote was only the second time since 1964 that a Democrat managed to obtain a majority of the popular vote in a presidential election until Barack Obama won 53% of the vote 32 years later.

APPENDIX B

THE SPIN MASTERS

THE SPIN MASTERS ON THE RIGHT

The proliferation of "talking heads," "political pundits," and other euphemisms for truth twisters or "spin doctors" has not been limited to television or to internet bloggers. You might not be able to watch TV while you're driving that truck (American-built, of course, and the biggest sonofabitch you can find), tractor, or SUV, but you sure as hell can *listen* to the radio, and become wise and knowledgeable in the process.

Welcome to the world of the "bottom feeders," the opinion makers who know very little of what they speak. Chief among them are Rush Limbaugh, a disk-jockey-turned-"statesman," probably the most listened-to "political commentator" on radio today; Michael Savage, he of the "Savage Nation;" and Sean Hannity. There are others, of course. Here's a capsule bios of some of the most noteworthy these "shock jocks."

RUSH LIMBAUGH (BORN 1951)

Limbaugh, who hosts *The Rush Limbaugh Show,* the highest-rated talk-radio program in the United States (he recently signed a $400 million contract extension with Clear Channel) was born into a family with a long history of involvement in Republican politics. He first began working at a local radio station at 16. In 1984, Limbaugh began working as a disk jockey and later as a radio talk show host in Sacramento, California. One of my closest friends worked at the same station and was part of the group that decided to hire him. She reports that whatever else he may be, Rush Limbaugh "paid his dues." He worked hard and appeared at the "grand openings" of supermarkets, drugstores, even hole-in-the-wall mom n' pop places. His unique program featured no guests. He relied exclusively on his conservative political analysis for content. He moved to New York City in 1988, where his national broadcasts on WABC radio.

By the 1990s, Limbaugh's fame grew beyond radio, into publishing and television. He became a bestselling author and hosted a half-hour television talk show. Limbaugh frequently accuses the American mainstream media of having a strong liberal bias. He criticizes liberal policies and politicians and promotes conservative positions.

Rush Hudson Limbaugh III was born in Cape Girardeau, Missouri. His father was a lawyer and fighter pilot, who had served in the China-Burma-India Theater of World War II. Limbaugh began his career in radio as a teenager in his hometown of Cape Girardeau, using the name Rusty Sharpe. He graduated from Cape Central High School, then enrolled in Southeast Missouri State University. He left that school after two semesters and one summer. According to his mother, "He flunked everything," and "he just didn't seem interested in anything except radio." Limbaugh was not drafted during the Vietnam War draft lottery. He was later classified as "4-F" due to either a football knee injury or a diagnosis of Pilonidal disease.

After dropping out of college, Limbaugh moved to McKeesport, Pennsylvania. In 1972, he became a Top 40 music disc jockey on a small AM radio station that reached much of the Pittsburgh area. He started with an afternoon show and later did mornings, broadcasting under the name "Jeff Christie." He then moved to Pittsburgh and became an evening disc jockey. He was fired in late 1974, and was told by management that he would never make it as on air talent, and should consider going into sales. After failing to find another job in radio in Pittsburgh, Limbaugh moved back home to Cape

Girardeau. For the rest of the decade, he worked in music radio before settling in Kansas City, where he accepted a job as director of promotions with the Kansas City Royals baseball team.

In 1984, Limbaugh returned to radio as a talk show host at KFBK in Sacramento, California. By 1987, stations could broadcast editorial commentary without having to present opposing views. Rush Limbaugh was one of the first to proclaim himself "liberated from the East Germany of liberal media domination." On August 1, 1988, Limbaugh moved to New York City and began his national radio show. By December 1990, Limbaugh had more listeners than any other talk show host. One pundit described his style as "bouncing between earnest lecturer and political vaudevillian." But his style took hold and was eventually being broadcast on over 650 radio stations nationwide.

In late 2001, Rush Limbaugh acknowledged that he had gone almost completely deaf, although he continued his show. He was able to regain much of his hearing with cochlear implants. In 2003, he had a brief stint as a pro football commentator with ESPN. In April 2006, Limbaugh turned himself in and was arrested on a single charge of prescription fraud. His record was expunged after 18 months of rehabilitation.

Today, Limbaugh's radio show airs for three hours each weekday and is broadcast worldwide on the Armed Forces Radio Network. He owns a majority of the show, which is syndicated by the Premiere Radio Networks. His views are decisive, opinionated, and often controversial, something he has never denied.

In an attempt to undermine the 2008 Democratic primary campaigns, Limbaugh encouraged his listeners to vote for whoever was behind in the race, an effort dubbed "Operation Chaos." In Ohio, he encouraged his listeners to register as Democrats and vote for Hillary Clinton. Hoping that factions of the Democratic Party would cause disunity at their convention, Limbaugh said that

"The dream end of Operation Chaos is that this keeps up to the convention, and that we have a recreation of Chicago 1968 with burning cars, protests, fire, and literal riots and all of that, that is the objective here."

Limbaugh was the keynote speaker at the 2009 Conservative Political Action Conference. His speech attracted widespread attention. When CBS's *Face the Nation* asked White House Chief Of Staff Rahm Emanuel who he thought represented the Republican Party; Emanuel named Limbaugh as his choice. Republican Party Chairman Michael Steele said that Limbaugh is "an entertainer" and his rhetoric at the convention was "incendiary" and "ugly." On March 4, 2009, Limbaugh challenged President Barack Obama to a debate on his radio program. Limbaugh offered to pay all of Obama's expenses including travel, food, lodging, and security. Rush Limbaugh has been married four times and has no children. His fourth and present marriage is to Kathryn Rogers, a party planner from Florida, whom he married on June 5, 2010. After the ceremony, Elton John entertained wedding guests for a $1 million fee. Limbaugh is a well-known cigar afficionado.

MICHAEL SAVAGE (BORN 1942)

Michael Alan Weiner, better known by his pseudonym Michael Savage, is an American radio host, author, and conservative political commentator, whose program, *The Savage Nation*, is syndicated throughout the United States and has an audience of 8 to 10 million listeners on 400 stations across the United States. He holds Master's degrees in medical botany and medical anthropology and he earned a Ph.D. from the University of California, Berkeley, in nutritional ethnomedicine. As Michael Weiner, he has written books on herbal medicine and homeopathy. As Michael Savage, he has written four *New York Times*-bestselling political books.

Savage has summarized his political philosophy as, "To the right of Rush and to the left of God. He outspokenly opposes illegal immigration to the United States, supports the English-only movement and argues that liberalism and progressivism are degrading American culture

Savage, born Michael Alan Weiner in the Bronx, comes from Russian Jewish heritage. He describes his childhood as difficult, due to his father's "gruff and profane" personality and frequent verbal abuse. After graduating from Jamaica High School, Savage attended Queens College, where he earned a bachelor's degree in education and sociology. After college, he taught high school for several years in New York City. His first marriage ended in divorce. He remarried after meeting his current wife, Janet, in 1967. During this time, Savage worked for Timothy Leary as keeper of the stone gatehouse on Leary's Millbrook estate. Savage earned two master's degrees in ethnobotany and anthropology from the University of Hawaii and a Ph.D. in 1978 from the University of California, Berkeley, in nutritional ethnomedicine. Savage spent many years researching botany in the South Pacific and has a background in alternative medicine. As a result of being outside of the US, he was not subject to the Vietnam draft.

Savage and his second wife Janet have two children, a daughter and a son; his son Russell Weiner, is the founder of the company that produces the Rockstar energy drink. In the early 60s, Savage befriended and traveled with Beat poets Allen Ginsberg and Lawrence Ferlinghetti. Another acquaintance was poet and author Neeli Cherkovski, who says Savage dreamed of becoming a stand-up comic in the mold of Lenny Bruce. Savage became alienated from the North Beach scene in the early 1980s and had intense arguments with his liberal friends.

In 1996, Savage applied to become the Dean of the Graduate School of Journalism at the University of California, Berkeley. The University instead selected award-winning journalist and China scholar Orville Schell. Savage sued the University, contending he was discriminated against because he was a conservative. He later dropped the lawsuit. The rejection of his 1994 manuscript prompted him to record a demo tape with a mock radio talk show about illegal immigrants and epidemics. He mailed this tape to 250 radio stations in an attempt to change careers and become a radio talk show host. On March 21, 1994, Savage began his radio career on San Francisco's KGO (my own favorite news/talk radio station) as a fill-in host for the liberal Ray Taliaferro. Less than a year later, he was given a weekday show on KGO's sister station, KSFO.

During his tenure at KSFO, Savage reached #1 in Arbitron ratings and became the top talk host in his time slot in Northern California. In 1999, he came to the attention of the Talk Radio Network, which currently syndicates *The Savage Nation* radio program. He says that he tries to make a show that has a "hard edge combined with humor and education. Those who listen to me say they hear a bit of Plato, Henry Miller, Jack Kerouac, Moses, Jesus, and Frankenstein."

Michael Savage calls himself an "independent-minded individualist" and says he "fits no stereotype." He criticizes big government, homosexuality, and "Liberalism," accuses the media of liberal bias, and champions environmentalism and animal rights. He has said that there are three aspects that define a nation: borders, language, and culture. Liberal advocacy group and media watchdogs accuse Savage of fascist leanings, racism, homophobia, bigotry and Islamophobia because of his controversial statements about homosexuality, Islam, feminism, sex education, and immigration.

SEAN HANNITY (BORN 1961)

Radio and television host, author, and conservative political commentator, Hannity is the host of *The Sean Hannity Show*, a nationally syndicated talk-radio show that airs throughout the United States on Premiere Radio Networks, as well as the cable-news show, *Hannity*, on Fox News Channel. Hannity has written three *New York Times* bestselling books: *Let Freedom Ring: Winning the War of Liberty over Liberalism*, *Deliver Us from Evil: Defeating Terrorism, Despotism, and Liberalism*, and *Conservative Victory: Defeating Obama's Radical Agenda*.

Hannity grew up in Franklin Square, New York and attended Sacred Heart Seminary and St. Pius X Preparatory Seminary high school in Uniondale, New York. He dropped out of New York University and Adelphi University to pursue his broadcasting career. During the late 1980s, Hannity was a general contractor and bartender in Santa Barbara, California. In 1993, he married Jill Rhodes, a columnist for *The Huntsville Times*. They have two children.

Hannity hosted his first talk radio show in 1989 at the volunteer college station at UC Santa Barbara, KCSB-FM. His weekly show was canceled after less than a year by station managers upset with his remarks about gays and lesbians. The station later reversed its decision, due in part to a campaign conducted by the Santa Barbara Chapter of the American Civil Liberties Union, but Hannity decided against returning to KCSB. After leaving KCSB, Hannity placed an ad in radio publications presenting himself as "the most talked about college radio host in America." Radio station WVNN in Athens, Alabama hired him to be the afternoon talk show host. From He moved to Atlanta in 1992. In September 1996, Fox News co-founder Roger Ailes hired Hannity to host a TV program, *Hannity & Colmes*. In 1997, WABC New York put Hannity on the air full-time.

Hannity has been described as a leader of the pack among broadcasting political polarizers, "those who have an intense commitment to a candidate, culture, or ideology that sets people in one group definitively apart from people in another, rival group." In November 2008, Colmes announced his departure from *Hannity & Colmes*. After the show's final broadcast, Hannity took over the time slot with his own new show, *Hannity*. In April 2009, Hannity said he'd allow himself to be waterboarded for charity. The statement generated attention, though there was no public follow-up by Hannity. Hannity's radio program is a conservative political talk show that features Hannity's opinions and ideology related to current issues and politicians. The program is heard by over 13 million listeners a week.

GLENN BECK (BORN 1964)

Glenn Lee Beck is a self-described conservative radio and television host, political commentator, author, and entrepreneur. He is currently the host of a nationally syndicated talk-radio show that airs throughout the United States on Premiere Radio Networks and the host of a self-titled cable-news show on Fox News Channel.

Beck was born in Everett, Washington and raised as a Roman Catholic. He obtained his first broadcast job as a disc-jockey at the age of 13. When his mother died, Beck moved to Bellingham, where he attended high school. After graduation, he worked as a disk jockey at radio stations in Provo, Utah, Washington D.C. and New Haven, Connecticut. While working at WPGC, Beck met his first wife, Claire. They had two daughters, Mary and Hannah. Mary developed cerebral palsy. The couple divorced in 1994 amid Beck's struggles with substance abuse. Along with being a recovering alcoholic and drug addict, Beck has been diagnosed with Attention Deficit Hyperactivity Disorder. By 1994, Beck was suicidal, and imagined shooting himself to the music of his fellow Washingtonian, Kurt Cobain. He attended his first AA meeting in November 1994, the month he stopped drinking alcohol and smoking cannabis.

After getting clean, Beck claimed he had gotten high every day for the previous 15 years, since the age of sixteen. After marrying his present wife Tania in 1999, the couple joined the Church of Jesus Christ of Latter-day Saints. He and Tania have two children, Raphe, who is adopted, and Cheyenne. Beck currently resides in a $4.2 million dollar colonial mansion in New Canaan, Connecticut, with his wife and four children.

In August 2010, Beck commented, "We are definitely at a crossroads. We will either be a third world country that looks more like Latin America, or we will have totally reinvented ourselves. We're not going back to the way it was ten years ago, nor should we." Beck has described himself as a conservative with libertarian leanings. Among his core values Beck lists personal responsibility, private charity, the right to life, freedom of religion, limited government, and family as the cornerstone of society. Beck also believes in low national debt, and has said "A conservative believes that debt creates unhealthy relationships. Everyone, from the government on down, should live within their means and strive for financial independence." Beck supports individual gun ownership rights and is against gun control legislation. He has asserted his business is not political, but is an entertainment company. In 2010, he addressed the Conservative Political Action Conference by stating, "What's the difference between a communist or socialist and a progressive? Revolution or evolution? One requires a gun; the other eats away slowly."

Glenn Beck has supported Tea Party protests from their inception and held a broadcast from one of the April 2009 rallies in San Antonio, Texas. In June 2010, *The Weekly Standard* named Beck "one of the fathers of the Tea Party." In April 2010, *Forbes* calculated Beck's earnings for the period March 2009 - March 2010 to be $32 million. Despite millions of viewers, more than 200 companies have joined a boycott of Beck's television program, making it difficult for Fox to sell ads.

After moving to the Fox News Channel, Beck began to host *Glenn Beck* airing weekdays at 5 p.m., beginning January 19, 2009. His first guests included Sarah Palin and the wives of Jose Compean and Ignacio Ramos. As of September 2009, Beck's program drew more viewers than all three of the competing time-slot shows on CNN, MSNBC and HLN combined. However, his show's high ratings have not come without controversy. *The Washington Post's* Howard Kurtz reported that Beck's use of "distorted or inflammatory rhetoric" has given him a "lightning-rod status," that in turn has complicated the channel's and their journalist's efforts to neutralize White House criticism that Fox is not really a news organization. Television analyst Andrew Tyndall called Beck an "activist" and "comedian," whose incendiary style has created "a real crossroads for Fox News," stating "they're right on the cusp of losing their image as a news organization." Eric Burns, the former host of *Fox News Watch*, has also been very critical of Beck, whom he refers to as "Huey Long without the political office," "Father Coughlin without the dour expression," "John Birch without the Society," and "an embarrassment to all true conservatives."

JAMES CORSI (BORN 1946)

Jerome Robert Corsi is best-known for his two *New York Times* bestselling books: *The Obama Nation* and *Unfit for Command.* Both books attacked Democratic presidential candidates and were strongly criticized for including numerous factual errors. In other books and columns for conservative websites such as WorldNetDaily and Human Events, Corsi has discussed topics that are considered conspiracy theories in some circles, such as the alleged plans for a North American Government, criticism of the United States government for allegedly covering up information about the terrorist attacks of September 11, 2001, promoting the theory that oil is produced from chemical reactions in the Earth, in contrast to the scientific community's consensus that oil is produced from the bodies of animals and/or plants, and alleged United States support of Iran in its attempts to develop nuclear weapons.

Jerome Corsi was born in East Cleveland and graduated St. Ignatius High School in 1964. He earned a B.A. from Case Western Reserve University in 1968 and a Ph.D.in Political Science from Harvard University in 1972. He married Joy Dugan in 1970. After the marriage ended in divorce. he married Monica Corsi in 1991. In January 2005, Corsi told the *Boston Herald* that he planned to bid for John Kerry's Senate seat in Massachusetts in 2008 as a Republican or Independent candidate. He later said his wife had "vetoed" this plan. Corsi has written about a variety of subjects, including Democratic politicians and conspiracy theories. Corsi, who is Catholic, has been accused by the press of being anti-Islamic, anti-Catholic, anti-Semitic and homophobic, and of exploiting racial prejudices in an attempt to scare white America. Corsi has also referred to Martin Luther King Jr. as a "shakedown artist." Corsi claimed that "President Bush was pursuing a globalist agenda to create a North American Union." In 2007 he predicted an amero currency to replace dollar for this union would happen within 10 years.

MICHAEL MEDVED (BORN 1948)

Michael Medved is a radio host, author, conservative political commentator, and film critic. His Seattle-based nationally-syndicated talk show, *The Michael Medved Show*, airs throughout the United States on Salem Radio Network. Medved was born into a Jewish family in Philadelphia and raised in San Diego, where his scientist father David Medved worked for Convair and later for NASA. He attended Palisades High School in Los Angeles, entered Yale University as a sixteen-year-old undergraduate, and graduated with honors in 1969. He entered Yale Law School, but after his first year there, he left to work as a head speechwriter for Democratic U.S. Senate candidate Joe Duffey, and then for four years as a speech writer and political consultant. After political campaign work, including a position as an aide to Congressman Ron Dellums, Medved worked in advertising, and coordinated a campaign to recruit more African Americans and Hispanics to the police departments of San Francisco, Oakland and Berkeley.

After writing more than forty articles for the book *The People's Almanac*, Medved wrote *What Really Happened to the Class of '65?* with David Wallechinsky (son of best-selling novelist Irving Wallace).The book became a bestseller in 1976 and the basis for a weekly TV series on NBC. Medved continued his involvement in politics, becoming a friend of Ford's chief of staff, Dick Cheney. He affiliated himself with the Republican Party, and campaigned for Ronald Reagan in 1980. He has become, and still is, a well-respected, nationally known movie critic.

While focusing on the theme of *Hollywood vs. America*, radio talk show host Rush Limbaugh interviewed Medved, then asked Medved to guest-host his talk show. Medved served as a regular guest-host for Limbaugh on 30 occasions. In 1996, he was offered his own local show on a major Seattle radio station. Medved welcomed the chance to speak to a wider audience about politics and morality. His three hour daily show is now broadcast on 200 stations coast to coast and reaches more than 7.25 million listeners weekly. Medved describes his show as "Your Daily Dose of Debate," often focused on listeners who call in to debate issues with the host.

Medved writes a regular column for *USA Today* and occasional op-ed pieces for *The Wall Street Journal.* He has argued that voters in the American Jewish community don't necessarily embrace candidates based on their support for the state of Israel as much as they passionately oppose candidates based on their identification with Christianity, especially the fervent evangelicalism of the dreaded *Christian Right*. Medved also notes that the Orthodox community, which he states represents less than 10% of the American Jewish population, "gives nearly as disproportionate support to Republicans as their Reform, Conservative, and secular Jewish neighbors give to Democrats," and argues that the main reason for this different response is that "the Orthodox feel no instinctive horror at political alliances with others who make faith the center of their lives."

Medved co-founded the Pacific Jewish Center, a synagogue in Venice, California, with his friend and teacher, Orthodox Rabbi Daniel Lapin. For fifteen years, Medved served as president of PJC, which states that its mission is outreach to unaffiliated and disconnected Jews. In his book *Right Turns: Unconventional Lessons from a Controversial Life*, he states that his commitment to religion led to his conservative political outlook. He is a *baal teshuva* (returnee to traditional Judaism) and a vegetarian.

ANN COULTER (BORN 1961)

Ann Hart Coulter is a lawyer, conservative social and political commentator, author, and syndicated columnist. She frequently appears on television, radio, and as a speaker at public events and private events. Well-known for her right-wing political opinions and the controversial ways in which she defends them, Coulter has described herself as a polemicist who likes to "stir up the pot" and, unlike "broadcasters," does not "pretend to be impartial or balanced." She was born in New York City. Her family later moved to New Canaan, Connecticut, where Coulter and her two older brothers were raised. She graduated New Canaan High School in 1980, *cum laude* from Cornell in 1984 with a B.A. in history, and received her J.D. from University of Michigan Law School in 1988, where she achieved membership in the Order of the Coif and was an editor of the *Michigan Law Review*.

After a short time working in New York City in private practice, where she specialized in corporate law, Coulter left to work for the United States Senate Judiciary Committee after the Republican Party took control of Congress in 1994. She later became a litigator with the Center for Individual Rights. Coulter is the author of seven books, all of which have appeared on *New York Times* Best Seller list, with a combined 3 million copies sold. Her first book, *High Crimes and Misdemeanors: The Case Against Bill Clinton*, details Coulter's case for the impeachment of President Bill Clinton. In the late 1990s, Coulter's weekly syndicated column for Universal Press Syndicate began appearing. Her column is featured on six conservative websites. She has a loyal fan base of conservative readers who look forward to reading her columns in their local newspapers.

Coulter contracted with *USA Today* to cover the 2004 Democratic National Convention. She wrote one article that began, "Here at the Spawn of Satan convention in Boston..." and referred to some unspecified female attendees as "corn-fed, no make-up, natural fiber, no-bra needing, sandal-wearing, hirsute, somewhat fragrant hippie chick pie wagons." The newspaper declined to print the article. She has criticized former president George W. Bush's immigration proposals, saying they led to "amnesty." In one column, she claimed that the current immigration system is set up to purposely reduce the percentage of whites in the population. Overall, Coulter's columns are highly critical of liberals and Democrats.

Coulter made her first national media appearance in 1996 after she was hired by the then-fledgling network MSNBC as a legal correspondent. She was fired from that network at least twice, but her troubles with MSNBC only freed her to appear on CNN and Fox News, whose producers called often. Coulter has also made frequent guest appearances on many television and radio talk shows, including *American Morning*, *The Fifth Estate*, *Glenn Beck Program*, *The Mike Gallagher Show*, *The O'Reilly Factor*, *Real Time with Bill Maher*, *Red Eye w/ Greg Gutfeld*, *The Rush Limbaugh Show*, *The Sean Hannity Show*, *The Today Show*, *Lou Dobbs Tonight*, *Fox and Friends*, *The Laura Ingraham Show*, and *The View*.

Coulter has been engaged several times, but never married. She has dated publisher Bob Guccione, Jr. and conservative writer Dinesh D'Souza. In October 2007, she began dating Andrew Stein, a liberal Democrat. When asked about the relationship, Stein told the paper, "She's attacked a lot of my friends, but what can I say, opposites attract!" Three months later, the relationship ended, both sides citing "irreconcilable differences." Coulter owns a condominium in Manhattan and a house in Palm Beach, Florida. Coulter says that she holds Christian beliefs. She has stated, "I'm a Christian first and a mean-spirited, bigoted conservative second, and don't you ever forget it! Being a Christian means that I am called upon to do battle against lies, injustice, cruelty, hypocrisy – you know, all the virtues in the church of liberalism."

On September 14, 2001, three days after the September 11 attacks, Coulter wrote in her column, "Airports scrupulously apply the same laughably ineffective airport harassment to Suzy Chapstick as to Muslim hijackers. It is preposterous to assume every passenger is a potential crazed homicidal maniac. We know who the homicidal maniacs are. They are the ones cheering and dancing right now. We should invade their countries, kill their leaders and convert them to Christianity. We weren't punctilious about locating and punishing only Hitler and his top officers. We carpet-bombed German cities; we killed civilians. That's war. And this is war."

BEN STEIN (BORN 1944)

Before talking about Ben Stein, I must here confess that I really *really* like the man, even if our politics don't always jive. He is an oddity in *The Politics of Hate* in that I do not believe he truly hates anything or anyone. He just happens to be a brilliant lawyer, speechwriter, economist, and *raconteur* who can poke fun at himself and whose worldview is a trifle skewed. He is the irascible uncle that everyone likes to joke about. Before he graduated to his present position as talking head on CNN, his best previous roles were as the stuffed-shirt teacher in *Ferris Bueller's Day Off* and as the hilarious protagonist of the Comedy Central quiz show *Win Ben Stein's Money.* (I actually qualified to be a contestant on that show - you can ask Jimmy Kimmel, who was the warm-up guy for Ben Stein, and who now has risen to the very pinnacle of success as a late-night TV host). Unfortunately, although I was on the list, I never got called, and thus never had the chance to challenge the *Maestro* for the munificent sum of $5,000.

Benjamin Jeremy "Ben" Stein is an actor, writer, lawyer, and commentator on political and economic issues. He started out as a speechwriter for Richard Nixon and Gerald Ford before he morphed into acting. He is the son of economist and writer Herbert Stein, who worked at the White House under President Nixon. While as a character actor he is well-known for his nerdy monotone, in real life he is a public speaker on a wide range of economic and social issues. Stein was born in Washington, D.C. and is Jewish. He graduated from Montgomery Blair High School in 1961 along with classmate journalist Carl Bernstein. He went on to major in economics at Columbia University. After graduating with honors from Columbia, Stein took his J.D. at Yale Law School.

Ben Stein started his law career as a poverty lawyer in New Haven, Connecticut, and Washington, D.C. before becoming a trial lawyer for the Federal Trade Commission. His first teaching job was as an adjunct professor at American University in Washington, D.C., then at University of California, Santa Cruz. He was a professor of law at Pepperdine University Law School in Southern California from 1990 to 1997, where he taught libel law and United States securities law and its ethical aspects.

Stein writes frequently on a variety of topics, including politics, investing and economics. He was fired from his position as Sunday Business columnist at *The New York Times* in August 2009 due to a policy forbidding writers from performing product endorsements or advertising. Stein has stated his belief that the real reasons for his firing were budget cuts at the *Times*, his criticism of President Obama, and pressure from those critical of *Expelled*, who "bamboozled some of the high pooh-bahs at the *Times* into thinking there was a conflict of interest." Stein became a Hollywood consultant before he moved into acting. His film career was launched by his performance as the monotonic economics teacher in the 1986 movie *Ferris Bueller's Day Off*. Stein played similarly bland and unemotional characters. He had a recurring role in the TV series *The Wonder Years* and played himself in *Dave*. He has done, and continues to do, myriad commercials.

On March 18, 2007, Stein famously proclaimed at the beginning of the subprime mortgage crisis that the foreclosure problem would "blow over and the people who buy now, in due time, will be glad they did," the economy was "still very strong," and the "smart money" was "now trying to buy, not sell, as much distressed merchandise" in mortgages as possible.

Stein is a pro-life activist. He has criticized the U.S. tax code for being too lenient on the wealthy. He has repeated the observation made by Warren Buffett, that Buffett pays a lower overall tax rate than his secretaries (who pay income taxes). Stein has advocated increasing taxation on the wealthy. Ben Stein endorsed Democrat

Al Franken in the 2008 Minnesota Senate race, calling him an "impressive guy." Stein has publicly denounced the theory of evolution, which he and other intelligent design advocates call "Darwinism." Stein is twice married to entertainment lawyer Alexandra Denman, with whom he has an adopted son. He lives in Beverly Hills and Malibu, California. He also has a summer home in Sandpoint, Idaho and an apartment in the Watergate complex in Washington, DC, which he inherited from his parents.

BILL O'REILLY (BORN 1949)

William James "Bill" O'Reilly, Jr., TV host, author, syndicated columnist and political commentator, is the host of *The O'Reilly Factor* on the Fox News Channel, which is the most watched cable news program on American television. During the late 1970s and 1980s, he worked as a news reporter for various local television stations and eventually for CBS News and ABC News. From 1991 to 1995, he was anchor of the entertainment news program *Inside Edition*. O'Reilly is widely considered a conservative commentator.

O'Reilly was born in the Washington Heights section of Manhattan. In 1951, his family moved to Levittown on Long Island. After high school, O'Reilly attended Marist College. He received his B.A. in history in 1971, then moved to Miami, Florida, where he taught English and history at Monsignor Pace High School from 1970 to 1972. He returned to school in 1973 and earned an M.A. in Broadcast Journalism from Boston University.

O'Reilly's early television news career included stints in Scranton, Pennsylvania, Dallas, Texas, Denver, Colorado, Portland, Oregon, Hartford, Connecticut, and Boston, Massachusetts. In 1980, he anchored his own program on WCBS-TV in New York. In 1982, he was promoted to CBS News correspondent and covered the wars in El Salvador and the Falkland Islands from his base in Buenos Aires, Argentina. O'Reilly joined ABC News as a correspondent in 1986. At ABC, O'Reilly hosted daytime news briefs that previewed stories to be reported on the day's *World News Tonight* and worked as a general assignment worker for *Good Morning America, Nightline,* and *World News Tonight.*

In 1991, O'Reilly joined the nationally syndicated program *Inside Edition*, a tabloid/gossip television program in competition with *A Current Affair*. He became the program's anchor after David Frost's termination. When he left that program, he went back to school and received a Master of Public Administration from Harvard University. After Harvard, he was hired by Roger Ailes, chairman and CEO of the then startup Fox News Channel, to anchor *The O'Reilly Factor.* The program is routinely the highest-rated show of the three major U.S. 24-hour cable news channels and began the trend toward more opinion-oriented prime-time cable news programming.

O'Reilly's life and career have not been without controversy. He is often accused of distorting facts and using misleading or erroneous statistics. After the September 11 attacks, O'Reilly accused the United Way and the American Red Cross of failing to deliver millions of dollars in donated money, raised by the organizations in the name of the disaster, to the families of those killed in the attacks. Actor George Clooney accused O'Reilly of misstating facts and harming the relief effort by inciting panic among potential donors. O'Reilly is the main inspiration for comedian Stephen Colbert's satirical character on the Comedy Central show *The Colbert Report*, which features Colbert in a parody of *The O'Reilly Factor*. On the show, Colbert refers to O'Reilly as "Papa Bear." O'Reilly and Colbert exchanged appearances on each others' shows in January 2007.

O'Reilly has long said that his inspiration for speaking up for average Americans are his working-class roots. Liberal talk-show pundit Al Franken accused O'Reilly of distorting his background to create a more working-class image. O'Reilly has also said, "You don't come from any lower than I came from on an economic scale" On *The O'Reilly Factor*, Bill O'Reilly has focused on news and commentary related to politics and culture. O'Reilly has long said that he does not identify with any political party. On December 6, 2000, The *Daily News* in New York reported, however, that he had been registered with the Republican Party in the state of New York since 1994. When questioned about this, he said that he was not aware of it and says he registered as an independent after the interview. Despite being registered as an Independent, many view him as a conservative figure. O'Reilly married Maureen E. McPhilmy, a public relations executive, in 1996. They have a daughter, Madeline and a son, Spencer. O'Reilly currently resides in suburban Manhasset, New York.

STEVE SCHMIDT (BORN 1970)

Steve Schmidt, an American campaign strategist and public relations worker for the Republican Party, specializes in political "message development and strategy." He was the senior campaign strategist and advisor to the 2008 McCain presidential campaign. Schmidt grew up in North Plainfield, New Jersey. He first handed out campaign materials for Democrat Bill Bradley's 1978 Senate campaign. Schmidt attended the University of Delaware but left three credits short of graduating because he did not pass a math course.

In 1995, Steve Schmidt managed Will T. Scott's unsuccessful campaign for attorney general of Kentucky. In 1998, he ran Tim Leslie's unsuccessful race for lieutenant governor of California. That year he was also the Communications Director for the unsuccessful U.S. Senate campaign of Matt Fong. In 1999, he was communications director for Lamar Alexander's presidential run, leaving in June when the campaign reduced its senior staff.

Schmidt joined the Bush administration as a Deputy Assistant to the President and Counselor to Vice President Dick Cheney. In 2004, he was a member of the senior strategic planning group led by Karl Rove that ran President George W. Bush's re-election campaign. Schmidt oversaw the reelection "war room." In 2005 and 2006, he was the White House strategist in charge of the U.S. Supreme Court nominations of Samuel A. Alito and Chief Justice John Roberts. In 2006, he left the White House to become the campaign manager in the re-election campaign for California Governor Arnold Schwarzenegger. On July 2, 2008, Schmidt was appointed to head up day to day operations of the McCain campaign in response to concerns that the campaign lacked coordination and a clear message. Schmidt's management transformed the McCain campaign into an "an elbows-out, risk-taking, disciplined machine." He aggressively responded to press criticism and found creative methods of manipulating the news cycle.

In a CNN interview with John King, when asked about the debut of Sarah Palin's upcoming book release, he stated, "My honest view is that she would not be a winning candidate for the Republican party." He said Sarah Palin was dishonest as the GOP's vice-presidential nominee and that her untruths have done long-term damage to her public image. "There were numerous instances that she said things that were not accurate that ultimately, the campaign had to deal with. That opened the door to criticism that she was being untruthful and inaccurate. And I think that is something that continues to this day." Schmidt cited an ethics report on the then-Alaska governor from her home state on an investigation into whether she had improperly used her government position. "She went out and said, you know, 'This report completely exonerates me,'" Schmidt said. "And in fact, it didn't. You know it's the equivalent of saying down is up and up is down. It was provably, demonstrably untrue." Schmidt's withering depiction of Palin was aired in a "60 Minutes" segment devoted to the release of a long-anticipated book on the epic 2008 campaign, "Game Change."

THE SPIN MASTERS ON THE LEFT

I must here admit that on the whole I find the talking heads on the liberal side of the spectrum to be, with the exception of Ben Stein, possessed of a much better sense of humor than their Conservative counterparts. For one thing, they don't tend to take themselves as seriously. For another, they generally take more of a "live and let live" attitude. To be sure, there are dirty tricksters among their number, but I'm talking about the *public* face these spin doctors put on for the media. The only problem with their attitude is that Americans tend to take the Conservative pundits more seriously than they do the Liberals. Which is a shame, because politics without laughter is dull and drab indeed. Since I've provided mini-biographies of Conservative "luminaries," a "fair and balanced approach" means I should equal time to a similar number of master communicators from the left side of the aisle.

JON STEWART (BORN 1962)

Jon Stewart (Jonathan Stuart Leibowitz) is a political satirist, writer, television host, actor, media critic and stand-up comedian. His program, *The Daily Show*, airs on Comedy Central. He has gained great traction as a satirical critic of personality-driven media shows, in particular the coverage of CNN, Fox News Channel, and

MSNBC. He critiques other news shows from the safe, removed position of his "fake news" desk. In spite of its self-professed entertainment mandate, *The Daily Show* has been nominated for a number of news and journalism awards. He hosted the 78th and 80th Academy Awards. He is the co-author of *America (The Book): A Citizen's Guide to Democracy Inaction*, which was one of the best-selling books in the U.S. in 2004.

Stewart was born in New York City to a Jewish family. He grew up in Lawrenceville, New Jersey, where he attended Lawrence High School. His mother is an educational consultant and teacher, and his father is a physics professor at The College of New Jersey. The couple divorced when Stewart was eleven years old and Stewart no longer has any contact with his father. He has said that he was subjected to anti-Semitic bullying for being Jewish. After graduating from the College of William & Mary in 1984, Stewart held numerous jobs. He was a contingency planner for the New Jersey Department of Human Services, contract administrator for City University of New York, puppeteer for children with disabilities, caterer, busboy, shelf stocker at Woolworth's, and bartender at a local blue-collar bar, the Franklin Corner Tavern.

With a reputation for being a funny man in school, Jon Stewart moved to New York City in 1986 to try his hand at the comedy club circuit. He made his stand-up debut at The Bitter End, the same place where Woody Allen, began. Stewart became a regular at the Comedy Cellar where he was the last performer every night. For two years, he would perform at 2 a.m. while developing his comedic style. In 1989, he landed his first television job as a writer for *Caroline's Comedy Hour*. In 1991, he began co-hosting Comedy Central's *Short Attention Span Theater* along with Patty Rosborough. When David Letterman left NBC in 1993, Stewart was a finalist to replace him, but Conan O'Brien was hired instead.

In 1999, Stewart began hosting *The Daily Show* on Comedy Central. The show, which has been popular and successful since Stewart became the host, blends humor with the day's top news stories, usually in politics, while simultaneously poking fun at politicians and many newsmakers as well as the news media itself. In April 2010, Comedy Central renewed Stewart's contract to host *The Daily Show* into 2013.Stewart is paid a reported $1.5 million for one season of *The Daily Show*. According to the Forbes list of Celebrities, he earns $14 million a year. Stewart again became a viral internet phenomenon following a March 4, 2009 *Daily Show* sequence. CNBC cancelled Rick Santelli's scheduled appearance but Stewart still ran a short segment showing CNBC giving bad investment advice.

For years, Stewart has regularly lambasted Fox News for distorting the news to fit a conservative agenda, at one point ridiculing the network as "the meanest sorority in the world." In November 2009, Stewart called out Fox News for using some footage from a previous rally during its report of a more recent one. The show's anchor, Sean Hannity, apologized the next night. A month later, Stewart criticized *Fox & Friends* host Gretchen Carlson, a former Miss America and Stanford graduate, for claiming that she googled words such as "ignoramus" and "czar." Stewart believed that Carlson was dumbing herself down for "an audience who sees intellect as an elitist flaw." Stewart stepped up his criticism of Fox News in 2010. As of 24 April, *The Daily Show* had had 24 segments criticizing Fox News' coverage. Bill O'Reilly, host of *The O'Reilly Factor*, countered that *The Daily Show* was a "key component of left-wing television" and that Stewart was a fan of Fox News because the network was so interesting to watch.

Although best known for his work on *The Daily Show,* Stewart has also had roles in several films and television series. In 2000, when he was labeled a Democrat, he generally agreed, but described his political affiliation as "more socialist or independent" than Democratic. Stewart married Tracey McShane, his girlfriend of four years, in 2000. He proposed to his future wife through a personalized crossword puzzle created with the help of the crossword editor at *The New York Times*. The couple had their first child, Nathan Thomas Stewart in July 2004. Their second child, a daughter, Maggie Rose Stewart, was born in February 2006. They also have a cat named Stanley and two pit bull terriers.

BILL MAHER (BORN 1956)

William "Bill" Maher, Jr. is a stand-up comedian, television host, social critic, political commentator, author, and actor. Before his current role as host of HBO's *Real Time with Bill Maher*, he hosted a similar late-night talk show, *Politically Incorrect,* on Comedy Central and later on ABC. He targets religion, politics, bureaucracies, political correctness, the mass media, greed among people, and the lack of voters' intellectual curiosity – *which is exactly the target of this book*. He supports the legalization of marijuana and gay marriage and serves on the board of PETA.

Maher was born in New York City, the son of a Jewish nurse and a Catholic news editor and radio announcer. He was unaware that his mother was Jewish until his early teenage years. He subsequently self-identified himself as ethnically half-Jewish. He received his Bachelor of Arts in English and History from Cornell University in 1978.

Maher began his career as a stand-up comedian and actor at the New York City comedy club Catch a Rising Star in 1979. Thanks to Steve Allen, he started appearing on the Johnny Carson and David Letterman shows in 1982. He rose to prominence as host of *Politically Incorrect with Bill Maher*, a late-night political talk show that ran from 1993 until it was ultimately cancelled in June 2002. Jerry Seinfeld, a regular guest on the show, stated that *Politically Incorrect* reminded him of talk shows from the 1950s and 60s "when guests interacted with each other as much as with the host." ABC cancelled Maher's contract after he made a controversial on-air remark shortly after the September 11th attacks, whereby he agreed with his guest, conservative pundit Dinesh D'Souza, that the 9/11 terrorists did not act in a cowardly manner. Maher replied, "We have been the cowards. Lobbing cruise missiles from two thousand miles away. That's cowardly. Staying in the airplane when it hits the building. Say what you want about it. Not cowardly." Although Rush Limbaugh came to Maher's defense in pointing out the distinction between physical and moral cowardice, several companies including FedEx and Sears pulled their advertisements.

Maher is a frequent political commentator on CNN, MSNBC, and HLN. He is a frequent guest on the Larry King show, and was a special guest on the June 29, 2010 edition when Larry King announced his retirement. He regularly appears on CNN's *The Situation Room with Wolf Blitzer* and is also a frequent guest on MSNBC's *Hardball with Chris Matthews, The Rachel Maddow Show, Countdown with Keith Olbermann,* and on HLN's *The Joy Behar Show*. Since May 2005, he has been a contributing blogger at The Huffington Post.

Maher describes himself as a libertarian who believes that, "government is really there to do the things that people absolutely can't do for themselves." Maher has also called for the creation of a new progressive party "to represent the millions of Americans who aren't being served by the Democrats." He favors partial privatization of Social Security, ending corporate welfare and federal funding of nonprofits, and legalization of gambling, prostitution, and marijuana. He is highly suspicious of corporations and often criticizes figures with close ties to industry. Maher supported Bob Dole in the 1996

U.S. presidential election on the basis that Dole was a war hero and the kind of "old-fashioned" Republican he admired. In 2000, he voted for Ralph Nader in the election.

Maher has expressed his distaste for the pharmaceutical and health care industries on the grounds that they make their money out of curing people who are made sick by consuming unhealthy food that society urges upon the public. He is not a vegetarian, but claims he doesn't eat a lot of meat. He says he has a "very eccentric diet."

Before the 2004 U.S. presidential election, Maher clearly opposed George W. Bush's reelection and went so far as to publicly kneel on his show, with director Michael Moore, and beg Ralph Nader to drop out of the race. Maher says that the word "liberal" has been unfairly demonized. Another word Maher claims has been unfairly demonized by the right-wing is "elite." On his show, he has highlighted the hypocrisy of distrusting elite politicians while at the same time wanting elite doctors to treat you and elite lawyers to represent you in court. Maher supports the death penalty, the legality of abortion and euthanasia, and racial profiling at airports.

Bill Maher was originally against the Iraq War. He now views the Iraq War as a failure. In an interview promoting *Religulous* Maher stated: "People say 'The surge worked now, we got rid of Saddam.' But the cost was 4000 American lives, untold Iraqi lives, ethnic cleansing, four million refugees, a trillion dollars of U.S. money that could have rebuilt every road, bridge and school in America, started a Manhattan project for energy alternatives, and given health care to everybody. Did the surge work compared to that?"

In 2008, Maher announced his support for Barack Obama. He was very critical of John McCain, and called Sarah Palin an extremist who was completely unqualified for the presidency. He also called Palin a "Category 5 moron," who was not even qualified to be the mayor of Wasilla, Alaska. On September 12, 2008, Maher declared that Levi Johnston, the father of Bristol Palin's unborn child, was "America's number one political prisoner," and offered to turn control of his website over to Levi should Johnston wish to use the site as a way of raising money to purchase his freedom.

While Maher welcomed Obama's election, by June 2009, he criticized Obama for not being aggressive enough in tackling health care reform, the banking crisis, and energy legislation. With the Democrats controlling both Houses of Congress and the Executive Branch, Maher argued that significant health care reform should have been accomplished within the first year or two of Obama's presidency, before the mid-term elections. Maher is highly critical of religion, which he often describes as a neurological disorder that justifies crazies and stops people from thinking logically. He has said many times that religion works under the guise of morality but that its tenets generally have nothing to do with morality, that religious prohibitions are being confused with moral law. In Maher's view, just because a religion prohibits abortion or decries homosexuality, that does not mean that having an abortion or having homosexual sex are immoral acts. Instead, an immoral person is one who harms others through murder, rape, or greed.

In answer to the suggestion that a divine moral authority is necessary, he says, "Couldn't we just get together and agree on the few basic Commandments that are laws? Like 'I won't slaughter you, and don't take my shit.'" On August 15, 2007, on *Larry King Live*, he stated it was impossible to know what happens after death. He compared Christian promises of an afterlife with the promises made by politicians trying to get elected. Maher and director Larry Charles teamed up to make the feature film *Religulous*, a documentary that spoofs religious extremism across the world, in 2008.

Maher has stated that the AMA is a powerful lobbying group and one of the primary reasons why the United States has failed to enact health care reform. On August 24, 2009, on *The Tonight Show,* Bill Maher stated, "Obama should forget about trying to get 60 votes for it. He only needs 51. Forget getting the sixty votes or sixty percent, sixty percent of people don't believe in evolution in this country. He just needs to drag them to it. Like I said, they're stupid; get health care done, with or without them." He has expressed the view that most illness is generally the result of poor diet and that medicine is often not the best way of addressing illness. "The answer isn't another pill."

Maher has never married. In 2003, he began dating former Playboy Cyber Girl Coco Johnsen. At the end of their 17-month relationship, she sued him for pain and suffering for allegedly insulting, humiliating and degrading racial comments. Her suit claimed that Maher promised to marry her and father her children, support her financially, and purchase her a Beverly Hills home. Her lawsuit against Maher was dismissed on May 2, 2005. In 2005, he began dating author Karrine Steffans, an actress, former music video performer and hip-hop model. Maher lives in Beverly Hills. As of 2009, he is dating Cara Santa Maria, who has a masters degree in neurobiology.

MICHAEL MOORE (BORN 1954)

Film maker, author, and liberal political commentator, Moore produced and directed *Bowling for Columbine*, *Fahrenheit 9/11*, *Sicko*, and *Capitalism: A Love Story*, four of the top highest-grossing documentaries of all time. In September 2008, he released his first free movie on the Internet, *Slacker Uprising*, documenting his personal crusade to encourage more Americans to vote in presidential elections. Moore is a self-described liberal who has criticized globalization, large corporations, assault weapon ownership, the Iraq War, George W. Bush and the American health care system.

Moore was born and raised in Davison, a suburb of Flint, Michigan by his parents, a secretary and an automotive assembly-line worker. At that time, Flint was home to many General Motors factories, where his parents and grandfather worked. Moore, who was brought up Roman Catholic, has described his parents as "Irish Catholic Democrats, basic liberal good people." He achieved the rank of Eagle Scout and, at the age of 18, he was elected to the Davison school board. After dropping out of the University of Michigan-Flint, following his freshman year, Moore got a job at the Buick plant. In 1986, when Moore became the editor of *Mother Jones*, a liberal political magazine, he moved to California and shut down *The Michigan Voice*, a paper he had founded. Moore was fired after four months at *Mother Jones*, because he refused to run an article, believing it to be inaccurate. Moore believes that *Mother Jones* fired him because of the publisher's refusal to allow him to cover a story on the GM plant closings in his hometown of Flint. He responded by putting laid-off GM worker Ben Hamper (who was also writing for the same magazine at the time) on the magazine's cover, leading to his termination. Moore sued for wrongful dismissal, and settled out of court for $58,000, providing him with seed money for his first film.

Moore first became famous for his 1989 film, *Roger & Me*, a documentary about what happened to Flint, Michigan after General Motors closed its factories and opened new ones in Mexico, where the workers were paid much less. In 1995, Moore released a satirical film, *Canadian Bacon*, which features a fictional U.S. president (played by Alan Alda) engineering a fake war with Canada in order to boost his popularity. This was Moore's only non-documentary film and one of the last featuring Canadian-born actor John Candy. Moore's 2002 film, *Bowling for Columbine*, probes the culture of guns and violence in the United States, taking as a starting point the Columbine High School massacre of 1999. It won the

2002 Academy Award for Documentary Feature and became the highest-grossing mainstream-released documentary. *Fahrenheit 9/11* examines America in the aftermath of the September 11, 2001 attacks, particularly the record of the Bush administration and alleged links between the families of George W. Bush and Osama bin Laden. *Fahrenheit 0/11* was awarded the *Palme d'Or*, the top honor at the 2004 Cannes Film Festival. *Fahrenheit 9/11* is the second highest-grossing documentary of all time, taking in over $200 million worldwide.

Moore next directed *Sicko*, a film about the American health care system, focusing particularly on the managed-care and pharmaceutical industries. At least four major pharmaceutical companies – Pfizer, Eli Lilly, AstraZeneca, and GlaxoSmithKline – ordered their employees not to grant any interviews to Moore. The film premiered at the Cannes Film Festival on 19 May 2007, receiving a lengthy standing ovation, and was released in the U.S. and Canada on 29 June 2007. The film is currently ranked the third highest grossing documentary of all time and received an Academy Award nomination for Best Documentary Feature.

On September 23, 2009, Moore released a movie titled *Capitalism: A Love Story*, which looks at the financial crisis of 2007–2010 and the U.S. economy during the transition between the incoming Obama Administration and the outgoing Bush Administration. Moore said, "Democracy is not a spectator sport, it's a participatory event. If we don't participate in it, it ceases to be a democracy. So Obama will rise or fall based not so much on what he does but on what we do to support him."

Moore has authored three best-selling books, *Downsize This!* (1996), about politics and corporate crime in the United States; *Stupid White Men* (2001), a book of political humor; and *Dude, Where's My Country?* (2003), an examination of the Bush family's relationships with Saudi royalty, the Bin Laden family, and the energy industry, and a call-to-action for liberals in the 2004 election. Though Moore rejects the label political activist, he has been active in promoting his political views. Moore is known for his fiery left-wing populism, and the political left have hailed him as the "new Tom Paine."

Despite having supported Ralph Nader in 2000, Moore urged Nader not to run in the 2004 election so as not to split the left vote. On April 21, 2008, Moore endorsed Barack Obama for President, stating that Hillary Clinton's recent actions had been "disgusting." Since 1990, Moore has been married to producer Kathleen Glynn, with whom he has a stepdaughter, Natalie. They live in Traverse City, Michigan. Moore is a Catholic, but has said he disagrees with church teaching on subjects such as abortion and same-sex marriage.

JAMES CARVILLE (BORN 1944)

Buffoon, svengali, skeleton-in-the-closet, big mouth, dirty-trickster, and more – James Carville, the mastermind behind the Clinton victories, has been called all those things and much worse. Carville, political consultant, commentator, educator, actor, attorney, media personality, and prominent liberal pundit, gained national attention for his work as the lead strategist of Bill Clinton's successful presidential campaign.

Carville was a co-host of CNN's *Crossfire* until its final broadcast in June 2005. Since its cancellation, he has appeared on CNN's news program, *The Situation Room*. As of 2009, he hosts a weekly program on XM Radio titled *60/20 Sports* with Luke Russert, son of the late Tim Russert who hosted NBC's *Meet The Press*. He is married to Republican political consultant Mary Matalin. In 2009, he began teaching political science at Tulane University.

Carville, the oldest of eight children, was born Chester James Carville, Jr. at Fort Benning, Georgia, the son of a former school teacher who sold World Book Encyclopedias door-to-door, and a postmaster as well as owner of a general store. Of Irish-Cajun ancestry, he was raised in Carville, Louisiana and received his undergraduate and Juris Doctor degrees from Louisiana State University. He was a marine for two years. Before entering politics, Carville worked as a high school teacher, then as a trial lawyer in Baton Rouge from 1973–1979. Prior to the Clinton campaign, Carville and his consulting partner, Paul Begala, spearheaded the gubernatorial victories of Robert Casey of Pennsylvania in 1986, and Zell Miller of Georgia in 1990. In 1991, Carville and Begala led an appointed incumbent Senator, Harris Wofford of Pennsylvania, back from a 40-point poll deficit over White House hand-picked candidate Dick Thornburgh. That was the first time Carville and Begala used the now famous, "It's the economy, stupid!" strategy which they perfected during the 1992 Clinton campaign.

In 1992, Carville helped lead Bill Clinton to a win against George H. W. Bush in the Presidential election. He pounded on three themes: (1) Change vs. more of the same. (2) It's the economy, stupid!; and (3) Don't forget health care. After 1992 Carville began working on a number of foreign campaigns: (1) Prime Minister Tony Blair of the United Kingdom; (2) Ehud Barak of Israel (3) the Liberal Party of Canada; and (4) A strategist to help Gonzalo Sánchez de Lozada win the presidency in Bolivia. Carville was the executive producer of the 2006 film *All the King's Men*, starring Sean Penn and Anthony Hopkins, which is loosely based on the life of Louisiana Governor Huey Long.

In 2009, it was reported that Carville, Begala, and Rahm Emanuel devised the Democratic Party's strategy to cast Rush Limbaugh as the face of the Republican Party. Carville was particularly critical of Limbaugh for saying he wanted Barack Obama to "fail." Afghan presidential candidate Ashraf Ghani hired Carville as a campaign advisor in July 2009. When asked about similarities between politics in Afghanistan and politics in Louisiana, Carville responded, "Yeah, I felt a little bit at home, to be honest with you."

James Carvuille was an advisor to Hillary Rodham Clinton's ultimately unsuccessful 2008 presidential campaign. Even as Clinton's campaign began to lose steam, Carville remained loyal and positive in his public positions, stoutly defending his candidate, but in May 2008, a few hours before the primary in West Virginia, Carville remarked to an audience at Furman University in South Carolina, "I'm for Senator Clinton, but I think the great likelihood is that Obama will be the nominee." That moment marked a shift from his previous and often determinedly optimistic comments about the state of Hillary's campaign. After Barack Obama's clearly showed he was headed for victory, James Carville said he was ready to open up his wallet to help Obama build a political war chest to take on John McCain in November.

Carville is a best-selling author. His most recent book is entitled *40 More Years: How the Democrats Will Rule the Next Generation.* He married Republican political pundit Mary Matalin, who had worked for President George H. W. Bush, in 1993. They have two daughters: Matalin Mary "Matty" Carville and Emerson Normand "Emma" Carville. Carville publicly acknowledged that he has adult attention-deficit disorder. In 2008, Carville and Matalin relocated their family from Virginia to New Orleans. He is currently on the faculty of the department of political science at Tulane University. James Carville is a notoriously famous master of the quip. Some of those *bon mots* attributed to him are:

☺ On the odds of John McCain beating Obama: " It would be the biggest comeback since Lazarus"

☺ "One of Clinton's problems was, the interest groups don't care about the working poor. The Republicans don't care about the working poor — they don't know any."

☺ About Paula Jones "Drag $100 bills through trailer parks, there's no telling what you'll find."

☺ "I was against gay marriage until I realized I didn't have to get one."

☺ "I used to think that if there was reincarnation, I wanted to come back as the president or the pope or as a .400 baseball hitter. But now I would like to come back as the bond market. You can intimidate everybody."

STEPHANIE MILLER (BORN 1961)

Host of *The Stephanie Miller Show*, a liberal talk radio program produced in Los Angeles and syndicated nationally by Dial Global, she was ranked as the 36th most important radio talk show host in America for 2007. She is the daughter of former U.S. Representative William E. Miller, Barry Goldwater's running mate in the 1964 presidential election and Chairman of the Republican National Committee. After completing her secondary education in private Catholic schools, she attended USC, earning a degree in theatre. After graduation, she performed stand-up comedy at the Laugh Factory, the legendary Hollywood comedy club. Later in her career, she performed at many comedy clubs around New York and Los Angeles.

In the autumn of 1995, Miller became one of the few women to host her own late night television talk show, *The Stephanie Miller Show,* syndicated by Buena Vista Television. The show was cancelled after 13 weeks. She returned to Los Angeles radio in 1997, where she began co-hosting the CNBC television show *Equal Time*, as the liberal counterpoint to conservative Bay Buchanan. In September 2004, *The Stephanie Miller Show* was launched by

Democracy Radio. The live show is broadcast weekdays from 9 a.m. to noon in Los Angeles, San Francisco, Chicago and Seattle and on XM Satellite Radio's America Left channel. She often appears on cable news shows, such as *Larry King Live*, to represent the progressive political point of view. From April 30, 2007 to May 2, 2007, Miller filled in for Don Imus on MSNBC's 6AM–9AM ET time slot. Miller and her on-air staff received generally favorable reviews for their appearance. A fan petition was started to make the show the permanent replacement for Imus. Her present show boasts 2.5 million weekly listeners as of March 2010. On August 13, 2010 Miller announced on her radio show that she is a lesbian and credited country singer Chely Wright with helping her come out.

PAUL BEGALA (BORN 1961)

Paul Begala is a Democratic political consultant, political commentator, and former advisor to President Bill Clinton. He gained national prominence as half of the political consulting team Carville and Begala. Until June 2005, Begala was co-host of CNN's political debate program, *Crossfire*. He is Research Professor at Georgetown University and currently teaches at the University of Georgia School of Law. Begala was born in New Jersey to a Hungarian-American father and an Irish-American mother. He was raised in Missouri City, Texas. Begala is married to Diane Friday, with whom he has four sons. He is a practicing Catholic.

Paul Begala earned both his B.A. and J.D. from the University of Texas at Austin, where he taught briefly. Begala, along with his business partner James Carville, helped then-governor of Arkansas Clinton win the 1992 presidential election. After working on Clinton's campaign, he served as a consultant and aide to the President, who helped defend the Clinton-Gore agenda and served as the administration's public spokesperson.

Before becoming a co-host of *Crossfire*, Begala co-hosted a show, *Equal Time*, with Oliver North on MSNBC. He was a contributor to John F. Kennedy Jr.'s political magazine *George* in the late 1990s. As an author and co-author, Begala has written a handful of bestselling political books. His writings include *Is Our Children Learning?: The Case Against George W. Bush*; *Buck Up, Suck Up and Come Back When You Foul Up*; and *It's Still the Economy, Stupid*. Paul Begala has an over-the-top style of commentary that has led him to be parodied on *Saturday Night Live*, where he has been a repeated guest. Many conservative radio personalities including Rush Limbaugh have nicknamed Begala "the forehead," highlighting his receding hairline. Begala was a supporter of Hillary Clinton during the 2008 primaries. However, after she dropped out of the race, he became an Obama backer. Begala was a paid consultant for mortgage lender Freddie Mac. That arrangement ended in September 2008.

DONNA BRAZILE (BORN 1959)

Brazile is an author, professor, and Democratic political analyst. She was the first African American to direct a major presidential campaign, for Al Gore in 2000. She was born in Kenner, Louisiana, the third of nine children. After graduating from Louisiana State University, Brazile worked for several advocacy groups in Washington, D.C., and was instrumental in the successful campaign to make Martin Luther King, Jr.'s birthday a national holiday. Donna Brazile has worked on several presidential campaigns for Democratic candidates, including Jimmy Carter in 1976 and 1980, Jesse Jackson in 1984, Walter Mondale in 1984, and for Richard Gephardt in the 1988 Democratic primary. After Gephardt lost the primary, Brazile served as deputy field director for the Michael Dukakis. She made headlines by telling a group of reporters that George H.W. Bush needed to "fess up" about unsubstantiated rumors of an extramarital affair. The Dukakis campaign immediately disavowed her remarks and Brazile resigned the same day. She advised Bill Clinton's campaign for the presidency in 1992 and for re-election in 1996. In 2000, she was promoted to campaign manager of the Al Gore campaign.

In 2008, as a superdelegate to the Democratic National Convention, Brazile consistently refrained from declaring her preferred Democratic presidential candidate. In an interview with political satirist Stephen Colbert, Brazile stated, "Look, I'm a woman, so I like Hillary. I'm black; I like Obama. But I'm also grumpy, so I like John McCain. In fact, I have pissed off just about every state in my career." Brazile has been a lecturer at the University of Maryland, College Park, a fellow at Harvard University's Institute of Politics, and she is currently an Adjunct Professor of Women and Gender Studies at Georgetown University. She is a weekly contributor and political commentator on CNN's *The Situation Room* and *American Morning* and in CNN's Election Coverage, as well as being a contributing writer for *Ms. Magazine.*

AL FRANKEN (BORN 1951)

Alan Stuart "Al" Franken, currently the junior Senator from Minnesota, is a Democrat. He was. a writer and performer for *Saturday Night Live* from its inception in 1975 before moving to writing and acting in films and TV shows. He then became a political commentator, author of five books and host of a nationally syndicated radio show on the Air America Radio network. In the 2008 national election, Franken narrowly defeated incumbent Republican Senator Norm Coleman, by 312 votes, after a mandatory statewide manual recount. The Minnesota Supreme Court unanimously upheld

Franken's victory and Franken was sworn in to the Senate on July 7, 2009.

Franken was born in New York City, had a Jewish upbringing, attended Harvard College, and graduated *cum laude* in 1973 with a B.A. in political science. He his wife, Franni, met in his first year of college. The Frankens have two children, daughter Thomasin, a Harvard-educated former elementary school teacher turned food educator and private chef," and son Joe, who holds a degree in Mechanical Engineering from Princeton. Franken and his long-time writing partner, Tom Davis, honest their skills at Minneapolis' Brave New Workshop theater, specializing in political satire. He and Davis soon went west to "a life of near-total failure on the fringes of show business in Los Angeles." They were recruited as two of the original writers on *Saturday Night Live* Franken was associated with *SNL* for over 15 years.

Franken is the author of five *New York Times* best-selling books, three of which reached #1, including *Rush Limbaugh Is a Big Fat Idiot and Other Observations*. In 2003, Penguin published Franken's book *Lies and the Lying Liars Who Tell Them: A Fair and Balanced Look at the Right*, which included a cover photo of Fox News commentator Bill O'Reilly and a chapter accusing O'Reilly of lying. In August of that year, Fox News sued, claiming infringement of its registered trademark phrase "Fair and Balanced." A federal judge found the lawsuit to be "wholly without merit." The incident with Fox focused media attention on Franken's book and greatly increased its sales.

Franken is a Grateful Dead fan, and he used their songs as bumper music on his radio show. Since 2005, Franken has been a contributing blogger at *The Huffington Post*. His most recent book, *The Truth (With Jokes)*, was released in 2005. On January 29, 2007, Al Franken announced his departure from Air America Radio. On the day of his final show, Franken formally announced that he would run for the United States Senate from Minnesota in 2008. In a July 2008 interview with CNN, Franken was endorsed by Ben Stein, the noted entertainer, speechwriter, lawyer and author who is known for his conservative views and generally supports Republican candidates. Stein said of Franken, "He is my pal, and he is a really, really capable, smart guy. I don't agree with all of his positions, but he is a very impressive guy, and I think he should be in the Senate." On September 9, 2008, Franken won the Democratic primary for the Senate seat.

Preliminary reports on election night November 4 had Coleman ahead by over 700 votes; but the official results certified on by November 18, 2008, had Coleman leading by only 215 votes. As the two candidates were separated by less than 0.5 percent, the Secretary of State of Minnesota authorized the automatic recount stipulated in Minnesota election law. In the recount, ballots and certifying materials were examined by hand, and candidates could file challenges to the legality of ballots or materials for inclusion or exclusion with regard to the recount. On January 5, 2009, the Minnesota State Canvassing Board certified the recounted vote totals, with Franken ahead by 225 votes. On January 6, 2009, Coleman's campaign filed an election contest, which led to a trial before a three-judge panel. The panel ruled that 351 of 387 disputed absentee ballots were incorrectly rejected and ordered them counted. Counting those ballots raised Franken's lead to 312 votes. Coleman appealed to the Court. The Court agreed to hear the case. On June 30, 2009, the Minnesota Supreme Court unanimously rejected Coleman's appeal and said that Franken was entitled to be certified as the winner. Shortly after the court's decision, Coleman concede. Franken was sworn in to the Senate on Tuesday, July 7, 2009

Franken had initially supported the Iraq War but opposed the 2007 troop surge. However, since then he had come to believe that "we were misled into the war" and urged the Democratically-controlled Congress to refuse to pass appropriations bills to fund the war if they don't include timetables for leaving Iraq. Franken favors transitioning to a universal health care system, with the provision that every child in America should receive health care coverage, immediately. He has spoken in favor of protecting private pensions and Social Security. He has also advocated cutting subsidies for oil companies, increasing money available for college students, and cutting interest rates on student loans.

On August 6, 2009, Senator Franken presided over the confirmation vote of Sonia Sotomayor to be an Associate Justice of the United States Supreme Court. A year later, he presided over the confirmation vote of Elena Kagan. Senator Franken's first piece of legislation was the Service Dogs for Veterans Act, which he wrote jointly with Sen. Johnny Isakson (R). The bill, which passed the Senate via unanimous consent, established a program with the United States Department of Veterans Affairs to pair disabled veterans with service dogs. In August 2010, Franken made faces and hand gestures and rolled his eyes while Senate Minority Leader Mitch McConnell delivered a speech in opposition to the confirmation of Elena Kagan to the Supreme Court. Franken's actions prompted McConnell to remark, "This isn't 'Saturday Night Live,' Al."

KEITH OLBERMANN (BORN 1959)

News anchor, sportscaster, writer, and political commentator, Olbermann hosts *Countdown with Keith Olbermann*, an hour-long nightly news and commentary program on MSNBC. Olbermann spent the first twenty years of his career in sports journalism. After leaving Fox, Olbermann joined MSNBC, hosting *Countdown with Keith Olbermann* in 2003. Olbermann has gained prominence for his pointed criticism of major politicians and public figures, directed particularly at the political right. He has feuded with Bill O'Reilly and strongly criticized the George W. Bush administration and John McCain's unsuccessful 2008 Presidential candidacy. Although many have described Olbermann as a liberal, he has said on at least one occasion "I'm not a liberal; I'm an American."

Olbermann was born in New York City and is of German descent. He grew up in a Unitarian household in Hastings-on-Hudson in Westchester County. Olbermann enrolled at Cornell University at the age of 16, graduating from Cornell with a B.S. in communications arts. Olbermann began his professional career at UPI and the RKO Radio Network before joining CNN in 1981. In 1992, Olbermann joined ESPN's *SportsCenter*, a position he held until 1997, when he abruptly left ESPN under a cloud of controversy, apparently burning his bridges with the network's management. This began a long and drawn-out feud between Olbermann and ESPN. When he left ESPN, Olbermann hosted his own prime time show on MSNBC, *The Big Show with Keith Olbermann,* a news-driven program. The show covered three or four topics in a one-hour broadcast.

On Olbermann's current *Countdown,* his stories usually involve celebrities, sports, and, regularly and somewhere in the middle, the bizarre. Olbermann has been criticized for only having guests who agree with his perspective. In a technique similar to that of former CBS News anchor Walter Cronkite in connection to the Iran Hostage Crisis, Olbermann closes the program by counting the days since May 1, 2003, the day President George W. Bush declared the end of "major combat operations" in Iraq under a banner that read "Mission Accomplished," and then crumpling up his notes, throwing them at the camera and saying "Good night and good luck" in the mode of another former CBS newsman, Edward Murrow. Olbermann co-anchored NBC's coverage of the death of Tim Russert on June 13, 2008. During the 2008 presidential election, Olbermann co-anchored MSNBC's coverage until he and Chris Matthews were replaced by David Gregory after complaints from both outside and inside of NBC that they were making partisan statements. Despite this, *Countdown* was broadcast both before and after each of the presidential and vice-presidential debates, and Olbermann and Matthews joined Gregory on MSNBC's election day coverage. Olbermann and Matthews also led MSNBC's coverage of the inauguration of President Barack Obama.

Since beginning *Countdown*'s "Worst Person in the World" segment in July 2005, Olbermann has repeatedly awarded Bill O'Reilly that dubious honor. The feud between the anchors originated with Olbermann's extensive coverage of a 2004 sexual harassment suit brought against O'Reilly by a former Fox News Channel producer, during which Olbermann asked *Countdown* viewers to fund the purchase of lurid audio tapes allegedly held by that producer. O'Reilly avoids mentioning Olbermann's name on the air, and once cut off a caller who mentioned Olbermann. O'Reilly has also led campaigns against MSNBC's political coverage without ever specifically mentioning Olbermann. The rivalry continued when in 2006 at Television Critics' Association in California, Olbermann donned a mask of O'Reilly and made a Nazi salute, leading to a letter of protest from the Anti-Defamation League.

As of June 2009 the "combat" between the two hosts abruptly ended due to instructions filtered down to Olbermann and O'Reilly from the chief executives of their respective networks. Although it began as a traditional newscast, *Countdown with Keith Olbermann* eventually adopted an opinion-oriented format. Much of the program has featured harsh criticism of prominent Republicans and right-leaning figures, including those who worked for or supported the George W. Bush Administration, Republican presidential nominee Senator John McCain, and his running mate Governor Sarah Palin. During the 2008 Democratic Party primaries Olbermann frequently chastised presidential aspirant Hillary Clinton for her campaign tactics against her principal opponent, Senator Barack Obama, and made her the subject of two of his "special comments."

Before the 2010 Massachusetts special election, Olbermann called Republican candidate Scott Brown "an irresponsible, homophobic, racist, reactionary, ex-nude model, Tea Bagging supporter of violence against women, and against politicians with whom he disagrees." Jon Stewart criticized him about this attack by noting that it was "the harshest description of anyone I've ever heard uttered on MSNBC." Olbermann the apologized, saying, "I have been a little over the top lately. Point taken. Sorry." He has accused the Tea Party movement of being racist due to what he views as a lack of racial diversity at the events, using photos that show overwhelmingly Caucasian crowds attending the rallies. In response, the Dallas Tea Party invited Olbermann to attend one of their events and also criticized his network for a lack of racial diversity, pointing out that an online banner of MSNBC personalities that appears on the website shows only white personalities. Olbermann declined the invitation, citing his father's prolonged ill health and noted that the network has minority anchors, contributors and guests.

Olbermann briefly dated conservative talk show host Laura Ingraham (who has won the "Worst Person in the World" Award numerous times on *Countdown*) in the 1990s. In June 2006, Olbermann began dating Katy Tur, now a reporter with WNBC-TV. The couple broke up in 2009 after three years of cohabitation. Olbermann suffers from a mild case of celiac disease, as well as restless legs syndrome. In August 1980, he suffered a head injury while "leaping" onto the NYC subway. This head injury permanently upset his equilibrium, resulting in his avoidance of driving.

RACHEL MADDOW (BORN 1973)

Radio personality, television host, and political commentator. Maddow hosts a nightly television show, *The Rachel Maddow Show*, on MSNBC. She is the daughter of an attorney and a school program administrator from Newfoundland, Canada. Maddow earned a degree in public policy from Stanford University in 1994. At graduation she was awarded the John Gardner Fellowship and a Rhodes Scholarship. She earned a Doctorate in Philosophy in politics from Oxford University. She is the first openly gay American to win a Rhodes scholarship. In June 2005 Maddow became a regular panelist on MSNBC's *Tucker*. During and after the November 2006 election, she was a frequent guest on CNN's *Paula Zahn Now*. In January 2008, Maddow was given the position of MSNBC political analyst and was a regular panelist on MSNBC's *Race for the White House* with David Gregory and MSNBC's election coverage, as well as a frequent contributor on *Countdown with Keith Olbermann*. MSNBC announced in August 2008 *The Rachel Maddow Show* would replace *Verdict with Dan Abrams* in the channel's 9 p.m. slot. Since its debut, the show has topped *Countdown* as the highest rated show on MSNBC on several occasions. After being on air for more than a month, Maddow's program doubled the audience that hour.

To distinguish herself from the left in one aspect, Maddow said she's a "national security conservative" and in a different interview that she's not "a partisan." During the 2008 presidential election Maddow did not formally support any candidate. Concerning Barack Obama's candidacy, Maddow said during the primaries, "I have never and still don't think of myself as an Obama supporter, either professionally or actually."

Maddow lives in Manhattan and western Massachusetts with her partner, artist Susan Mikula. The couple met in 1999, when Mikula hired Maddow, who was then working on her doctoral dissertation, to do yard work at her home. Maddow does not own a television set, but does sometimes watch streaming broadcast content on her computer. However, she is reportedly committed to getting one so that Mikula can watch her show. Although Massachusetts recognizes same-sex marriage, as of 2009 Maddow and Mikula had no plans to marry.

www.ingramcontent.com/pod-product-compliance
Lightning Source LLC
Chambersburg PA
CBHW072104270326
41931CB00010B/1456